STRENGTH IN NUMBERS

INSIGHT FROM TOP COACHES ON HOW TO BUILD YOUR CAREER, HANDLE FAILURE, AND ACHIEVE LONG-TERM COACHING SUCCESS

JOHN BLOOM

FOREWORD BY DARBY RICH

ISBN 979-8-9918865-0-5 (hardcover)
ISBN 979-8-9918865-1-2 (paperback)
ISBN 979-8-9918865-2-9 (ebook)

The information provided in this book is for informational purposes only. The author and publisher are not liable for any actions taken based on the content of this book.

JohnBloomCoaching.com

To my mentors, my athletes, all the coaches I have worked with, and all the coaches in this book.

To my family, and to my wife Josie.

This book is not here without you. I am not who I am without you.

CONTENTS

FOREWORD

In the now-famous scene from *Ted Lasso*, the world's most lovable soccer coach borrows Walt Whitman's quote, "Be curious, not judgemental" before burying his darts in the hearts of both Rupert Mannion and the Crown and Anchor dartboard. Had Rupert been curious, and done his homework, perhaps he would have never underestimated Ted. The rest is streaming television history.

The author in this book, *Strength In Numbers*, will never be accused of not being curious. In fact, John Bloom might be the most inquisitive, norm-challenging young coach I've ever been around. In his quest to be the best coach possible, John consumes every form of education available, always looking to evolve and grow. I can't remember a single day that John came into our facility without a book in his hand, a course on his laptop, or a podcast in his earbuds. His thirst for improvement and knowledge often caused me to look deeper into my own self, challenging me to make sure I was never too comfortable and always striving to grow in my own ways. This book is simply an extension of his daily life, and not only that of his desire to improve himself, but to offer back everything he acquires for the betterment of others.

Whenever I have the opportunity to hire assistants, my goal is to hire people with different strengths and skill sets than my own. I know what "buckets" need to be filled for me to improve as a coach, as well as to offer my athletes an elite standard of care they seek and deserve. And as much as I enjoy mentoring young coaches and moving them along in their careers, I also want to learn and grow myself. I believe mentorship should be mutual. John was an easy choice from an outstanding group of candidates when I first interviewed him in 2021. I could tell right away that he had something special in his makeup. I knew he would make me a better coach, and thus make both our team and overall program better.

Strength In Numbers is just the tip of the iceberg in what John will mean to both the S&C and coaching communities. But what exactly is it? In short, it is the ultimate book of mentorship. What started out as a project to acquire answers from a select group of S&C coaches grew into an incredible compilation of experiences and advice from coaches across the entire sporting spectrum. Coaches of Olympic medalists, national champions, professional athletes, and years in the trenches all gave their time to provide answers for the current and next generation of coaches.

For a multitude of reasons, great mentors can be hard to come by for many coaches, both young and old alike. This book literally gives you a cheat code (or a personal Rolodex for older coaches like myself) into how coaches with more and differing experiences have handled the important questions you'll need to ask, and the problems you'll need to stare down in the coming days, months, and years of your coaching journey. Imagine having Lee Taft, Anson Dorrance, Mike Boyle, Kevin Eastman, Phil Beckner, and Dan John on speed dial. *Strength In Numbers* gives you just that (well not quite that, but you get the picture). I have already gleaned a wealth of information from just the handful of chapters that I've had the privilege to read in preparation of this foreword. I look forward to getting the final copy in my hands so I can continue my quest to become both the coach and person my athletes deserve and expect each and every day.

–Darby Rich
Head Strength and Conditioning Coach
Men's Basketball, University of Texas

INTRODUCTION

The idea hit me and I knew I had to do it...

In September 2023, I went to reread Tim Ferriss's book *Tribe of Mentors.* Tim's book is filled with answers to 11 questions sent to the best in the world, questions developed from answers he was struggling to find. Rather than continuing to struggle on his own, he searched for a Tribe of Mentors—a group to carry him further than he could go alone. His tribe filled the book with priceless wisdom.

As I read Tim's introduction and reasons for writing his book, an idea shot into my head.

Why don't I write a book like this for strength and conditioning?

I'm always searching for answers. Endlessly exploring books, articles, podcasts, conversations, my own thoughts.

Why not create a resource packed with wisdom from the best strength coaches in the world to help answer the questions I struggle with?

Names of people to reach out to and questions to ask began flooding my mind. But after a day or two of thought, I realized this shouldn't *just* be for strength coaches. Why not include all types of coaches? Different fields of coaching will interpret the same question with a different lens. Different roles lead to different struggles, and different struggles lead to different viewpoints. Use the perspectives in this book to more fully understand the lenses of those around you.

When you see an elite coach in action, do you ever ask yourself, "How did they get where they are today?" I know I do. This book reveals that blueprint for over 100 top coaches—insight into their career journeys and the principles that guide them. Not to copy them, but to create your own roadmap from the myriad of successes and failures they have experienced.

Adam Grant writes in his book *Hidden Potential*:

> **"Just as it's unwise to seek rudimentary instruction from the most eminent experts, it's a mistake to rely on a single guide. No one else knows your exact journey. But if you collect directions from multiple guides, they can sometimes combine to reveal routes you didn't see. The more uncertain the path and the higher the peak, the greater the range of guides you'll need. The challenge is to piece the various tips together into a route that works for you."**

No one gets to the top on their own. No one. Coaching is a craft where you need mentorship. Guides point you in the right direction for *your career* through the struggles you will inevitably face as a coach. My goal is that this book provides you with a multitude of guides you can turn to for wisdom.

Some guides in this book are household names, legends of coaching, yet some are names you've never heard. Don't value their words because of the logo they wear, value their words by *the value of their words.* Some of the greatest wisdom in this book comes from coaches wearing logos you couldn't pin on a map.

Whether you are a strength coach, sport coach, or anyone else picking up this book, take the time to explore insights from outside your profession or sport. Uncover the stuff that's not included in your textbooks, that they don't tell you before you start coaching. Go beyond the X's and O's and learn how to build your career, sustain your career, and be the best damn coach you can be.

QUESTIONS

Here is the list of the 12 questions that I sent to each coach. Underneath each question, I have explained *Why* I asked the question. Why does asking this matter? What is the intent of the question, and what value does each response provide?

Because of this book's length, I left out parts of many coaches' responses. I would have loved to keep every single word, but I'm afraid we would've run out of paper!

Disclaimer: I recorded some of the coaches' responses over a Zoom or phone call. Their bio mentions this. Because of the live nature of those calls, you will sometimes find bonus questions in their sections.

1-Who do you go to when you need advice? Why them?

Who do the best go to when they need advice? That is probably a good place for us to go as well. How should we choose the people we lean on?

2-What early job was pivotal in your career? Why?

I have always been fascinated with the story of how someone got where they are today. You will see common threads here that can impact how we shape our own path.

3-What are your first steps when you start a new job? What do you need to figure out, what do you need to get done, who do you need to get to know?

There are many moving parts when taking a new job. Seeing how those who have most likely done it many times think about this question will help you create an actionable plan when starting a new position.

4-What advice do you have for a college student looking to break into coaching? Who are the best mentors in the world to work for early in your career?

The advice given in response to this question is invaluable to young coaches. Initial mentors can have a massive domino effect on careers.

5-If you only had two 30-minute sessions a week to train your team, how would you prepare them?

This question forces prioritization. What will you do to get the most out of your limited time? Understanding what these coaches prioritize shows what they think is most valuable and will get the most ROI.

6-What goes into your decision to leave or stay at a job?

Frequent job change, especially early in your career, is common in coaching. Creating a framework on when and why to move is crucial.

7-What do you do to overcome times of struggle, burnout, or overwhelm? Who do you turn to?

I asked this question because these are three things I have faced in my career. How have these coaches overcome these obstacles and kept longevity?

8-What do you think about immediately after one of your athletes is injured? What is your mindset in the following week?

Injuries are probably the most difficult part of my job. It pains me to see anyone get hurt, and I take injuries very personally. If you're like me, you think over and over about what you could have done differently and will do differently going ahead. I wanted to know if these coaches have similar mindsets, how they reframe that mindset, and how their mindset changes within that first week.

9-How do you approach difficult conversations with athletes, coworkers, or your boss?

In sport, in life, difficult conversations repeatedly pop up. How have these top coaches navigated hard talks and conflict to push towards success? Do they have a framework for these conversations or certain timing they use? Successfully having hard conversations is crucial in coaching.

10-Do you have a "failure" that was critical to your long-term development or success?

The ability to turn struggle to success, loss into gain, and failure into an opportunity to grow is a trait I believe you will find in most high-performers—in coaching and in life. How have these coaches pulled themselves out of rock bottom to propel themselves forward in their path to the top?

11-What traits or skills do your most successful athletes have in common?

These coaches have been around many of the best athletes we see performing on our TVs. What are the common threads between these athletes in the way they live their life and approach their craft? Player selection and recruitment is an aspect I love to think about. How can we better select athletes to fit our program and develop long term? Understanding the makeup of the best athletes that have succeeded in your program, along with the make-up of the best athletes that have succeeded in all of sports, can help you develop a better framework for understanding who will be most successful. You can then turn this framework into a blueprint to further develop and refine those traits and skills within the athletes you select.

12-What books or resources do you most often recommend to coaches?
This question provides immediately applicable insight to everyone who reads this.

MY REQUEST

If you read a coach's section that impacts your life, coaching journey, or decision making—send a note letting them know. Call or text them. Email them. Shout them out on social media. *Let them know they are making a difference.*

This book was written through the generosity of over one hundred coaches that strive to impact the coaching profession. It is about a community of coaches—building *STRENGTH IN NUMBERS*. As a reader, you are just as much a part of this community as anyone that contributed. For each coach's section that affects you, try to impact one coach in your life. Share the advice or principles that you discovered. Share this book with other coaches! Build our community of coaches—build our Strength In Numbers.

HOW TO MAKE THIS BOOK VALUABLE

I know...this is a REALLY big book. I encourage you to view it more as an encyclopedia of coaching wisdom, not as a large book to be overwhelmed with, feeling like you have to read it front to back. Jump around. Go straight to reading the sections with coaches you are most excited to learn from. Read all—or only some—of a coach's section. Skip all of my writing and read from better coaches (I wouldn't blame you!). Make the journey your own and read this book the way that helps you the most.

At the end of the book, I've included themes for each question highlighting answers that repeatedly popped up. You could read these first if you are dealing with that specific problem, and then go dive deeper into the references for each theme. OR, you can read it front to back if that's what you want to do! I am confident that however you read it, in whatever order, this book will influence your career and, more importantly, your life. One thing I would HIGHLY encourage is to not only read the chapters of coaches you are familiar with, but to read and learn from new coaches—to find new perspectives.

I cannot wait for you to dig into this book and the incredible wisdom it holds. I say that humbly because the wisdom is not from me! It is from this uniquely incredible collection of coaches.

FREE BONUS---*Strength In Numbers: The Highlights*

Scan the QR Code below to access *Strength In Numbers: The Highlights*. Since the book is packed with insights, I've created this free bonus with ONE powerful answer from each coach. It's a quick way to find wisdom, insights, and inspiration at a glance—and to discover coaches whose full stories you might want to explore further.

> *"There's an old saying, 'Don't F with happiness,' and if you are at a place in your career where money is no longer the driving force, the logo on your polo is not nearly as important as the time spent with your family."*
>
> ## *-Darby Rich*

Darby Rich is in his first year as the Head Strength and Conditioning Coach for Men's Basketball at the University of Texas. One of the most respected strength coaches in college basketball, Rich has worked with the men's basketball programs at Memphis, Texas Tech, Texas A&M, Oklahoma, and South Carolina. Over his career, his teams have made four appearances in the Sweet Sixteen and one in the Elite Eight, while winning SEC (A&M) and Big 12 (Oklahoma) regular-season championships. Rich has the unique experience of working as an assistant basketball coach at Hutchinson Community College and Sam Houston State before an internship with the Dallas Cowboys launched his career as a strength coach. He has developed numerous NBA players, including Alex Caruso, Khris Middleton, Robert Williams, Danuel House, James Wiseman, Precious Achiuwa, and 2009 No. 1 pick Blake Griffin.

Who do you go to when you need advice? Why them?

I realize that not every coach still has this option, but I still go to my father for advice on anything and everything important in my life and career. Even though he may not have expertise in my chosen career, we will talk through other narratives that will be impacted by my decisions. It is actually comforting to have someone I can turn to that won't advise me to make decisions based on what others in the industry might think, or how it might advance my career, but give me honest input on making sure I do the right things for those people I am responsible for.

As it pertains strictly to our profession, I most often reach out to an extremely small circle of colleagues who I trust wholeheartedly. Whether it is a question about training, rehabbing an athlete with an injury I've never had experience with, or even how to handle an internal situation in our program, there are people I know I can turn to and trust. Still, if there is a question I need answered to help an athlete, and I cannot get that answer from one of my trusted colleagues, there is not a single person in our industry I wouldn't try to reach out to for help.

What early job was pivotal in your career? Why?
Without question, my first job at a community college shaped the rest of my career. Working as an assistant basketball coach for room and board only, my responsibilities covered everything that could possibly happen in a program. On-the-floor coaching, recruiting, S&C, academics, scheduling, scouting, video, mailouts, camps, bed-checks, laundry, equipment ordering, fund-raising, and everything in between was a part of a normal week. Not only did it allow me to learn how to do all those things, it made me more appreciative of others around me as I moved on and no longer had to fulfill all of those duties. I also worked for a HC and with an AC who were totally driven and possessed elite work-ethics. It was the only way they knew how to operate, so I had no choice but to fall in line and do the same.

What are your first steps when you start a new job? What do you need to figure out, what do you need to get done, who do you need to get to know?
The most important thing to do when starting a new job is finding out exactly what your new boss expects from you in your role. This may have been clearly outlined during the interview process, and you have clear direction and initiatives before you ever walk in the building. However, in those cases where you were being pursued, there may have been more recruiting of you than a detailed vision of what exactly was wanted from you. And while you may have received a healthy raise and lots of autonomy, nothing is more important than having a clearly defined set of expectations from your new boss. It will allow you to set a direct course for meeting those expectations, as well as giving your new boss a voice and assuring him/her they hired the right person.

Another very simple but meaningful thing you can do is to learn the name of every person you come in contact with as quickly as possible. It may never affect a single win/loss, but you could literally make someone's day by unexpectedly addressing them by their name before you've ever met them. Make some time to go online and learn names and faces in the staff directory. Remember, you only get one chance to make a first impression.

What advice do you have for a college student looking to break into coaching? Who are the best mentors in the world to work for early in your career?
My first advice would be to ask yourself, "Why do you want to coach?" If it is for the glory of running out of the tunnel on Saturday afternoons, or the paycheck that comes

with being the Head S&C Coach at a P5 football or basketball power, then you need to stop and rethink your goals. There are very few of those jobs, and only a small number change hands from year to year. However, if you really enjoy training young people, and hopefully impacting their lives both inside and outside of the weight room, then a career in coaching could be very rewarding. Some of your most rewarding results may not show up until years down the road (and very likely not even in the athletic arena), but those will be even more gratifying than any championships won along the way.

As for mentorship, I would look for someone truly respected in the industry. There is nothing more valuable than time spent watching, learning, asking questions, and growing as a young coach. A recommendation from a respected mentor who believes in you and will vouch for you is priceless. As an employer, I always weigh experience and who/where that experience was gained far more than a candidate's education and certifications.

If you only had two 30-minute sessions a week to train your team, how would you prepare them?

There are so many variables and parameters that could frame this situation. What sport are we training for? Is it in-season or off-season? Are your teams doing additional speed training? Plyometric training? Conditioning? All of these would factor into my choices, and all would eat up lots of time if done properly. So for the sake of this book, I am mandating that this "any sport" team is getting the aforementioned work done outside of these two sessions, and we can concentrate on the nuts and bolts of constructing strong, healthy, powerful athletes.

With only 30 minutes, maximizing time without turning your training sessions into glorified circuits will be important. Setting up your two training days so that your athletes can get an adequate dose of exercises needed, within the flow of your weight room, is paramount. Therefore, if traditional pairings of exercises don't fit your space, don't worry about that. Here would be my must-haves for each week: 2 power movements (one each day), 2 bilateral squat exercises (OED), 2 unilateral squat/lunge exercises (OED), 2 unilateral lateral lunge variations (OED), 1 vertical (overhead) push/pull (one day), 1 horizontal push/pull (OD), 1 bilateral hip-dominant hinge (OD), 1 unilateral hip-dominant hinge (OD). Any extra time can be used on specialty, accessory, or core work. Obviously, there are countless exercises I would (and do) add into our training blocks, but given only 30 minutes, twice a week, these are staples I would never go without.

What goes into your decision to leave or stay at a job?

Early in my career, all job-movement decisions were based around money or career advancement. Who could pay me the most, or how would this job position me to move on to my next one? After getting married and having kids, every decision now revolves around what is best for our family. Is the HC someone who will allow my boys to be around the gym or in the facility? Will my wife be happy around the other wives? Is it in a great community with excellent schools? There's an old saying, "Don't F with happiness," and if you are at a place in your career where money is no longer the driving force, the logo on your polo is not nearly as important as the time spent with your family.

What do you do to overcome times of struggle, burnout, or overwhelm? Who do you turn to?

I am probably not the person to turn to for this answer. I think it is one of the biggest challenges facing our industry. We work long hours. Our job is to be vibrant, strong, enthusiastic, and consistent in our appearance, attitude, and demeanor. We are paid to be the Supermen and Wonder Women of our programs. When we leave the building, we need to be all of those things and more for our families as well. How do we unplug? There is never really an offseason. I have no real answers for this question, but I will offer some suggestions.

If possible, try to leave winning and losing at the office. Be "present" when you are around your spouse and children. Put the phone on the counter and listen to them talk about their days. As hard as it is, try to take a vacation every year. Don't be the first in the building and the last one to leave when it's not completely necessary. Get your work done. Do the absolute best job you can for every one of your athletes. Prepare for the next day. And then get the hell out of the facility and don't let anyone make you feel guilty for doing so.

What do you think about immediately after one of your athletes is injured? What is your mindset in the following week?

Without fail, the first thing I think of when a player gets injured, especially if it is a severe injury, is, "Was there something in training we could have done differently?" I think it is very natural for us as strength coaches to want to shoulder the blame. Depending on the severity of the injury, it is almost impossible not to be gutted, for both the athlete and the team (and yourself if we are being totally honest here). It is at this time, however, that you must display your ultimate face of courage and hope. Your players, and even staff, may feel despondent and stressed. It is now up to you to set the course (along with your ATC) for the injured athlete's road back, but also to get the team moving forward. Be compassionate with your words, but let there be no misunderstanding that both the team and the injured athlete must move forward.

How do you approach difficult conversations with athletes, coworkers, or your boss?

Difficult conversations need to be held, when possible, when emotions are not running rampant. I try to set meetings when all parties involved have had the opportunity to completely gather their thoughts and process all information or feelings that may come forth during the meeting. In more recent years, I have even started having a 3rd-party "witness" attend any meeting that I think might stray into an emotional place, as well as to lessen the chance of any "he said / she said" coming out of the conversation. Approaching difficult conversations with a cool head and clear mind should always be the goal, whether it is a one-on-one with your boss, or if you are mediating a meeting between two independent parties.

Do you have a "failure" that was critical to your long-term development or success?

I don't have a monumental coaching failure that was critical to my long-term development, but I truly believe that it was my lack of individual success as a collegiate athlete that helped develop me into who I am as a coach. Like most college athletes, I spent my elementary and secondary school years as normally the best player on the field or court. Success came fairly easy, even though I was still a decently hard worker. The SEC, however, was a totally different animal. I found myself a very small fish in a big tank of sharks. Not only did I have to learn how to really work, I also realized that if I wanted to be happy and feel like I was contributing to the overall success of the team, I had to find ways to make my teammates better. This self-awareness of my lack of individual prowess, and realization that the team's needs were more important than my own, set the stage to spend the rest of my life pushing others to maximize their potential. I guess you could say I learned early that my value was much more as part of the backstage crew and not as the lead singer.

What traits or skills do your most successful athletes have in common?

The number one quality that my most successful athletes have shared over the years has been the ability to make those around them better. Of course, they were all blessed with God-given ability and almost insane work-ethics. However, what makes the best athletes/players the most successful is their ability to raise others up with them. You see, my most talented athletes have not always been the most successful. Neither have they been my most athletic, nor my hardest working. It is the rarest of all these individuals who can combine those qualities, and still have the personality, charisma, and leadership to draw people in and almost will them to be the best version of themselves, therefore making the team, and ultimately that athlete, the most successful of all.

What books or resources do you most often recommend to coaches?

My path to becoming a strength coach was very different than that of most people coming into our business today. I had already been a sport coach, but had very little background in exercise science, biomechanics, or programming. Therefore, learning and being sound in the basics was always very important to me. The first book ever given to me by my mentor, Joe Juraszek, was the original *Periodization: Theory and Methodology of Training*, by Tudor Bompa. It has been updated several times through the years, and is still a great resource for someone who didn't come through a traditional S&C regimen. Both *Practical Programming for Strength Training* and *Starting Strength: Basic Barbell Training* by Mark Rippetoe are books that every young strength coach should take the time to fully digest.

In recent years, I have become a huge fan of Aaron Horschig. Both *Rebuilding Milo* and *The Squat Bible* are great resources for young S&C's as they are building their personal toolboxes. Being able to blend solid technique training along with physical therapy is a path that will open many doors along the way, as well as allowing coaches to give their athletes the best training and care possible. *Becoming a Supple Leopard* by Kelly Starrett is another book that blends PT into S&C, and will allow you to add another layer of expertise that your athletes will find valuable, which often leads to better buy-in.

Being an older coach in our profession, I also feel like it is imperative for me to "stay current" on the latest findings and studies in our field. As a basketball S&C resource, I try to read everything gathered in the NBA-NBSCA Sports Science Research Update published monthly by the National Basketball Strength Coach Association. It is packed with valuable information from the highest levels of both academia and sports performance.

"Having peers who I TRUST and who do what I do every day and can empathize with the pressure, stress, and constant weight of public judgement of your job performance is critical to my wellbeing. I come away from those phone calls feeling better, probably because I feel like I'm not alone with the struggle."

-Tim Doyle

Tim Doyle returned to Virginia Commonwealth University in 2022 as the Head Women's Volleyball Coach after serving as an assistant coach there from 2014-2017. He was a part of the staff in 2017 that led VCU to a thirty win season, the longest win streak in the nation (27 matches), the program's first A-10 regular season and tournament titles, and an appearance in the NCAA tournament. After his time as an assistant at VCU, Doyle was named the Head Coach at William & Mary University. In the 2022 season, he led the program to its most wins since 2012 and an appearance in the CAA league-championship semifinals for the first time since 2009. Doyle was selected to the AVCA Thirty Under 30 list in 2017.

Who do you go to when you need advice? Why them?

Mentors who have given to me in the past, people who have historically given me their time, advice, or resources without anything of benefit to them. I can count on them for honest, concise, straightforward opinions without a lot of the extra chatter other people give. No hemming and hawing, just advice for me that they're giving after sincerely listening and appreciating whatever circumstance I find myself in. Coaches that have mentored me in my past.

What early job was pivotal in your career? Why?

Without a doubt being a volunteer assistant for the men at Ohio State for ~2.5 years. I learned everything there is to know about the game, tactically and technically, from an assistant coach there. I learned the value of humility, consistency, work ethic, and paying attention to your people from the head coach. And my exposure to a high standard still lasts to this day.

What are your first steps when you start a new job? What do you need to figure out, what do you need to get done, who do you need to get to know?

Oh gosh, a ton of stuff. I'll answer as a volleyball coach and let you draw conclusions, but my list is usually something like:

- Meet with and hire immediate staff.

- Conduct a team meeting to discuss my background and provide an opportunity for team members to ask questions to clarify any uncertainties.

- Meet with every student-athlete (outgoing seniors included). These meetings focus on getting to know each student-athlete, their background, aspirations, and insight into what life is like as a player. This meeting should also cover their personal and team goals.

- Meet with every immediate member of the volleyball family—strength coaches, sport administrators, academic advisors, sports medicine, sports info, facilities managers, development, marketing, and compliance to discuss program strengths, weaknesses, and objectives. Share my communication strategy and expectations for each area.

- Establish a training timeline for the remainder of the semester/time period we're in, focusing on culture growth, skill development, team training, and strength and conditioning.

- Formulate a recruiting calendar for the remainder of the year.

- Review the program budget and plan appropriately.

- Identify and meet with advocates and mentors of the program to aid in gaining perspective and making decisions.

- Meet with members of Development to review alumnae outreach operations.

- Establish a spring leadership council with representatives from each class to build a weekly communications and feedback infrastructure.

Basically, my first couple of months are just information seeking. Ask a lot of questions, don't rush to show what I know, don't rush to say, "This is where we're going." I want to find out where we are, where we've been, what people like and dislike, what they want for themselves, and what the climate for change is before introducing any. I'm very modest when I implement new things, and usually only ask for one change at a time, a few months in.

When I started at William & Mary, I didn't even ask them to come to practice wearing the same color shirt [a basic SOP I thought every team did] for a few weeks because I found out the old coach was indiscriminately personal, so I wanted to build some trust before asking them to do even the smallest of things. Way more investigative out of the gate than decisive. Slow crescendo to "this is the way we'll do things." I'm one year in now at VCU and we're just now getting to that point, for perspective.

What advice do you have for a college student looking to break into coaching? Who are the best mentors in the world to work for early in your career?
I heard an older coach reflect on her career recently and she said, "If I could tell myself in my 20s to slow down and enjoy it, I would. Don't let it consume you." I couldn't disagree more!! It depends on what your goals are. So my advice is to determine your goal, your career aspiration. Mine was to be head coach at Ohio State one day. That goal prescribed how hard I would have to work; that prescription for me meant constant work, reflection, and preparation for future job opportunities. I wouldn't take back a minute of the insane hours I spent trying to get where I am. Life plan #1 is to work your ass off to get where you want to go and Life plan #2 is to sustain wherever you are once you've made it.

Show up way early, volunteer for the hardest jobs, do the small things to make it a professional operation, take physical notes in meetings, follow up on those notes, make your phone invisible, ask a lot of questions, listen 4x to the amount of what you say, be enthusiastic, reflect on your learning, read a ton and look for that learning to play out in real life, find your own way to lead and impact [even in the smallest ways], take time to develop your own plan.

The best mentors are those who [I mentioned this earlier] give their time, advice, and resources without care for getting anything in return. Look for programs with successful young "alumni" coming out of their spots. Look for signs of an organized infrastructure/learning platform.

If you only had two 30-minute sessions a week to train your team, how would you prepare them?
Session 1 would be designed around the themes of: leadership, small group operability, situational problem-solving, adaptability, and as Jocko Willink calls it, "decentralized command." My goal would be to develop a team with lots of leaders and comfort in

VUCA environments [volatile, uncertain, complex, ambiguous].

Session 2 would focus on team culture and cohesiveness, the goal of which being to get the team rowing all in the same direction

My thinking with this response is to use the sessions for things which our team can't teach/do themselves—these are skills I know I can impart that need a facilitator.

After each session, I would send our group leaders home with packets for what they should lead the team through the rest of the week—conditioning circuits, practice plans, and training goals for the week. After all, we did so much leadership training they should then have a chance to implement it...

What goes into your decision to leave or stay at a job?

Am I happy? Is my family happy and set up for the future?

What do you do to overcome times of struggle, burnout, or overwhelm? Who do you turn to?

My personal therapies are: journaling, working out, meditating, reading, and listening to music. Also, a 12-pack of Bud.

I usually turn to other colleagues that have become trusted friends who I can talk about anything with, without fear of it leaking somewhere or getting back to anyone. As much as I want to say my wife, she doesn't really understand the intricacies of my professional life. Having peers who I TRUST, who do what I do every day, and can empathize with the pressure, stress, and constant weight of public judgement of your job performance is critical to my wellbeing. I come away from those phone calls feeling better, probably because I feel like I'm not alone with the struggle.

A side note: I think I struggle more with censoring myself and my own work habits. I love what I do so much, and constantly want to be doing it, that I find myself saying, "OK, wait to send this email." Because if I send an email to an assistant coach at 10:00pm on a holiday, or 7:00pm on a Sunday, what do they think? Even if I pressure them to take time off, I'm not signaling that it's OK to. I don't personally want time off but I need to self-impose a boundary for them to have space and time away, because they need it and aren't obsessed at my level. I want them to be all in when they're here, so I try to do that more these days.

I also see people stay in positions too long—that will inevitably lead to burnout. Working 12-15 hour days for minimum wage is not sustainable no matter how much you love your career and athletes.

What do you think about immediately after one of your athletes is injured? What is your mindset in the following week?

"Continue mission." There's no good time for it to happen. And when it does, our team always has something 'more important' in that moment for them to focus on. The team comes first. So I encourage everyone to press pause, get their mind right, then be ready to step back up to the plate and take action. There will come a time after the "mission" to sympathize, spend time with, and exhibit our compassion. But not in that moment.

The following days and weeks are about establishing a support structure for that athlete. Consistent check-ins, spending time with them in the training room or at PT, going with them to appointments, ensuring they feel the same level of support and personal attachment even when their on-court abilities have been temporarily taken away. I find it's helpful to involve teammates, too. I remember we had two athletes suffer ACL injuries within three weeks of one another. We came up with a letter-writing chain where each girl with an ACL injury would receive two letters a week from two of her teammates (different each week) expressing what she meant to the team, how important she was, and words of encouragement. It's a program-wide effort to keep that person feeling valued. I also try to find in-practice and in-match job duties for them to give them a new mission and purpose while out.

How do you approach difficult conversations with athletes, coworkers, or your boss?

I love this line from Lencioni's book *The Motive*—confront difficult, awkward issues quickly and with "clarity, charity, and resolve." It's so spot-on for me. We've also outlined a four-step process for our team when there's an issue that encourages ownership and conflict resolution:

1. Make the request known for a conversation.
2. State your observations, not your judgements.
3. Seek understanding and acknowledge your role.
4. Resolve with clarity and charity.

With ANYONE, I find these conversations easiest when falling back on a previously established expectation or standard, explicitly defined. This is why group sessions on culture and leadership are so important. When I can bring an athlete in and say,

"Go to page 3. See what the position expectations are? And the criteria for me making a decision? How can I go against that?" It makes the conversation much easier. I've also learned to not linger. Be candid and empathetic but be ready to hold the line and don't over-explain. Establish expectations/norms for group behavior and hard conversations early/first thing.

Do you have a "failure" that was critical to your long-term development or success?

I failed to get a new job after year two at VCU [when I was an assistant in 2015]. VCU was in a bad spot, our program was in turmoil, lots of players transferring, and one of the worst postseason finishes we've had in a long time. Our other assistant coach left. I put my name out there for 1-2 other jobs and didn't get them. Best thing that ever happened to me. I had to stick with VCU. I HAD to make it work for my career, for my wife, for my life. I didn't have deep connections and wasn't [I'm still not] a household name. I had nowhere to go, so I had to do whatever it took to make it work. Combined with reading *Extreme Ownership* around that same time, everything turned around. It's like it suddenly all clicked how to dig myself out of the s**t. So, after staying a 3rd and 4th year, the 4th year being epic for the program, I could promote myself as a head coach candidate that knew what it took to not just turn a program around, but what a 4-year lifecycle should look like in D1 volleyball. I got a HC job, did well there, and that eventually positioned me to go for one of my two dream jobs, back here at VCU.

What traits or skills do your most successful athletes have in common?

- The ability to learn and implement quickly.
- An intrinsic motivation to learn, study, reflect, grow, and be a master at their own craft without urging.
- Consistency in habits.
- Take care of the small things.
- Selfless teammates.
- Sacrificing short term "fun" for long-term success.
- Jump high, hit hard, quick first step.

What books or resources do you most often recommend to coaches?

Too many to count to be honest. I created an "assistant coach development guide," and as part of that a standalone recommended reading list, broken down by Culture; Personal Philosophy and Leadership; For Your Athletes; Impactful Biographies. So some of my favorites plucking from that list:

- *The Five Dysfunctions of a Team* [Lencioni]
- *The Four Agreements* [Ruiz]
- *LEAD...For God's Sake* [Gongwer] ... side note, it's not a religious book
- *The 360 degree leader* [Maxwell]
- *Extreme Ownership* [Willink]
- *The Inner Game of Tennis* [Gallwey]
- *Team of Rivals* [Goodwin]
- *The Soul of a Butterfly* [Ali]

"It wasn't necessarily burnout, but I felt like, 'Am I being fair to my family? Am I being fair to my kids? Should I go in a different direction so that I have more time at home?' But then you get that reminder that you're doing exactly what you're supposed to be doing. You may not have the most time, but you can find ways to make the most of your time together."

-Marissa Young

Marissa Young was named the first Head Softball Coach in the history of Duke University, achieving a record of 263-106 since building the program. She has led the program to three straight NCAA Super Regional appearances, including their most recent record breaking season in 2024 where they reached the Women's College World Series, won 52 games, and won the ACC regular season and tournament championships. Young won ACC Coach of the Year during this season, while the team earned the No. 1 ranking in the nation for the first time in school history. Before building an elite program at Duke, she was an assistant at North Carolina, Eastern Michigan, and the head coach at Concordia University in Ann Arbor, Michigan. **(Young's responses were transcribed from a phone call)**

Who do you go to when you need advice? Why them?

First and foremost my faith, clinging on to prayer and guidance, along with my pastor or someone within the church that is a mentor for me. Carol Hutchins, my former coach and a decorated Hall of Famer. She is somebody with a lot of knowledge and experience that she's willing to share. You can learn a little bit of something from everyone around you. I try to be a lifelong learner and pick up things from successful business people, people outside of athletics, and coaches of different sports. I try to learn something from everyone around me.

What early job was pivotal in your career? Why?

My parents had a janitorial service when I was young, and watching the hard work and grind they had to put in, doing the lowest of the low, gave me an appreciation for hard work, but also for paying attention to the details. You're the person that walks around looking at the baseboard and the dust and cobwebs in the corner, the things that most people don't notice. Your eyes have to be drawn to the little things most overlook. That has helped me keep perspective—no matter what my role is, I'm still able to take a step back and look at the little things that are an integral part of success.

How we were treated as people while being janitors—people really look down upon it, and people look at you and say, "It's their job to pick it up or their job to clean up after you." To me, it doesn't matter what your title is, how powerful you are, or how much money you have. It's everybody's job to take care of your facility or home. In my role, I work to go out of my way to make sure that people don't feel valued just based on their title, that everybody is a key contributor to the program.

What are your first steps when you start a new job? What do you need to figure out, what do you need to get done, who do you need to get to know?
Reach out to the people that have been there and have had sustainable success at that institution. What is their cheat code, or what they've learned over the years to best navigate the environment that you're in. It's also important to take time with all of the people that are going to touch different parts of your program. You want them to know that they have value and highlight their impact. You also want them to understand your vision, so that when adversity strikes, you've built that common bond and vision with everybody, even if you're not interacting with them on a day-to-day basis.

What advice do you have for a college student looking to break into coaching? Who are the best mentors in the world to work for early in your career?
Find the right balance of getting in as a GA or student manager in a great program where you can learn in a successful environment, but also being in a place where maybe you're not as historically successful, but you have a lot of responsibility. You have your hands in a lot of different things that are going to give you the experience that you need to be successful. You're not going to know what you don't know until that responsibility is on your shoulders. But I also think being in a place where you have quality examples and role models, where you've been able to see people navigate the difficult things ahead of you, is really important.

What goes into your decision to leave or stay at a job?
To a fault, I'm very much a person who wants to finish what they started. As long as I

feel like I have the resources and the support around me to enable me to be successful, I'm willing to continue overcoming the challenges that particular job or place comes with. A lot of us think money will be the cure all, but it's not. It also has to be a place that I want to raise my family first and foremost, a place where I'm gonna be surrounded by great people. And I want to be successful—is it a place that you feel like you can go win?

What do you do to overcome times of struggle, burnout, or overwhelm? Who do you turn to?

The biggest source of that is being a working mom. College athletics never stops, you're never off the clock. There were a lot of times when it wasn't necessarily burnout, but I felt like, "Am I being fair to my family? Am I being fair to my kids? Should I go in a different direction so that I have more time at home?" But then you get that reminder that you're doing exactly what you're supposed to be doing. You may not have the most time, but you can find ways to make the most of your time together.

Also, the impact daily exposure to a college environment and the insight it provides to your children is invaluable. You have to constantly remind yourself of the big picture, weigh the pros and cons, and understand that you being a great mom is not going to look like the mom who is running the PTA, Teacher Appreciation Week, or field trip chaperones, and all those things. But you can be a great mom if you give love and teach them life lessons. It's going to look a little bit different, and you have to be okay with that.

How do you approach difficult conversations with athletes, coworkers, or your boss?

I try to find a middle ground. You have an agenda that you're trying to accomplish, but what is going to resonate with that person? How can you navigate the conversation in a way that's going to create more buy-in? I've done a much better job over the years of going in with an open mind and asking questions so that we can work collectively towards a common goal.

Do you have a "failure" that was critical to your long-term development or success?

When I first started the program, the focus was so much on the nuts and bolts, the X's and O's, and taking care of the things that needed to be done to get the program up and going. Over time, I realized that more of the emphasis needs to be on the relational piece. You're working so hard to get it right and you want everything to be perfect, but you need to delegate and give others ownership so you have more time available to connect with those you are coaching and working with.

What traits or skills do your most successful athletes have in common?

Being a great competitor is something they have to have, but you can't give it to them. Self-awareness and a hunger to learn and grow are critically important. So many athletes take coaching as a personal attack. The kids that are really hungry to learn and grow are the ones that have the most success.

Bonus: How do you try to identify if athletes have those qualities in the recruiting process?

Wow, it's tough. Sometimes you can see it—they stand out differently than others, they're willing to run into the wall or make a dive that most kids wouldn't do, and you can see the physical piece. But a lot of it is asking the right questions, trying to dig deep and not get too caught up in physical ability, but to ask more about the intangibles and the choices they make outside of softball.

Bonus: How do you weigh character and talent when recruiting athletes to your program?

If you divide it into a pie, the biggest chunk of the pie are the kids that have the athleticism, the character, and the grit all together. Then you're gonna have some others that you're taking a chance on—maybe really high character, but less talent. You'll have some that are really talented, but you're going to have to keep the guardrails on them to keep them in line. It's definitely a balance. You can have a few that fall into each of those categories, as long as you have a really strong core that you know is going to pull the less talented or the wild ones towards the middle.

What books or resources do you most often recommend to coaches?

Legacy brought to light for me a different way of approaching building culture from within. I've always been somebody with high standards that demands the most of my players, but to read that book and to hear how the players demanded it from each other was really powerful.

"He answered, 'We've learned that even with the toughest warfighters in the world, with any kind of human, you can't assume resilience.' I think the great piece of advice here for coaches is—don't assume resilience. Don't assume that you can just keep not showing up at night, and having your wife or your spouse handle all the little kids. Don't assume she's that resilient. We've all got our breaking points."

-Rod Olson

Rod Olson is a nationally recognized speaker and leadership consultant. After almost 20 years of coaching college football, he has now spent more than a decade coaching teams and leaders from collegiate and pro sports, the corporate sector, and our United States military special forces. Olson is the founder of the Coaches of Excellence Institute and the Coach O Consulting Group. He also authored three leadership fables: *The Legacy Builder, Wisdom Lunch Warrior,* and *Greatest Motivation Tool.* **(Olson's responses were transcribed from a phone call)**

Who do you go to when you need advice? Why them?

We call it building your Mount Rushmore. Who are four people you can call anytime, anyplace, anywhere, and they'll take your call and speak truth into your life? They won't tell you what you want to hear. They're going to tell you what you need to hear for your life. They love you more than they care about your career. My Mount Rushmore now is 12, 13 guys. There are different guys I call for different things.

Early on, my Mount Rushmore was my high school basketball coach, because I loved how he coached and I loved how he lived. Another one was Jerry Moore at App State. Another one early in my career was John Stiegelmeier. He was at South Dakota State when I was there, now John's retired and won a national title. John's just a rock and a great man of God. I also had colleagues too, like Jed Stugart, who's the head coach at Lindenwood right now. Even though we're the same age, he had great wisdom for me on a lot of different things. I also found guys that were outside my industry. Bob

Parry was a long time track coach in college and then he was a high school teacher—but that guy had been around the block.

Those are just a few of mine, and a guy named Scotty Kessler too, but right now I've got friends, colleagues that I call that are aligned with me and my values. That's the key too, find people that either have the same values or have the values you aspire to in order to build your Mt. Rushmore and to put those people into your life. People always ask me, how do you find those people? Look for people who have the values you have or you want, and then go talk to them.

What early job was pivotal in your career? Why?

I didn't come from a family of coaches, I didn't have a dad who could help me, I didn't know anybody, but back then we could work camps and I met people that way. I was a small college guy, NAIA guy, and I played JUCO, but then I had some knee injuries and that got me to coach right away.

Especially in today's world with the portal and work ethic, when we recruited at the NAIA level, it's non-stop. You recruit 400 guys to get 50. Our motto is always first one in, last one out. If we had a great player, like an All-American, we figured he's probably going to transfer in two years to D1. I think my work ethic and my mindset were formed at that NAIA small college level where you have to do everything. It's no different than an entrepreneur or starting out as a strength coach where you're doing every sport, and I think that gives you such an advantage when you have to be a jack of all trades. Just like my youngest son, he's a lacrosse coach. He's a head coach at a D2 school in Georgia, and he's having to do everything.

When I got to Appalachian State, everything changed for me. Jerry Moore made us go home at night after practice, and I had never experienced that. That was the first time I really experienced, and my wife experienced, a schedule that was somewhat family friendly in a very difficult, time-consuming world.

What are your first steps when you start a new job? What do you need to figure out, what do you need to get done, who do you need to get to know?

When I was young, I had no clue. I'm just taking jobs, trying to move up and get the head coach to like me. But I always tell people this, even SEAL team commanders when they take over a new SEAL team or a new group, the first thing you have to do is build trust. The way you build trust is by assessing and gathering intel, especially when you become a head coach. One activity I have new head coaches, new CEOs or presidents, and SEAL Team Commanders do when they come in—I call it the note card exercise. Ask them two questions in your very first meeting with everybody. Write on one side of the notecard, what are the things that you love about this culture that we shouldn't change? These are staples and really impact you, and makes us who we are. On the backside of that note card, I want you to put down one or two things that we need to change right away in this culture. Or operations that you think we've got to really look at and change—it's almost a red flag and it's really holding us back.

It's like the Ted Lasso thing, it was his suggestion box. Then he fixed the shower. What you do is you take the low hanging fruit off of those cards and fix it, and quickly. Like the shower without enough water pressure, or the way we do our reimbursement for our receipts is ridiculous. You do some low hanging fruit stuff to gain trust, and then people also feel heard. It's "Man, they actually asked my opinion. This guy has got a clue." You drive your credibility by building trust right out of the gate, and conversely, the worst thing you can do is come in and be a dictator immediately. Even in the worst cultures, there's something probably decent they're doing that you could build off of in some area.

What advice do you have for a college student looking to break into coaching? Who are the best mentors in the world to work for early in your career?
I just did it with my son. He played at Limestone University and got his MBA, had a lot of success in lacrosse, and then he got an internship one summer in the hospitality industry because he wanted to be a general manager of hotels. That company did a great job, they flew him all around the country doing these four or five day internships where he had to do every job from housekeeping to sales. He was about 24, and we were having a cigar on the deck and talking about it. He said, "Dad, I just loved it, but I didn't LOVE it, like all in, this is my passion." I said, "Do you love it as much as you love lacrosse?" And he goes, "Oh no." I said, "If you had to string lacrosse nets for $25,000 a year, 40 to 50 hours a week and maybe help coach a little, or work your way up at a hotel, being a front desk person, what would you rather do?" He goes, "I string nets all day long and coach." There's your answer.

My advice is to find things that give you three things. One is joy. It just gives you joy. You feel God's pleasure when you do it. You feel like you were made to do it. Two— fulfillment. When you're a strength coach, I'm sure it fulfills you to see your athletes making gains, but then seeing transference from the weight room to the field and to the court, that transference is fulfillment. Then the last part—it better not seem like work. I don't know how many jobs I went through in high school or college that were awful. I couldn't keep a job because I wasn't passionate about it. It felt like work.

I'm a faith guy, so a big piece for me too is I gotta trust God's nudge. If I feel like God's opening a door over there, I need to walk through and see where it leads. A good friend of mine, now he's a friend and a colleague, but I trained him in high school in my quarterback school one on one for four years. He ended up going to Oklahoma State, got drafted, and played in the NFL for a little while. Then he started doing quarterback lessons on his own, and now he's the offensive coordinator for the Atlanta Falcons. His name is Zac Robinson, and if Zac hadn't walked through the doors that God was opening, he wouldn't be where he is today either.

You also have to take advantage of what door is open for you and not look for the perfect job. This is the last thing I'll say—my son was an assistant and he liked that. Then he got a chance to be a head coach at this school that's been awful for the last decade. He said, "Dad, do you think I should take it?" I'm like, "Yeah! At 25 years old, you don't get good jobs. You get bad jobs that you have to turn into a good job." You've got to see the upside of something too, realistically. You can't walk into the electric chair, but you gotta just walk through those open doors and go for it.

What do you do to overcome times of struggle, burnout, or overwhelm? Who do you turn to?

A lot of Navy SEALs are killing themselves now, and a lot of combat veterans are killing themselves, almost 30 a day now in our country. Think about the SEALs. They're the greatest warfighters on the planet with arguably the greatest training pipeline in the world. It's tried and true. It's an 18 month process. It's brutal and the cream only comes out. These are the guys now that are killing themselves. There was a guy named Job Price who was a commander over in Afghanistan. I've worked with a lot of guys that knew Job and were teammates of his, and I also coached the commander that took over for him after he committed suicide.

I said, "Hey, what's the story on Job?" He goes, "Oh Rod, you don't know? Job was the poster child for Navy SEALs. He was the toughest guy. He was the most skilled guy. He was a brilliant commander. We all thought he'd be an admiral some day and maybe Medal of Honor. He was the guy Rod. Every time they called him for a mission, he took it and he crushed it, and so did his team." I go, "Why did he kill himself?" He goes, "Exactly...Exactly." I asked him, "So what's the biggest lesson you've learned in all this?" He answered, "We've learned that even with the toughest warfighters in the world, with any kind of human, you can't assume resilience." I think the great piece of advice here for coaches is—don't assume resilience. Don't assume that you can just keep not showing up at night, and having your wife or your spouse handle all the little kids. Don't assume she's that resilient. We've all got our breaking points. We all do.

That's a fine line though, right? Because I see a lot of young coaches today that think they're working really hard and they're not. They make fun of the Gen X's like me. They're like, "Don't mess with those Gen X's, man. They will give you no slack. They won't feel sorry for you at all." And it's true. I'm like, "Yeah dude, get off your ass and go recruit more." "I don't have enough players. I don't have...get on the phone more." What are you doing? I don't want to hear that you're going on vacation when you don't have enough players or good enough players yet, or the portal isn't working out. You got to work your ass off, bro. That's the main thing.

There's that fine line where I think you have to understand—don't assume resilience. Then as quickly as you can, figure out—what are the indicators or the yellow flags that you're starting to not be resilient? You're starting to not recover. You're starting to deplete. For me, a great indicator that I'm getting run down is that I'll be a lot less patient with people. I will not listen to people all the way through. I'll just freaking cut them off, whether it's at home or at work, I'll just cut them off and solve their problem so I don't have to freaking listen to that crap anymore. And that's not right. Alcoholics Anonymous has a great term, it's called HALT. They believe that negative coping mechanisms are driven by one of these four things: you're hungry, angry, lonely, or tired. Everybody's gotta figure out what their own indicators are. What's your own kryptonite? And the sleep thing is off the charts crazy important now. It's way more important than we ever thought.

The other piece of this, and we teach this to players all the time now, especially basketball players in college because the season is so long, we teach the players when they get a week off to go find a healthy recharge. You better know what your healthy recharge is. Getting hammered and smoking dope is not a healthy recharge. Even though it might relax you, partying is not a healthy recharge. We differentiate between a healthy recharge versus an unhealthy recharge. Going on a bender might be fun, but your body's being torn down. It's just like some people on a break, "I'm gonna go run five miles." No, you're in mid-season here. You need to relax. "I love to run though. It relaxes me." Now you're just being stupid. That's not a healthy recharge.

As I got older, I had a guy challenge me. If you don't want to burn out, we call it the third thing. What's your third thing? This isn't just a hobby. Your first thing is your faith and your family, the second thing is your job, and your third thing is whatever is your healthy recharge. For some guys, it's golf. For some guys like me, it's fishing. I've got a cabin out by a mountain, and I love working on it. I'm not the handy guy, I never have been, but now I can YouTube anything and I can do it. I found out I like doing that and it recharges me.

How do you approach difficult conversations with athletes, coworkers, or your boss?

There's a principle that we teach coaches that's absolutely pivotal: the longer it's been since you've played the game or competed, the easier it gets in your head. The first question we have to ask to make sure we put ourselves in an empathetic state is, "What's it like to meet with me right now?" What's it like to be pulled in by the head coach and be reprimanded? What's it like to miss four workouts and now he might kick me off the team? What's it like to get a DUI and now I have to meet with the head coach? I'll do it with my wife in the middle of a disagreement. We've been married for almost 35 years and in the middle of the conversation, I'll think to myself, "What's it like to argue with me right now?" Because I'm an ass. I don't want to lose when I get into those situations. Ask yourself that question, "What's it like to talk to me right now after my fourth strikeout in the day, and I'm the hitting coach?"

Think about as a strength coach, power cleaning is a great example. I trained my kids how to power clean since they were six. They go in the weight room and the strength coach is like, "Oh, this is great. They already know how to power clean." Then think about the kid that just can't figure it out. The rhythm, the movement— your ability to remember, "Hey, what was it like for me to have to learn something I wasn't good at?" That's what master teachers do. That's why sometimes it's hard for a super talented athlete to be a great coach. Not to say that they can't be, but it's, "I don't know dude, I could just always power clean, I don't know what the problem is."

You can't be over empathetic though, because when you're over empathetic, you'll start helping people and doing things for people that they should do for themselves. That's that parenting piece too, where I want to always think with the end in mind whenever I meet with a player. Just like my kids, where do I want them to be in 20 years? That gives you a much better perspective on the current conversation, and I don't want to lose the relationship just because I have to discipline them or punish them.

Do you have a "failure" that was critical to your long-term development or success?

Tons of them. We actually do an exercise with executives, leaders, and SEAL leaders called Epic Fail, where we talk about our epic fails and what we learned from them. We all have epic fails. Frosty Westering, probably the greatest coach you've never heard of, won four national titles at NAIA and Division III and played for eight while at Pacific Lutheran. Frosty's big thing is you better have a mistake plan, and there's only three things you can do when you make a mistake in our program. Admit it, fix it, and don't repeat it. That's great advice for parenting. To admit it means to take ownership, and in today's world we've got a major problem with taking ownership. We love to play the victim. And then fix it, it's an unemotional fix. You missed something on the checklist, that's probably all that happened, so quit being emotional about it and let's just talk about it. Quarterback would throw an interception, he comes to the sidelines, and instead of ranting at him, I think, "I'm either coaching it or I'm letting it happen." So, "Hey, what'd you see Zac? Alright, you misinterpreted it, here's what we gotta do next time." And then try not to do it again. That's a spiritual plan too.

Again, being a faith guy, one big mistake for me was when I took this one job. I'll cuss every once in a while, and I remember I hired this assistant. He was a young assistant and he came in after about the first month of working for me. He said, "Coach, I want to talk to you about something." I said, "What's that?" I could tell he was crazy uncomfortable with the conversation. He goes, "You keep saying you're a Christian and you want these kids to be kingdom building leaders and follow Jesus, you want us to emulate Jesus and all that. You're talking out of both sides of your neck." I said, "What are you talking about?" He goes, "You cuss all the time. I'm not saying that you're not a Christian because you cuss all the time, but I don't understand the hypocritical behavior." I wanted to fire that guy. Who the hell are you to tell me how I'm...But I looked at him and I asked that question, "Man, how hard was it for him to come in and tell me that?" So I said, "You know what, I appreciate you bringing that to my attention, and I'm gonna address it."

There's something else that I teach that I really believe in. Again, there's nothing new under the sun, but we believe that there are no elite coaches or leaders who aren't mature humans or aspiring to be a mature human. There's nobody elite that is immature. There's a direct correlation to determine a leader's maturity by how long it takes them to admit a mistake once they find out. When I was a young coach, if I suddenly found out that it was my fault it might take me a month to own up to it because of my ego. As you mature—and this is going to happen in your marriage too—if I'm in a fight with my wife and I figure out it's my fault, it'll take me about three seconds to go, "Honey, I'm sorry." Hopefully the more mature we get, the less time it takes for us to admit our mistakes. As I get older and hopefully more wise, it's less time where I try to hold on to it for my ego.

What traits or skills do your most successful athletes have in common?
Number one, and they're very rare today, is they have to be a gym rat. Elite people have a gym rat mentality. They can't wait to work out. Anything that has to do with the game or making them better, they can't get enough of it. That's singleness of purpose. Out of the gate, that's number one. Finding gym rats now is like finding unicorns. And we're talking about elite players, not just good ones. We're talking about the elite.

Number two, they're either a mentally stable individual, or they're willing to work on it. Meaning they're not manic. They're not super high and super low. They're resilient, yes, but I don't have to get on a roller coaster or a merry-go-round with them every freaking day. They have a consistent attitude, and it's a positive mental attitude. That's old school, nothing new under the sun kind of stuff, but I don't see elite guys being pessimistic. I don't see elite people that aren't relentless and don't have great attitudes.

The third thing is they help other people get better. The common term now is we call it a we guy, not a me guy. But there's more to it than that. The elite ones want their teammates to get better too. They want to help people. They understand that they're a man or a woman who's also built for others. The elite ones—that's why they're great leaders and great teammates. As jacked up as Michael Jordan was on how he motivated, he wanted to help other people get better. He just didn't have enough tools in his toolbox, so he bullied everybody. He just needed more tools, but he wanted his teammates to get better, and not just so he could win.

There's one more that I want to give you. With the SEALs, they call it propensity for violence, but we call it a propensity for competition, and a propensity to win. That's the fourth one, I want people who want to fricking win too. There are a lot of great players that have great character that won't compete to win. Everybody wants to call it the Kobe killer instinct, and like I said, the SEALs called it propensity for violence, meaning you're okay with the violence. You're good with it. You're okay with fricking getting on the mound and fricking competing against that guy.

We have this thing called FATC. I want players and leaders who are faithful, available, teachable, and courageous. It's in my first book, *The Legacy Builder*, and I was taught that a long time ago by a good friend. Faithful means they trust the organization, they trust the coaches, and they're not going to whine about the organization out loud. You got a problem, come to me. We'll work on it. Available means they're going to be available to do the work. They're going to make time—it's that important to them. It's a priority. Teachable means they have a teachable and coachable spirit. We call it the white belt mentality. They don't think they know it all. They're very coachable and malleable. The last one is courageous, which means they have to be willing to step up when it's not comfortable. They have to be willing to do the right thing when it might not be the cool thing to do. If any one of those four is missing, their leadership is going to shipwreck, so we won't put them in that position or we won't recruit them.

Bonus: In recruitment, how should coaches weigh character and talent?

The Navy SEALs spent millions of dollars on selection. How can we find the right guys? And just to show you how much of an inexact science it is—they spent millions of dollars trying to figure out—who are the guys we can bring into our training pipeline and into BUD/S that would be great SEALs, but we don't have to waste our time with all the others? Today there are YouTube videos, they have added two pre-training courses to BUD/S, books, SEALs that will train you before you go to BUD/S—and the percentage of candidates that make it through and are selected is not any higher than it was before we had all these things. That tells you two things. One, the training pipeline is good. The process is good. It still is hard enough and weeds out people. The second thing is...we really don't know. It's just like the NFL and they draft Tom Brady in the sixth round—they don't know. I spent almost 15 years in pro baseball, and my son is in the mental skills part, and looking at people's ability to handle adversity at the pro level—they think people can, but they don't know. You really won't know until they're in it. That's the same thing with the SEALs.

You better have your bare bone criteria. I want a kid with a great attitude. I want a kid that's got a good value system or is open to having one. I gotta have a kid that's coachable and teachable, and I gotta have a gym rat. Now, do I have to have talent? Yes, especially at the collegiate level. I've gotta be a developer too, and that's where coaches are pretty frustrated right now with the portal because development takes time. Things that are built to last are not built fast. What happened to development? Especially if you got into college coaching to be a developer.

I think talent is in there, and I love that quote by Zig Ziglar. "Money's not that important. It's just like oxygen." I think talent's not that important, skill's not that important, it's just like oxygen. But I can't put it above character. I can't have someone that might tear down my culture, that could cost me my job, that could hurt another human, or hurt the university. Character to me is still number one. Character really is what are your values? If integrity is not one of their values, I'm not going to recruit that kid. I don't care how good he is. One of the biggest mistakes I've made—I gave you that FATC criteria—is I thought I could make them faithful, available, teachable, and courageous. Now, do some kids evolve and change and grow and mature? Sure they do, you've seen that. But if I can help it, I don't want to have a lot of those edge people. I don't want people with an unhealthy edge. I want them with a healthy edge.

Bonus: With so much pressure to win, with the landscape specifically in college sports of NIL, the transfer portal, and condensed timelines to work with athletes— how can coaches focus on both character AND winning? How do they avoid the trap of thinking Character and Competing can't coexist?

I think you just hit the nail on the head. It's not an either or, it's an and. Your mindset, number one, is everything. You still can develop. I throw the BS flag when guys go, "We just can't develop anymore." Yeah you can. You just have to do it faster. And unfortunately, those of us who really understand development know that it takes a lot of time. What Lou Holtz says, as bad as we want freshmen and sophomores to be, to act, and play like juniors and seniors, they won't. They just won't. It takes time, it takes reps, it takes game experience. But can I still develop? Yes. I just have to recalibrate my expectations.

Number one, your mindset. Yes, I can develop and I can win. Number two, I have to recalibrate my expectations. Right now, I'm going to Colorado State at the end of this month because that's a whole new team, which everybody's dealing with. I call it my portal integration process. I've got to help him accelerate the integration process and assimilation process. That's the third thing. You've got mindset, then you've got to recalibrate, and then you've got to have a process for speeding up integration, synergy, and assimilation. That includes technical, tactical, and culture. If you don't have those three things, you're freaking screwed.

Bonus: What are the critical aspects of your Portal Integration Process?

The number one thing you have to do is build trust and relationships, and realize we don't know each other. Don't take interpersonal relationships and communication for granted. Don't just think guys are going to get along. Don't just think it doesn't matter if they get along. It does, and I've got to raise their awareness of the importance of communication and human interaction. How do I do that? Through assessments. Here's what this guy's personality is. Here's how this guy handles conflict. This is how this guy communicates. This guy is more of an introvert, he's more of an extrovert. That's why all the personality profiles and assessments—if you have them at your disposal, you should use them. They're worth the investment to pay $70 to get a player's personality assessment and then go through it with the team.

Coaches have to really work hard on interpersonal communication. But what's the first thing we do? We go to technical and tactical because we're scared. We won't get our offenses or defenses in, and those are important. But if they don't know how to communicate and they don't know how to get along with each other, and you don't give them those skills or that knowledge, you're freaking asking for problems. I'll tell you who understands this better than anybody—coaches of females. Not because women are more emotional and all that, but they understand how important relationships are with these girls. If you're good, you understand that it's important for all of us, not just women. Even in the workplace, how fast can I get people to know each other, understand each other, trust each other, and respect each other? Not be best friends, but to help understand each other. I had all my kids take DiSC tests and then when they got married, I had them do conflict assessments with their spouses so they understand how they fight and how they handle disagreement. Those are major tools.

What books or resources do you most often recommend to coaches?
When I wrote my books, I wrote those because I didn't think they were covered very well in other books. There are some things in mine that can really help coaches, especially when you're talking about finding your sweet spot in regard to work–life balance, and also understanding the importance of valuing people, and then tools and tactics on how to really value people. That probably goes into your last question too, I gotta teach my players how to value each other. That's massive in that process of assimilation. Because it's not natural, it's just not.

Frosty Westering's book, *Make the Big Time Where You Are*, not many people know about it. That's a great book. Everybody talks about *Legacy*, and that's a great book. But at the end of the day, you've got to find and emulate people you like and that are your personality. I think the books are being overvalued. I'm not saying reading isn't important, I'm not saying that listening to books isn't important. But if you can go visit people—that's what we don't do anymore. Like this conversation you and I are having, could I have written you an email with all these answers? Yeah, but it's not the same. It's not even close. And it's not even close as if you followed me around for a year. Even better, right? The Jews call it the Rabbinic Process, where what did Jesus do? The best thing you can do is have them follow you around for three years. What's the second best thing you can do? Watch a bunch of Zooms. Go visit.

I visited Pete Carroll a couple of times because he was my personality. I watched how he coached, and I had a role model. Today there's so much information, but I think watching interviews is huge, like Zooms and podcasts, listening to people, I think they're way more important than books. Not that reading books isn't important, but man, I just think get at the feet of the master. All these people are open to it now. Geno Auriemma, you can go watch his practice. I used to send my strength coaches to Mike Kent when he was at Louisville. I said, "Go spend a week with Mike. Go sleep in the freaking weight room, because just a week with that guy could change your life."

If you find an author or you find a coach or a podcast, go ahead and start digging. Just lock yourself up in that room and watch and listen and read everything you can on that person and what they do. It's different now than when I had to go visit Pete Carroll to get the information on him.

There's one more book that is really good, *Excellence Wins*, written by the founder of Ritz Carlton. It's one of the best books I've ever found on how to galvanize teams and how to set up your core values. I think of Ritz Carlton and how customer service driven they are, but at the same time, they're the best on the planet. That did not happen by accident. There's intentionality in how that guy did it.

Bonus: Final Thought

I'm going to tell you one last thing—everything I've learned I was taught—and they're all Biblical principles. I don't think there's anything new under the sun. All these things we're talking about have been taught for 2,000-3,000 years, and Jesus taught them. I just teach them in a secular format. The bottom line is Jesus—think about it, He coached them so well. He coached them through everything that even after He left, which is a great sign of a coach, they were willing to die for what He taught them. That's what we want our players to do. They believe in what we're doing so much that they'll reproduce it. They're so convicted by it that they'll stick with it, and they'll build that legacy into other people.

"I describe passion as the willingness to suffer and sacrifice for that which you love, and if you would eagerly do it for free then you have found a passion inside of your soul and you are obligated to fulfill that passion during your time on earth."

-Sundance Wicks

Sundance Wicks is in his first year as the Head Men's Basketball Coach at Wyoming University after one year as the Head Coach at Green Bay. At Green Bay, Wicks was honored as the 2023-2024 Horizon League Coach of the Year and Joe B. Hall National Coach of the Year, an award presented to the top first-year head coach in NCAA Division I college basketball. He led the team to an 18-14 record following a 3-29 season the year before. Wicks previously worked as an assistant at Wyoming for three seasons before heading to Green Bay, helping the program earn their first at-large bid to the NCAA tournament since 2002. Before joining the Cowboys, he was the Head Coach at Missouri Western, Associate Head Coach at Northern State University, and Assistant Coach at San Francisco, Northern Illinois, and Colorado.

Who do you go to when you need advice? Why them?

I believe you should have a circle of 3-5 "Accurate Observers" in your life—those people who see you daily or you stay connected to more regularly than anyone else in this life. They must truly know you and know your soul and your story. They are the ones you should absolutely trust when it comes to advice or mentorship because they can see beyond that which is superficial and dive deeper into the truth.

What early job was pivotal in your career? Why?

Working as a GA for Don Meyer at Northern State University. $500/month stipend living out of a garage with two other GA's. I learned hours do not exist, only execution exists in this profession. You get the job done right no matter how long it takes you. The more you do it, the better you get at it, much like any skill, and the more efficient you become at it. I learned that if you have passion, it will provide you with purpose and if you live your purpose, payment will find a way to you as well. I describe passion as the willingness to suffer and sacrifice for that which you love, and if you would eagerly do it for free then you have found a passion inside of your soul and you are obligated to fulfill that passion during your time on earth. Most people seek payment first, and that is why they fail. They feel like compensation = competency, and that could not be further from the truth.

What are your first steps when you start a new job? What do you need to figure out, what do you need to get done, who do you need to get to know?

Rule #1: You don't have to have all the answers, you must know the people who know where to find them. Connect with the people in the positions that matter most to your transition. They are the experts in their field, and you are the expert in yours. Have the humility to know you don't know it all.

Rule #2: Tie up all loose ends as quickly and efficiently as possible so you can work like a lion and not get distracted by the odds and ends that eat up all your time and make you think you are working when really you are just busy. The goal is to be impactful, not busy!

Rule #3: Make peace with not being at peace for at least a calendar year. Get to work.

What advice do you have for a college student looking to break into coaching? Who are the best mentors in the world to work for early in your career?

First off, don't look for your break, make your break. If you only had one chance to make it in this profession, what would you do to make sure you didn't fail? People want safety nets or back-up plans, but if you want to get into this profession, you better have passion, and that passion better fuel your purpose. If you are looking for a fast track to become a big-time college coach, your ass better wait in line.

Second, the best mentors are the ones who care enough about you to help you grow and not just use you for their own gain. I don't care who your mentor(s) are, but pick someone who cares enough to invest in you achieving your dreams!

What goes into your decision to leave or stay at a job?

Happiness—don't mess with happy.

What do you do to overcome times of struggle, burnout, or overwhelm? Who do you turn to?

Burnout happens when you do something you are not passionate about. I don't get burned out because I stay on fire for my vocation. If you are doing something because you absolutely love it and you have an insane amount of passion for it, then burnout doesn't exist.

What do you think about immediately after one of your athletes is injured? What is your mindset in the following week?

Empathy first for the young man—uncontrollable event secondly—improvise, adapt, and overcome third. You have to be able to pivot in times of unforeseen circumstances and you must always be thinking about contingency plans.

How do you approach difficult conversations with athletes, coworkers, or your boss?

Fierce conversations are all about credible confrontation. To confront anyone, there must first be a credible human being behind that confrontation. You cannot sell what you don't own. There is no dancing around the hard, and there is only one way through and that is the truth. Become a truth teller by first establishing a trustworthy connection with those under your supervision or care. It sounds cliché, but there can be no correction without first a connection.

Do you have a "failure" that was critical to your long-term development or success?

My four years working at Northern Illinois as an assistant from 2007–2011 made me understand the value of having a plan and putting that plan into action. Our staff was let go in 2011 for not winning enough games, and I can most certainly attribute that to our lack of execution on a daily basis. Getting over the fear of getting fired was pivotal for me early in my career. You never fully become the best version of yourself until you have felt what it was like to be the worst version of yourself.

What traits or skills do your most successful athletes have in common?

Every Day Dudes who value their service to others over their own self-interest.

- They show up every single day, the same way, regardless of circumstance.

- They do the right work...not just the work...anyone can do "the work." High Clarity = High Performance.

- They serve others—Managing is telling others what to do—Leading is showing others what to do—Serving is telling them, showing them, and then doing it with them.

What books or resources do you most often recommend to coaches?

Most often my books will have double meanings—less strategy—more deeper meaning and enlightenment.

- Ryan Holiday books: *Ego Is The Enemy – The Obstacle Is The Way – Stillness Is The Key*

- Paulo Coelho: *Warrior of the Light – The Alchemist*

- Seth Godin: *The Icarus Deception – Make Better Art*

- Robin Sharma: *The Monk Who Sold His Ferrari*

- Timothy Galloway: *The Inner Game of Tennis*

"The day I lost my Dad, my mindset shifted. I started asking myself this question: will those athletes or coworkers be at my bedside when I draw my last breath? Signs point to no. So, in spite of caring a great deal about the people that I work with, I no longer give them more than a moment's thought when making a decision about a career move."

-Missy Mitchell-McBeth

Missy Mitchell-McBeth is the Director of Sports Performance at the Fieldhouse Volleyball Club in DFW and the owner of Missy Mitchell-McBeth Sports Performance. Before her current positions, she was the Head Strength and Conditioning Coach at Byron Nelson High School for almost six years. Mitchell-McBeth came to Byron Nelson after serving as the strength coach for Women's Basketball, Volleyball, and Women's Golf at TCU. She began her career at Copperas Cove ISD as a track, volleyball, and powerlifting coach. Mitchell-McBeth is a featured writer and speaker, most recently publishing her first book *Developmental to Division I: Strength and Conditioning for the Volleyball Athlete.*

Who do you go to when you need advice? Why them?

I always go back to my mentor, Reb Brock, who I met during the first year of my coaching career. In addition to being a great strength coach, Reb *always* shoots me straight when I call for advice. When I'm wrong? He tells me, even when I don't want to hear it. When I have an issue? He's there to help me find the best way to navigate it. When I need to call and vent? He's there for that too, but always follows up with actionable advice.

Circling back to my earlier statement: an echo chamber is not an advisor. An advisor is, for me at least, someone who can help me navigate the icy waters of "people-ing" in the coaching profession. Most strength and conditioning coaches have a pretty solid grasp on the X's and O's, but many lack the soft skills that allow for effective communication.

Find an advisor that understands both. Having technical knowledge can make you a good coach, but only those who can communicate that knowledge will become great.

What early job was pivotal in your career? Why?

I started my career as a high school volleyball coach in Copperas Cove, Texas. In addition to volleyball, I coached girl's powerlifting, girl's high jump, and taught 10th grade biology. On top of the roles and responsibilities that were listed in my job description, there were a number of other duties as assigned. This meant coaching during my conference period and spending lunch fielding 101 questions from freshman volleyball players. Who has time to eat when solving the world's problems one forgotten locker combination at a time?

Weekdays were non-stop from 5am to 8pm and weekends typically included a tournament or meet. If there wasn't a tournament or meet? I spent the weekend grading papers, setting up science labs for the week, and doing exciting things like going to the grocery store. There was no time off, vacations, or social life. It was the early 2000s, and you would have been laughed out of the building for proposing any semblance of work:life balance. The coaching profession at the time was all work, no life.

Though you couldn't pay me enough money to live this specific life again, I'm forever thankful that I experienced it. Not only did I learn the volume of work that I'm capable of, I also learned very early on that the coaching profession isn't just showing up to the weight room and doing the things that you like. There's a lot more to it than that. As coaches we should never consider ourselves too good or too big to roll up our sleeves and work.

What are your first steps when you start a new job? What do you need to figure out, what do you need to get done, who do you need to get to know?

This is typically context specific, so I'll keep this short and discuss one of the most valuable lessons I learned from the first head coach I ever worked for at Copperas Cove High School.

The people that run the school are the administrative assistants, maintenance workers, and custodians. These are the people you need to get to know and should always be treated with the utmost respect.

More specific to the strength and conditioning world: our most important ally on staff should be the athletic trainer. They have eyes and ears everywhere and know what's going on with our athletes and coaching staff at all times. As an added bonus, they can fix our broken strength coach bodies when we once again do something stupid in our own training programs.

What advice do you have for a college student looking to break into coaching? Who are the best mentors in the world to work for early in your career?

Liking your sport or, in the case of strength and conditioning coaches, the weight room, is not enough. The road to career longevity is littered with individuals who "liked to work out" so they started coaching. Your "why" has to be bigger than that. I can't tell you what your "why" is. For me, strength and conditioning is the tool I use to cultivate a relationship that I hope allows me to positively impact someone's life.

If you only had two 30-minute sessions a week to train your team, how would you prepare them?

Since my departure from collegiate athletics in 2016, I've served in two capacities. From 2016–2022, I was a high school strength and conditioning coach managing around 400 athletes across 12 sports. In the Fall of 2023, I began serving as the Director of Sports Performance at a volleyball club training 19 different teams across eight different age groups. In both cases, two 30-minute sessions a week was all that was available. However, the two situations were different, so I took two very different approaches.

In my role as a high school strength and conditioning coach, I managed two weight rooms and was rarely able to leave one of those two rooms to lead a field or court-based workout. The sport coaches were expected to lead these field/court sessions with me advising as requested. It certainly wasn't the best model, but anyone who claims they have a perfect model for high school strength and conditioning has probably never worked in that setting.

Given the above information, along with the constraints of our facility, the two 30-minute sessions per week consisted of:

- 3–5 minute in-place dynamic warm-up.
- 25–27 minute lift with maximal intent jumping and mobility interspersed.

In my current scenario as the sports performance director at a volleyball club, many of the athletes that I train already lift at school. With that being the case, I've taken the approach of trying to supplement what they do at school versus trying to one-up or replace it.

Which looks like this:

- 2-3 minutes of fundamental movement skills.

- 6-8 minutes of extensive plyometrics and/or speed drills.

- 6-8 minutes of med ball throws, intensive plyos, fly 10s, or change of direction work.

- 10-15 minutes in the weight room.

However, we nuance the above plan by age group. On the field, our younger athletes will do more gamified versions of things while our older athletes train with more structure. Conversely, we tend to spend a bit more time in the weight room with the younger athletes, since fewer are getting adequate time in a resistance training program at school, and less time in the weight room with the older ones as that bucket tends to be a little more full.

To reiterate, neither of these are "perfect" systems, but they are optimal given the context. 60 minutes a week is quite the constraint, so you have to look at the specific circumstances to determine what will have the highest return on investment within your training program.

What goes into your decision to leave or stay at a job?

I'm very old now. My willingness to stay in a position that lacks any semblance of growth potential is zero, unless that position affords me the opportunity to generate enough side income that makes it worth my time.

Additionally, I use what I have termed my "deathbed mentality" to help guide these decisions. In younger years, I would consider how my departure might impact my athletes or coworkers. How will this make them feel? How will I ever replace them? Were a few questions I would ask myself during the process.

The day I lost my Dad, my mindset shifted. I started asking myself this question: will those athletes or coworkers be at my bedside when I draw my last breath? Signs point to no. So, in spite of caring a great deal about the people that I work with, I no longer give them more than a moment's thought when making a decision about a career move.

Instead, my family, my life, and my career goals are the primary considerations when determining whether to stay or move on. A few questions I ask myself in this process as it relates to these considerations:

- What will staying/leaving do for my career?
- What will it do for my family?
- How does it get me closer to my career goals?
- How does it get me closer to the life I want to live?

And there is one final question:

- What am I willing to tolerate?

Hard truth: there is no perfect job. All jobs have parts that suck. Job hopping to get out of one type of drama only sends you into another type, so carefully evaluate whether the not-so-great parts of your job truly make the grass greener elsewhere.

What do you do to overcome times of struggle, burnout, or overwhelm? Who do you turn to?

Full disclosure, I'm in one of these times right now with no end in sight. Entrepreneurship isn't easy. Watching as your personal calendar fills with all of the things you need to do to grow a business can be overwhelming. Being in the final stages of publication and feeling like you're crawling towards the finish line is exhausting. It seems like every time I check off one task, four more emerge to replace it.

Woe is me, right? Wrong. The first thing I do during these times is to recognize that all of the above "problems" aren't actually problems at all. They're a product of hustle and the fact that others respect the work I've put in enough to believe that I can be a value add. So in this current time of overwhelm, I'm choosing gratitude. Sort of.

If you're a pragmatic thinker like me, choosing gratitude isn't going to cut it. I can be grateful, but still tired. Grateful, but still irritable. Grateful, but still only have 24-hours a day.

So here are a few tactical strategies I use to manage these times:

- Keep a calendar. That's not really an earth-shattering recommendation, but nothing makes a busy time worse than a lack of organization.
- Knowing when to say no. In the early stages of your career or of building a business, you probably need to say yes to most, if not all, opportunities. As you progress, you need to be more selective about what you take on.
- Done is better than perfect. As a perfectionist, this one is a challenge for me.

Sometimes things need to be done at a really high level. But other times you just need to get something done and not worry so much if it's not the best thing ever. The challenge is in figuring out when to use each of these approaches.

- Get away from your phone and devices. People can wait for you to take some time for yourself. Remember the "deathbed mentality."

- Walk away. There are times to power through a project, and there are times to set it aside, take a break, and come back with renewed energy. When I say walk away, I literally go outside and walk, phone free, to clear my mind more these days than ever before.

- Go to therapy. It's okay to get help managing the stressors of life. Coaches need coaches too.

Finally, somewhere in the last few months I heard a coach on a podcast discuss work–life balance in terms of periodization. Let my lack of citing a specific coach and podcast serve as an example that "done is sometimes better than perfect," because I have no idea where I heard it.

Anyway, just as our training programs don't emphasize every physical capacity equally at all times, there will be certain times in our lives where work takes the front seat. Other times where family time and free time will be our priority. The important thing is that we plan for this and ensure that even if a particular element of our lives isn't the primary emphasis of our current phase of "training," that we still keep it in our program at a level that ensures we are able to maintain it.

What do you think about immediately after one of your athletes is injured? What is your mindset in the following week?

Most would never be caught on record with this take, but I'll say what many of us feel. If it's one of those athletes that never does a single thing you ask of them that sustains an injury? I wince, knowing I'm about to spend even more time in misery working with them through their painstakingly lazy return to play. This doesn't mean I don't feel empathy, it simply means I'm realistic about the likelihood that we're all in for a bumpy ride.

Conversely, if it's an athlete who does everything that's asked of them? I'm beside myself believing that I've failed them. I pour over every program I've ever written for that athlete trying to find the missing piece of the puzzle.

Curiously, I've never successfully located this elusive puzzle piece and, to my knowledge, no one in strength and conditioning has. Sometimes, despite careful programming and monitoring, injuries happen. So ultimately, I give myself the same 24-hour pouting window that my good friend and G.O.A.T. athletic trainer Val Hairson gave to our athletes. After the 24 hours have expired, we no longer focus on the injury, only the recovery. Of course I modify programming for the athlete as needed, but I try to keep the training process as "normal" as possible for everyone involved. Mentally, injured athletes don't need to be treated like an invalid. They need to be treated like they're in the weight room training, because they are, even if that training looks different than it did previously.

How do you approach difficult conversations with athletes, coworkers, or your boss?

First, I want to preface this by recognizing the enormous number of times I've gotten this one wrong in my lifetime. As you have likely surmised in reading some of my responses, I don't often mince words. While it tends to be my preferred way to communicate, it can also be an absolutely foolproof strategy for being told you need to "sand down your edges" because you're "difficult to work with" by those who don't share the core value of transparency, which anecdotal evidence leads me to believe is roughly 90% of the population.

Having done it wrong so many times, I've had ample opportunity to sit back and reflect upon better ways of operating. This doesn't mean I get this right all the time, it simply means I make an effort to get it right.

The first step is knowing your audience and their preferred communication style. It is incredibly challenging and often abrasive to have a difficult conversation with someone when there is no prior relationship. It becomes even more abrasive if there are opposing communication styles at play and no one seeks a middle ground. Sometimes, despite valuing transparency, you may need to sugarcoat things to be better received, or vice versa.

The second step is to choose your battles. An overarching question I try to consider: what action would I like the other party to take as a result of this exchange? If I'm not able to answer that, it's likely not a conversation that needs to happen. A second question: is there a step I can take in the other person's direction that can assist in resolving this issue without compromising my values?

Here's an example. This year I started working with a group of athletes that I didn't know. Giving them the benefit of the doubt, I allowed them the autonomy to choose their own weight room groups. Five out of six groups handled it really well. Group six? Not so well. In a former life I would have stormed over, yelled at them for being immature, dispersed them to other groups (inadvertently spreading the immaturity to more groups), and marched away triumphantly having solved the problem. The irony is that I would have created more problems using this tactic than I actually solved.

Fortunately, Present-Day-Me is sometimes more evolved. I took a step in their direction and asked what I could do better to help them be more successful, provided them with a couple of possible solutions, and gave them the space to provide some of their own.

Which ties into another governing principle for navigating difficult conversations: everyone involved usually knows there's a problem. Rather than continuing to point it out, come to the table with potential solutions. If you can't think of any? That's okay too, but be transparent about it and be open to the proposed solutions of others.

A final way I try to approach difficult conversations is by having thick skin. Every problem won't always get solved and it definitely won't always get solved the way you want it to. When things don't go your way, understand that most workplace interactions aren't personal. Athletics are a business. At times you need to treat it as such.

Do you have a "failure" that was critical to your long-term development or success?

I don't know that this is a "failure" in that I opted to leave, but leaving collegiate strength and conditioning was one of the most difficult decisions I ever made. At one point, I believed I would retire from where I was at. But circumstances changed, and as much as my salary allowed me to pay my bills and still have fifty-seven cents left over to spend, it was time to move on. So I got a job as a high school strength and conditioning coach.

My assumption was that this transition would make me fade away professionally. A once promising career at the collegiate level was now tarnished by a regression back to my days as a lowly high school coach. How embarrassing.

Except that it wasn't. At the first CSCCa conference after I left the collegiate level, I met David Neill, another defect from the collegiate S&C ranks who was working down the street from me at another high school. I realized there were more people like me. I also met other coaches who had tons of questions about the transition because they were looking to make the same transition for themselves. The money was better, and the work/life balance was better.

At some point I started getting asked to do speaking engagements, podcasts, and even to serve on the board of the National High School Strength Coach's Association due to my unique blend of experiences. What I formerly saw as a weakness, I leaned into and branded as a strength. Ultimately, it was these experiences that led me to recognize the opportunity to create my own business.

What traits or skills do your most successful athletes have in common?

Here's what everyone wants to read: "My most successful athletes were such great people! I truly enjoyed working with them. They had outstanding attention to detail, were great teammates, worked hard, and were coachable!"

Those words apply to some. But honestly, many of my most successful athletes over the years had some less than desirable tendencies. One was averse to hard work, unless it was her exact event. Then she would go all in. Another had roughly zero sense of urgency in training, but when the whistle blew to start the match? She would rip someone's head off their shoulders. Another was just a genuinely unpleasant human being to work with. But also the most talented athlete I've ever trained in her sport. So what's the common thread aside from not being a strength coach's pet?

These were athletes that didn't seek validation from me, their sport coach, or even their teammates. They played for themselves, and they played hard. Usually. Sometimes they only played hard enough to win, but if we're being honest, many would take that approach if they had the luxury of doing so.

However, with that being said, there was a way to reach them. I believe they each intuitively knew what they needed to do to outmatch their competitors, or at least they believed they did. If you butt heads with that belief as a coach, you'll rarely win. But if you lean into it just a little, gain their trust, and use that trust to show them that with a little more work they could be even better, you've got a shot.

And for what it's worth, no, I'm absolutely not promoting this as a great mindset for athletes. It may work for certain high performers, but not for the rest of us. Those who are less talented have to do more to achieve less than their superstar teammates. An unfortunate reality, but reality nonetheless.

What books or resources do you most often recommend to coaches?

At the time of writing this, I am in the end stages of publishing a book of my own:

Developmental to Division I: Strength and Conditioning for the Volleyball Athlete.

Typically, I find that those seeking books and other resources are sport coaches who lack a background in strength and conditioning but are tasked with designing and implementing a strength and conditioning plan for their team. With that in mind, D2D1 is a culmination of 20 years of trial and error, organized and simplified to take the guesswork out of the what, why, and how of program design for the sport coach, parent, or young strength and conditioning professional.

Other books that will always be on my list of recommendations are Joe Kenn's *The Strength Coach's Training Playbook* and Zach Dechant's *Movement Over Maxes.*

Beyond books, the best resource I can recommend is to build a network of other coaches who *do not think like you.* This network should expose you to different perspectives and challenge your thought process. Networks that serve as echo chambers can feel validating, but rarely elicit growth.

"The most successful athletes have a high basketball IQ to go alongside their impressive physical qualities. They know their bodies better than me and I've leaned on them to help me best program for them as athletes."

-Matt Aldred

Matt Aldred is in his first year as the Head Strength and Conditioning Coach for Men's Basketball and Men's Golf at the University of Michigan. He comes to Ann Arbor after spending the last six years at Furman, where he most recently earned the title of Assistant Head Coach/Director of Basketball Performance, the first coach in the nation to gain this title within basketball strength and conditioning. Aldred helped Furman have incredible success during the six seasons he was there, including a Southern Conference Tournament Title, a first round upset in the NCAA tournament along with a record 28 wins in the 2022-23 season, and four 20-win seasons. He has contributed to the education of many other coaches through his articles and social media, while also co-producing the course *Fascial Mechanics.*

Who do you go to when you need advice? Why them?
My mom is my role model, so I speak to her often about all areas of my life. My wife is my best friend, so every day we talk through personal and professional stuff. My twin brother is an incredible Christian man, so I have a high respect and care for the advice he gives me. I also have a very close relationship with our athletic trainer so often I see him for both personal and professional advice. I'll only seek advice from people I trust and that I know care about me, but it's like anything in life, the more you give attention and care to something the better outcome you expect, it's the same way with relationships, two-way street.

What early job was pivotal in your career? Why?
I was a personal trainer in England before I came to the states to do a graduate assistant job. It was my first time really programming for multiple clients and using a commercial gym space to train them. I learned a lot of valuable skills then that still apply to my job now. Perhaps the biggest skill was being able to sell my vision to them of what their physique and health would look like after consistent training and

lifestyle changes. Another skill was being comfortable one on one with clients, both training them and interacting before and after sessions. I frequently train athletes one on one now, which is essentially personal training!

What are your first steps when you start a new job? What do you need to figure out, what do you need to get done, who do you need to get to know?

Learn everyone's names as fast as possible. Nothing shows you're more ready to work than getting to know the people you work with as quickly as possible. Learn the lay of the land while slowly inputting your system and philosophy of how you want the training culture to be. I'm fortunate to have been at Furman six seasons now, we have our system in place, guys know our training culture and how I operate. *(This was before he left for Michigan)*

What advice do you have for a college student looking to break into coaching? Who are the best mentors in the world to work for early in your career?

Email coaches you respect and want to work for, tell them why you respect their work, and ask to come in and shadow them for an hour/half day/full day. That's then your opportunity to impress them and work towards becoming an intern for them where you can work for that Coach for an extended period. I was very fortunate when working at The University of Alabama in Huntsville (D2) to not only work for a great head Strength Coach (Tyler Shimizu) but also to work with multiple great coaches at The University of Tennessee in Chattanooga (D1) for three summers. Collin Crane (now with Georgia MBB) was a huge role model for me early in my career and is a close friend to this day. He taught me so much about work and life balance, training, and the S&C industry. For me, he's the best S&C mentor I've ever had.

If you only had two 30-minute sessions a week to train your team, how would you prepare them?

This sounds a lot like in-season training to me! Make these 30 minutes as individual as possible for the athletes so that they are getting the max ROI from those sessions for their development both short and long term. Barefoot warm up, unilateral training, force plate tests, and multi-planar movements gets the job done for me.

What goes into your decision to leave or stay at a job?

Who I work for and who I would work for. Knowing the character and morals of a Head Coach is the most important thing for me. All things will flow down from that.

What do you do to overcome times of struggle, burnout, or overwhelm? Who do you turn to?

I have a checklist of daily tasks on my office wall that changes depending on the time of the year (early off-season, pre-season, in-season, etc.). Two things that are always on there—family check in and outside time. Speaking to my family back in England often gives me great outside perspective about the stresses in my life. If we won or lost a game of basketball, there's more to life than that. Outside time whatever the weather is key for my focus and mental well-being. Our campus is beautiful and whether it's a walk/run/ruck in the woods or around the lake, this is a much-needed mini escape from work and boost in mood for me.

What do you think about immediately after one of your athletes is injured? What is your mindset in the following week?

Did we do enough to prevent that injury from happening? Can we do an autopsy without blame and just see how we could stop that injury from happening in the future?

How do you approach difficult conversations with athletes, coworkers, or your boss?

I pray over the upcoming conversation and try to look at it from their perspective before my own.

Do you have a "failure" that was critical to your long-term development or success?

I have a story of struggle that is quite funny looking back on it. When I became an assistant Strength and Conditioning Coach for The University of Florida, assisting men's and women's basketball and being the primary coach for men's tennis, we had both lbs and KGs for weight plates. KGs were on the floor as bumper plates and on the racks were plates in lbs. Being from England I dealt with KGs only, to now use lbs and to load up bars multiple times a session with "170" being shouted at me with no clue what that meant for on the bar. I had to figure things out quickly.

I decided to go to the UF library on the weekends and study the plate colors so I knew what 155, 170, 142.5, 237.5 looked like and could at least put the right weight on the bar. That first month I didn't feel like I was good enough to be there. I felt out of my depth. It was a feeling I've only had once in my career and there's a reason why—I was determined not to let a small thing get in the way of my progress and the work that needed to be done. I'm grateful for the learning curve and often reflect back to this when new interns or assistants start working with me. I want to give them grace to work on things, but also I want to see them go out of their way to figure it out and get better. The small things we do or don't do at work matter. They accumulate over time into successful habits or distracting behaviors.

What traits or skills do your most successful athletes have in common?

They are the best movers on the court. Our weight room warriors over the years often haven't been our best athletes or basketball players, they've just really enjoyed the resistance training side of their development. The most successful athletes have a high basketball IQ to go alongside their impressive physical qualities. They know their bodies better than me and I've leaned on them to help me best program for them as athletes.

What books or resources do you most often recommend to coaches?

I love books by Adam Grant (organizational psychologist), especially his books *Think Again* and *Originals*. There are a lot of great coaching X's and O's books and periodization books, but to me, at this stage in my career (8 years in) I want to be challenged to constantly question what I do with my athletes and why I do it. These books are very thought provoking for me and challenge me to keep seeking best practice, not just doing what I've always done or what's always been done in our industry.

In terms of resources, I would encourage people to turn their social media into an educational resource rather than a black hole of procrastination. There are SO many great coaches that put out amazing content. I have used social media over the years to take ideas/concepts and improve my process and service to my athletes, it's free knowledge! Notable follows for me are: Danny Foley, Hunter Eisenhower, Daniel Bove, Cory Schlesinger, Zack Zillner, Nick DiMarco, Collin Crane, and Pat Lewis.

"If there's a talk that needs to happen but I really am not looking forward to it, I try to remember what things will look like in a week or two, or a month or two, if I don't do the hard thing. Author Brene Brown calls these meetings 'Rumbles.' As the boss of my small company, I have to be intentional about rumbling."

-Erika Lambert

Erika Lambert is entering her second year as the Head Women's Basketball Coach at the University of North Florida. She arrived at North Florida after spending seven seasons as the Associate Head Coach and Recruiting Coordinator at Abilene Christian, helping the program achieve four 23+ win seasons, their first Division I regular season and tournament championships, and their first appearance in the NCAA tournament. While in Abilene, Lambert was named one of 22 assistants ready to lead their own program by The Athletic, and was also one of only 30 coaches named to the Women Coaches NEXT UP program in 2020. Her stops before ACU include Charleston Southern and the College of Charleston. Lambert is also the co-founder of "Moms in Coaching."

Who do you go to when you need advice? Why them?
My go-to people for wisdom in coaching and in life are my own basketball coaches. I'm 38 but still reach out to my coaches from the College of Charleston and my high school basketball coach back in New York if I'm struggling with something and need advice. I also lean on coaching friends I've connected with over the years. My inner circle in the basketball coaching world consists of people I have worked with previously, coaches who are more experienced than me and whom I have a lot of respect for, as well as friends in the business who are at the same stage of the game as me.

The 2023-2024 season was my 16th year in coaching, but only my first as a head coach, so I really relied on my network to help me figure things out. Brooke Wyckoff (Florida State), Lindsay Edmonds (Rice), and Lisa Fortier (Gonzaga) are three head coaches I'm thankful to call friends who I often bounce ideas off of. Erika Lang-Montgomery (Longwood) is a head coach I think the world of because she has been in the business for a long time and has had a lot of success while leading her teams as a Christian coach and raising a family. We met years ago through an organization I co-founded called Moms in Coaching and we joked we would never forget each other's name. Ever since then, we run into each other on the recruiting trail or I'll give her a call and she's generous with her time to help me.

I worked as an assistant coach for Julie Goodenough (Abilene Christian) for nine seasons at both ACU and Charleston Southern University. A lot of the good parts of my program here at UNF came from her and she will always be like family to me. Weston Jameson (Harding University MBB) and I were assistant coaches alongside each other at ACU and both became first-time head coaches last season. It was really helpful to have a colleague and friend to talk through all the 'firsts' with because we have been figuring things out at the same time.

What early job was pivotal in your career? Why?

I believe I am the coach I am today because of my first job. I graduated from the College of Charleston in May 2008 and had the privilege of joining the coaching staff there in August as the Director of Basketball Operations. Working at my alma mater, for the coaches who poured into me as a student-athlete, was really special. I learned right away that there was a lot more to basketball coaching than what I had seen from the student-athlete side. There was a lot of grunt work involved in my first position and I'm thankful for that. I've worked with a lot of people since then who all claim to be hard workers but turn their nose up at tasks that seem beneath them. That won't get you very far in coaching. It's not as glamorous as it looks on ESPN. The work is the work. No job is not your job.

What are your first steps when you start a new job? What do you need to figure out, what do you need to get done, who do you need to get to know?

This depends on the position you're working in, but I have a few thoughts on starting new jobs. One thing I encourage young coaches to be clear about is why they were hired. Why did your boss bring you onto their coaching staff? Whatever strengths they saw in you, lean into those and bring your best in those areas every day. If you were hired for your recruiting prowess in a specific region or for your player development experience with a certain position on the team, be prepared to execute those things and dedicate a majority of your time to it. Also, assistant coaches need to hone in on where their head coach needs the most help. How can you make their life easier? Plan your early to-do lists around that.

Head coaches need to get to know their administrators. As a new head coach at North Florida, I asked my Athletic Director what the top priority would be in rebuilding the Women's Basketball program. The answer was: recruiting. So in the midst of all the newness and the stress of everything that needed to get done, I knew to prioritize recruiting above everything else. The most important people you need to get to know when you start a new coaching job are the players. Sure, it's important to reach out to notable alums, to connect with donors, and to start building relationships with key staff members across campus, but the team you've been entrusted with is most important. So if that means the other things need to wait, that's okay.

What advice do you have for a college student looking to break into coaching? Who are the best mentors in the world to work for early in your career?
My first question to them would be—"Are you sure you really want to try this?" A career in coaching is not for the faint of heart, haha. The actual day-to-day job and grind of the schedule looks and feels different from what you see just on the sidelines at practice and on gameday. So any college student interested in coaching should definitely get involved with opportunities to intern or volunteer with athletic programs on their campus to get a glimpse behind the scenes.

If you only had two 30-minute sessions a week to train your team, how would you prepare them?
One of those sessions would be dedicated solely to strength and conditioning. I'm a firm believer that if we're not in shape, the basketball coaching won't matter. The second session would be dedicated to basketball drills, both individual skill work and team offense/defense. Lastly, I'd use our closing huddle each day for a 5-minute talk about core values, competitiveness, mental health, nutrition, etc. You have to get the culture and off-the-court stuff right.

What goes into your decision to leave or stay at a job?
Pretty much my whole career has been dictated by putting my family first. Staying or going decisions were made based on what was best for my husband's career alongside my own, and where we felt good financially and geographically about raising our two daughters. My husband is a pediatric dentist, so some of our cross-country moves have been because of his residency and fellowship training. Even though I wasn't free to climb the ladder, so to speak, in a traditional way, my husband and I have made it

all work by the grace of God. When it comes to being a wife and mom first, I wouldn't change my career path for anything.

What do you do to overcome times of struggle, burnout, or overwhelm? Who do you turn to?

I pray. Coaching is a ministry for me, so when I start to feel burnt out, I need to be reminded of my kingdom purpose in all of this. The first six months of my first head coaching job were so overwhelming professionally and personally. For weeks (months, really), I was leaving the office after midnight in Florida, missing my family back in Texas, and struggling to keep up with everyone who needed something from me. I can't tell you how many times I verbally said to myself, "Just do the next right thing. That's all you can do. God's got the rest." And another thought that kept replaying in my mind was, "The people are the job." So no matter how long the to-do list was for the day, I still took advantage of opportunities to have personal conversations with the players on my new team or to help them with things they needed direction from me on. Keeping those human connections is so important during busy seasons because otherwise we tend to isolate ourselves.

What do you think about immediately after one of your athletes is injured? What is your mindset in the following week?

As a student-athlete, I was perpetually injured. My adult knees often remind me of that...As a coach, I'm keenly aware that the possibility is always there, and it can drastically change the course of a team's season. Last year I took over a team that was pretty shorthanded to begin with, and I would often think to myself that we would really be in trouble if one or two players in particular happened to go down. But I also planned for it. I hope for the best and plan for the worst. Injuries are bound to happen, but you just have to be mentally prepared to keep it moving. With an injured athlete, my first concern will always be for their well-being. I'm well aware of the increased chances of clinical depression among athletes with serious injuries, so I think it's important that coaches don't let kids on the IR list fade into the background.

How do you approach difficult conversations with athletes, coworkers, or your boss?

Confrontation is uncomfortable, but I have learned that uncomfortable conversations are necessary for a high-performing team. If there's a talk that needs to happen but I really am not looking forward to it, I try to remember what things will look like in a week or two, or a month or two, if I don't do the hard thing. Author Brene Brown calls these meetings "Rumbles." As the boss of my small company, I have to be intentional about rumbling. I approach these types of conversations with love and from a place of humility. Always start by listening. You may think you see the whole problem when in fact, there are important details unbeknownst to you. We're like a family and families don't get along all the time. That's okay. But we will always treat one another with respect.

From a practical standpoint, I rarely have difficult conversations with my athletes alone. Another coach is usually present in the meeting. I keep notes on these meetings with both my players and staff and also try to take notes if the discussion is one with my own superiors.

Do you have a "failure" that was critical to your long-term development or success?

One season many years ago, I was part of a new coaching staff. It was a unique situation because I had also been a part of the previous coaching staff there. When a new head coach gets hired in college basketball, it's very rare that any former assistant coaches get retained. I was extremely grateful that the new head coach kept me on. At the time, I was expecting my second daughter and my husband was finishing his last year of dental school, so I would not have had the opportunity to move and coach anywhere else. The year prior, our team had the most wins in D1 school history. But the following season, with the coaching transition, we barely won 10 games. It was a really hard year. Everything felt a little chaotic and I found myself as the middleman between old and new. It challenged me to remain professional and loyal to my head coach whenever the players might have wanted to complain to me about not liking the way things were done now.

That loyalty is a quality that has stuck with me as a coach and I value it above just about anything now in my own assistants. I also witnessed what a coaching transition looks and feels like from the inside. That was over a decade ago, but it informed some of my decision-making as I took the helm of my own program recently. For example, not once since I was hired at UNF did I refer to any players as "[Former Coach's] kids." And I don't distinguish the players I've signed as "My kids." I learned from experience that mindset can be detrimental to culture. Another thing about that losing season years ago is that while I was loyal to my head coach, I recognize now I didn't do my best work. I see where I should have done a better job as a communicator, recruiter, etc. and I've improved in those areas.

What traits or skills do your most successful athletes have in common?

Humility, mental toughness, and healthy nutrition/sleep habits are common threads between my most successful players. I have found that I love coaching kids who are not all about the hype. It's hard for me to connect with kids who care more about their own success and visibility than they do about the team. I appreciate kids whose parents never told their daughter they are the best thing in the world, but instead taught them that hard work and being a great teammate are the daily standard. Players who are mentally tough are those who don't make excuses, who choose gratitude instead of complaining, and who understand that coaching critiques are meant to help. The more mentally tough players are, the more efficient we can be to coach in practice and games without having to tiptoe around feelings or people taking offense.

And lastly, players who learn how to fuel their bodies well just tend to be more successful. The physical demands of our athletes' schedule are too great for sleep and nutrition to be left to chance. I have several international players on my team and they are far and away our healthiest eaters. They love to lift, run, and get up extra shots without complaining in a way that is so different from our American kids. There's more maturity there. I can't really explain the reason for that. But I know I will continue to recruit international players!

What books or resources do you most often recommend to coaches?

I don't really have go-to books that I recommend to coaches, but I do always encourage reading. 'Leaders are readers,' as they say. The very first leadership books I ever read are classics from when I first started playing basketball in high school. *Reach for the Summit* by Pat Summit and *Leading with the Heart* by Mike Krzyzewski are still on my shelf, all marked up, dog-eared and tattered from referencing over the last 25 years. Jon Gordon books are always in the rotation. This summer, my team at North Florida is reading *Atomic Habits* by James Clear and discussing together. I love reading and recommending autobiographies from successful women across all industries. I enjoy coaching resources that draw parallels between team-building in the business world to the like in college athletics. Nowadays, it's more likely that I share podcast episodes with my coaching peers rather than books. *The Andy Stanley Leadership Podcast* is my favorite, but I also love and often recommend *The Basketball Podcast* with Chris Oliver and the *Women Leaders in Sports Podcast.*

> **"Building a career is about progress and evolution, not perfection and revolution. Develop awareness, reflect on what works, what doesn't, and keep improving. Learn from others, watch the mistakes poor coaches make— you can always learn what not to do from poor coaches."**
>
> ## *-Fergus Connolly*

Dr. Fergus Connolly is one of the world's leading experts in team sports and human performance and is the only coach to have worked full-time in every major league around the world. He has served as Director of Elite Performance for the San Francisco 49ers, Sports Science Director with the Welsh Rugby Union, and Performance Director and Director of Football Operations for the University of Michigan Football. Connolly has consulted with organizations, coaches, and players from multiple other leagues, along with elite military units and companies around the world. His highly acclaimed books include *Game Changer* and *59 Lessons.*

Who do you go to when you need advice? Why them?

I've been lucky to have a huge network of mentors and advisors over the years in every conceivable field and domain. In sport, I've had many great mentors who gave me advice—most of the best known are mentioned in my book *59 Lessons.* Craig White, Phil Richards, Charles Poliquin, Charlie Francis were all world leading when I started and I was lucky to learn directly from them. Later Dan Pfaff, Henk Kraaijenhof, Mike Boyle mid-way through my career. Those guys are not just great coaches, but wonderful people. Then there's been a host of people and close friends from the SOF community that have always been there for me, and of course family.

What early job was pivotal in your career? Why?

Your first two jobs are always the most pivotal in directing your career. I always tell young coaches, Rule 1: Early in your career is find the best Coach to work for. Later you can worry about finding the best team or club, but starting out find the best coach. The best coach is someone who's actually coached and has experience. I was fortunate the first two coaches I worked for, Phil Richards and Craig White at Bolton Wanderers and Welsh Rugby, were two of the most open-minded and driven I've ever been around. I learned the value of continuous professional development from day one. They always found and learned from the best in the field, not the loudest. The other critical distinction was that they never let S&C get in the way of the most important thing—winning games.

What are your first steps when you start a new job? What do you need to figure out, what do you need to get done, who do you need to get to know?

Before you can, as Bruce Lee said, "Be Like Water," you need to "Be Like Sponge." Watch and learn everything you can.

(A) Perfect the basics and (B) get to know the people you're working with. Many coaches try to stand out by doing something special or unique. That usually backfires. They either fail or look like they're trying too hard and lose all credibility, which is impossible to regain.

The basics always win. Do the basics right, keep doing the basics right, and remember winning is and always will be a people business. You need to be able to understand, listen to, connect, and communicate with people. It doesn't matter how smart, qualified, or intelligent you are—if you have poor people skills you'll forever struggle to progress.

Building a career is about progress and evolution, not perfection and revolution. Develop awareness, reflect on what works, what doesn't, and keep improving. Learn from others, watch the mistakes poor coaches make—you can always learn what not to do from poor coaches.

What advice do you have for a college student looking to break into coaching? Who are the best mentors in the world to work for early in your career?

The best advice I have for young coaches who really want to make it is: Start Coaching. There's been a trend to stay on and do further education. That was a good idea a number of years ago, but today it's almost a disadvantage. The biggest gaps in the skill sets of young coaches are (1) problem solving and (2) people skills. These will not be developed spending longer in higher education in a way that will assist in the real world in this industry.

If I had to hire between two people, 26 years of age, one coming out of university with a PhD after four or five years and one or two years experience or someone who has been working full-time since their degree and perhaps has registered for a masters or

PhD part-time—I'm always taking the person with more real-world experience.

You can always hire a PhD to help solve your problems, you can't hire one to identify them or even solve them on their own. You can continue further education in your spare time. But getting into the field, learning from experienced coaches is a priority today. You'll understand the ACTUAL problems coaches really face, the ones that matter. You'll learn how to communicate with the people and backgrounds you need to coach. You'll develop buy-in, listening, and communication skills. Even when it comes to technology, you'll learn to apply the technology to solve real problems as needed by your team, that actually solves problems. Get coaching and keep improving.

If you only had two 30-minute sessions a week to train your team, how would you prepare them?

My experience is only with team sport. Based on what most teams are doing today, practice will cover the 'middle zone' physically. Lots of anaerobic work, agility, routes, etc. Speed endurance, coordination, endurance, anaerobic, etc. should all be covered during the team training. All the middle ground work will be taken care of in practice.

I'd do one max strength or max speed (depending on position) with full rest. And I'd do one low intensity, mobility session. Address the two outer extremes of the training continuum. Max Strength/Speed is not going to be touched on in team practice and will detrain fast over a season. Also, if all you have available is 2 x 30 mins, that suggests mobility (flexibility through the desired ROM) will be sorely lacking in the players.

What goes into your decision to leave or stay at a job?

There's three ways to answer that question.

First, in your 20s I'd encourage young coaches to change as soon as learning starts to plateau. You want to learn from completely different types of coaches early in your career—especially those who train with completely different philosophies. Challenge your thinking.

One mistake I see young coaches make early in their career is they work for one coach and almost fall in love with that one way of doing things. Nothing is more risky for a long career. You want to search out opposite methodologies. I've learned as much from Mike Boyle as I did Louie Simmons—and I saw the similarities, not just the differences. This is important because in your career the demands will change and if you have only one way of doing things you'll struggle to be flexible and adapt.

In your 30s you want to look at working for organizations and leaders that you can learn from. You should have good people skills at this stage, but as your maturity develops you will need to learn management and leadership skills. The best way to learn this is not just from the person you choose to work for, but from the organization as a whole.

Secondly, I believe every coach personally should have their own ethical code. Every coach talks about how they'll do 'whatever it takes to win,' do anything to win or anything to be successful. That's easy. Even easier to say. I want to know what you won't do. For me it's always been four: Doping, Discrimination, Abuse, Compromising long-term athlete health. To each their own, but trust me, it's better to know your line and code BEFORE you start coaching than trying to decide when you're in a situation where you have to decide on the spot.

Finally, if you're genuinely not happy, get out. We all have bad days, but if you're unhappy over an extended period of time, either your values don't align with the leadership or organization OR you've lifestyle and relationship issues away from work that you need to take time to address.

What do you do to overcome times of struggle, burnout, or overwhelm? Who do you turn to?

I've gotten much better at this now. Before I just toughed it out. Now I've a whole series of close friends, most actually not in the industry who I'll call and speak with. I plan time off, down time away from work to regenerate.

I think the bigger challenge for most coaches is to spot when those things are happening or starting. Know yourself.

Over time you can almost blunt your own awareness, so you need people around you who are NOT in the business who can tap you on the shoulder and say, "Hey, you're not yourself, let's grab coffee."

What do you think about immediately after one of your athletes is injured? What is your mindset in the following week?

Opportunity. I can point fingers, cry and b***h about it. But it's happened. Now it's opportunity. Opportunity to figure out why it happened. Opportunity to make sure that same reason never occurs again. Opportunity to create protocols to ensure no other player gets injured the same way. Opportunity to understand that injury better than anyone else. Opportunity to return that player to play better than they were before they got injured. Opportunity to develop areas of that player's performance I hadn't time to previously. Opportunity to get to know that person better while rehabbing. Opportunity.

How do you approach difficult conversations with athletes, coworkers, or your boss?

Early and honest. The longer you leave something unsaid, the more combinations and permutations your mind runs through. Most are inaccurate and just speculative. With that time and speculation comes pressure you're only putting on yourself. You end up making mountains out of molehills.

If there's an issue, or you think there might be an issue, have a quiet word to clarify and move on. I personally haven't time for BS or disingenuous people, so I don't understand why people wouldn't be forthright, but there's plenty of it. Surround yourself with people who will just tell you the truth, whether you like it or not, ignore the ones who won't.

Be respectfully honest and get it out there. In many cases, real issues I see could have been solved long before with a quiet chat over coffee or the end of practice and are in most instances a case of misunderstanding or something taken out of context. Address it fast and honestly, move on.

Do you have a "failure" that was critical to your long-term development or success?

Sure. Too many to list. But "The man who never made a mistake never made anything." I have no problem with mistakes providing two things: (1) the intent was sincere and well-intentioned and (2) the mistake is learned from and isn't repeated.

If you're trying to improve you're always pushing boundaries, you're testing and setting new limits, you're seeing what works, what doesn't. It's called 'Action-based Research,' that was the basis of my PhD. You find ways that work, ways that don't work— but it's a process of constant iterative improvement. That's not an excuse to recklessly make change, you're taking probability based risks to explore possible improvement.

The alternatives are drones and robots, copy cats, that never truly improve. They have no initiative, independent thinking, or creativity. Nothing is a greater obstacle to winning or success. Nor boring!

What traits or skills do your most successful athletes have in common?

Triple H. Honesty, Hard work, Humility.

It's the very same for coaches. You need to be honest enough to know your strengths and weaknesses. Brutally honest with yourself to see them and acknowledge those areas of development. Honest with colleagues and teammates. Honesty is the basis of trust. People think you have to be liked. Ideally sure, but you need to be trusted most of all. And honesty is the basis of trust.

No one achieves anything without hard work. And that's hard quality work. Not simply going through the motions or putting in hours or time with the office lights on. That's purposefully deciding to focus on something to improve it.

Humility is the key to improvement. To find and understand your role, respect others, respect teammates, and have a long career, humility is a key. That doesn't mean being bashful, but it certainly means avoiding arrogance and complacency.

Triple H. That's the starting point.

What books or resources do you most often recommend to coaches?

I get asked this question a lot and the answer rarely changes, they're never sports books. *The Four Agreements, Five Regrets of the Dying, Letter to Garcia, Who Moved My Cheese*. Each are short simple reads, but with powerful lessons for the reader. Those are the starting point. After that, in terms of sport-specific reading, it always depends on the area of most need for the coach. That's too long to list honestly. I've a library of over 1,500 books, it depends very specifically on the area the coach needs to develop.

A few things I do now that I wish I'd learned sooner about books and reading:

· Keep a list of each book you read, and organize it simply by theme (my list is over 1,500 books) such as 'Talent ID & Development,' 'Innovation & Creativity,' 'Communication & Expression,' etc. It will be a great help later when you need to solve a problem that comes up.

· Change your mindset from 'reading' books to 'using' books. Every time you buy a book, ask yourself how am I going to use or apply this book. Reading is a passive activity, using the book is about making the content work for you.

· Start with the problem first. Don't just buy a book that's 'popular' or trending. Buy books on the issue you're currently trying to address, otherwise you'll never solve what you need to solve, you'll be like a headless chicken.

· Don't ignore older books. Because publishing is more accessible to more people, 90% of books published today should have been free articles. Older books are not only cheaper but often much richer in content and value.

· Never write on a book. Rewrite it in your notebook. Underlining makes you feel good, but unless it moves from the book to your pages, that knowledge is going nowhere.

"When we talk about the book of Romans, where God turns all things to the good of those that follow Him and believe in Him, I've seen that in my own life. You remind people that these things, these failures, God's going to use them. If you're abiding in God, if you're invested in God, if you're open to God, he will take any failure, any damage, and reconcile it on his timeline."

-Charlie Melton

Charlie Melton is a recognized Master Strength and Conditioning Coach entering his 20th season as the Director of Athletics Performance for Men's Basketball at Baylor University. He has helped to elevate the program to an elite level, including multiple trips to the Sweet Sixteen, multiple trips to the Elite Eight, and a National Championship victory in 2021. Melton worked at Florida State and Memphis before heading to Baylor. While at Baylor, he has coached 46 players that have gone on to have professional careers in basketball, including 16 NBA players, six 1st Round Draft Picks, seven current NBA players, and three other players who played in the NFL. **(Melton's responses were transcribed from a Zoom call)**

Who do you go to when you need advice? Why them?

I've got a great support system with our basketball staff and other staffs at Baylor, but to really flesh out that question, it would be who do you go to when you need advice for...this situation...for that situation. I've got people I go to for personal advice and counsel on our team chaplain staff. If it's advice on a player, I might go to volleyball to see how they're dealing with it, because maybe we have a similar problem. I tailor my counsel depending on the particular problem, when I need particular insight.

What early job was pivotal in your career? Why?

At Memphis I interned my senior year in the weight room with the football staff. I was competing in olympic weightlifting, I'd made nationals, and I was really disciplined in my training. I had just wrapped up earning the senior award of the year for my exercise science department, I had a 3.9 GPA in my core curriculum—but I needed to get my hands dirty. I was looking at the route of going into cardiac rehab, but getting that internship early led to them offering me a grad assistantship that summer. The GA position was a dual role position. I was a strength coach with football during the lift, and then 15 minutes prior to the end of the lift, I'd scramble over to my milkshake station, and we had our two-year research study going on creatine. I got the ability to be a strength coach, but also get school paid for by doing lab work. It was a great position that opened the door for me to see, do I really want to pursue a PhD, or do I want to be in the trenches? Ultimately, I wanted to be in the trenches.

The strength coach I was a GA under in the weight room was a former Florida State defensive lineman, Todd Stroud. He still had ties to Florida State, so when I finished that GA spot at Memphis, I got the opportunity for a GA spot at Florida State, which gave me a springboard to a better level, a new conference, a big time football program, and an expanded network.

I worked at Florida State for five seasons until 2005, and then I got a call from Dr. Richard Kreider, my professor and mentor at Memphis who had gone to Baylor. He said, "We need a strength coach for men's basketball. There's a new guy here named Scott Drew. It's his second year and he needs an exclusive strength coach. They're doing a rotating strength coach, multi-team approach, where everybody helps everybody." That doesn't work in the world of basketball, because you had big time programs like Texas, Kansas, and Duke that all had an exclusive men's basketball only strength coach. I was able to get my foot in the door on that interview for Scott Drew from my graduate assistantship professor from Memphis from five years earlier. That GA spot really opened up Florida State and Baylor, which was life changing.

What are your first steps when you start a new job? What do you need to figure out, what do you need to get done, who do you need to get to know?

I learned a great lesson from Dave Plettl—the Florida State Women's Basketball strength coach. He told me his first year with the former basketball coach, he had a bunch of stuff he wanted to implement that she wasn't ready for. Rather than force the issue, he jumped on what they were doing and made a slow change every semester. Gradually by giving them what they wanted and getting a little bit of what he wanted, five years down the road it was the bulk of his program because he had gained their trust.

Relationships are the utmost concern coming into a new job. You've got to know who's got the juice, who's got the power, who's got the influence, who you can trust, who's going to not be trustworthy. It's the old adage—you've got two ears and one mouth. Come in, listen, observe. When I started with Coach Drew, he didn't know what to do with a strength coach. He was used to not thinking about it, but now I was working for him. It started off where he'd give me five minutes to warm up the team for practice, because he used to say dogs don't stretch when they come off the porch to chase a car. I'm like, "Coach, I get it, but we're not dogs. We're actually human beings and we need more time to warm up all these different qualities that we need to perform well for you." But it's not about coming in and making a bunch of waves at first. Still be great at your job, be a coach, be authoritative, but learn the culture that you're in.

Bonus: How has your relationship with Coach Drew evolved over the 20 years you have worked together?

I'm able to anticipate his moves better. If he says we're gonna have to have a hard practice today, I know what that means in his terms. When I say, "Hey Coach, I'm going light in the weight room today, go heavy on the floor," we don't have values assigned to it, but we know each other's tendencies. Communication is a lot more efficient. I'm also able to fill in some of the gaps that he doesn't know he needs in terms of keeping the practice gym and locker room clean.

The trust from his side to me has grown tremendously. He doesn't care what the weight room lift is. He doesn't care what we're doing for conditioning. He just trusts me to get it done, which is great. Now in the warmup, if I need 15 minutes, I can just say, "Coach, they don't look good. I'm going to keep going." He'll say, "Yeah, keep going because you know what you're doing." That's been one of the biggest areas of growth in our relationship over 20 years—there's more trust and an easier line of communication.

What advice do you have for a college student looking to break into coaching? Who are the best mentors in the world to work for early in your career?

First of all, don't pursue being a strength coach. You're going to bite off more than you can chew. But the way I started was in the exercise science department. I volunteered to do every activity the department was doing. I would help run a research study and I would be a participant in the research study. We formed a student chapter of the NSCA in our department, and I was the treasurer and vice president. We formed the Tiger weightlifting club where we all competed against each other.

LIFT AND TRAIN. Nobody trusts a skinny cook. You don't have to be the strongest person in the room. You can be great at conditioning, speed, powerlifting, olympic lifting, kettlebells—but there has to be some aspect about you that shows competence in that field. We're getting an influx of young strength coaches that know everything there is to know about data and devices, but they don't know how to adjust a daily workout when everything falls apart, when what they had planned two days ago isn't working. Be able to know the weight room and the flow of activity. At the end of the day, a strength coach is really a physical educator. It comes down to pedagogy. If their cleans are off, if their bench press is off, do you know how to change the movement pattern? Do you know the right cues? Do you know how to sub out a squat for a single leg press at the right time? All that comes through being in the weight room yourself. If you're not training, if your athletes don't see you train, you're missing a big part of the validity of your influence.

Work with as many teams as possible. A lot of intern candidates want to work with just men's or women's basketball because it's cool, but that's going to hamper your knowledge base. When I got to Florida State, I had women's soccer, track and field, and assisted with football, but that drove up my ability to understand different team cultures, different athletes. Early on, you don't know where life's going to take you. I had no basketball experience when I took the basketball position at Baylor, but I could show in a presentation how the work I had done with agility and conditioning fits basketball, just in a smaller playing surface. The work we did with throwers, with Olympic lifting, with rotational strength, fits our post players. The track and field first step quickness and sprint mechanics also fits.

Having the experience with a multitude of teams teaches you the way to work with a water polo player, even if you've never worked water polo. It's understanding the human body, programming, and adaptation. It's also big to get a wide experience, not only from the athletes, but from the coaching staffs. The women's basketball staff here—same game, same court, same gear—is a completely different animal than the men's staff. Learning how to communicate with those people is important.

I learned from Jeff "Mad Dog" Madden, a legend in the field, a great piece of advice. In 1997, I went to a strength clinic at Tennessee and asked him what I should do as a young guy trying to break into the field. He said, "Be there before the doors open and leave after everybody's gone" kind of thing. Just work your tail off. That was great to hear at the time, because it's about work ethic. Are you going to be willing to lift guys? Yes, of course you love lifting, but are you going to clean the floor? Are you going to clean up all the water bottles? Are you going to make sure the towels get washed if your managers are slipping? Immerse yourself into the world of athletics.

If you only had two 30-minute sessions a week to train your team, how would you prepare them?

You're speaking our in-season basketball language. We're doing two lifts a week from December through March. There are times with your travel schedule where you've got a heavy lift on the calendar because it meets your game schedule, but that might be a heavy lift on Monday week one, because you've got a Wednesday/Saturday split for your games. But the next week you might have a Saturday/Monday. That Monday lift has to slide. I'm looking at the end of the week to get a feel of how hard was practice the day before, and what games or practices are coming up on the schedule. It's about being fluid, malleable, and adaptable.

If I'm going two days a week, I'd better get in a dense training model to check all the boxes I need. Knowing where we've been, where we are now, and where we are going dictates those shorter training sessions. In the summer it doesn't matter. The summer is for the strength coach, and you can train through some harder situations that you wouldn't do in-season. One of the things I do in that situation is use supersets, be it a speed contrast, be it upper body/lower body splits, but we're usually linking two to four movements per set. We did our dynamic effort work yesterday, eight sets of three on squat, bench, pull up, and kettlebell swing. You've got two minutes to do three reps on all four movements. In 16 minutes, we get eight sets of three on four different exercises. It's super efficient. If it's summer training, we run all those percentages up in the 70s and 80s. In-season, I'm still going to do that eight by three, but rather than get to 70-80 percent, I might be at 40 or 50 percent where everybody's got a 10 kilo plate on bench and a 15 kilo plate on squat. By the end, they feel like they got some work, but we didn't overload their nervous system or demand too much metabolically so they can't practice. If coach says it's going to be a light practice, I can ramp that up. If I want to ramp it up, but I'm seeing what the practice plan is, I can pull it back really quick. Being able to adjust in real time is the most important aspect in those kinds of situations.

What goes into your decision to leave or stay at a job?

For me, it's really simple. I got divorced in 2011 and there's a geographic clause in there. If I leave town to work down in let's say Austin at UT, I'm going to have a good job that pays a lot of money, high profile, but I'm never going to see my children. So life decided I'm Baylor for life. If a new basketball coach came in, I would hope and pray that he would retain me as the basketball strength coach. Otherwise, I'd be begging golf to let me be their strength coach, or I'd work at a physical plant and turn wrenches for a living. I was going to do whatever it took to stay at Baylor, and God has really been favorable. He's blessed us where I haven't had to move.

Do you fit the culture? I fit really well with Scott Drew. We have similar belief systems. We have similar expectations for where we want to be. We want nothing but a national championship. Losing breeds losing, and winning breeds winning.

If you're going to leave, what's the shelf life of the staff? You can take a great job, move yourself and your family halfway across the country, and that guy gets fired the next year, and you're back in the same position. It's a really tough decision to move. Part of why I went from Florida State to Baylor was that it was a chance for me to be the head strength coach over a revenue sport, men's basketball. It was a chance to move to a new conference. But in my mind I thought it was a buy-low, sell-high opportunity. The shelf life for Baylor looked pretty grim because they were waiting to get all the penalties handed down from the NCAA. My thinking back then was even if Baylor only lasts for two or three years, I've moved into the Big 12 Conference, I've got a better network, and I have access to basketball jobs. If that was going to crash and burn, I was going to be able to get out before the ship went down and convert that risky investment. Because it was a risky investment to come to Baylor, but looking at the return on investment now blows my mind.

What do you do to overcome times of struggle, burnout, or overwhelm? Who do you turn to?

If I don't get my mind right in the morning and read a devotional, get some prayer time, and try to digest what the Lord's Word says that morning, I'm not as balanced spiritually going into the day. To take a phrase from NBA trainer Phil Beckner, "Lead yourself well." We can burn ourselves out by not taking time to do self care stuff, like getting quiet time, going fishing, or going on a date with your significant other. All those things help you not get burned out, but inevitably when it hits, that's when I'm picking up the phone and calling Darby. I'm calling Andy Kettler at Xavier. I'm calling Vinny. I'm calling other strength coaches that I trust to give me a good answer, or at least tell me that I'm being stupid and suck it up.

There's a gentleman named Drake McLean, and he runs McLean shipping. Our new football stadium is the McLean stadium—this guy's a billionaire and he spoke to the team one day. One thing he said he does is drive a different way to work and home from work every day. Change up your routine. Sometimes I get stuck driving down the same streets to get to work, parking in the same parking spot. All of a sudden it becomes mundane. I can get to work in 18 minutes from my house. There are other days after a really hard day at work, I'll take every frontage road possible, not touch the interstate, and it takes me about 45 minutes to get home. That gives me time to see different things, think different ways, to change up that external stimulus I'm getting with a new way home. That's a small example, but maybe you change up your training routine. Maybe you're getting stale because you're running the same lift for your team.

Self-reflection, self-correction, redirection. In my younger years, I was quick to point out what was causing things to be hard, laying blame. "I just moved and took over a basketball team, I've got a two-year-old daughter and a newborn son, I'm gonna get burned out." I could easily say, "Look what I'm going through. Of course it's a bad day." Or I could self-reflect and ask, "Why am I thinking this is so horrible? Where's my head at right now? Why am I going down these negative paths?" The older I get, the more time I spend in self-reflection and reading scripture. I write a daily poem as my response to my devotional. By doing that, I'm able to get out some of the things I'm thinking. Writing is a big way to get out what's inside.

Going through divorce, I was burned out, I didn't want to go to work, I couldn't see my kids as much as I wanted to, and obviously I had the pain of losing a marriage. That's when the team became my savior, because when I went into work, they just saw me as Coach Charlie. I was able to step outside of that. But some of those emails I wanted to send my ex-wife to tell her to go fly a kite, I would write in my notes or in an email and save it but not send it. I'd wake up the next day, read it, and go, "I'm not sending that." If I feel a certain way about where the team's at, rather than voice it on social media or go bark at them, I'll go home and think about what's going on and talk to some people. I'm learning now to sleep on things more. Cooler heads prevail. Let yourself get out of that emotion and step back to get a better perspective.

What do you think about immediately after one of your athletes is injured? What is your mindset in the following week?

Mental health is getting a lot of attention, but it's always been something that's important. I lost my brother, Andy, in 2004. He took his own life. Two years later, my dad got killed on the job. He was a railroad mechanic and got hit by a train car. That was my second year at Baylor, and I was still grieving from the loss of my brother. Then you look at the ramifications: I can't be there to help my family because I'm all the way in Texas and they're in Tennessee. My mom's a widow, and it's hard enough to lose a child. That nearly broke our family.

In 2007, I blew out a quad tendon on a shot put attempt. Going through that massive injury in the emotional state I was in, it was really hard because the way I coped with life was by training and throwing—and that was taken away. Thinking about my athlete, I automatically start running down a checklist of, is this a tough athlete? Is this a gritty athlete? Is this somebody I'm going to have to go by their apartment and check on them? Is this somebody I'm going to have to call and text and encourage? Finding out where they are first, what's the severity of the injury.

Having gone through a quad tendon blow out, and since then I've blown out the other quad tendon, blown out both shoulders, but I've had to continue to find a way to train and push through it. To adapt exercise, adapt activity, and adapt my daily life. I'm a single dad in a second-floor apartment with a blown out quad tendon trying to take care of my kids when I got custody of them. Brutal. I had my right shoulder blown out in 2011. I was a single dad that was right-handed with a blown out right shoulder, having to take my kids to the pool, the zoo, and go grocery shopping with one arm. Learning how to drive through that and not let life keep me down is something I've been able to impart to other people.

At first I thought it was a sign of failure, "I'm a terrible strength coach because I broke myself. I'm supposed to be Superman." I was thinking everybody's looking at me like, "He doesn't know what he's doing. He's a bad strength coach." Nobody thought that way. They felt bad because they knew how hard I was training and injuries happen. But I learned how to get back on my feet, and that's been a huge blessing dealing with injured athletes. I can tell them, "Hey, I know how that feels. I REALLY know how it feels." One of the best things that's ever happened to me as a coach is knowing what it's like to be healthy, and knowing what it's like to have everything snatched away.

Do you have a "failure" that was critical to your long-term development or success?
More of a life failure, but divorce. I'm remarried. We're both formerly married, and we repented from divorce when we dated and were engaged for 18 months. I had three kids, she had two kids. We were in our late thirties, and we decided that during that period of time before we got married, there was going to be no alcohol and no sex. That's really hard when you've been a married man, but we were tremendously blessed by honoring God with getting remarried. Divorce is one of the worst things,

but that failure in divorce has led to a great marriage with Julie and an example of how marriage should be.

I've been able to counsel three or four coaches and friends like my brother Joey—all of a sudden out of nowhere, after 20 years, his wife walked out on him two Christmases ago. Now similar to the injury, because of that failure of divorce in my life, I'm able to give great counsel to people. "Hey, here's what I did wrong, or here's what to be ready for." When we talk about the book of Romans, where God turns all things to the good of those that follow Him and believe in Him, I've seen that in my own life. You remind people that these things, these failures, God's going to use them. If you're abiding in God, if you're invested in God, if you're open to God, he will take any failure, any damage, and reconcile it on his timeline. It might not be your timeline, but if you trust God with your life and God with your failures, that's the secret to success.

What traits or skills do your most successful athletes have in common?
They better be pretty athletic, number one. I learned at Florida State, it's not about your weight training or your speed work. It's about the dudes you recruited. We had the most basic strength programs at Florida State, and I look back and wonder, "How did we get better with that?" It's not even close to where it is now, but we were defending for a national championship because we had a bunch of five star football players.

The first trait is Grit. What is grit? My mother, who's about to be 70 and is 5'2, raised four boys, and was married to my dad who was crazy, is one of the grittiest people I know. We have a former athlete, Jonathan Tchamwa Tchatchoua. We call him Everyday Jon. He had a horrific knee injury, and they didn't think he was going to walk, let alone play basketball. But I just helped him the entire month of May because after returning to playing, now he was flying out to do NBA workouts, and now he's been picked up as a player development coach for the Spurs. He went straight from a player to a coach, which rarely happens to anybody, and the predominant reason is because he's so gritty.

Discipline over motivation. You'll see early in the summer, the first two or three weeks, it's a new team. It's summer. There's no class. It's really fun. But by the end of that first month in the summer, it turns into work. Then in July, it's not fun anymore. Everybody's in pain. We've got ankles, we've got knees, we've got backs, the coaches are frustrated. It's coming in everyday under duress, under pain, under stress, not being in the right headspace—and still having the ability to do it. That takes people from being a good athlete to a great athlete, or a good coach to a great coach.

Humility is another one. I went to Charles Stephenson's Vegas clinic in 2014, and he picked me up from the airport. I'd never met him face to face, but at the airport he goes, "THE Charlie Melton—Baylor!" We had been to an Elite Eight, and I said, "Man, come on. I'm just my mom's oldest son." I keep that mentality. I am the father of my children. I'm Julie's husband. I'm my mom's oldest boy. A cool Phil Beckner moment that I just had—and he's big time, he is THE Phil Beckner. He sat in on our session that we had with the coaches and the players on Wednesday. He said, "Baylor is an elite program. You used to be this, but now you're elite." Some people see us as elite, or our coaches will say, "Charlie is the best strength coach in America." People want to inflate your ego and say, "You've got a national championship. Look at who you've worked with." We've sent a bunch of guys to the NBA, but at the end of the day, I still have to come home and take out the trash. I was just scrambling to finish the dishes.

But Phil Beckner blew my ego up. He's with the team and he pulls out his phone. He says, "Look at these voicemails. I save encouraging voicemails." He showed one of our players—it was a voicemail he saved since 2014, which is really cool. Then he holds up the phone and says, "I'm going to play you guys a voicemail. I want you to listen and tell me who this is." It was from a year earlier, 2023, and it was me! He saved a voicemail that I sent him randomly. All of a sudden I was like, "Yeah, Phil respects me. If Phil respects me, I must be good!" But people get caught up in it. I've been off social media since 2021. I got off in February, and we won the national championship that spring. I'm sure my Instagram and Twitter have tons of messages saying congratulations. I've never seen them. It helps not to be somebody that's after likes and responses.

The last one ties into athletic intelligence and your ability to learn. Show me a great athlete and I'll show you a great compensator. You look at athletes with long careers—they've had surgeries. I want an athlete that will fight through an ankle, and even though their back's tight, they'll learn to stretch it themselves and keep going. To hit on that high athletic IQ, I've got guys that have been with me since last year and they still can't do the RDL skip properly. I've got guys that have been with me just this year that I've told two times how to do a movement and they do it perfectly and don't have to be reminded.

What books or resources do you most often recommend to coaches?
Old and New Testaments of the Bible. CSCCa and NSCA textbooks. *Supertraining* (Mel Siff). *Encyclopedia of Weightlifting* (Arthur Dreschler). *Original Strength* (Tim Anderson). *Enter the Kettlebell* (Pavel Tsatsouline).

"Who do you need to get to know? Everyone. The equipment people, the custodians, the cooks. Get to know support staff and show them the respect they deserve. My dad was a high school principal. His second in command at the school was the head custodian and everyone knew it."

-Mike Boyle

Mike Boyle is the co-founder of Mike Boyle Strength and Conditioning (MBSC), a gym recognized as one of America's top 10 gyms by Men's Health magazine. A pioneer in the strength and conditioning industry, Boyle's work has influenced countless coaches and training methodologies. Through MBSC, he has trained numerous Olympians and professional athletes, while also serving as the Strength and Conditioning Coach for the Boston Bruins from 1991-1999. Boyle played a key role in the U.S. Women's Olympic Ice Hockey Team's historic gold medal win in 1998 and has consulted for the World Champion Boston Red Sox. He was Boston University's Head Strength and Conditioning Coach from 1984-1997 and continued with the Men's Ice Hockey team until 2012. His books, including *Advances in Functional Training, New Functional Training for Sports,* and *Designing Strength Training Programs and Facilities, 2nd Edition,* are widely recommended resources in the field (as seen by the number of times they are referenced in this book).

Who do you go to when you need advice? Why them?
At 64, it gets tougher to find advisers. The majority of my peers are retired or retiring. We have a wonderful business manager, Carrie Burns, who has become a great sounding board for me. Why her? Carrie has a good business mind, lots of experience (both business and life) and thinks like me.

What early job was pivotal in your career? Why?
For a very long time I only had my Boston University job. I went from volunteer to full-time coach, and from coaching one team to an entire athletic dept. I was on the ground floor of an entirely new field and I was able to grow a program from one team

and 600 sq ft of space to 20+ teams and 7,000 sq ft.

What are your first steps when you start a new job? What do you need to figure out, what do you need to get done, who do you need to get to know?

Step 1 is analyze the landscape. Who am I working for? Who am I working with? Who are the decision makers? I want to know who the boss is and I want to know the backgrounds of the athletes. In college, this might be the AD, athletic trainer, etc. What type of kids? Scholarship? Non-scholarship? At the pro level, young guys? Old guys? Married? Single? New dads? All these play a part. What languages are spoken? What are the cultural differences?

Who do you need to get to know? Everyone. The equipment people, the custodians, the cooks. Get to know support staff and show them the respect they deserve. My dad was a high school principal. His second in command at the school was the head custodian and everyone knew it.

What advice do you have for a college student looking to break into coaching? Who are the best mentors in the world to work for early in your career?

Show up early, stay late. Do more than you're asked. Always have a notebook. Dress professional, act professional. What do they say—dress for the role you want. Brush your teeth, wear deodorant. Shower every day before work. It's a simple world.

My best mentors weren't people that I worked for. I was the one and only strength coach from 22 years old on. However, I was lucky to go to college with Mike Woicik (NFL Hall of Fame Strength Coach 6 Super Bowl rings). He was my first mentor. I was then lucky to work at Boston University with and for Coach Jack Parker. Coach Parker is the winningest coach in one sport at one school in NCAA history with almost 900 wins, all at Boston University.

If you only had two 30-minute sessions a week to train your team, how would you prepare them?

That's a tough one. Do I get them before or after practice? With 30 minutes twice a week you have to really go with big bang-for-the-buck stuff but, you also want them to be ready. Probably sprints, jumps, and throws, and then a superset of something like bench press and Trap Bar one day and chin-ups and skater squats the next day.

What goes into your decision to leave or stay at a job?

For me it was always about people and family. I had lots of pro offers but loved Boston.

Money was never a huge motivator for me. I turned down an amazing job in the NHL in the 90s. My dad had passed away and I couldn't imagine leaving my mom alone.

What do you do to overcome times of struggle, burnout, or overwhelm? Who do you turn to?

I play pretty hard. I love to have a few beers after a game. I also try to take regular naps. It also helps when you really love what you do and have a patient spouse.

What do you think about immediately after one of your athletes is injured? What is your mindset in the following week?

I immediately think, "Could I have done more?" My first ACL crushed me. It was a kid named Sean Brown in the 80s. I visited him in the hospital (In those days you stayed overnight). I became obsessed with prevention because injuries ate at me. In the following week, my mindset was always to dig in more, learn more, and figure out who was the expert on that area.

How do you approach difficult conversations with athletes, coworkers, or your boss?

Make some notes so you're prepared. Put those notes in your pocket in case you get flustered. Set up a time to meet. Take a deep breath and let it go.

Do you have a "failure" that was critical to your long-term development or success?

Many. Jobs I wanted but didn't get. Athletes injured. The biggest "almost" was almost getting divorced. Marriage counseling made me realize that my motivation toward my job made me a poor partner.

What traits or skills do your most successful athletes have in common?

Talent. I'd love to say work ethic but, I've had so many great ones that I had to motivate and encourage. Motivation will get you a long way, but probably not in sports. Talent rules.

What books or resources do you most often recommend to coaches?

I find the top two are *How To Win Friends and Influence People* by Dale Carnagie and *Goals* by Brian Tracey.

"It only gets harder with time as more responsibilities get piled onto your plate...Dial in now and get as good as possible as quickly as possible by committing as much time as possible to your craft. There is no such thing as 'balance' early in your career if you want to separate yourself from the other thousands of coaches wanting the same jobs as you."

-Alan Bishop

Alan Bishop is in his eighth year at the University of Houston as the Director of Men's Basketball Sports Performance, playing a key part in the program having the most wins in all of college basketball since 2020. Bishop has also helped the program achieve six American Athletic Conference Championships, the 2024 Regular Season Big 12 Championship, multiple Sweet Sixteen appearances, and trips to the 2022 Elite Eight and 2021 Final Four. Prior to Houston, he worked as the Director of Olympic Sport Strength and Conditioning at Utah State, along with stops at UT Arlington and Southern Utah. Bishop has helped develop NBA players Damyean Dotson, Quentin Grimes, Marcus Sasser, Jarace Walker, and Jamal Shead.

Who do you go to when you need advice? Why them?

If I need advice on something from a training/nutrition/data analysis/research, etc. I will typically go straight to the source to get better clarity. That may be in the form of consulting with the person who wrote the book on the topic, or putting out a quick email/call to the researcher/author asking for clarity.

If I need help from a practical application standpoint, I will reach out to colleagues in a similar situation to me to ask for perspectives on how they've navigated the problem.

What early job was pivotal in your career? Why?

Working at Utah State University was probably the most pivotal. It allowed me to work directly for the mentor who has been most influential in my career, it forced me to think like an administrator as I was dealing with bigger budgets and projects than at previous stops, and I was able to continue developing my coaching/teaching craft by working with multiple teams both as a lead and as an assistant.

What are your first steps when you start a new job? What do you need to figure out, what do you need to get done, who do you need to get to know?

My first step is understanding why I'm there to begin with, meaning what is the head coach paying me to accomplish? Every organization has a different expectation out of their S&C, and our job is to bring as much value as possible to the organization within our role.

What advice do you have for a college student looking to break into coaching? Who are the best mentors in the world to work for early in your career?

There will never be another time in your career where you'll be more overworked and less appreciated than you are at the beginning. There will also never be a time in your career where you're as bad at your craft as you are right now, and that's okay, you're supposed to get better with time. That said, embrace it. You aren't the first and you won't be the last. We've all gone through it. Do everything you can to get as many hours on the floor as possible coaching, as many hours in front of a computer writing programs, and as many hours in front of books and articles reading.

It only gets harder with time as more responsibilities get piled onto your plate. Right now, you're probably only responsible for yourself, but in the future that will likely include a spouse, kids, mortgage, etc. Dial in now and get as good as possible as quickly as possible by committing as much time as possible to your craft. There is no such thing as "balance" early in your career if you want to separate yourself from the other thousands of coaches wanting the same jobs as you.

What goes into your decision to leave or stay at a job?

Too many variables to list, but remember that if you're happy in the job you've got, don't be quick to mess with happy.

That said: Salary, Benefits Packages and Bonus Structures, Professional Growth, Strategic Career Longevity and Advancement, etc.

What do you do to overcome times of struggle, burnout, or overwhelm? Who do you turn to?

The work is always going to be there. Take time when you can get it to recharge your batteries, but the job doesn't get easier and it'll be waiting for you when you get back.

The strength coaches I admire most seem to have something in common, and that is that they love the grind of the job. It isn't for everyone.

What do you think about immediately after one of your athletes is injured? What is your mindset in the following week?

My mind immediately goes to putting a plan in place to get them back as efficiently as possible. Remember that injuries can really mess with people. REALLY mess with people. People aren't machines, so just like any good physician, maintain a good bedside manner during rehab.

How do you approach difficult conversations with athletes, coworkers, or your boss?

Be direct and solve the problem. We're all on the same team and the goal is to make sure we're resolving whatever the issue is and moving forward to keep working towards winning games. Don't beat around the bush, be a professional.

What traits or skills do your most successful athletes have in common?

Control what you can control, and keep the main thing the main thing.

What books or resources do you most often recommend to coaches?

- Speed – James Smith
- Strength – Poliquin, Hatfield, Thibaudeau
- Nutrition/Health – Antonio, LaValle
- Leadership – Willink, Carnegie
- Finance – Stanley, Ramsey

> *"They have to have absolute clarity because high clarity equals high performance, but then high clarity also leads to high accountability. Now I could hold them accountable, and they could hold themselves accountable."*

> ## *-Phil Beckner*

Phil Beckner is an elite NBA player development coach and high-performance consultant for athletes, sports teams, and business organizations through his business Be Better. Be Different. Beckner works closely with All-NBA player Damian Lillard, going all the way back to coaching him in college at Weber State. Some of the top organizations he has recently consulted with include the Philadelphia 76ers, Texas Tech Men's Basketball, the United States Military Academy, Oregon Football, Blazer Electric, ZeroFox Inc, and Apex Systems. Beckner also leads Formula Zero with Damian Lillard, an elite camp for top high school and college basketball players that instills character, work ethic, and accountability. **(Beckner's responses were transcribed from a Zoom call)**

Who do you go to when you need advice? Why them?

We need someone coaching the coaches. A big phrase from one of my mentors is you can't give away what you don't possess. If you're asking players to be coachable, but you're not being coached yourself, or you're not willing to hear criticism or feedback yourself, it's going to be hard to give that away to your player. If you're tough, it's easy to help your athletes get tougher. If you're soft, that's probably not going to work too well. If you don't show up on time and your players are always late, well that's probably because you can't give away what you don't possess.

What I try to do is have two or three people, sometimes almost three or four, in my life as mentors, as coaches, with different titles. A spiritual one from a church. A life one, that's Brian Dwyer, a guy in Utah. Rod Olson is a coach of the coaches, leadership expert, he's in my life. Then you gotta have someone above you, someone on your level, someone below you. I have a couple people who are similar in age or who have gone through what I do, like Craig Smith at Utah or Jeff Linder at Wyoming, who we could talk to and work through problems together who have similar battles or similar things we're working on. You need someone personally, spiritually, life wise working with you; you need someone professionally, leadership wise working with you; then you need a couple people who you could trust and you could work through things together.

What early job was pivotal in your career? Why?

My grandpa was in the beekeeping business, and he had a rule that when every boy graduated from the eighth grade he started working, and my dad actually did that with me. It was pivotal in my career because when you're in eighth grade, you just want to go to the summer rec program all day in town. I didn't get to go in the morning with all the kids. I only got to go at night when they play men's league basketball. Having to have a job like that at an early age taught me three things. One, show up early to impress your boss. Be there early, do your job the best you can while you're at work. You've got to do the stuff no one wants to do. Then the 3rd thing is do what's asked of you within those hours. Even though I only worked four hours a day, you were still working those 20 hours a week. You don't leave early. You work the whole time.

What are your first steps when you start a new job? What do you need to figure out, what do you need to get done, who do you need to get to know?

I mentor a lot of coaches now; we have coaching development programs. They all think they're going to be doing drills or a scouting report. The first thing you have to do at any new job to make a difference for that program, to make a difference for the head coach—is do the s**t no one else wants to do. For instance, when I got to Weber State, I was the ops guy, but I was also your video, your GA. I always tell the story, when the coaches would go pick up the recruits from the airports, the guy who cleaned our arena and our offices always came in late, so I would vacuum our offices myself. I would dust off all the computer monitors. I made sure that when the recruit walked through there it was clean, because the cleaner of the arena might not show up.

Looking back on it, you have to ask the right questions. There's so many times people want to ask questions about drills and skills and everything for the next steps, but ask the question, "What can I do to help you more? What can I do to take this off your plate? What should I be doing when I have nothing else to do? When I've got all my work done?" Those are questions I think when you're first starting out, if you just have the balls and go ask somebody who's been there a while, or you ask your boss or the head coach, now you're going to know what to do, which will ultimately help the program or help the players.

What advice do you have for a college student looking to break into coaching? Who are the best mentors in the world to work for early in your career?

If you think you want to do something like that, just surrender, throw caution to the wind, and go do it. You can't have one foot in and one foot out. If you want to try coaching, don't be like, "Well, I kind of want to be an executive for this financial firm, and I kind of want to coach." If you're going to coach, throw caution to the wind, show up, impact people, help people, coach your butt off, give whatever talents and gifts you have to that coach or the player that you're working with, give it to that program, and just see what happens because you're never going to know.

I tell this to coaches all the time. You're never going to know if you like something or if you want to do something until you really do it. If you're going to do it for a year or two years, it's not like we're just stepping on this path and we can never change the path. I think that's really important to know. Go throw caution to the wind and go try it.

Mentors, that's too tough of a question for me because I always think an answer to that is more individual specific. I would flip the question to a young coach, "Who are the people in your life that have been impressive to you, that you want to be like, and have had success the right way, that you would want to follow or build a career similar to?" Go find those people because there are a lot of different ways to be successful, and too many times we just want to be with a Jay Wright at Villanova, Tom Izzo at Michigan State, Bill Self at Kansas, and they might be successful, but they might not be about what you're about. Some coaches are hard-nosed. Some coaches are super easy. Find people who are aligned with your values and your vision and try to get them to mentor you.

If you only had two 30-minute sessions a week to train your team, how would you prepare them?

Number one, the first thing that I think helps players so much is working with them on their approach. How do they approach the workout? How do they approach life? How do they approach coaching? How prepared are they? Teach these guys how to have a winning approach or a professional approach. I don't care if we're doing skill development, weight room stuff, or a character session in an office. If we get two 30-minute sessions, the first thing we're going to talk about is their approach.

The second thing we're going to talk about is having clarity on what they're doing and why they are doing it, so they know what to do, how to do it, when to do it. They have to have absolute clarity because high clarity equals high performance, but then high clarity also leads to high accountability. Now I could hold them accountable, and they could hold themselves accountable. I had a meeting with one of my employees today. I'm like, "When are you doing that fundraiser? What's the date?" And he's like, "We're going to do it June or July." That's not a date. That's not clear enough.

The third thing I want them to have is a level of—we talk about it all the time with Formula Zero and Dame, but that relentless work, that powerful passion, that energy, excitement. We're going to do the s**t other people aren't willing to do, and we're going to do it all the time. So clarity, but then that mindset, that willingness. Those things that produce that passion, that energy, that ability to work, we're going to emphasize that every 30-minute session we have.

What goes into your decision to leave or stay at a job?

You have to know who you want to be and what you want to have. That's not always a materialistic thing, but who do I want to be in this profession, in this life? And then what do I want to have? Do I want to have freedom of my own schedule? Do I want to have championships? Do I want to have a nice car and a nice house, or do I want to have relationships that will last a long time? You gotta know who you want to be and ultimately, when you're done, what you want to have, and that could be the driver of most of your decisions.

People always talk about mission, vision, values, but to have a clear vision of what you're about and what you want to be known for will tell you whether you should take the next job or not, or should tell you what position you want to be in, whether that's an ops guy, an assistant coach, me running my business, consultant, whatever. Part of our mission statement is, "Impact people, impact performance. Build people, build careers." If we impact people, we're going to impact their performance. If we build people, we're also going to build their careers or build their life. If you know what you're about, what you want, who you're going to be, that's going to be the driver. I know Nick Saban and a lot of other high performers have talked about this stuff too before—decision making becomes so easy. If you decide what you want, what you have to do after that is already decided too. If you want to be a champion, you have to show up early, you have to stay late, all that cliche stuff. But it's true. If you know who you are and what you want and who you want to be, the decisions are made for you. There are not a lot of choices you have to make.

What do you do to overcome times of struggle, burnout, or overwhelm? Who do you turn to?

Number one, you have to know where to look. If you feel burnt out, or you feel frustrated or tired—the first place you look is within. We have a game plan for Be Better, Be Different. I talk to teams about, if you bring me out, the first time we talk about the game plan. Come out two months later, we talk about the separators. Come out two months later after that, we talk about the guardrails. To have a game plan—if you give your team a game plan, here are a few keys that we could win the game. The first key to winning the game individually, to not getting to burnout and to being able to take care of yourself, the first key we have to our game plan is you have to lead yourself well.

Know where to look. You look within and ask, "Am I leading myself well?" Whatever those things are, mine are reading, praying, running. I gotta be able to read stuff or connect, podcasts even now tend to count, but fueling our mind. Praying, just taking quiet time away, solitude. The third thing, moving your body. I feel like absolute s**t today, to be honest with you. I've been sick for two weeks. The one thing I haven't done because I've been so low energy, is I haven't been able to move my body. If you are ever feeling burnout, usually what's happening is you're pouring into everyone else except yourself. You have to pour into yourself, you have to fuel yourself because the best way to pour into others is through your overflow. If you're filled up and your cup's just overflowing, "Like man, I'm on fire, I'm doing skill development. Now I'm going to go check in with John. Like it's just flowing out of me." Then you're never empty, and I think that's the key and that's the best place to look.

The other part, do you know what your filters are? If you run water through a filter, it keeps all the bad stuff out. We want to filter those bad things out. Do you have anything set up in your life to filter out negativity, to filter out—one for me is busyness. Saying no is one of my filters. As much as you have to lead yourself well and know those things that excite you, you also have to know those things that electrocute you and zap you, and try to have a filter to keep those—I call poisons—but keep those poisons out all the time.

What do you think about immediately after one of your athletes is injured? What is your mindset in the following week?

I'm a little different because I'm so much in the player development side and getting people to go from point A to point B. As a coach and as a leader, our job ultimately is to help someone, not do it for them, but help someone get to a place they could not have got to on their own. That's our job. So injury, immediately it goes to, "Hey, who do we need help from?" Too many people in our profession are always isolated, and the team doctor needs to be connected with the trainer, needs to be connected with the strength coach, needs to be connected with our ops guy. What team can we put around this player so they know they're taken care of, they know they're going to get better, and they know we're all pulling in the same direction, because that will probably accelerate the progress of them coming back. That's one—connection, communication with everybody.

Number two, now I start thinking of the athlete, and what are they going through? What plan do they want? What do they want to work on? I think when you show an athlete a plan, and it's old school, but even just on a piece of paper, whether, "Here's where you are, here's where you want to be in two weeks. Here's what we fill in during those two weeks." Showing someone a plan goes back to exactly what I was talking about a little bit ago. Now they could work on their approach. We're providing clarity, and then we could develop this mindset, this confidence, this relentless work ethic within that framework. Having a plan for that kid and showing them—that increases hope, that increases confidence, that allows them to not feel left out.

That's something I think we excelled at when I was with the Oklahoma City Thunder. When I go out and meet with college programs now, we're gaining clarity on things. And it's not Phil Beckner's answers, but I'm able to help. I've gone to Baylor this year, I've gone to Army—it's Army's language, it's Army's values, but we're able to streamline it. Get these kids connected more, speak on it. Again, I don't care if it's you, if it's me, high clarity equals high performance.

If I just said, "John, you're going to go from Tulsa to Oklahoma City, and you're going to meet me at the Waffle House in Edmond." You could probably get out of Tulsa. You could probably get on the freeway, but then after that, what are you going to need? Some directions. We need to be like, "Okay, Waffle House. Well, there's two in Edmond. Is it this one or that one? Do I get off on this road?" If you're trying to figure it out all day, it's going to be a four-hour trip instead of the hour and a half it usually takes. Also, you don't know what time. "Well Phil, are we going at 11 or we going at 9 am?" If you know how you're supposed to get there, when you're supposed to get there, which one, it's an hour and a half trip. If you don't, that's going to take you three hours, and you can probably see that with your program or players. "Man, why is it taking this kid so long to develop, or why is it taking our defense so long to improve? Or why do we take one, two steps forward, one step back?" A lot of it's because of clarity, alignment, and organization.

How do you approach difficult conversations with athletes, coworkers, or your boss?

I wish I would have been way better at this throughout my career. Number one, this is a skill set coaches need to work on, that I didn't work on, but now as a consultant I've had to get better at because I want to reach more players, I want to reach more coaches. What I would encourage everyone is—what do you do before that? Before that, you gotta have a strategy for how you have difficult conversations, and different people are going to have different strategies.

Here are the things that I think go into your strategy, and some of it sounds very basic. One, you have to know the person and know the situation they're in. You gotta have empathy. Empathy is a huge deal. You gotta have the emotional intelligence to know, "Hey, I know this is an issue," but Tony Robbins always says this, "If you want to change behavior, you have to know what influences behavior." What's influencing their behavior, what's going on in their life right now? You have to know the person because everyone's different, and you have to talk to people in a different way. I could go in there and be direct with Damian Lillard and take a hammer and hit him between the eyes and be like, "Hey, we're on, it's going." But you grab a young guy who hasn't trained with me as long, he doesn't know some of these standards.

Now I'm getting to the strategy. When do you tell them? When do you have this conversation? Where do you have the conversation? Is it on the court? Is it in the classroom? Some guys will be way less insecure and willing to hear it if everyone's getting warmed up, and you could have it at half court. Some other people are going to flip their lid and not be able to do it. Do you have it in an office? When do you have it? Where do you have it? And then how do you have it?

It's great to ask them questions first. You think about it, even Jesus would ask people questions first, let them kind of tell on themselves without being manipulative, but ask them or give them feedback. Here's the thing I think is lacking too with hard conversations, but also just in coaching. For some reason, communication has died so much, whether it's cell phones, social media, whatever. Coaches used to be teachers almost all the time. You're a high school teacher, so you know how to teach. Well, part of being a great teacher, which leads to being a great coach, is you ask performance based questions. How did that feel? What could you have done better? What could we add to this drill?

Yesterday I watched film with Ochai Agbaji from Kansas. We get off. I'm like, all right, what are your three biggest takeaways from this film session? I do that. His NBA coaches don't. I think that makes me better than them because now I hear what he heard and what's stuck in his mind and it doesn't always work this way, but he was three for three on what we emphasized, what I wanted him to do, and what he needs to take away. Where sometimes you don't ask performance based questions, they might be one for three. They may be like, "Yeah, I gotta rebound better, I gotta show up to the weight room on time. And, you know what, I need to high five my teammates more." Bro, no one is talking about you getting to the weight room on time. Why did that come up? We wanted you to pass the ball, whatever it may be.

What traits or skills do your most successful athletes have in common?
The first thing I'm going to say is they're mature and secure. They have a level of maturity and a level of self security to them. The second thing they have is a willingness to be coached and held accountable. Number one before all of this, to be honest, the best—they have talent and great genetics. They really do have s**t we can't put into them. That's why they're the best. They're built a different way.

Number three is one of our separators for Be Better. Be Different. Everyone thinks it's all about their success and what they do great, but the best ones I've been around, they could take a freaking punch. Championship level boxers, everyone talks about all their knockouts and that they won all these rounds. What no one talks about—Floyd Mayweather went 50-0, do you know how many punches he took, kept fighting, and didn't lose? How many rounds he lost and bounced back?

The ones I'm around, they lose and they get back up. They get punched, the next time they get swung at, they don't flinch. They know how to embrace the punch. That's something people aren't talking about enough with the high performers, everyone's preparing them to be successful. One thing I prepare my guys to do is fail. How do we respond? I know you're going to hit a shooting slump. You know how I know? Everybody does. I know you're going to lose two or three games in a row. Why? The majority of teams do. So instead of just preparing to be successful, preparing to be great, and we want to speak life and do all those things, what else can we do? We know we're going to get punched. Can I teach them how to take a punch better and how to respond from that?

"I've had millions of failures. Probably most important was my experience as a head basketball coach when I was in my twenties. My record in my first five years was 28-90. This forced me to become a lifelong learner. I feel sorry for coaches who have immediate success."

-Tony Holler

Tony Holler is the Head Track and Field Coach at Plainfield North High School. Widely known for his Feed The Cats approach to sprinting and sport and as the Co-Director of the Track Football Consortium, Holler has impacted thousands of coaches at multiple levels on *HOW* to train, think, and coach in a more efficient, effective, and engaging way. Holler is a member of the Illinois Track and Field Hall of Fame with over 40 years of coaching experience spread across football, basketball, and track.

Who do you go to when you need advice? Why them?
I don't seek advice. If a man knows the difference between good advice and bad advice, he doesn't need advice. However, people around me feel free to offer advice. I tell those surrounding me, don't bring me problems, bring me solutions.

What early job was pivotal in your career? Why?
I worked at Copley Hospital in Aurora six days a week when I was home from college. I worked every job in the Dietary Department, from dishwasher to secretary to cook. I learned I didn't like having "a job." I wanted to do stuff I liked. This made teaching and coaching a no-brainer.

What are your first steps when you start a new job? What do you need to figure out, what do you need to get done, who do you need to get to know?
As a teacher and a coach, the first thing is to have a great first day. Sounds trivial, but meeting people and remembering their names is fundamental.

What advice do you have for a college student looking to break into coaching? Who are the best mentors in the world to work for early in your career?
Visit people who do things well. Buy someone breakfast. Watch people do their work.

If you only had two 30-minute sessions a week to train your team, how would you prepare them?

I'm a sprint coach. I would sprint with tons of recovery.

What goes into your decision to leave or stay at a job?

If a new opportunity is a "HELL YES!", take it. If not, grow where you are planted.

What do you do to overcome times of struggle, burnout, or overwhelm? Who do you turn to?

Reading and Running. When I am struggling, I'm always missing reading and running in my life.

What do you think about immediately after one of your athletes is injured? What is your mindset in the following week?

Injuries are a nightmare. My first thought is always, "Is this a result of our training?"

How do you approach difficult conversations with athletes, coworkers, or your boss?

If they are upset with me… Let them talk! Don't defend. Seek common ground. You don't have to win. Apologize sincerely. If I'm upset with them… Sleep on it first. Breathe. Take the high road. Seek common ground.

Do you have a "failure" that was critical to your long-term development or success?

I've had millions of failures. Probably most important was my experience as a head basketball coach when I was in my twenties. My record in my first five years was 28-90. This forced me to become a lifelong learner. I feel sorry for coaches who have immediate success.

What traits or skills do your most successful athletes have in common?

Great athletes, first and foremost, have talent. Great athletes have a mission mindset. They look forward to practice. They love belonging to a team. They have the ability to exaggerate their wins and forget their losses.

What books or resources do you most often recommend to coaches?

Essentialism (McKeown), *The Subtle Art of Not Giving a F*ck* (Manson), *The Twin Thieves* (Jones), *Chop Wood Carry Water* (Medcalf), *The Practice of Groundedness* (Stulberg), *Atomic Habits* (Clear).

> *"Save as much money as possible in as many ways as possible. The more money you have for the essentials, the easier, the quicker, the faster you can jump at an opportunity that comes across...Money buys you options and patience and room for error."*
>
> ## *-Charlie Weingroff*

Charlie Weingroff is one of the most sought-after professionals world-wide in physical therapy and athletic performance. He is a Doctor of Physical Therapy, a Certified Athletic Trainer, and a Certified Strength and Conditioning Specialist who has worked with countless A-list celebrities, professional athletes and organizations, as well as the general population. During his career, Weingroff has held roles as the Head Strength and Conditioning Coach of for the Philadelphia 76ers, the Director of Performance and Head Strength and Conditioning Coach for Men's Canada Basketball, the Lead Physical Therapist for the United States Marine Corps Special Operations Command (MARSOC), a Member of the Nike Executive Performance Council, and a consultant for the Beijing Yanding Training Company, Oura Ring, and Equinox Fitness Club. His Training=Rehab series is often discussed as a thought leading model that highlights the value of medical, fitness, and science professionals all collaborating as one unit.

Who do you go to when you need advice? Why them?

It's different every time based on where my head is at and what space the advice is for.

What early job was pivotal in your career? Why?

It was actually my college internship, which became a PT Aide job, and that 100% led right into my first job in sports, Head Athletic Trainer for the New Jersey Shorecats in the USBL. And then literally every job or role after that tumbled from that relationship.

What are your first steps when you start a new job? What do you need to figure out, what do you need to get done, who do you need to get to know?

I'm sure there are lots of right answers for different people here. I want to suggest that I would be highly observant, as much as possible without skirting primary responsibilities, and try to categorize who-what-where-when-how about everything and everybody. This way, when you get your only chance to make a first impression, you are a little more armed or prepared to nail it.

I need to figure out how to recruit PTs to work and develop in my models. I need to be "louder" and more frequent in making it known that these opportunities are available for the right people.

What advice do you have for a college student looking to break into coaching? Who are the best mentors in the world to work for early in your career?

Save as much money as possible in as many ways as possible. The more money you have for the essentials, the easier, the quicker, the faster you can jump at an opportunity that comes across. You can quit something that is sour. You can move across the country. You can take something low paid or even unpaid. Money buys you options and patience and room for error.

As far as a mentor, there was no one that I worked for that I would now consider a mentor. There was no one that 1) genuinely cared about me, my growth, my success, 2) would tell me things so that I would not make the same mistakes they did, and 3) they would tell me things not necessarily caring how I felt after hearing their words.

If you only had two 30-minute sessions a week to train your team, how would you prepare them?

Warmup for 5 minutes and parse the 25 minutes with varying combinations of Kettlebell Ballistics (Swings/Cleans/Clean to Press/Snatch) and Get-Ups.

What goes into your decision to leave or stay at a job?

First and foremost, if you dread going to work, those voices almost never get softer, so that 100% is the most important thing in leaving.

Using a business concept of "burn rate," if you simply can not accomplish what you absolutely have to accomplish in your life outside of work, the considerations to move on have to start to be formulated.

What do you do to overcome times of struggle, burnout, or overwhelm? Who do you turn to?

Again, there is not a name that I can offer that I always go to in these times. But the system to run is stop, analyze, organize resources, and attack the problem(s). There is no timetable for how this system progresses; it happens as fast as possible, just no faster.

If there is anyone that at least is always a part of these times for me, it's me. I turn to me and put my head down and figure it out. That doesn't mean I won't search for or accept help from others, but top to bottom, it's on me.

What do you think about immediately after one of your athletes is injured? What is your mindset in the following week?

First thing I think of is what could I/we have done differently. I immediately feel like I committed an error, made a bad pass, dropped a ball. My role in the machine is to make sure no one gets hurt. That's how my worth is measured.

The following week is simply rewriting the script and contributing to the machine in a different way to get this player as close to full training and practice as possible. We fix it.

How do you approach difficult conversations with athletes, coworkers, or your boss?

It may look different in each situation, but there are a whole host of concepts that are consistent throughout any difficult conversation.

The absolute key(s) are honesty and transparency with what everyone wants when the discussion is over and always recognizing that multiple things can be true.

Do you have a "failure" that was critical to your long-term development or success?

I've had about five life-changing events that could be considered failures as they were all undesirable circumstances. But each time, over time, life got better than it was before. It helped me believe such comments as "things happen for a reason," and "you'll be better off in the end" because they are/were unequivocally true.

What traits or skills do your most successful athletes have in common?

1) Enormous desire to win and doing (almost) whatever it takes to accomplish their version of victory.

2) Exceedingly elite physiological profiles of endocrine gland mass, volume of cytotoxic T-cells, an activity-specific heart, and high oxidative function of all type 1 and type 2 fibers.

3) An ability to continue despite imminent failure, loss, or danger.

What books or resources do you most often recommend to coaches?

The one book that I seem to recommend without much discernment is *How to Win Friends and Influence People* by Dale Carnegie. I mean, the title alone should get anyone excited and be like, "There is no way this book won't help me." Personally, I read that book once a year.

"Absolutely no one is successful alone. The narrative of solo genius is factually untrue, and yet is lauded in our culture to the point where people think they succeed or fail on their own stream alone."

-Miranda Holder

Miranda Holder is the Founder and Principal Coach of Holder Leadership, working with clients as a leadership and career coach. She is frequently brought in to speak with groups and organizations on various topics, ranging from leadership and self-awareness to the science of somatic approaches. Holder transitioned to founding Holder Leadership after almost 10 years as a rowing coach, with her last stop as the Head Women's Rowing Coach for four years at Georgetown University.

Who do you go to when you need advice? Why them?

I most often go to my own coach for advice, although my need for advice has gone down as my confidence and trust in my own internal compass and decision-making ability has gone up. Many times we ask for advice to pressure-test our own feeling or decision about something, and there is nothing wrong with this as long as we know the difference between what is ours and what is someone else's perspective.

I go to my coach for advice when I am specifically looking for knowledge I do not have, or a skill set I have not yet developed. As a coach myself, I have had many coaches at different times of my life for different reasons, based primarily on the skills I wanted to strengthen or cultivate. I go to my current coach because she is trustworthy, knowledgeable, experienced, and emotionally neutral. She is able to hold my goals and the truth about my skills and abilities apart from my own emotional roller coaster. It's one of the most important things a coach can do.

What early job was pivotal in your career? Why?

My first coaching job set the stage for everything else, and revealed how much I loved teaching and bearing witness to someone else's developmental journey. I was training in a pre-elite group at a local rowing club in 2006 when I was diagnosed with a genetic heart condition that ended my rowing career. Another coach in the group offered me a volunteer assistant coaching job, which led to my first collegiate assistant coaching job at Northeastern University five months later. I never would have sought out coaching as a vocation or career, but I followed what I loved and what energized me. My path revealed itself.

What are your first steps when you start a new job? What do you need to figure out, what do you need to get done, who do you need to get to know?

In some ways, my last first job was nearly nine years ago when I started my leadership coaching practice in 2015. In other ways, every time I get a new client or project, I get a new job. My take may be a little different.

1) You need to understand from all the stakeholders what success looks and feels like in that job. What are they expecting? Do not be afraid to ask very specific, seemingly dumb questions. Assuming you know doesn't make you look smarter, but we often think we need to know. Don't assume your stakeholders know or have thought deeply or carefully about it. It's not their job. Notice the assumptions you make about their language when they tell you and make sure to clarify, even if it seems obvious. For example, "So when you say you want a successful team, that looks like..."

2) I need to get done what is important, and be mindful of what is urgent relative to the overall goal or goals of the organization/relationship. They are not always the same, and knowing the difference is critical. Every day, week, month, and quarter is dictated by that awareness.

3) I need to get to know my clients, to understand who they are, and how they think and feel. When I was a rowing coach, my athletes were my clients. In previous jobs, this might have included coworkers and bosses, or sponsors, athletes, alumni, etc. I would visualize the system like a solar system, seeing who was at the center and who was more removed. This helped me prioritize whose feedback and opinion mattered most.

What advice do you have for a college student looking to break into coaching? Who are the best mentors in the world to work for early in your career?

Start with the places where you are known and trusted (your club, high school, or collegiate program). Let your former coaches know what you're looking to do and why. Do they need help, or are they willing to let you volunteer for a period? Do they know people who they can connect you to?

Don't be afraid to swing for the fences and imagine where you'd like to be. Reach out to those coaches/programs as well, either through leveraging your network if you have connections or even going in cold. Tell them your intentions and why you're interested in being a part of that program. It can't hurt to try. You never know what will happen, and I've learned never to say "no" for someone else until they have said it to me first.

If you only had two 30-minute sessions a week to train your team, how would you prepare them?

I would have them do visualization and mindfulness exercises. Everything starts and ends in the mind: your view of yourself, your ability to reach your goals, the story of yourself and your team on the journey to those goals, your ability to be present to and feel—proprioceptively—your body's shape in space. So much of the time, it's our minds that get in the way.

What goes into your decision to leave or stay at a job?

Am I doing the job out of duty and obligation or from a place of energizing joy? This is critical in coaching, but any job goes better if you are there because it's the right one for you. I always promised myself that if I became what I saw in other older coaches (burned out, exhausted, disengaged, defeated), I would leave because it wasn't fair to the athletes to have a leader in that state. Now I look at it with a bit more nuance. If I were in that state again as an athletic coach, I would hire a leadership coach to help me shift that state or move on to the next thing.

After many years, coaches can feel trapped in coaching, and lose sight of the way their skills are transferable beyond athletic coaching. But doing a job because you are afraid or feel trapped isn't a great example to set for your team, so the moment is an opportunity to grow, either within the role or into a new one.

What do you do to overcome times of struggle, burnout, or overwhelm? Who do you turn to?

Absolutely no one is successful alone. The narrative of solo genius is factually untrue, and yet is lauded in our culture to the point where people think they succeed or fail on their own stream alone.

I have intentionally cultivated relationships with people who I can turn to in times of struggle, both coaches, mentors, and friends. Most of the time, we need others who will believe in us when we are having difficulty believing in ourselves. Sounds simple, but most stories of difficulty boil down to that. I have many, many people I can call and be with when things are hard. They know if I need advice, I'll ask, but if I don't, I need their presence and encouragement to keep going.

I have also purposefully cultivated a relationship with what I call my Wise Self. We all have it, and we all have access to it. I've watched hundreds of people in workshops I've run do it every day without any prior training or skill. And, like a muscle, this connection benefits from use, repetition, and challenge to strengthen it. It also often requires getting still or quiet, and trusting that the best answers lie inside.

I often get in touch with this aspect of myself best out in nature, after meditating or exercising, or even in writing a letter to myself from that perspective.

One easy way to get in touch with it is to get clear on the question you want to ask. Close your eyes, and drop your awareness down into your body (out of your head). Turn on your senses more acutely. What can you hear? Taste? Feel (physical sensations)? Smell? Put your hand on your heart. If your Wise Self could speak, what would s/he say to you right now? Trust what comes up and write it down. What do you notice?

When I invite my clients or workshop participants to share their experiences with this exercise, their Wise Selves are uniformly compassionate, loving, encouraging, clear, and patient. It never fails to blow my mind.

Short story long: it's important to be able to go inside (Wise Self) and outside (support system) for help. Both are necessary.

What books or resources do you most often recommend to coaches?

I most often use a short video about the Ladder of Inference. In about five minutes, it explains how quickly our brains work to tell stories and make assumptions that we think are facts. How we think, feel, and act is significantly influenced by that internal mental narrative, and without our awareness, it controls many aspects of our life and performance.

"If an athlete is not committed, I can't help them. If an athlete is committed, I can't stop them. There's power in making up your mind to complete a task and not giving yourself any outs or chances to make an excuse."

-Mike Nilson

Mike Nilson has been the Director of Performance and Nutrition for the Gonzaga Athletic Department since 2004, working directly with the Women's Basketball program. Beyond his role as a strength coach and sports nutritionist, Nilson is also a leadership coach, implementing an 18-week leadership program with the Women's Basketball staff. He launched HoopCommitment.com in 2019, where he shares his passion for basketball nutrition, training, and leadership, while hosting the *Hoop Commitment Podcast.* Nilson also helped found U-District Physical Therapy and the U-District Foundation.

Who do you go to when you need advice? Why them?

When I have an important decision to make, I reach out to my brother Marc because of his wisdom and willingness to ask difficult questions. Instead of giving advice, he shares life principles that provide perspective and allow me to make better informed decisions. I tend to shy away from people who want to give solutions to problems. I benefit more from hearing a thought process and experiences so I can understand the "why" behind the "what." It's also helpful to be challenged with clarifying questions on my past decisions. My brother cares enough about me to point out my successes and failures.

What early job was pivotal in your career? Why?

I worked at a shoe store in the mall when I was in college. There were stretches throughout the day where not a single customer would enter the store, and I would just stand and stare at the clock. I've never experienced time moving so slow in my life! That job taught me that if my body doesn't move throughout the day and my mind isn't consistently challenged, my spirit will suffer. My days fly by as a S&C coach because I'm constantly demonstrating exercises, strengthening relationships, and problem solving. There's always something new to learn about the human body and any job I pursue in the future must be in an environment that brings out my passion.

How do you approach difficult conversations with athletes, coworkers, or your boss?

Before I approach a difficult conversation, I review how the situation is positioned in my mind. If I don't feel good about initiating the talk, that's a sign that I'm not looking at the problem through the correct lens. This usually means that I'm too focused on what happened instead of how to move forward. I feel best when I've produced at least one positive solution of how we can right the past wrong. If I can "begin with the end in mind," I'll know how to navigate times of high emotion or when the talk strays off path.

What traits or skills do your most successful athletes have in common?

A skill that is foundational to success is commitment. If an athlete is not committed, I can't help them. If an athlete is committed, I can't stop them. There's power in making up your mind to complete a task and not giving yourself any outs or chances to make an excuse. It's the equivalent to burning the ships behind you. This skill not only works in athletics, but also in music, business, and relationships. You can learn to play any instrument by committing to practicing it every day for a year. You can become a better partner by giving compliments and asking questions every day for a lifetime. If you want to gain weight, don't make a goal of eating breakfast every day, commit to it! A goal is something you want to do, while a commitment is something you have to do. I've turned every important habit in my life into a commitment.

What books or resources do you most often recommend to coaches?

I was so excited to land a Division I strength and conditioning job that I never thought about the financial side of coaching. My first coaching opportunity was a part-time position at Gonzaga, training 20 hours a week. A friend congratulated me and then asked, "Now, how are you going to make money?" I was crushed, wondering how I could support my family while following my passion. Since then, I've been reading books and taking courses on wealth building. The book that got me started on the journey was Robert Kiyosaki's *Rich Dad, Poor Dad*. It taught me the importance of investing in assets, and this one concept has allowed me to support my family while being in the strength and conditioning profession for over twenty years. I now play the board game, Cashflow, with my three kids so they'll have options for building wealth regardless of their occupation.

"If you are working for a good person, which I fortunately have over the years, they have always led me in the right direction. To me, asking them for advice builds rapport and maintains loyalty by staying in-house for advice."

-Erik DeRoo

Erik DeRoo is an Assistant Coach for the Texas Tech Women's Basketball program, while also assisting with recruiting operations. Before working in Lubbock, DeRoo was an Assistant Coach and Recruiting Coordinator for the Women's Basketball team at Abilene Christian University for five seasons. He was a part of two conference championships at ACU, and the program's first NCAA tournament appearance in Division I history. After the 2019-2020 season, DeRoo was named to the WBCA 30 under 30 list while also being a finalist for the D1 Assistant Coach of the Year.

Who do you go to when you need advice? Why them?

My current Head Coach. If you are working for a good person, which I fortunately have over the years, they have always led me in the right direction. To me, asking them for advice builds rapport and maintains loyalty by staying in-house for advice. The next person I run most everything by is my dad. He is experienced in managing people and making decisions. He has always led me in the right direction or offered questions to ask myself.

What early job was pivotal in your career? Why?

Being a Graduate Assistant at Fresno State. This program had seen success at the highest level over a long period, therefore there were high expectations with good resources, but relatively limited staffing. I was able to serve in a bunch of roles and see every element of the program. This job allowed me to learn the foundations of operating a college basketball program with limited hands-on opportunities to actually coach basketball. Very humbling position!

What are your first steps when you start a new job? What do you need to figure out, what do you need to get done, who do you need to get to know?

I get my job responsibilities from my head coach (usually formally written out) and my goal is to become as competent in those spaces as possible over the first year. I then try to find out what elements of my job are not on that piece of paper, but still fall under my responsibilities so that nothing falls through the cracks. The goal is by the end of year one, be knowledgeable in my job so that year two I can become more efficient. I then try to meet anyone that is directly attached to our program that helps any aspect of our program more forward on a daily or weekly basis.

What advice do you have for a college student looking to break into coaching? Who are the best mentors in the world to work for early in your career?

The first thought is the higher level of the sport you can play the better. If you aren't fortunate enough to play at the highest level, finding a way to get in the door with an athletics program at a low-end position will provide you with experiences and references for your next stop. The best mentors are the ones willing to help beyond just one call or interaction! Not everyone you reach out to will get back to you or will be the best person to align your career with.

If you only had two 30-minute sessions a week to train your team, how would you prepare them?

One simple offensive action, then skill develop the elements to that action so you can be solid in knowing and executing the scoring opportunities. (I am an offensive-minded person, so this likely is not the best answer for everyone)

What goes into your decision to leave or stay at a job?

Long-Term Stability! If I am in a place of stability it will always be harder for me to move on. If I am looking at a job that does not have a certain level of stability I cannot consider it. Stability offers a level of peace for myself and my family that you cannot put a price tag on.

What do you do to overcome times of struggle, burnout, or overwhelm? Who do you turn to?

I see my therapist every six weeks to help guide me in any personal struggles I am facing at that time. I'm a big advocate for mental health and I think opening oneself up to a therapist offers a great opportunity to help each of us grow!

What do you think about immediately after one of your athletes is injured? What is your mindset in the following week?

Honest answer is: Who will be able to fill their role?

The follow-up is: How can we help this athlete through recovery and their return to play protocol? Injuries are tough for any athlete and team. Helping the athlete and the coaches cope through injuries is the area that I believe needs more education across the sports landscape beyond just physical recovery with an AT or PT.

How do you approach difficult conversations with athletes, coworkers, or your boss?

Each of the three take emotional awareness! Each person and each position probably needs different conversations with different tones and timing.

Do you have a "failure" that was critical to your long-term development or success?

I have had micro-failures in every position and season throughout my career. I believe all of them helped me grow and learn how to be better or more efficient. The ones that affect the entire team or head coach are the ones that sting the most in the moment, but as long as I made sure these mistakes didn't happen again or consistently, I felt like I was learning.

What traits or skills do your most successful athletes have in common?

I believe that high-level, successful athletes have: Multiple Elite Skills, they Play and Work Hard, they can Defend multiple positions and they have adequate size and athleticism for their position. That is the foundation of being a successful athlete. The traits that continue to move the needle forward for athletes are their IQ for their sport, their love of the game, and their Leadership capabilities.

What books or resources do you most often recommend to coaches?

Coaching Better Every Season by Wade Gilbert. This book incorporates so many elements of team building, sport psychology, practice planning, etc. into it. If you have any questions on how to build the bones of a program, this is for you! For college coaches, I would push any book or the blog of Dan Tudor. He offers high levels of recruiting resources backed by research.

"Keep your aim on 'being less wrong,' rather than 'being right'; you will respond more favorably to actual outcomes not meeting your expected outcomes from a particular training program you wrote, to being challenged or questioned by colleagues or your athletes on what you're doing, and every other situation where you may find yourself in where the possibility of being wrong exists."

-Scott Kuehn

Scott Kuehn is the Manager of Applied Sport Science with LSU Football, helping the program achieve back-to-back 10 win seasons while working to prepare Jayden Daniels to win the 2023 Heisman Trophy. Kuehn previously worked at the University of Arizona as a Performance Enhancement Coach-Coordinator of Performance Sciences, spending time with both the Football program and with Women's Soccer, Men's Golf, Men's and Women's Tennis, and Diving. Before Arizona, he worked at the College of William & Mary as the Assistant Athletics Performance Coach-Coordinator of Data Science. Kuehn also has experience with the University of Tulsa, the University of Kentucky, Acceleration Sports Performance, and Metea Valley High School.

What early job was pivotal in your career? Why?

The first one as a head strength and conditioning coach at a high school in my hometown, because it gave me the confidence to know 1) this was the field that I was meant to be in and 2) that I was good at it. I had enough wherewithal at that point to know I wasn't doing everything right (I know this even much more so now), but it was still all the validation I needed that I was exactly where I was meant to be in my professional life.

What are your first steps when you start a new job? What do you need to figure out, what do you need to get done, who do you need to get to know?

No matter what pretense you are coming into a new situation under, it is paramount to spend a lot of time listening, observing, and asking questions before moving in any one direction. Either you are being brought in as part of a new staff, with an impetus to change things from the way they were previously done, or you're being brought in to fill an opening on an already established staff, where it is understood that you'll fill a role, just with more of your spin on it. No matter which, the quote, "If you're going to run against the grain, you better understand why the grain runs the way it does first" has always been front of mind for me, as I've come into both situations in my career, and it's always been a strong reminder to pause for a second, take in the totality of your new surroundings, and then move in the direction you believe to be best. To me, this general guidance answers the first three aspects of this question.

As for the final part, get to know your athletes asap. Names, where they're from, who they are; all of it. They're the most important relationships you have in coaching, and if being athlete-centered is a pillar for you (which it should be), they are the first ones that should command your time and energy in getting to know. Beyond them, getting to know your superiors, namely the Head Coach and Head Strength Coach (if you are not the Head Strength Coach yourself) is a critical and concurrent step to take, as their directives are going to serve as your professional north star for how you go about the job and work to underpin what they're about. Sports Medicine staff is always next for me, just given the proximity with which you'll work with them, especially when it comes to working with athletes returning from injury. Establishing quality relationships and trust there is essential in being able to give the athletes the care they need in coming back from injury, so you want your athletic trainers to know what you're about to maximize the collaboration that is requisite at mid and long-term rehab stages. Everyone else naturally comes with time, provided you are intentional about meeting the people you work in close proximity with on the day to day; don't avoid getting to know assistant sport coaches, as some become future head coaches and are the relationships you want to have if you aspire to be a Head Strength Coach someday.

What advice do you have for a college student looking to break into coaching? Who are the best mentors in the world to work for early in your career?
Start coaching yesterday. If you are in undergrad, reach out to your school's strength and conditioning department, and ask if you can observe/volunteer your time and aid a few times a week. Just being immersed in the day to day, seeing how coaches coach and run sessions, and gaining an understanding of the prep that goes into

a S&C program is invaluable experience to get. As you earn their trust, they may start to afford you small opportunities to coach—if they don't because you are just a volunteer, find opportunities to get experience coaching. Just like is discussed in exercise modifications, keep plan B as close to plan A as possible; if you can't coach in a S&C program, look for a sports performance facility. If that isn't an option, find a public gym that maybe has a sports performance program associated with it that you can start working in. Obviously with college students/immediate post grads, you aren't expecting them to have a wealth of experience, but it always stands out on application materials if someone has ANY sort of experience coaching athletes, as opposed to none at all or coaching general population.

If you only had two 30-minute sessions a week to train your team, how would you prepare them?

Depends—if they are concomitantly practicing their sport, I would seek to fill in the gaps of what the sport/sport practice doesn't give them with reverence to competitive demands, typically higher intensity actions/movements. If that time includes sport practice, then I'm allocating all of that time to practicing the sport.

What goes into your decision to leave or stay at a job?

Succinctly, when my reaction to the opportunity being presented is "F*** yeah." If it's anything less than that, I don't leave. To elaborate a bit more, one of my good friends and mentors, Keir Wenham-Flatt, boiled down career decisions to 4 P's: Pay, Progression, Personal life, and Purpose. Pay—obvious financial compensation, but also hidden value of time demands and supporting human resources of the job, and ability to earn additional streams of income. Progression—does the opportunity move you up or down the career ladder relative to your professional goals? Personal Life— does the job add or remove from your ability to exist in the ways you want to outside of the job? Purpose—does the job give you meaningful direction and alignment with your morals and principles? If you've got all 4, you're in the dream job and should never leave; 3 out of 4, only leave for the dream job; 2 out of 4, you should be actively looking; anything less than 2 out of 4, what are you doing there? Use that framework as an evaluative mental exercise to ensure you are appraising the opportunity appropriately, and always lean on your gut reaction as to whether the opportunity is a "F*** yeah"; if it isn't, you probably shouldn't pursue it.

What do you do to overcome times of struggle, burnout, or overwhelm? Who do you turn to?

I've been there before frequently, and it's been a point of emphasis for me in learning how to better balance work and life so I don't reach that point. Inevitably, there are times of the year where the work mounts up and the pressure is on, and you have to condition yourself to take that as a signal that it is time to find opportunities to decompress/relax to balance that out so it doesn't reach a bad point. Vizi Andrei is a modern thinker that I enjoy, and he heavily speaks to the value of downtime/relaxation for what it contributes to the time when you are working; don't be afraid of taking time to relax, or conflate it in your head as laziness. Talk with family, friends, or colleagues to air your thoughts out. There is a lot of benefit that comes with getting the thoughts swirling in your mind out of there so your mind can clear and feel better about it all. During those times, I take it as a signal to be especially diligent about my nutrition, sleep, and workouts. Those are high priority times to kick those things into gear and take care of yourself so you don't end up in a downward spiral. If we are going to preach health, wellness, and recovery to our athletes, we have to be about it as coaches ourselves.

What do you think about immediately after one of your athletes is injured? What is your mindset in the following week?

There is a delicate balance of introspection and acceptance of uncontrollable factors that has to be considered. No matter what, I think you're doing the job the right way if you have a strong gut reaction to an athlete getting hurt. If your first instinct is to shrug your shoulders and say, "It happens," I think you've got the wrong mindset towards the work you do. I always start looking inward; revisiting relevant athlete data to see if I missed a workload spike, significant asymmetry or output decrement, or significant inflection in subjective data points, look at what had been prescribed from a physical preparation standpoint prior to the injury, or from a practice load standpoint if the injury occurred in practice. I look to fill in the gaps of these objective data streams as well by talking with the athlete and getting more information from them: what happened, did you feel anything at the injury site prior to getting hurt, how'd you sleep the night before, has anything stressful happened recently, etc...

These conversations can be illuminating, such as an athlete saying they felt a sensation in the affected area going into the session, but didn't say anything and just tried stretching it instead, or that despite reporting they had 8 hours of sleep on their wellness survey, they actually only got 2 hours because they were up late studying for a test, and thought they would get in trouble if they reported sleeping that little. All of this information together gives you an opportunity to audit your data systems; maybe the athlete didn't accurately report their sleep duration, but they did report a massive spike in their stress levels that was overlooked or unflagged. Maybe the athlete was symmetrical on a performance test, but the output was dropping bilaterally due to accumulated fatigue, and the tissue finally gave out and it just happened to be on that side. No matter what, there is always a lesson to be learned from injuries, you have to be willing to do the work to uncover it, learn from and move forward with it, and then ultimately give yourself the grace of acknowledging that its part of the risk undertaken by working in sport.

Ships are safest in the harbor, but that's not where they're meant to be; you could have an injury rate of zero if your athletes did nothing but sit on the bench every practice and workout, but that's not the point of athletics. Learn the lesson, give yourself grace, and then do right by the injured athlete to work with them and the athletic trainer to help them get back to their sport as quickly and safely as possible.

Do you have a "failure" that was critical to your long-term development or success?

All of them. I'm still failing today. Nassim Taleb talks about two kinds of learning: via positiva and via negativa. Via positiva is learning what something is. Force equals mass times acceleration; this is a law of physics that you can learn and definitively know. Improvement of the ability to produce force, however? Anything but a law; you can have two athletes do the same training program and have one who adds 40lbs to a lift, and the other one doesn't increase their max at all. You can either turn a blind eye to the one who didn't improve and pat yourself on the back for the 40lbs increase, or you can dive into the one who didn't go anywhere to better understand why that didn't occur, so you can lessen the likelihood of that happening next time. Failures are opportunities to learn and grow by learning what something isn't, or via negativa; there is very little about this field we know with 100% certainty, but there is infinitely more knowledge to be gained by learning what not to do or what doesn't work.

I heard a podcast the other day that talked about successful people viewing failure/being wrong as positives because it means they learned something new—I wish I was there mentally, and it's something I aspire towards after hearing how it was talked about. Keep your aim on "being less wrong," rather than "being right"; you will respond more favorably to actual outcomes not meeting your expected outcomes from a particular training program you wrote, to being challenged or questioned by colleagues or your athletes on what you're doing, and every other situation where you may find yourself in where the possibility of being wrong exists. Another mental model I enjoy is a friend of mine named Frank Barone who always asks himself, "What if I'm wrong?" about his programs to shoot holes in his approach. It's an outstanding thought experiment that keeps yourself accountable to knowing how you know what you know and finding any gaps in your approach that need shoring up.

What books or resources do you most often recommend to coaches?

In order: *Game Changer* by Fergus Connolly and then *Governing Dynamics of Coaching* by James Smith. Both texts illustrate the very holistic lens with which sport preparation needs to be approached with. The first time reading through them isn't easy; the first time through is best meant to illuminate the complexity of humans and sport—subsequent revisits to those texts are when you begin to learn and understand the concepts they both speak to, and how to apply them. As a continuing education resource, Strength Coach Network is unmatched in terms of the variety, depth, and practicality of information available. Being able to watch no fluff presentations from coaches who are working at high levels of sport, then engage with them in Q&A and discussion on the site makes it a goldmine of knowledge, all of which serves to bridge the immense gap from academia to working in the field.

"Move on and do not make a big deal out of who's missing. Always prepare the exact same way for the next game. Let the team know that our expectations never change no matter what the circumstances may be."

-Randy Rahe

Randy Rahe retired in May 2022 after 16 seasons as the Head Men's Basketball Coach at Weber State University. With 316 wins, he is the winningest coach in the history of Weber State Basketball and the Big Sky Conference. Rahe led Weber State to five Big Sky Championships, three appearances in March Madness, and nine 20+ win seasons—including a school record 30 wins in 2012-2013. He was named Big Sky Coach of the Year four times and coached five Big Sky MVPs, including NBA draft picks Damian Lillard (2x MVP), Joel Bolomboy, and Dillon Jones. Rahe had multiple stops as an assistant before Weber State, including Colorado, Denver, Colorado State, Utah State, and Utah.

Who do you go to when you need advice? Why them?
Stew Morrill, Retired Utah State Coach. My mentor.

What are your first steps when you start a new job? What do you need to figure out, what do you need to get done, who do you need to get to know?
Number one priority was to develop a culture, who are we going to be and what are we going to stand for. I would meet with everyone that will be involved with our program and educate them on what our culture will be and how important it is that they uphold that culture. To me, that was the most important thing we had to have in our program.

What advice do you have for a college student looking to break into coaching? Who are the best mentors in the world to work for early in your career?
Develop a philosophy of what type of coach you want to be. Be who you are and always stay true to your core values.

Any mentor that has high character and strong integrity. Mentors that are committed to doing things the right way.

If you only had two 30-minute sessions a week to train your team, how would you prepare them?

I would use those sessions to develop a team cohesiveness and mental and physical toughness by pushing them hard doing difficult tasks. Emphasis on everyone giving themselves up for the team and playing for each other.

What goes into your decision to leave or stay at a job?

Am I happy and is my family happy? Am I supported by our administration and do we have the resources to be successful?

What do you do to overcome times of struggle, burnout, or overwhelm? Who do you turn to?

I put my trust in God and always stay true to who I am and what I believe in. I turn to my wife to help me stay balanced and keep things in perspective.

What do you think about immediately after one of your athletes is injured? What is your mindset in the following week?

First thought is...next man up. Move on and do not make a big deal out of who's missing. Always prepare the exact same way for the next game. Let the team know that our expectations never change no matter what the circumstances may be.

How do you approach difficult conversations with athletes, coworkers, or your boss?

With total honesty and total transparency. No time for bulls**t.

Do you have a "failure" that was critical to your long-term development or success?

Not just one failure, but a number of them. How I dealt with them led me to becoming a better coach.

What traits or skills do your most successful athletes have in common?

Mental toughness, work ethic, humility, and high character.

What books or resources do you most often recommend to coaches?

- *The Legacy Builder* – Rod Olson
- *Training Camp* – Jon Gordon

"One of my favorite quotes from Andrea Hudy is, 'Experience doesn't create higher standards; exposure to higher standards creates a heightened experience.'"

-Nicole Jimenez

Nicole Jimenez is in her third year as the Head Strength and Conditioning Coach for Women's Basketball at Missouri State University. She's helped the program win at least 20 games in her first two seasons, appearing in the WNIT, WBIT, and 2024 MVC Conference Tournament Championship game. Jimenez was the strength coach for Women's Basketball, Women's Rugby, and Women's Volleyball at Sacred Heart before Missouri State. She also gained experience as the primary intern for the UConn Women's Basketball team.

Who do you go to when you need advice? Why them?

- Catherine Lass (Duke University: Assistant Director of Athletic Medicine; Women's Basketball)
- Andrea Hudy (University of Connecticut: Director of Sports Performance; Women's Basketball)

Catherine Lass and Andrea Hudy both exemplify what it means to work and be successful at an elite level. Everything they are about is what I hope to become someday, not only as a coach but as a person. One of my favorite quotes from Andrea Hudy is, "Experience doesn't create higher standards; exposure to higher standards creates a heightened experience." Because of these ladies I have been fortunate enough to have the experience of what high standards look like day in and day out.

What early job was pivotal in your career? Why?

The most important thing is to be honest with what your goals are and if you are doing everything necessary to reach those goals. Once I graduated from graduate school, I knew I needed another year of observation and learning. Although I was offered a few jobs after graduating and I could have used the money, I knew what I needed to do to be better prepared to reach my professional goals. It was extremely difficult to not get paid and to be away from family, but I knew if I continued to be persistent, then the right opportunity would eventually come. It was the best decision I made.

I ended up interning for Andrea Hudy, one of the top strength coaches in the field, at the University of Connecticut, one of the top women's basketball programs in the country. I learned the best ways to train elite athletes, how to collect and analyze data, and observed how to have hard conversations with sport coaches and athletic trainers. It opened my eyes to a lot of new concepts and allowed me to make new goals for myself. The next step was to challenge myself to do the same or better.

What are your first steps when you start a new job? What do you need to figure out, what do you need to get done, who do you need to get to know?

The first steps for me are to observe, listen, and learn. I observe how coaches interact with each other, how the players interact with one another, and how the players interact with the coaches. I listen to what the head coach wants and what his/her goals are. At the end of the day it is their program. As a strength coach, I am an extension of the coach, and my job is to execute what the coach wants. Lastly, I try to learn all that I can from the coaching staff, athletic training staff, and student athletes— everyone can learn from those around them. As you listen, you gain respect from your colleagues and players, and you can begin to build relationships with them.

My goal is to do my job and to do it with excellence. It is the reason I was hired. I need to be confident regarding the knowledge I possess and educate those around me. It is essential they understand why we train the way that we do. Also, it is important to get to know everyone who is involved with the program; it does not matter who it is, everyone plays a crucial role in the athlete's success.

What advice do you have for a college student looking to break into coaching? Who are the best mentors in the world to work for early in your career?

If you have chosen the coaching career, you need to be all in. This career comes with long hours, low income, hard work, personal sacrifices, and continuing education. You must love coaching to help you get past the difficult days. You also need to understand that everyone's path is different. Some take longer than others to reach the "dream job" that you envision, and some never even end up with their "dream job."

Intern for a coach who allows you to have coaching experience and not a coach who only has you clean and set up. Make sure you are networking with coaches and maintaining connections, you never know who will give you an opportunity. It is a small world and the more people you know and build relationships with, the greater your chances for the opportunity for which you are waiting. Once you discover your training philosophy, seek coaches that share the same philosophy and ask for their mentorship. You should learn from those that share the same views. Some coaches who come to mind: Andrea Hudy, Glenn Cain, Justin Roach, Eric Cressey, Vernon Griffith, Megan Young, Kelly Dormandy, Mike Guevara, Cory Schlesinger.

What goes into your decision to leave or stay at a job?

I decide whether I stay or leave a job according to the freedom I am given to do my job; it is essential for me to work for a coach that trusts and values my strength and conditioning philosophy and believe it is a crucial component to be successful in the sport. I do not enjoy being in a position where I am micromanaged. Another factor is the distance to my family. Lastly, being in a position that allows me to get closer to my "dream job."

What do you do to overcome times of struggle, burnout, or overwhelm? Who do you turn to?

I enjoy being involved in the outdoors by hiking, fishing, canoeing, lifting, running, playing basketball, or pickleball to help me relax. Spending time with my family also helps me disconnect. We are in a profession where we are constantly pouring into the athletes we work with. We must have the discipline to find time to fill our cup so we can continue to be our best.

What do you think about immediately after one of your athletes is injured? What is your mindset in the following week?

It is one of the worst feelings to watch one of your athletes get injured—the last thing you want to see is an athlete sitting out. After the injury, I make sure the athlete receives everything necessary to get healthy. It is my job to get them back on the court. "The best ability is availability," although there are many factors that play a role in the athlete getting injured and many times, it is out of our control. A strength coach once told me, "You can't catch all the raindrops."

What traits or skills do your most successful athletes have in common?
- Consistency
- Confidence
- Discipline
- Competitiveness
- Mindset

"There are problems everywhere, but luckily you have the power to choose WHICH problems you want to co-exist with. The answer to this question is what should ultimately help empower you to decide on whether to stay or leave a job."

-Thomas Lené

Thomas Lené is in his third season as the Strength and Conditioning Coach for Women's Basketball at LSU, where he helped the Tigers win the program's first National Championship in 2023 and advance to the 2024 Elite Eight. He first won a National Championship with Kim Mulkey as the Interim Director of Athletic Performance for Baylor Women's Basketball in 2019. Before heading to LSU, Lené worked as the Director of Sports Performance for Women's Basketball at VCU and the Associate Strength and Conditioning Coach at Drake University. He has helped coach multiple WNBA draft picks, including recent top 10 draft pick Angel Reese.

Who do you go to when you need advice? Why them?

God first. Going to Him is even more important when you don't understand why things are the way they are. Especially when you are doing everything you can or in a season of doubt. He will always provide hope and an answer when the time is right. Not great timing, but PERFECT timing. It may not make sense to you, but you are not God, and God will give you everything you would've wanted in time if you knew what he already knows.

Secondly, I go to my mentors when I need to talk shop or discuss ideas about strength and conditioning. I need to ask those who are extremely knowledgeable about the fundamental processes of the human body to discuss innovative ideas and then add in the "known" strength principles and practices that we use daily.

What early job was pivotal in your career? Why?

Working at Drake University. Going from winning a national championship at Baylor with elite athletes and essentially unlimited resources to less talented athletes who all share the same weight room. Two complete opposite ends of the spectrum will really challenge your understanding of bioenergetics, biomechanics, and physiology. It will also force you to get creative with your lift sessions when two other sports are in the weight room at the same time as you, and you don't have access to the same equipment as what Baylor had. It will also challenge your ability to adapt to new communication styles with coaches and learn them and their vision for the program and how you need to assist their vision. Be respectful to your new "boss" and their dreams. Help create and guide alongside them.

What are your first steps when you start a new job? What do you need to figure out, what do you need to get done, who do you need to get to know?

Build a relationship with your coaches and admin. Understand their vision for the program and university and ask questions. Figure out their expectations of you to support their vision, and then look internally for ways to innovate and grow it based on your experience. You also need to set the standards in the weight room for the athletes on how your program operates on a day-to-day basis. What is acceptable, what is not, and why. Explain how your vision will supplement their performance and goals based on these set daily standards.

Build a relationship with those athletes and people that revolve around your philosophy and make sure you live it day in and day out. That will create an authentic culture and that needs to be done more than anything. This will make buy-in and provide intentionality in their lives to do what is asked of them, as well as allow for a culture of inspiration rather than one of needing motivation.

After that you need to get a lay of the land. What you have to work with, a list of future purchases, and how to program around what is in front of you. Then it is a matter of sticking to your philosophy in the weight room and adapting along the way to support your vision, but also the head coach's—which will likely change throughout the course of the season.

Then program design. Program design your philosophy that fits with the structure of the weight room. You may not be able to create a great circuit the way you want to because of the design of the weight room. You'll have to get creative and restructure your program around it, so give yourself plenty of time to design and experiment to work through errors.

Set up one-on-one meetings with your athletes. Get to know who they are as a human being. You need to find something you can relate with them on from their personal life that doesn't revolve around basketball, then you can introduce the strength and conditioning aspects into the conversation. This will help with quick buy-in because they will see that you care for who they are, helping them believe in what you offer.

What advice do you have for a college student looking to break into coaching? Who are the best mentors in the world to work for early in your career?

Study a ton on your own. Look into everything and everyone's program with open eyes for how they use it to fit their program. Never look at someone's program to find something wrong. Look at it to learn how you can see through another lens of why that may be the way it is, and how it can benefit you by learning not to use it or how to implement it into your philosophy. The more judgmental you are, the less you'll learn, the more arrogant and egotistical you'll become, which will blind you and make you more susceptible to long-term frustrations in this career in a multitude of ways. Not to mention the lack of success and actual impacts you will make along the way.

Be willing to take any job you can get off the rip. Don't be picky about where you want to live or how much money you want to make. It is a journey, not a race. You will lose if you are picky.

The best mentors are the ones you ask the most questions to. Learning how to ask questions and what questions to ask will take you just as far as learning from a specific mentor. If you don't know how to do those things, then it doesn't even matter who you train under. Most strength coaches "know" the same stuff. It is the philosophies and the specificity of their approaches to the demands of their specific coach that differ. THAT is the difference, and knowing how to ask questions that relate to that, along with "specific" strength and conditioning questions, is what will ultimately dictate your level of success.

If you only had two 30-minute sessions a week to train your team, how would you prepare them?

Considering I live this with my program year after year, I micro-dose during the entire season. Last "off-season" did not exist, and we went into the season with only 6-8 lifts under our belt. So, no foundation what-so-ever. Enter the micro-dose. Frankly, all season long, regardless of a summer foundation or not, this is what I do. I always lift the team after practice in-season to make sure I do not apply too much excess stress to the body by accident. We run 5x2's, 5x3's, 6x3's, 7x3's, 8x3's, 10x2's. I have a dynamic effort focused day, which is usually two days after our last game and two days before our next game. The day after the 1st game of the week is usually lower body recovery focused with heavy upper body. For example, Tuesday lift (2 days out) would be dynamic effort chain squats to the bench along with chin-ups for a 8x3 and that is it. No second circuit with it unless there is time to recover properly and they entered the session recovered well enough to add more stress.

What goes into your decision to leave or stay at a job?

Now this is a million-dollar question. No phoning friends or asking the audience on this one. For me, it has changed over and over and over again. When you are young, excited, and full of hope, you don't "truly" know what you are aiming for. Your eyes automatically look for bright and shiny things such as salary and clout. Your focus is narrow and blind. You turn down options because they aren't "cool" enough, and then accumulate frustrations about where you are currently positioned in life. When those frustrations boil, whether it is due to coaches, feeling under-valued, not happy, not enough money, not winning, etc. you start to think that life could "easily" be better if I leave and go to one of those "cool big-time" schools that win it all and get paid more.

Keep dreaming. I have found that no matter where you are or what your current frustrations are...it doesn't actually "get better." It will just manifest itself into something different, and the same intrusive thoughts you had before you left your last job will creep back in and tell you the same thing. "Leave. You don't get paid enough to deal with this. You aren't happy." This is coming from someone who has won two national championships and has multiple Elite Eight and Sweet Sixteen appearances. It feels the same either way. But why? Exactly. Why? There are problems everywhere, but luckily you have the power to choose WHICH problems you want to co-exist with. The answer to this question is what should ultimately help empower you to decide on whether to stay or leave a job. Foundation. What are YOU rooted in.

Stop all those other intrusive thoughts formerly mentioned. That is ego and emotion speaking. It provides ZERO true direction for you. Those things help you pursue what you think is "happiness" and that is fleeting and ever-changing with each new day. You constantly want more than you have and you promise yourself that "if only you get this," you will be "happy" and love your job. Wrong. Those are short-term goals/answers that will leave you un-fulfilled. You have actually received quite a few things you have wanted in the past, but you are not grateful enough in the present to realize it. Your foundation in who you are as a person is the only thing that will give you the strength to make the best decision for your future career.

I will use myself as an example to best illustrate what I mean by this "answer." I have been through and felt everything mentioned above. I emotionally detached myself from the effects of losing OR winning. This allows me to have proper mental clarity in decision making that won't be emotionally based, which rarely presents the best solutions. My foundation is my faith, and it is deeply rooted. Unwavering, undisturbed, immovable, all around unbreakable. THAT is MY answer for you and here is why. As a Christian we are called to something bigger than ourselves and our career. It presents me with a proper moral and ethical foundation and with that it gives way to a true and fulfilling direction no matter where you are at. It dictates everything I do and how I treat people, and if that is truly the case, then it makes decision making much easier. Don't get it twisted. It does not make the emotional feelings that come with decision making easy, but it makes it bearable and sustainable. It is a moral obligation to pursue meaning and purpose. That is how you create and sustain "happiness."

What do you do to overcome times of struggle, burnout, or overwhelm? Who do you turn to?

I turn to the Lord. I get down on my knees and pray. I tell God everything that I am upset about and how I want things to change. I get real specific with Him. He wants to hear these things from you. He wants to be the only thing/one you turn to in times of need. He will provide.

I also get out in nature. Sit on the dock and read and write. Relax in the grass. Soak up the sun. Simply put, JUST SLOW DOWN. Surrender your worries and uncontrollables. Show up everyday doing what you know to do and be content with that. The pieces WILL fall where they may. You just HAVE to do your part to the best of your ability, and with that you have to let the rest go. Now, if you provide a weak link in the chain, then you need to do some self-reflection and figure your stuff out. You better make sure you are on top of your stuff, and then let the rest go, because that is all you can do.

Get out of your normal routine of go home and go to work. Go do some work, reading, writing in a coffee shop, a smoothie shop, at a park, etc. Get out of your everyday element and connect with the rest of the world while still completing the things you need to get done.

Call or visit friends or family. Have game nights with co-workers or other friends. Go to church. Better yet, invite athletes or co-workers to church.

Volunteer and have your eyes opened to what real struggle and need looks like.

Write a gratitude journal, or journal about anything.

Go enjoy a movie, ice cream, or take yourself out to a nice dinner. Forget your macros for a meal. You will survive.

Don't forget to enjoy life.

What do you think about immediately after one of your athletes is injured? What is your mindset in the following week?

Most of the time I take an unhealthy approach of, "What could I have done better to prevent this?" But as we know, that is not helpful nor realistic. I allow myself to think that way for about 24-48 hrs. Why? Because I want to let it fuel me to research and learn anything and everything about that injury mechanism as well as the rehab for it. After that, it is simply time to get to work programming and get out of your own ego of thinking you could have prevented everything. Turn your focus on this kid who needs you to be who you are day in and day out so you can be there for them over the next few weeks to months when they are mentally questioning everything.

How do you approach difficult conversations with athletes, coworkers, or your boss?

Approach it from a place without expectation. Approach it with grace, forgiveness, and unconditional love. You approach it with all these and it will make your career and life so much more invigorating and tremendously less stressful. Let go of control, and even the potential for control, and the expectation to get things where they "need" to be, and just be guardrails with arrows. Meaning, know the boundaries placed by you based off your knowledge, and do not let coaches or athletes cross that line, but rather draw and redraw arrows pointing them in the right direction.

Do not be afraid to have discussions based on your philosophies and knowledge. You are the expert in your field and you're hired to be that part. Coaches won't understand and they will often oppose what you know to do. That is when you need to be the professional and ask for that one-on-one meeting to discuss why you should or should not do certain things. Leave emotion out of it and it will be productive. As soon as emotion gets involved, then it is time to end the conversation and try again another way, or put it into writing for them to process on their own. If it is a discussion with your coach, then you need to provide everything they need to know, and how what you are saying is the right thing for the athlete's body in that time and place. But, when the conversation is over, you need to allow the coach to have the last word and do what they ask of you. If it is against your beliefs, knowledge, and wisdom, then it is up to you to decide whether to continue to do what is right by the athlete behind the scenes, or move on to somewhere else where you are utilized to the extent you desire.

Do you have a "failure" that was critical to your long-term development or success?

I do not have a primary failure that propelled me forward. Rather, I learned early on to know that I am going to fail daily with things. Kids will get injured, family members will die, people will suffer, you will lose games, you will lose relationships, you will program poorly one day, you will lose your voice and be embarrassed, you will forget to do something very important, you will get yelled at, and so on. I allowed myself to know that this will happen at some point, but I did not and do not allow myself to let it be defining or permanent. I use failure as a tool and not an outcome. Failure allows me to learn to improve or to know there are worse outcomes, and to prevent me from complacency.

What traits or skills do your most successful athletes have in common?

This changes generation to generation but the MOST successful, in which there are few, are the ones who like to focus on showing up and giving the day what they have to offer. Focused on work ethic. The outcomes are going to be in your favor if you take care of what you need to take care of.

What books or resources do you most often recommend to coaches?

- *Easy Strength* – Dan John
- *Ultimate MMA Conditioning* – Joel Jamison
- *The Quick and the Dead* – Pavel Tsatsouline
- *Triphasic Training* – Cal Dietz
- *Courage is Calling* – Ryan Holiday
- *Discipline is Destiny* – Ryan Holiday
- *The Prayer of Jabez* – Bruce Wilkinson
- *Supertraining* – Mel Siff and Yuri Verkhoshansky
- *Weird*
- *Ruthless Elimination of Hurry* – John Mark Comer
- The Bible

"Being a professional means you have a routine and you follow that routine no matter what. Most of life is a struggle. Amateurs allow the hard times to change their practices. Pros don't f***ing care about external factors."

-Pat Davidson

Dr. Pat Davidson has a PhD in exercise physiology and is a strength and conditioning coach, author, consultant, and traveling lecturer. A former professor at Springfield College and Brooklyn College, Davidson possesses an incredible amount of knowledge paired with the experience of pushing his own limits in training, nutrition, strongman, and bodybuilding. The creator of the Rethinking the Big Patterns seminar series, he was formerly the Director of Continuing Education and Training Methodology at Peak Performance in NYC. Davidson is the author of *A Coach's Guide to Optimizing Movement, Mass,* and *Mass* 2.

Who do you go to when you need advice? Why them?
I don't go to anybody for advice to tell you the truth. I figure s**t out.

What early job was pivotal in your career? Why?
The most pivotal jobs I ever had were working in a grocery store, doing landscaping, and working in wholesale fish sales. Those jobs sucked so much that I knew I didn't want to work them or anything like them for the rest of my life. It motivated me to read, write, train, and work hard with my mind.

What are your first steps when you start a new job? What do you need to figure out, what do you need to get done, who do you need to get to know?
I haven't worked for someone else in a long time. I'm pretty unemployable as a person. I'm going to do things my way whether you like it or not. I observe things, I research things, I tinker, and I ultimately land on something that I believe is best practice. I'm always willing to modify things in either small or large ways from there based on learning new things. I'm not a particularly social person, so I don't bother with trying to get to know people to advance myself.

What advice do you have for a college student looking to break into coaching? Who are the best mentors in the world to work for early in your career?

They need to find someone who's doing what they want to do, introduce themselves to that person, and spend time with that person.

What goes into your decision to leave or stay at a job?

There's only two things I think about: money and not having to work with someone I don't respect. I can't work with or for someone I don't respect. There's very few people I respect professionally, so it really limits the possibilities.

What do you do to overcome times of struggle, burnout, or overwhelm? Who do you turn to?

I just continue to work. Being a professional means you have a routine and you follow that routine no matter what. Most of life is a struggle. Amateurs allow the hard times to change their practices. Pros don't f***ing care about external factors. I turn to nobody but myself.

How do you approach difficult conversations with athletes, coworkers, or your boss?

I approach difficult conversations head on. I find the point of greatest resistance and lack of comfort and I focus on that and push through it.

Do you have a "failure" that was critical to your long-term development or success?

I've failed more times than I can count. Most of my life has been failures. They don't matter. You just push on.

What traits or skills do your most successful athletes have in common?

They're genetically gifted. Both in body structure and physiology, and in hard work mindset.

What books or resources do you most often recommend to coaches?

There are some classic books everybody needs to read. *Supertraining* and *Science and Practice of Strength Training* come to mind. For training books, Boyle's *Functional Training* books are great. Cal Dietz's *Triphasic Training*, Joel Jamieson's *Ultimate MMA Conditioning*, Mike Israetel's *Science and Development of Muscle Hypertrophy* is pretty unparalleled. I think my book, *A Coach's Guide to Optimizing Movement,* is worth reading.

Then you need to read outside your domain. For movement, *The Janda Approach* is a great book. Shirley Sahrmann's books are amazing. People need to familiarize themselves with Bill Hartman. Zac Cupples is a great source for info similar to Bill's as well. The best resource is getting in the trenches and competing in things or working though.

> *"When I look in the mirror, I remind myself—only 351 people in the world are lucky enough to have this job. That reminds me that it's time to WORK and GET BETTER."*
>
> ## -Steve Englehart

Steve Englehart is the Director of Sports Performance for Olympic Sports at the University of Colorado, currently in his ninth year of working with Men's Basketball. Englehart has also worked with Football, Women's Soccer, Men's and Women's Golf, and Tennis during his 14 overall years at Colorado. Prior to Colorado, he worked as the Assistant Director of Strength and Conditioning Coach at SMU and the Head Football Strength and Conditioning Coach at Portland State. Englehart has developed multiple future NBA players including Derrick White, Jabari Walker, and three 2024 draft picks—Cody Williams (No. 10), Tristan da Silva (No. 18), and KJ Simpson (No. 42).

Who do you go to when you need advice? Why them?

I always talk to my twin brother Chad Englehart, an NFL head strength coach, or to one of my two mentors in Strength and Conditioning, Tommy Hefferenan or Kurt Hester. As well as Arnie Kander with the Orlando Magic and Dr. Carlos Daniels. I turn to one of these individuals for one reason—I trust them.

What early job was pivotal in your career? Why?

Early in my career, I was the Head Strength Coach for football at Portland State. This was a pivotal point in my career, specifically because I had to operate individually. I had no interns, so I was on my own with 105 football players. This will humble anyone quickly, while also making clear whether or not you love the field.

What are your first steps when you start a new job? What do you need to figure out, what do you need to get done, who do you need to get to know?

My first priority is taking care of business for my family, including insurance, living situations, and moving. From a job standpoint, assuming I know the head coach's priorities and the staff, these are my top five priorities:

- Set the culture from Day 1.

- Establish a relationship with the Athletic Trainer. Get to know your returning athletes and their existing injuries.

- Learn what injury prevention programs are in place. If none, set them.

- Emphasize Habits and Discipline.

- Set goals with your players and talk to them DAILY.

What advice do you have for a college student looking to break into coaching? Who are the best mentors in the world to work for early in your career?

Get as much hands-on experience as possible, and be willing to learn, grow, and work hard! WORK HARD.

Tommy Hefferenan, Kurt Hester, and Arnie Kander.

If you only had two 30-minute sessions a week to train your team, how would you prepare them?

This would never happen on my watch. If a coach wanted to train only one hour a week, I would talk to them and let them know what I need in order for our players and team to be successful.

What goes into your decision to leave or stay at a job?

- Family

- Staff

- Compensation Package

- Location

What do you do to overcome times of struggle, burnout, or overwhelm? Who do you turn to?

I turn to the mirror. This may offend some people, but the reality is that NO ONE CARES. I have a family I need to support. Burnout? I love this job. Overwhelmed? I love the pressure. It's a privilege to have this pressure. When I look in the mirror, I remind myself—only 351 people in the world are lucky enough to have this job. That reminds me that it's time to WORK and GET BETTER.

What do you think about immediately after one of your athletes is injured? What is your mindset in the following week?

Injuries happen. When they occur, I ask myself two things: 1) Did we do everything in our control to help this athlete? 2) Did the athlete do everything in their control to avoid this injury? In the long run, it doesn't do any good to point fingers. Instead, get to work and start building a rehab program to get the athlete better.

How do you approach difficult conversations with athletes, coworkers, or your boss?

I view a difficult conversation like any other conversation. It's critical to always have your homework done and information prepared, and most importantly, to be upfront and honest.

Do you have a "failure" that was critical to your long-term development or success?

Throughout my young career, I had some coaches tell me I wasn't ready for the role I was taking on. Some people take that and believe it. Instead, I tell myself to stay the course, and I ALWAYS bet on myself, because I know I have a willingness to work hard and continually adapt and learn, and that continues to set me apart.

What traits or skills do your most successful athletes have in common?

They work hard, want to be coached hard, and they never complain.

What books or resources do you most often recommend to coaches?

I recommend anything with Christian Thibaudeau. *Black Book of Training Secrets* is my all-time favorite.

- *Science and Practice of Strength Training*—Vladimir M. Zatsiorsky
- *Ultimate MMA Conditioning*—Joel Jamieson
- *God x Basketball*—Nick Graham

"My tagline for years is I don't coach basketball, I coach people. If you don't grasp that, you're never gonna make it. Or you will by accident. You'll be unconsciously competent. I prefer to be consciously competent, knowing what the hell I'm doing, why I'm doing it, when I'm doing it."

-Brendan Suhr

Brendan Suhr coached for almost 30 years in the NBA, winning back-to-back NBA Championships as an assistant with the Detroit Pistons "Bad Boys," along with a Gold Medal while coaching with the 1992 "Dream Team." Suhr also coached 13 seasons of collegiate basketball. During his career, he coached superstars like Isiah Thomas, Joe Dumars, Michael Jordan, Dominique Wilkins, Magic Johnson, Larry Bird, Charles Barkley, David Robinson, Karl Malone, Dennis Rodman, and Ben Simmons. Suhr now runs Coaching U, a renowned program for basketball knowledge that utilizes clinics, videos, podcasts, and other online resources. He also coaches and consults with leaders from all types of industries. Suhr is certified as a Master Strengths Coach by Gallup's StrengthsFinder—one of the only coaches in the world to hold that distinction. **(Suhr's responses were transcribed from a phone call)**

What early job was pivotal in your career? Why?

I got into coaching when I was probably 19 years old and still playing in college. In the summers, I would work in basketball camps as a coach. That's how I learned how to coach. When I was 19 years old, I was working at the great Five Star Basketball Camp, which was the best basketball camp in the country. I was coaching players two years younger than me who were high school All-Americans. That helped me learn to connect very early with very talented guys. When I was 21 years old, I became an assistant coach in college, with Dick Vitale as the head coach. There were only two coaches on the staff back then, so here I am working with Dick, who was in his first time as a college head coach. I was in college for six years and then went to the NBA when I was 27. Every stop I made was pivotal, but it was really about as an assistant coach, learning from my head coach.

What I try to teach in coaching now is that coaches are the most influential person sometimes in a young person's life. It's a huge responsibility. A teacher in school or a coach probably will be—outside of a parent, or even more so than a parent—the most influential person in a kid's life. I take the responsibility incredibly serious, even after 50 years of coaching. I understand the impact I have on young people and I love it. Coaching is the same skill set as parenting. You can't be a really good coach and be a horses**t parent. I know coaches that have four girls, and then they come in and motherf**k their players left and right. I always say, "Is that a good idea? And if you think it is, go home and practice on your family. Talk to your wife and your kids like that, see how it works." They go, "No, I would never do that." Why would you do it to someone else's kids?

That's the stuff that I'm most concerned about. I'm not concerned about X's and O's right now. You can be the best X's and O's coach, but if you can't connect to the young boys and girls that you're working with, it doesn't matter. Right now we're at a crossroads because we have a lot of good coaches leaving their sports because of age, sometimes because of parents, and sometimes because of the kids. My contribution now later in life is—how do I make coaching better? I don't care what the sport is. I was a professional basketball coach, but my daughter was a world class gymnast, my son was a professional golfer. I had a huge impact on them and I don't know how to do either one of those, but I helped them mentally. I did a clinic two weeks ago in Alabama, and a really phenomenal coach—Bucky McMillan, the coach of Samford University who was a great high school coach, was giving his core values of coaching for his players. The last one was confidence. A really great coach instills confidence in his people, just like you would with your own children. To me, that was one of the most brilliant things I've heard. That gives you a summary of what I wanted, where I'm at, what I want to do.

I work with coaches now, head coaches in the NBA, college football, basketball coaches, CEOs of companies. My tagline for years is I don't coach basketball, I coach people. If you don't grasp that, you're never gonna make it. Or you will by accident. You'll be unconsciously competent. I prefer to be consciously competent, knowing what the hell I'm doing, why I'm doing it, when I'm doing it.

What are your first steps when you start a new job? What do you need to figure out, what do you need to get done, who do you need to get to know?
If you go in as an assistant coach, I always say that 80-90% of all the coaches in the world are assistant coaches. How about that? You first better learn who you're serving.

I'm big on servant leadership, as all coaches should be. All servant leaders understand who they're serving. It's not yourself, it's the school or professional team I work for, the owner, but most importantly, my players and my head coach. I have to establish incredible relationships, the ability to connect with everyone.

A coach needs to learn how to coach up to your head coach, owner, or athletic director, down to my players, and sideways to the other assistants on my staff. If you're a head coach that only coaches downwards, you're missing the boat. You gotta develop your staff, and then you have to understand that you better learn how to coach upwards to get buy-in from people above you to get things. There's an art to doing that. It's not going in and telling them, "Hey, I need this." I have to convince them. I have to influence them to help them understand why it's good for my players.

What advice do you have for a college student looking to break into coaching? Who are the best mentors in the world to work for early in your career?

Young people want to skip steps. I worked for 10 weeks at basketball camp as a college student to learn how to coach. When I graduated, I was ready to coach at a major college because I was coaching high school All-Americans from the time I was 18 years of age. I would work at a camp for $75 for a week at an overnight camp, and nowadays, they expect to skip all those steps and just become a college assistant without ever being a coach. You have to do the little things and you have to understand that there's a path to get there.

As far as a mentor, just having a mentor is not going to help you. What are you going to contribute to being mentored? First of all, you gotta find someone that's willing to do it, willing to give up himself to you. And then are you willing to receive and take coaching? One of the things I tell every player, coach, business executive I work with—I don't care who you are, I coach people who make 25 million a year; I coach a person who has 26 bestselling books—the first thing I say to anyone is—are you coachable? I don't care what field you're in. If you're not coachable, if you're not willing to get better, I can't help you. Of the 8,000-9,000 people I've asked that question to, no one has ever said they're uncoachable. The second question is—can I be truthful with you? It's a very simple question. No one's ever said, "No, I'd really appreciate if you'd lie to me." They all say, "Yeah, I'd like you to be truthful." What that does is it gives me permission to give them advice, to tell them what I feel, what I observe. You might not like it, but you asked for it. You asked for my help. You wanted to get better.

Young people, players in particular, confuse coaching as criticism. It's not. Now, the delivery of it, the tone of it, dictates whether it's received better than others. If you have a really bad tone in your voice, if you're condescending, if you act arrogant above the person you're coaching, you won't have a connection with them. Your player might be coachable, and he might want you to be truthful, but you're not delivering it. For the guys that are married, I always tell them to think about how you're going home and asking your wife to do something. You're not walking in and saying, "Hey, let me tell you what we're doing." No, it's the opposite. You say, "Honey, I got a great idea for us. A really fun vacation for you and the kids." As a coach, you have to sell it all the time. The best coaches are the best salespeople. Every day, I'm selling my philosophy. All these young players in every sport now have trainers. Let's just take basketball—there is no player development coach out there that I know of that works on defense. All they do is work on skills. They work on offense, shooting, dribbling, ball handling. No one says, "Hey, get in a defensive stance. We're going to play defense for 30-40 minutes of your whole session. Game on." That's hard work. Every coach will tell you that we're going to win because we have great defense, yet we don't work on it in the off-season. We have to really be good salespeople, because I have to convince them that if we're going to win now, that's how we're going to do it.

Bonus: Has the transfer portal created an even higher need to be able to sell in college athletics, especially as athletes come in and out every year now?
The transfer portal has developed a very unusual situation that is very new to the profession. The best college coaches would have a plan to develop young men or women over a four-year period, but now you might have them for eight months. What I'm coaching my coaches to do is—I love that you have a development plan for four years, but now you gotta condense that to eight months. You say, "No, I can't do that." Then you're going to die. You have to adapt or you're going to die, in sport and in life. The rules change, there are people that grew up with me that wrote everything on a yellow legal pad. All practice plans were written on index cards, and now everything's done on a computer. It's just a natural progression of life. Everything in life and the world is about improvements. But here's what the problem is—many coaches, they haven't progressed and they haven't changed.

Bonus: When you talk about condensing down the timeline of development, does that come down to getting greater clarity on individual needs and attacking those areas, as opposed to a more systematic process for all players?
What I'm saying about in one year is it has nothing to do with X's and O's. It's simply

about the individual. I need to know all I can about the individual. I use different technology, different assessments to learn that. I'm a big StrengthsFinder person. I want to know what a player's strengths are. Then I coach them, not to my strengths, but to their strengths. Some people use the DiSC profile. Whatever it is—I need all the help I can get. I need it to help coach my staff. You don't want a staff where everyone's the same. I need people that fill in my gaps as a head coach, and I got a lot of them, so I need to have people that do things better than I do. I want to find out about my players so that I can understand what makes each one of them tick. The hardest thing to do in coaching, leadership, running a business, or running a sports team is figuring out that every one of my players must be coached differently. There's some people that need to be driven. There's some that you just need to pat on the backside once and tell him, "I believe in you, go after it." You have to be so good as a coach to understand every one of those players and all their needs.

You better be competent in this field that you're coaching, because the players will see it in a heartbeat. The thing about players—I don't care what their grades or SAT scores are—they know if you know what the hell you're doing. You want to be a coach? You better be a leader, you better be competent, you better have credibility, and you better know how to communicate. That's the starters. Then they gotta be able to trust you. Then they have to understand, do you have integrity? Do you love them? Do you care about 'em? If you don't have those things, you don't even get to first base.

Bonus: With StrengthsFinder, I know you are one of the only Master Strengths Coaches in the world. Do you use that in the evaluation process?

StrengthsFinders is a developmental tool, it's not an assessment we use to hire people. When I hire someone, there's nothing wrong with having someone take it. But I will then find out who they are so I can say, "You know what? He's going to be hard to work with. But I love what they're about. I love that they're a maximizer. I love that they like to take things that are good and make them great. I love as a coach that they individualize." Individualization is a talent where people can basically perform an MRI on people and figure out all the gifts that someone has. Amazing quality to have as a coach. A lot of people just look and say, "I'll tell you everything that's wrong with someone." That's not that helpful to be honest with you.

The evaluation skill and talent of seeing how they are in the sport is huge. In the NBA, they're doing so many interviews now with kids to find out about them because all they did was evaluate them in college and watch them play, but they don't know anything about them as a human being.

Bonus: In those interviews, how do you really get to the truth of who someone is, what their character is, when a lot of them know the answers to the test?

I'm rarely going to get that in an interview. I'm going to get it in my vetting process of doing background research on people. Interviewing other people about them. A lot of kids now have had problems. They've been arrested, they've used drugs, they've had domestic violence things. Something that used to be an outlier, and you were discarded, now it's more commonplace. You better find out what really happened. Sometimes domestic violence complaints are ordered against you for various reasons, so you better find out what really happened, and boy, you better be connected to be able to do that. I like to go into my interviews knowing the answers to this. And frankly, I'll ask them something knowing, as soon as he answered it, he just lied to me. That tells me a lot about character. I really want someone to come up and say, "You know what Coach, I F'd up. This is what happened. We were all out. Everyone was smoking weed. They passed the joint around. I took it." There's no black and white anymore, and you have to really go in depth.

Bonus: How do you establish identity, culture, and alignment within a program, especially if the roster is frequently turning over?

You better have a philosophy. You better be able to team build. You better understand how to get young people to buy into a culture. That is something that we're teaching all the time because a lot of coaches aren't equipped to do that. We have different exercises that we do, one is the 3 H's. In a given week, we might have every player and staff member talk about their history, but they're only allowed to talk for one minute. Now the other 20 people in the room found out a lot about something they didn't know. Then we'll ask them, "Who's the hero in your life?" All of a sudden, you find out it's their mom, their grandmother, because she raised them. Another one is what's a highlight? All of a sudden, you find out he is the first person in their family to ever graduate high school.

I've had players that are the first person ever to go to college in their family. When I was coaching last in college, I had a player from Africa. Because he wanted to come to the states to learn and get a college education, he had to leave his family, and he had not been home in 11 years. Imagine being away from your folks for 11 years? What happens is that it now becomes a rallying point for the team. Even though they practice with him every day, they knew nothing about it. What you've done is just provide a way to bond as a team, to build that culture. You have to have your pillars that you believe in. Whether it be brotherhood, sisterhood, love, care, servanthood, truthfulness—they start to understand why those are important to our team, because now they saw it in action. You do these things especially in the off-season, and you do one letter a week.

What goes into your decision to leave or stay at a job?

It's not money. It's about the opportunity to work with someone, learn from someone, new responsibilities, growth in the profession, or moving to a higher position. I have never in 50 years of coaching once been paid my value. Ever. There were times for 15 or so straight years I was the highest paid assistant coach in the NBA, but no one's ever come close to paying me what I'm worth. I didn't understand that then, but I understand now that if you're really good at something, you're never going to get paid what your value is. So get over it. Also, you deserve what you negotiate. Don't tell me how much you deserve—they offer you X, and then you have your free will to decide whether to take it or decline it.

I'm always searching for opportunities where I have a growth mindset and I can get better. If I can learn from someone, contribute to someone, or do something at a higher level or with a new challenge, that's something that's really intriguing to me. For people that are strictly chasing money, they're going to be happy until they don't get what they want. Two things about that—if you make a lot of money, you can't spend it all. Number two, you can't take it with you when you die. It's overrated. You need enough to lead a good life, ideally. Some people can't do it on the salary they get from their school. Hubie Brown was my high school coach, and he worked three different jobs. He was a teacher in our high school, he coached football, basketball, and baseball, and then in the summer, he ran a pool in one of the nearby communities to make enough money because he had a wife and three kids. He ended up leaving a meager salary and took a $10,000 pay cut to become a college coach. He knew that there had to be a journey, and it worked out pretty darn amazing for him. Your journey is more important than your money.

What do you do to overcome times of struggle, burnout, or overwhelm? Who do you turn to?

You always need a circle of friends. Life is a world of relationships. You better have people you can turn to and ask for advice, men or women that you trust. It's also important that you don't fall into vices of drinking, drugs, etc. Exercise is a much better idea, whether it be to walk, jog, swim, or to work out daily. When you finish doing that, you feel so much better. It was my thing where I could think every day, it'd be an hour jog or an hour walk to clear my mind. When my home was in Windermere, Florida, I would take my hour walk through our subdivision every day. But I was also doing professional speaking and consulting, so I would walk through our neighborhood and practice my speeches. One of our neighbors called my wife and said, "How's your husband doing? We see him walking every day and he talks to himself. Is he okay?" She asked me, "What the hell are you doing! Talking to yourself?" I said, "No, practicing my speaking!" She got to make a big kick out of it. Things like that are really good. A lot of people now walk and talk on the phone or listen to a podcast.

Do you have a "failure" that was critical to your long-term development or success?
No, to be honest with you. Did I have disappointments? Yeah. Failures? No. You lose jobs, you lose jobs because your head coach lost their job. There's disappointments every year when we didn't advance in the playoffs. But I don't call them failures, I call them disappointments and adversity.

What traits or skills do your most successful athletes have in common?
Talent is the price of admission for anyone to play at an elite level. But the other things that enter into it are all the intangibles. The enthusiasm, the work ethic, how good a teammate they are, the desire to win. All those things are difference makers. If you've coached Michael Jordan or Dominique Wilkins, which I have, they both jump out of the gym and everything like that, but they love to perform. They had that natural born thing, but they worked their ass off to get there, and they had such a passion to play. Right now, one of the biggest problems we're having in sport is kids don't love playing. Some play because it's a means to an end, but they don't love the game. Passion to me is a very big thing. The insatiable desire to win, the game chasers like Isiah, Magic and Bird, they just love to win. Jokic has it now, LeBron has it—those guys just love to win. And that's contagious. If you're like that as the best player in the team, it helps other guys.

People think that if you're the best player on the team, you should be a leader. That's totally untrue, because leadership is a whole different skill set. Just because you're the best player doesn't mean you should be a great leader. When I talk about filling in gaps, I have to put great leadership around those guys, because that's not their job. Their job is to play. God gave them incredible gifts, but he didn't give them everything. As a person building a team, you have to surround people and fill in the gaps that they don't have. Even Jordan didn't have that for seven, eight, nine years. He wasn't a leader. He then became a winner, but there were other guys on the team that helped him win. But as a competitor, the best. Leaders are people that take a group and make other people better. That's not what they're hired to do, they're hired to perform. It's rare when you get someone that can do everything.

What books or resources do you most often recommend to coaches?
Every Jon Gordon book. They're easy to read, and coaches aren't that smart. I say that being one! Jon Gordon just sent me his brand new book on difficult conversations the other day, and it was less than 90 pages. It took me less than an hour to read, and I'm the slowest reader that ever went to the Catholic School of America. I loved it because it was a simple story. I also love John Maxwell, as a human being, as a friend, and I love the things that he teaches. He's just such an incredible educator.

Chuck Daly taught me something years ago that was really cool. He was a big novel reader, but then he got into business books as he retired. I remember he said, "I just read the best coaching book ever. *Good to Great* by Jim Collins." I said, "Chuck, that's a business book." He said, "Brendan, no, it's a coaching book." Every book that he read, he said it was a coaching book, because through his eyes, it was how to help him coach. That's how I read books now. I went back and reread *Good to Great*, but I read it as a coaching book. It's one of the best coaching books I've ever read. Jim Collins' theory is, one of the keys to building a team is you have to get the right people on the bus, and then you better have the right person driving the damn bus. It's such a simple theory, but it's really what coaching's all about. Having good players on, getting all the energy vampires off the team, getting good leadership and a coach, and then hopefully he knows how to get you to the desired results. That's how I look at books nowadays and it's really helpful to me.

I'm always searching for new things. I'm not locked into certain ideas—I'm a big Carol Dweck fan with growth mindset. Part of the problem that we have in coaching is the coaches that have a fixed mindset and think that there's only one way to do it—their way. I've learned so much since our teams won two championships and the Dream Team won. I'm such a better coach now than I was back then. I tell Isiah Thomas all the time, "You really got screwed. I'm twice as good now." He said, "That's why you were lucky you had great players, we didn't need you and Chuck!"

> *"Choose people who will tell you the truth yet aren't too abrasive and certain—just listening and giving insight—it's an opinion."*
>
> ## -Todd Monken

Todd Monken is in his second season as the Offensive Coordinator of the Baltimore Ravens, finishing his first season there as a 2023 finalist for AP NFL Assistant Coach of the Year after engineering one of the top offenses in the NFL and helping Lamar Jackson win the NFL MVP. Before arriving in Baltimore, Monken won two straight National Championships as the Offensive Coordinator/Quarterbacks Coach at the University of Georgia. He has also served as the Offensive Coordinator for the Tampa Bay Buccaneers and Cleveland Browns, and the Wide Receivers Coach with the Jacksonville Jaguars. In college, Monken has also held positions as the Head Coach at Southern Mississippi (2015 Conference USA Coach of the Year) and Offensive Coordinator/Quarterbacks Coach at Oklahoma State.

Who do you go to when you need advice? Why them?

Go to the person that fits the scenario best—each situation is different. A variety of mentors, people, family. Choose people who will tell you the truth yet aren't too abrasive and certain—just listening and giving insight—it's an opinion.

What early job was pivotal in your career? Why?

Becoming a GA at Notre Dame. I went from a high school coach's kid and D2 part-time young coach to one of the best programs in the country (Lou Holtz), as well as being around assistant coaches getting head coaching jobs.

What are your first steps when you start a new job? What do you need to figure out, what do you need to get done, who do you need to get to know?

Realize that as a young coach, your greatest value is your diligence and effort. You are not expected to be elite yet at game planning or on the grass. You will advance early in your career because of the attitude you bring every day/diligence/effort.

What advice do you have for a college student looking to break into coaching? Who are the best mentors in the world to work for early in your career?

The supply is greater than the demand and you are in direct competition with other young coaches every day—first in and last to leave. The fun, partying, storytelling young coach might be most liked but is not likely to be hired and advance.

What goes into your decision to leave or stay at a job?

Best move for your future regardless of money. As kids get older—there are schools, education, friends, and comfort aspects that come into play.

What do you do to overcome times of struggle, burnout, or overwhelm? Who do you turn to?

I have copies of some self-talk info at my disposal to review—be it in books or notes I have kept.

What do you think about immediately after one of your athletes is injured? What is your mindset in the following week?

Pretty simple:

- What did we lose and how do we adjust?

- Who replaces him—What are his strengths and weaknesses?

- As a group, how do we make up for that individual's contributions?

How do you approach difficult conversations with athletes, coworkers, or your boss?

Not always easy, especially the younger you are—but always try to be on the front end—hit them head on with honesty.

Do you have a "failure" that was critical to your long-term development or success?

I was coaching at Eastern Michigan and the Head Coach left and took the job at Louisville. He didn't take me with him. It made me realize I wasn't where I needed to be as a coach, that I had gotten comfortable.

What traits or skills do your most successful athletes have in common?

- Mentally tough—it's not always going to go smooth.

- Only knows one speed—they have to be told to "slow it down."

- Humble but confident.

- Finisher—wants it in tough moments.

What books or resources do you most often recommend to coaches?

- *Don't Sweat the Small Stuff* – Richard Carlson

- *Great by Choice* – Jim Collins

- *What Drives Winning* – Brett Ledbetter

> *"Be a PRO because that is all about who you are and how you do things. A PRO is anchored in PURPOSE (the best in the world are the most intentional), RELENTLESS (average quits at some point, the best persist), and takes OWNERSHIP (dominates the controllables and leaves nothing up to chance)."*
>
> ## *-Kyle Stark*

Kyle Stark is the president of the leader development organization Stark Contrast. He created Stark Contrast after working with the Pittsburgh Pirates for 12 years, starting as the Director of Player Development and then working his way up to Assistant General Manager and eventually Vice President. He helped the Pirates snap a 19 year playoff drought. Stark spent over three years working with the Cleveland Indians (now Guardians) before Pittsburgh, spending his last two years as the Coordinator of Baseball Operations. He began his career as the Pitching Coach at St. Bonaventure University.

Who do you go to when you need advice? Why them?
My wife, Heather, as she is my best friend and closest confidant, followed by my Dad, and then I have a number of great resources in different areas that I know will speak truth and have expertise in that space.

What early job was pivotal in your career? Why?
1) Coaching summer camps as you had to do everything, had to nail organization, and got tons of free reps coaching kids and figuring out what works and does not.
2) Initial internship with Cleveland as it was a small front office with talented, good people who offered tons of opportunities to contribute.

What are your first steps when you start a new job? What do you need to figure out, what do you need to get done, who do you need to get to know?
Figure out WHO matters—your direct report, key influencers, informal influencers; WHAT matters—fight for clarity in expectations and objectives, as well as the principles and processes that actually happen vs. the ideals that are communicated;

and WHAT OBSTACLES might be present that you have to work around or work within.

What advice do you have for a college student looking to break into coaching? Who are the best mentors in the world to work for early in your career?

Anyone breaking into sports needs to know three things ... 1) You better have something that differentiates you (everyone works hard and wants to be in sports), 2) Who you know is tremendously valuable so be intentional about relationships, and 3) You better be willing to go above and beyond (which means you better love it for the right reasons).

As for mentors, rather than highlighting specific people, I would stress the importance of not chasing famous names or places, as some of the best are the furthest from the bright lights. Focus more on whether the person has a track record of success, is going to give you legitimate opportunities to grow and develop, and wants to pour into you while you're there.

If you only had two 30-minute sessions a week to train your team, how would you prepare them?

I would actually try to incorporate the physical training into the fundamental training as much as possible so that the athlete does not see it as something else, it is more connected to the skill you are developing, and you can be even more efficient with your time.

What goes into your decision to leave or stay at a job?

FAITH first ... followed by factoring in a number of factors, including (in no particular order) the BOSS (most people quit their boss, not their job), whether you are cared for and challenged (the two biggest factors in whether people are engaged), your motivation orientation and whether they are getting filled (cause, career, job), WHO you are doing it with (as the what will never outweigh the WHO), and personal dynamics.

What do you do to overcome times of struggle, burnout, or overwhelm? Who do you turn to?

FAITH ... followed by my wife.

What do you think about immediately after one of your athletes is injured? What is your mindset in the following week?

What is really going on, how do we get them back, and why did this happen so we can learn from it.

How do you approach difficult conversations with athletes, coworkers, or your boss?

Directly as too often the main message gets missed as we dance around it, BUT hopefully I have done the work necessary to approach things that way, meaning the person knows I care about them (have their best interests in mind) and clear expectations were communicated on the front end.

Do you have a "failure" that was critical to your long-term development or success?

Too many to count! In all seriousness, I have so many lessons along the way that I have learned from—getting lots of feedback on how I come across (too direct, too confident, too harsh, too fast, too much!), challenging tradition on some training approaches and not communicating up and across enough to ensure everyone was aligned to navigate the negative pushback, getting fired and learning how to navigate challenge without focusing on self and really leaning into identity, etc.

What traits or skills do your most successful athletes have in common?

I can answer this question several ways, but I will go back to a framework that I have used with players, coaches and leaders in terms of maximizing your potential ... Be a PRO because that is all about who you are and how you do things. A PRO is anchored in PURPOSE (the best in the world are the most intentional), RELENTLESS (average quits at some point, the best persist), and takes OWNERSHIP (dominates the controllables and leaves nothing up to chance).

What books or resources do you most often recommend to coaches?

The Bible (I recognize this one gets dismissed, but it is THE best leadership, coaching, performance manual there is) ... tons of other great books and podcasts with too many to list!

"At the University of North Carolina Women's Soccer Banquet, the highest award is not the MVP. The highest award is the Kelly Muldoon Award for Character. For us, the most important thing you can develop in your four years at the University of North Carolina isn't your ability to stick a ball in the upper corner and win games. It's your character, the way you treat people, the way you develop a resilience to withstand the chaos of the universe."

-Anson Dorrance

Anson Dorrance is a Hall of Fame soccer coach, recently retiring as the Head Coach of the University of North Carolina Women's Soccer program in the Fall of 2024 after 45 years of leading the team. He has won a combined 1,106 games (he coached the men's team for 10+ years), including 934 as the women's head coach—No. 1 in the history of the sport. With an astonishing 21 National Championships won in women's soccer, Dorrance is the all-time leader in Division I NCAA Championships in any sport. Claiming a 103 game unbeaten streak (1986-1990) and a 101 game unbeaten streak (1990-1994), his UNC program was named the sixth most successful sports dynasty of the 20th century. 19 of his players have won National Player-of-the-Year honors, highlighted by Cindy Parlow (current president of U.S. Soccer) and Mia Hamm, the selection for Greatest Female Athlete in the ACC's first 50 years. Dorrance has been awarded National Coach of the Year six times on the women's side and once on the men's side. He was the Head Coach of the United States National Team from 1986-1994, helping the team win the title in the first-ever Women's World Cup in 1991. Dorrance is a member of the National Soccer Hall of Fame, United Soccer Coaches Hall of Fame, North Carolina Sports Hall of Fame, and North Carolina Soccer Hall of Fame. **(Dorrance's responses were transcribed from a Zoom call)**

What are your first steps when you start a new job? What do you need to figure out, what do you need to get done, who do you need to get to know?

You need to meet the team that you're about to coach. Get a sense of who the leaders are in the room and then meet with them individually and make sure you're recruiting them to your perspective. Get the leaders together and sort out what they want their program to be like, because without the full cooperation of the leaders and the team, nothing's going to happen. Before you even recruit someone from outside the program to join you, the most critical thing is to recruit the kids you currently have. The first step is recruiting the leaders and making sure that they understand what your vision is, and to get full buy-in from them.

Once you get full buy-in from the leaders, then you have to recruit the entire roster. Get a sense of what your roster is, because every team has a different ethos, a different set of core values, and what you've got to get a sense of right out of the gate is—is it possible for you to establish your vision with these new players that you're now involved with? That's getting to know them and getting to know them very personally. If you don't make an effort to get to know them, they'll have a very good sense of that and then they won't be a part of the team that you're trying to develop.

Bonus: How do you determine who those leaders are on the team?

That actually is the question. There are all kinds of people that are leading the team and you've got all kinds of different levels of leadership. A lot of this first connection is about not just introductions with what you're going to do, but also with an understanding of who the real leaders are. Honestly, the easiest and simplest way to do that is to meet with the players individually, just briefly. Get a sense of who they respect on the roster and find out who from the individual players in the team, the leaders actually are. Then get that group together. Even within the leaders, there's going to be a leader or a collection of leaders. Then meet with those people as well to find out what their ambitions are. Find out if this is a group that you're going to effectively connect with, if this is a group that you think can help you lead the team in the direction you would love for it to go in, because there are all kinds of different leaders and some of them are not positive. One of the most important discoveries you're going to make is to find out which leaders you have that do not take the team in the right direction.

Then what's critical is for you to shape the new roster. Don't be married to people on the roster that were the former leaders if it's a toxic culture. Make sure you've decided, maybe this isn't the direction we want to go in with these kinds of leaders, and then separate your team from those players. If you come in, you're probably coming in for a reason. You're probably coming in because the previous leadership and administration that were running the team were not doing a very good job. You've got to come in and sort out why. Obviously, the coach is going to be ultimately blamed for this if there's an issue with the kids on the team already. They're going to make it difficult for the team to lead.

It's critical as you're coming in to sort out who those elements are. On every team, there will be kids that are going to be fantastic, positive life forces with the potential to lead the team in the right direction, because you're there to guide them in a better direction. Maybe that's why you were picked. Maybe your quality is that you've demonstrated that you're good at this. There are going to be kids on every roster you join that are going to be dying to join you by going in the right direction. You need to find out who those people are and attach to them as early and as fast as possible to get the team going in the right direction.

What advice do you have for a college student looking to break into coaching? Who are the best mentors in the world to work for early in your career?
I think most of us stumble on our mentors. They happen to be nearby and they happen to reach out. I've never been in a position where I've had to find a mentor. I've always been in positions where they were nearby, they were presented to me. When they reached out, I reached back. Almost all of us are mentored by the people that coached us. I think that's been an important part of anyone's mentorship are the people that actually trained and developed you. But once you end up in the workplace, there are going to be other people that can serve as wonderful mentors.

Fortunately for me, I had one of the greatest of all time. I came to UNC as a young coach when Dean Smith was our head men's basketball coach. He wasn't just an extraordinary coach; he was an extraordinary man. He reached out and invited me to come watch his team's practice, which of course I jumped on. The thing I loved about Dean Smith is the human element of his leadership. He valued everyone. He valued everyone from the Michael Jordans down to the lowliest manager. He didn't have this hierarchy of who he respected within his organization. They were all human beings, and he respected them similarly. He had this incredible culture of respecting the people around you. So when you're given that opportunity to be next to a great human being, your mission then is to connect with them to whatever extent they're willing to extend the connection back to you.

People are invariably amazingly busy. But there are ways they will reach back and reach out, and also there are ways you can study them. Certainly, being in the University of North Carolina's athletic department, we all knew how Dean led his team. There were sports information directors that shared this with us regularly. It wasn't just the Dean Smiths that we were in a position to study. Our bitter rival, the Duke Blue Devils, also had a brilliant person leading their team by the name of Mike Krzyzewski. Given the local media being so careful in their review of these two extraordinary men that were competing against each other, you can study your mentor's rival and find out why the rivalry is such a good one, why both teams are so successful, just because the local press will cover both for you.

Roy Williams and I had entered school at the same time at the University of North Carolina, and he actually was so poverty-stricken when he came to UNC that he was a ball boy for my soccer games. Whenever we're involved in some sort of speaking engagement together, he always brings that up. He was just this sort of humble, homespun, aw shucks personality that everyone loved, including me. Who was his mentor? Well, it was Dean Smith. And so all of a sudden you're associated with someone that also had huge respect for a man that didn't big time anyone. What was amazing about Dean Smith is the way he treated everyone. There was no reason for him to treat me like an equal. And yet he did, and that shocked all of us. Why would this great man even consider walking over when you were eating in a restaurant with a recruit and say, "Anson, who do you have visiting you right now?" Knowing fully well that I was involved in a life or death recruitment for a kid that if they came to us, we would be successful, and if they didn't, we would probably fail. He could recognize this. In those restaurants, when he saw me there, he would walk right over and suddenly he's recruiting for me and my collegiate women's soccer team.

These are different ways that these people can have an extraordinary impact on you. When we were hiring a new football coach, there was this press conference, and of course Dean Smith was involved in the press conference while we were trying to sort out who to hire in football. One of the press' core questions was, "Coach, isn't it going to be difficult for us to recruit a football coach to a basketball school?" Here's what he says, which is a part of almost every introduction I've been given for the rest of my life. He said, "No, we're not a basketball school. We're a women's soccer school." He's basically being wonderfully disarming and humble in a positive way and trying to deflect the question. That's a press question about what sort of football coach could we possibly recruit coming to a basketball school where we all know that the resources are rarely evenly divided. So how are you going to attract a great football coach when you have an incredible basketball program, and usually a school doesn't have great programs in both? Usually if they're a football school, their basketball team suffers, and if they're a basketball school, their football team suffers. This is a classic trap of a question that a reporter is going to extend to anyone. Watching Dean Smith answer this question so incredibly gracefully, but then feeding my program at the same time, was an incredible gesture of respect, but also an understanding of how to escape these questions where they're aimed to damage either him or the football coach that we ended up recruiting.

When you're surrounded by these kinds of people, the Dean Smiths and the Roy Williams, but also when you get to study the Mike Krzyzewskis, you learn a lot about our profession. They're in the limelight. They're under a scrutiny that I can't imagine, and for all these people to pay me such extraordinary respect in a way is ridiculous. They're under a stress that I would never experience in my life coaching the Women's Soccer team at the University of North Carolina. Yet they extend every opportunity to glorify our achievements and help us recruit. Those are the sort of mentors you want to be surrounded by. People that care about you, care about your success. They don't big time you. They don't ignore you. They support you, they reach out to you, they obviously nurture you in the most positive way. That extends to an entire athletic department of all of us that support each other. Why? Because the guy at the top supports you. How do you pay it forward? You support all the people around you as well, and then you've got a culture within the athletic department that's extraordinarily unique. It starts with the people that are in the most stress worthy positions, the positions of power, which generally in a collegiate environment are the men's basketball coach and the football coach. I just happened to have these extraordinary mentors right there available to me.

Bonus: You talked about Dean Smith not treating the walk-on any different than the star player. In today's age with the portal and NIL, how do we still keep that treatment fair to everybody while in one aspect we are signaling different levels of value with money?

You're asking the wrong coach because I don't have a collective that extends me an opportunity to pay every player. I'm sure it's a very challenging environment for those schools that have the money, although it's also an incredibly powerful weapon. All of us at the University of North Carolina, where most sports don't have NIL money, obviously the major programs do—football and men's basketball and women's basketball have NIL money—but the rest of us either don't, or the money is so small it doesn't really impact our recruiting. What's really interesting is to look at the success of a coach that isn't a blue blood basketball school, and that's the University of Connecticut. Suddenly, this gentleman that doesn't have the lineage that we have, or Duke has, or Kentucky has, or UCLA has, or Kansas, and I could go on and on about the Blue Bloods in basketball—he's won two in a row.

Here's what he's figured out: if he doesn't coach the parents and find a collection of parents that are coachable, he is not going to be able to compete at the highest level. Because what ends up happening is the parents end up hijacking the program. All of a sudden, everything is about the minutes their son or daughter gets or their NIL money. Before you know it, there are all these rampant jealousies within the roster itself. Who does he pick and why do I know this? Just like you, I have access to the same YouTube videos of him talking about what's critical for his success. He comes right out and says it. He wants parents that are parents. What's a real parent? A real parent has died in athletics. That parent died a long time ago. Every now and again you can find them, and apparently you can find a lot of them that have sons playing for Dan at the University of Connecticut. Who are these parents? These are parents that when their son isn't getting playing time, they call the son up and say, "Are you working hard in practice? Are you getting it done? Is everything Dan Hurley is telling you, are you absorbing that and taking that into your game?" This is a real parent. The real parent is putting responsibility for playing time and performance on the athlete, their son at the University of Connecticut. They're creating a culture where they're being real parents because a real parent doesn't side with the player and start whining about the coach and why they're not getting playing time.

Any parent with an IQ above 100 understands that every coach wants to win, there's no prejudice in who their starting lineup is. There's no push toward having their son on the bench. No, if their son were kicking rear end in practice, he'd be playing maximum minutes. If he doesn't, he's not going to play. It's just not complex. How all these parents come up with Republican conspiracy theories about why this isn't happening and that's happening, basically don't have any idea of how athletics works. Athletics is a meritocracy. If you want to play, you've got to kick rear end in practice. If you're the proper parent, you don't lay this at the feet of the coach. You lay this at the feet of your son. And if your son is playing at the University of Connecticut, here's what I know is true: if you're destroying people in practice, you're going to play. If you're not, you're not going to play. They have this understanding of this that's going on.

Even when you listen to Dan on YouTube about, "Do they pick this kid that's changed his AAU team seven times in the last five years?" No. You don't look at that player because Dan Hurley knows what's going on. He knows the parents are involved in trying to select the environment that's going to give their son the most minutes. Do you pick this kid that's bounced around four different high schools? No. You pick a parent that's willing to be a parent, someone that's willing to be loyal, that's going to be supportive, that's going to support the team and its mission. That's what a parent tries to do. A parent tries to raise their child so their child has an understanding that if you do things the right way, you're going to be able to navigate the chaos of the universe. I'm not here as your lobbyist. I'm here as your parent. I'm here to tell you that everything is on you. The way you treat the people around you, the way you work, the way you commit yourself to the team and its mission, the way you try to become a good teammate.

You're asking me about NIL money, I have no idea. I don't give any out. So does this hurt me in recruiting? Yeah, it does. I lose kids regularly to schools that have a fortune in NIL money. So what's my philosophy? I'm going to out coach them. I'm going to make sure the kid I have has the most extraordinary experience in becoming a human being that I can provide, and I'm not going to be able to buy a kid, I'm going to have to coach my kids in an old school fashion, the way Dan Hurley does.

How do you approach difficult conversations with athletes, coworkers, or your boss?

Most of my player conference is done with data, so it's very easy. Numbers that are data driven aren't my personal opinions. It's what the kid has achieved in practice. Since everything we do is data driven, it's me and the player against the data. This way, the player feels fully supported. So the hard conversation—a player conference based on opinion—is completely stripped away. That's the best way to have any kind of employer–employee conference, is to have it data driven. The hard work is actually constructing the model.

I've learned a lot from Sir John Whitmore's book that you should read called

Coaching for Performance. The GROW model is in there. G.R.O.W. is a mnemonic. G stands for goals, R stands for reality, O stands for options, and W stands for will you do it. Our player conference is constructed around this G.R.O.W. mnemonic. We always talk about the player's goals. Usually a kid that comes into my program, their goal is to make the US full national team and win gold medals in the Olympics and win world championships. Most of the kids that have these goals have that as an ultimate goal. Some kids that aren't as good, they want to start or they want to travel or they want to play maximum minutes. They all have different goals. The reality is data driven. We have 11 different categories where the kids are evaluated. These are serious categories where we have data attached to each category. All data has a number. An Olympic caliber athlete in this category would be a 5, a professional level athlete in this category would be a 4.5, a starter at UNC would be a 4, a kid that plays in every half would be a 3.5, a kid that travels would be a 3.

Everything is driven by data. We go through it. We talk about their goals, the G part. We talk about the reality, and this is the number part. The number part takes the most time. That's the athletic character part, because basically all these things can be manipulated by the player if the player can lead herself. That's what's critical. Then the O part, we know all the different things they can do to change the reality. If your player's not fit, you know what the player needs to do to get fit, and of course the player then knows what they need to do to get fit. The question is, is the player going to do it? It's not like a player can't get fit. If you're not fit, it's your fault. There's nothing complex about that. The numbers show it. But we also have numbers for every single thing on there. We have this thing called the competitive cauldron. You are ranked in the cauldron. You are ranked every single day. We have 28 different categories. You have a rank in all 28 categories. You can be number one in this, or you can be number 30. If you want to change your place if you're number 30, there are things you can do, and they're not hidden secrets. Then what's the question? The question is, are you going to do it? That gets back to the will thing at the end.

We ask them at the end, are you willing to do this? Of course, every one of them says yes, it's almost a rhetorical question. Then we ask them a harder question. On a scale of 1–10, 1 being I will not do it at all, to 10 being if I don't do this, I want you to take me and my family out and have us all shot at dawn, will you do it on a scale of 1–10? What's your number? And they all give me a number. Now, obviously what they're all trying to do is they're all trying to give me 10. Some don't. I had one girl that was wonderful. She gave me an honest answer. She gave me a six, and I was thinking, "Gosh, congratulations. You really know yourself." I didn't think she was going to do it either, and she confirmed it. But in this information, she's telling me she is not going to compete to start with her work in the summer. I predicted that before we started having this conversation, but I'm always curious to what a kid that doesn't lead herself is going to say.

Then the ones that say 10s, there's some I just don't believe. I challenge them on that. I'm saying, "Okay, holy cow, because if you do, this is going to be transformational. You're going to go to a completely different level as a player, because you've never done this in your life. If you commit yourself, let me tell you what your potential is. Your potential is off the charts." But the other thing is, even if you get after it and just kill yourself all summer, the rewards you'll get from making that effort, basically the effort to self-regulate, to lead yourself, will pay you back in so many ways, this is worth committing to. For me, it's done with numbers, for players and staff.

Bonus: It seems like over the years, it has been a struggle for some of your freshmen to adjust to the standard of competitiveness and the Competitive Cauldron in your program, but as they pushed past those struggles, they experienced incredible development over their career. With the current environment of the transfer portal, have you seen more athletes leaving during the initial struggle and missing out on that development?

Yes. If a kid doesn't think they can get on the field for me, they will certainly transfer and we encourage it. We have no issue with a kid that's struggling to get on the field coming in to talk to us about transferring. We don't have any issue with it, but there are all kinds of different approaches to this. Some kids will come in and they feel cheated. This is where I can sense from the way this player is leaving that the parent has been involved. There are some kids that come in and they know they can't get on the field of starters and they want to find a program where they can start. We get it. We support them fully, because honestly, it's more fun to play than to sit, and it's tough to get on the field for us. There are a lot of programs out there where it's not gonna be as tough to get on the field. We understand that completely and we support those kids entirely. There are other kids that if they would be patient and work hard, they would get on the field. These are the players that we try to convince to stay. These are the players where we are convinced the player's parents are involved. This is where the whole country seems to be going.

We have a country where grievance is everything. We're no longer taking responsibility. Everything is about a grievance. We blame this, that, and the other thing for our failure. Then all of a sudden, that seeps into the water. Now, grievance is the rule of law, that you've been cheated, not been treated with respect and everything else. It is a problem because those are the kids that I think can get on the field, but they've got to work. Those are the kids that I don't want to have transfer, and we've certainly lost some of those. I didn't want them to transfer because I think they had the potential to get on the field, but there were other kids in the program that were doing better than they were at the moment. But it didn't mean that the next year they would not get on the field.

This past year, we lost 11 kids that signed pro contracts. That's a lot of players. I'm very proud of the fact we had 11 signed pro contracts. That statement tells you how good last year's team was. We had a lot of holes available in the coming fall, but the players and parents that came in with grievances felt they weren't treated properly, and they jumped into the portal. We lost a whole slew in the portal, some of whom shouldn't have left. They would have gotten on the field their sophomore year and done very well, but we just had the entire team returning from the previous year, plus two kids that were injured that were All-Americans coming back, so it was really hard for these highly recruited players to get on the field their first year. There are two kinds of portal transfers. I fully embrace the kid that can't get on the field. But I don't embrace the kid that can, but then leaves because of some created grievance.

Do you have a "failure" that was critical to your long-term development or success?

All of us live and die by winning and losing. Every time we lost, it was difficult for me. Any loss, even like this past season, where we had a really good team and we were eliminated in the quarterfinals. This is a team that returned almost every starter from a team that was within 16 seconds and a blind referee from winning the national championship the previous year. We had a really powerful roster coming back. I'm still suffering from that end of season loss. It wasn't just the end of season loss where I thought we were a team that could win the national championship. It was the way we lost. We were winning 3-0 at the half. If a soccer team is winning 3-0, it's won the game. We end up losing to BYU In Provo 4-3 in the second half. I'm still reeling from that loss.

Now, I think I've come to an understanding of what I could have done to have changed it now, but I'm still suffering from that because in my opinion, that loss is on me. We had the talent to win not just that game, but every game. I look at last season and I've come to my own conclusions as to what I could have done to have made sure that was an even better season. I am now more or less at peace with that, but I'm still blaming myself for this great team that was eliminated relatively early from the NCAA tournament. So for me, every loss is a failure, and I get into the weeds of all the decisions I've made that took us there, because we're always going to have enough talent to win every game. I've got to sort out a way to resolve that.

We did some things this spring that I think really helped us a bit, and hopefully we'll carry this into the summer, into the fall. It'll put us in a position to compete again successfully in the fall. But I guess every loss for me is a very serious failure. Although I have had some losses where we totally outclassed the other team, and there was a fluke that caused us to lose them. One of the bad things about soccer is the best team isn't always delivered to the victory stand, unlike the NBA where you have a best of seven series and usually the best team wins.

Bonus: How do you balance your competitiveness and caring so much about the win or loss, but still being able to lose gracefully?

We try to instill in the kids that we recruit and the teams we develop that this isn't life or death. Again, this is a Dean Smithism. He used to say, "There are millions of people in China that don't even know you played yesterday." He had all these different ways to get his players to deflect the devastating impact of a loss. He understood that athletics—when you review the list of things that are most important on this earth—it's not incredibly high up there.

We have a similar sort of collection of statements that I make all the time. I tell these kids every single year, if I had a choice for you to cure cancer or win a gold medal in the Olympics, I want you guys to know it's clear what my choice would be—I would rather have you cure cancer. My kids know there are a lot of things that have a higher priority than the success of their performance in a soccer game. We talk about this all the time. In fact, we demonstrate it in our annual banquet. At the University of North Carolina Women's Soccer Banquet, the highest award is not the MVP. The highest award is the Kelly Muldoon Award for Character. For us, the most important thing you can develop in your four years at the University of North Carolina isn't your ability to stick a ball in the upper corner and win games. It's your character, the way you treat people, the way you develop a resilience to withstand the chaos of the universe.

The Viktor Frankl statement about the most important quality any of us could have is what he called the last of the human freedoms. To choose your attitude in any given set of circumstances, to choose your own way. For me, these are the most important things for a young player to learn when they're playing for me at the University of North Carolina. You could interview anyone on my team and ask, "In Anson's mind, what are the three most important things for your development at the University of North Carolina?" The players will rattle off for you—"Character development is number one, academic success is number two, and your soccer development is number three." There's no confusion in my program as to what's most important.

The kids can manipulate me if they like, they can say, "Anson, I've got a paper due tomorrow and I just haven't done enough work on it, or a test that I've got to study for, do you mind if I miss practice?" If they use academics as an excuse for missing something, I will always endorse it. I don't have a collection of narcs running around, sorting out why they're missing practice. No, I will trust them, and they know this. And I know the players that try to manipulate me in the system, and obviously I'm very disappointed. But I will never have my soccer program take a priority over someone's academic success. I will also never have it compromise their character in any way. Which is why for me, the core values and their recitation of the 13 core values we have, and the way they live them and their peer evaluations, are a very important part of my player conference.

It's so funny, we were just chatting about Dan Hurley. I'm trying to figure out a way to have a player conference with each of the parents now, just where the parents are coming from. I haven't figured that out yet. Basically for me, it's character number one, it's academic success number two, and then soccer development and commitment number three. I have no delusions of grandeur at the importance of what they're doing. As a result, I think our kids realize that a part of their character is demonstrating graciousness in defeat. Even if we were hacked to death and cheated, we're going to be gracious in the press conference following the game.

It was funny, in that game where we lost in the last 16 seconds, the press was in there and they couldn't wait to jump on the fact that my goalkeeper was smashed into the back of the net with 16 seconds to go when we were winning and there was no call on it. They were all dying to tee me up and ask me about that moment. I told them the truth. I said, "To be completely honest, I was sitting about 75 yards away from that, and it was hard for me to see what really happened." Because these press conferences are televised following the game, I got so many laudatory statements from people that saw the game. It was clear that my goalkeeper was smashed into the back of the net and there should have been a foul call. Then they heard me say that it was hard for me to see, and they're praising me, and I was just answering the question truthfully. Because I hadn't seen it.

Afterwards, I saw it, and saw what a mistake was made, but during the game that was my reaction. Again, I would love to always react that way and not say I saw what happened and clearly this, that, and the other thing, and blame everything on the referees. I'm so glad it happened that way because if I had seen that in the game, maybe I would have said something. To me, I think that would have lowered what I'm trying to teach if I had reacted that way. It's fortunate that I was just answering the question. "Yeah, it was too far away for me to see." I was given too much praise because maybe if I had seen that, I wouldn't have reacted that way because it was so clearly a foul. But for me, that's the way I would love for all of my players to react, to be gracious in defeat—and as a rule, we are. If you're gonna learn something in athletics, certainly being gracious in victory and defeat would be a wonderful character message to get from sport.

What traits or skills do your most successful athletes have in common?
The most important leadership skill is the ability to lead yourself, and that's difficult. It's very difficult to lead yourself because there are so many temptations to be lazy or not commit yourself to a worthy cause. There are so many incredible distractions that can take you away from this kind of mission, so many self serving things there. All of us are so tempted. There's so many excuses we could make to enjoy our days and not commit ourselves to becoming extraordinary. That's one thing—committing ourselves, leading ourselves. This is self-regulation. Self-regulation is very difficult in first world countries. We have so many freedoms to eat too much, to be lazy. We have so many distractions, and these are genuine first world problems, so that the majority of the people in the United States are obese. The weight loss industry is a billion dollar industry. Why? Because we can't self-regulate, and that's a major problem. The first principle is being able to lead yourself.

The other principles that tie into this, if you want to become absolutely extraordinary, is you have to have a personal narrative that's the truth. All of us are surrounded by people, and usually it's our parents, that are trying to protect us from the chaos of the universe. That are trying to protect us from the possibility that we're not as good, we're not working as hard, and we're not doing all these things that would deliver us to where we want to be. This is also one of the moral imperatives I have. I try to take every player's personal narrative to the truth as fast as possible, because as long as they have all these different excuses for why they haven't succeeded, they're going to be protected from committing themselves to taking responsibility. Again, I lay this at the feet of the parents that are out there.

There were these books written back in the day where they were telling us that one of the most critical things you can give to your child is self-esteem. This self-esteem movement started, and the self-esteem movement is to basically praise everything. There are two incredibly negative effects of the self-esteem movement. First, we shatter standards. When everything is praiseworthy, you eliminate high standards. The other interesting negative aspect of the self-esteem movement is that the child that's being praised for doing everything, the child that's now in the "everyone gets a trophy" culture, has no standards. What they also understand is that this is a bunch of BS, and now they lose their respect for authority, because they can sense way down deep that, "Oh, I don't think that was so good." Now all the authority figures in their lives, like their parents, no longer have credibility. Now this kid is in my program. Who's the authority figure? I am. What ends up happening to me? They have no respect for me, because they've never had respect for the authority figures that have been praising them their entire lives because they know this is a false front. There are all kinds of negatives for this self-esteem movement and the personal narrative, and the fact that very few of us have accurate personal narratives is an issue.

For me, this is also where Dean Smith came to the rescue. In the old days, what was really cool is that no one made decisions particularly early. Everyone went through a laborious recruiting process. A part of that recruiting process is you would visit the family in their home. This was Dean Smith's litmus test as to whether or not he would recruit the kid. This was his character test. He would go into a kid's home. He would watch and see how the kid treated his parents. If he treated his parents poorly in any way, he wouldn't recruit them. He knew that if he recruited that kid, that kid would become a problem relatively quickly. He's absolutely right. It's interesting, we have a wonderful leadership academy at the University of North Carolina, Jeff Janssen and Kara Cannizzaro run it and they do a wonderful job. I was listening to one of the coaches at UNC I genuinely respect by the name of Jenny Levy—our women's lacrosse coach. Her office is right next to mine. I really like her, love her kids, and I love Kara, who played for her, who is a part of our leadership academy. She was asked to speak at a coach's leadership academy meeting that was run by Jeff and Kara.

She was saying this is a problem that we're bringing in these kids that are world beaters. But here's what happens with that kid that's a world beater. This kid that's a world beater, we're not sure of yet because we don't have any sort of litmus test like Dean Smith had to sort out whether this young woman was a woman of character that had a team first mentality. This world beater is going to have a great freshman year because they're incredibly talented. But as they get more comfortable within your program, they're going to become more and more toxic, and by the time they're graduating and now real leaders in the team, not necessarily positive leaders in the team, but real leaders in the team, they're going to take this team down the wrong road, and they're not going to achieve their potential. I think that's absolutely true.

These days, this character piece is very difficult to sort out. This again gets me back to Dan Hurley. How do we sort out whether we want this kid? It's gonna be based on if we can sort out what the parents are like. Are they real parents? Do they hold their kids accountable for everything? Or are they cheerleaders for their kids, where they cheer for everything their kid does, and protect their kid from the possibility that they're not as good as everyone is telling them they are?

What books or resources do you most often recommend to coaches?
The biggest problem I'm having right now is developing leadership. I taught a course this past semester at the University of North Carolina called the Art and Science of Expertise. I'm learning a lot teaching this course. I've got two other absolutely brilliant professors, Erianne Weight from Exercise Sports Science and Jeff Greene from the School of Education. These are extraordinary professors, and we made a deal early in our relationship together that we would attend each other's lectures and support each other. Honestly, I love sitting through Erianne and Jeff's lectures because I've learned a lot. What's really interesting is we talk about the books that have impacted us and the way we're trying to shape ourselves, and I even share it with the class. I have admitted publicly in the class that I've struggled to develop leadership, and I am so convinced about this, that I don't think you can teach leadership. I think there's also a multi-million dollar industry out there that is teaching leadership, and I'm just not convinced it's teachable.

Jeni Shannon, our sports psychologist and absolutely brilliant woman that works with my kids, recommended a book to one of my spring captains, Bella Sember, and the book was *Dare to Lead*. I'm thinking, "Oh my gosh, even the title tells me this book is significant." The main problem in leadership isn't that you don't have the skill to be a leader. I think most people that lead have this inside them, and they have the courage to step forward and lead. I don't think it's—we have 30 kids in our roster, we sit down and we start to teach 'em the skills of leadership and suddenly, "Oh, so that's how you, that's the skill you need to lead. Oh my gosh, I wasn't aware of that, and I've got this skill now and I'm all set. Thank you!" I don't think that interferes with our lack of leadership.

I think we're terrified to lead. We're so afraid that if we open our mouths, what will everyone think of us? We're so afraid of being responsible for other people when we're not responsible for ourselves, we're terrified to step into that space because trust me, you can't lead someone else if you can't lead yourself, and most of us struggle to lead ourselves.

The books I would recommend right now, and a lot of this is through the course I'm teaching, but also through Jeni Shannon and Bella Sember, get Brene Brown. Get *Dare to Lead*. Teach the people that you're coaching to lead through *Dare to Lead*, because I think she's hitting on something. She understands the reason most of us don't lead isn't just because of the cliché I use: in order to lead someone else, you have to be able to lead yourself. Not that it isn't true. That is true. But I think the real fear most of us have is—I was asked to speak at a commencement, and I flew into Houston. I'm on a puddle jumper between Houston and College Station. The weather was bad and this plane was all over the sky. I'm thinking, "Oh my God, this is terrifying." So to calm my nerves, I pull out the inflight magazine and sure enough, they have this article in the inflight magazine about man's greatest fears. It was hilarious because I'm reading this and it says man's greatest fear is public speaking. You are afraid of public speaking even more than death.

Here I am, I'm about to die, and if I survive, I have to speak publicly. So the irony of the article was just all over me, and actually I began that commencement address with that story because it's a pretty funny story. But basically we're afraid of being out there. Public speaking is being out there. We're going to be ridiculed. We're going to be attacked for what we say. It's the same thing with leadership, and so I think the most critical book all of us should read if we want to develop leaders is *Dare to Lead* by Brene Brown. But in terms of coaching, I would recommend the Sir John Whitmore book (*Coaching for Performance*), which I think will have an incredibly powerful effect.

The most impactful book I've ever read is Viktor Frankl's *Man's Search for Meaning*. That's where the most important core value—and if you just type into your web browser, UNC Women's Soccer core values, those are the things I believe in. They are powerful. My kids memorize the quotes involved in all of those, and they recite them to me at the beginning of a player conference, and then they are evaluated against them by their teammates on a 1-5 scale. We take these things very seriously. I want them to live their core values because, as I've already shared with you, the highest award you can get at UNC is the kid that finishes on top of that in the fall. In the spring, those are the kids I honor most aggressively. They are demonstrating to me they're going to live extraordinary lives because of their character. Even though I've had a lot of the MVPs in soccer, the kids that I know are going to lead extraordinary lives are the ones at the top of my core value list.

Stephen Covey's *Seven Habits of Highly Effective People*. An absolutely brilliant book that I was using to teach this course with and then, when we asked for reactions from the student population, they didn't think that old book spoke to them, so we dumped it and we picked up Adam Grant's *Hidden Potential*, along with an absolutely amazing book by a friend of mine named Dan Lerner and that is *U Thrive*. He teaches at NYU, he's an absolutely brilliant professor. We bring him in to give two lectures in our class at UNC, and that book, *U Thrive*, is fantastic for any incoming freshman at the University of North Carolina. They all read that book, and I would recommend that to anyone. I've recommended that to my 14-year-old grandson. Then there are other books that my seniors read. We always read a book every year on anti-racism, I love Kendi's stuff in that. I love all these different authors in that because we want to have a culture that's anti-racist, not just, "We don't believe in racist," no, anti-racist, where the aggressive tenor of the book is we can't just exist, we've got to be against this in our culture officially.

The seniors all read David Brooks *The Second Mountain*. The reason I read that book is because I think Brooks may have originally been a conservative, but once he saw his own party go off the rails, I think he's a bit more liberal now. But we also brought in a radically liberal professor that gave a commencement address at Kenyon College, and the title of the address was *This is Water*. We have these two things for the incoming kids to read because if one was originally conservative, I want my noble Republicans that are coming into my program to understand that we're going to embrace them and we're going to embrace old school Republican values like family and spirituality and all those different elements that old school Republicans supported, and David Brooks talks along those lines. But in *This is Water*, in a way you've got a conservative and a liberal that start from different perspectives, but they end up in the same place. What I want everyone in my culture to understand is you're going to be embraced. I don't care if you're a radical liberal or a radical conservative, you're going to be embraced in my culture because the top values in both extremes can survive together. As long as we have a civil discourse, and we treat each other with respect at all times. By the way, *This is Water* is a commencement address, it's not a book, but they've turned it into a thin little book. You can read it before your lunch break is over, but it's extraordinary. I read it like scripture. I have so much respect for it and I read it every year because my seniors discuss it with me as they do *The Second Mountain* with David Brooks.

"Giving and receiving feedback can be one of the greatest gifts in life. It helps us grow. We all need feedback. If you want to accelerate your growth, ask for feedback. If you want to be elite in your field, learn to give feedback in a way that helps people get better."

-Henry Barrera

Henry Barrera is in his third year as the Head Strength and Conditioning Coach for Men's Basketball at the University of Alabama. In his first two seasons with the Tide, the program made trips to the Sweet Sixteen and Final Four while also winning SEC regular season and conference tournament championships. Barrera spent seven years at Liberty University before heading to Alabama, a period that included six straight 20-plus win seasons, three consecutive regular season and tournament championships, and the program's first ever NCAA tournament win in 2019. Before joining the college ranks, he worked as a performance training specialist at Nike World Headquarters in Beaverton, and also worked at the high school level for a decade. Barrera helped coach 2023 first round NBA Draft selections Brandon Miller and Noah Clowney, while also working closely with current Boston Celtic Payton Pritchard while he was in high school.

Who do you go to when you need advice? Why them?

I've built a board of directors in my life that I go to for life decisions and to look at things from different perspectives. They serve as a sounding board. The board is made up of a group of men that work in different disciplines from the medical field to advertising. I trust them. They've all earned a voice in my life by how they live.

What early job was pivotal in your career? Why?

My first real job was for the City of Grandview in Parks and Recreation. It taught me how to show up and serve people. If you learn how to serve people, you will be better at everything you do, including your career.

What are your first steps when you start a new job? What do you need to figure out, what do you need to get done, who do you need to get to know?

I typically read or go through this book called *The First 90-Days* to get a gauge of the people, environment, and overall vibe. Then I start building a priority list of what and how I can help. It all comes back to service. Finding ways to serve the people I'm working with. This doesn't mean just doing things for them, it means finding ways to help them operate at a higher level.

What advice do you have for a college student looking to break into coaching? Who are the best mentors in the world to work for early in your career?

Coaching is teaching. It's a different context because you're on the court, field, or in the weight room, but it is trying to help people get to where they want to go. If you want to coach, find a way to get involved, get around coaches. Find a way to coach at any level. The best mentors are those who find opportunities for you to learn and develop.

If you only had two 30-minute sessions a week to train your team, how would you prepare them?

I have three basic principles that guide everything I do in regards to performance:

- Master Movement to Maximize Power.

- Strategic and Progressive Overload.

- Build Capacity to Work.

I would break up the segment into three categories: Explode, Strong, and Build. Explode would be sprinting, jumping, loaded jumps, or some variation of Med Ball throws. Strong would be building up to heavy lower body strength work like trap bar deadlifts, split squat variations, or single leg squat or hinge movements. We'd finish up with an upper body push and an upper body pull.

What goes into your decision to leave or stay at a job?

It's probably a little different for me. Faith is a big part of my decision making. I consult with my family and my board of directors and pray on where God wants to use me. I consider fit, which includes people, the location, the organization, and what they are trying to build.

What do you do to overcome times of struggle, burnout, or overwhelm? Who do you turn to?

I'm probably the most extroverted introvert you know. I love working with players but know I need time to recharge. For me, that is being by myself, reading, writing, thinking, and just being still.

What do you think about immediately after one of your athletes is injured? What is your mindset in the following week?

What could I have done to help prevent this? When you work with athletes every day, it's hard not to take it personal. My mindset following an injury is how can we come back better? I operate on a 3D process that I've been working on for a while. Discover, Develop, and Deliver. Learn as much as possible about the injury and recovery process, develop a plan of action, and deliver that on a day-to-day basis.

How do you approach difficult conversations with athletes, coworkers, or your boss?

I try to be as transparent as possible. Giving and receiving feedback can be one of the greatest gifts in life. It helps us grow. We all need feedback. If you want to accelerate your growth, ask for feedback. If you want to be elite in your field, learn to give feedback in a way that helps people get better. It's something I'm working on every day.

Do you have a "failure" that was critical to your long-term development or success?

I have more than I want to admit, but the best one is not being good at something. It's humbling. When I was a young coach, one of my mentors told me I had to get better at communication, my organization, and my presence. He was right.

I don't see failure as negative; I see it as a growth opportunity.

What traits or skills do your most successful athletes have in common?

Genetics. Beyond that, it's a feel for whatever they do. They have an almost supernatural feel for their bodies and can translate that into skill in the context of what they do. In addition, they have an elite mental framework that spans mindset to understanding of the game.

What books or resources do you most often recommend to coaches?

Mind: The Creative Act by Rick Rubin; *Supercommunicators* by Charles Duhigg; *Atomic Habits* by James Clear.

"Putting my family before my career has perhaps kept me from advancing from a monetary standpoint to some degree. I would not have changed it, however. I trust that God has me right where he wants me and I would rather fail as a coach than as a husband and father."

-Eric Duft

Eric Duft is in his third year as the Head Men's Basketball Coach at Weber State University after spending 16 seasons as an assistant coach with the Wildcats. He led Weber State to the Big Sky Tournament semifinals in his first year as head coach, and won 20 games in his second season, including a road win at No. 23 Saint Mary's, the program's first win against a ranked team in 23 years. As an assistant, Duft was a part of five Big Sky Championship teams with three appearances in March Madness. He has helped coach six Big Sky Conference MVPs, including NBA draft picks Damian Lillard (2x MVP), Dillon Jones, and Joel Bolomboy. Before heading to Weber State, Duft coached at Hutchinson Junior College, Cowley County CC, and Central Community College.

Who do you go to when you need advice? Why them?

For coaching advice, I normally consult a few people that I trust deeply. Tim Duryea, Phil Beckner, and Jeff Linder are people that I have worked with, and who I know have my best interest in mind. Most of the time, it's not just asking for answers, but openly talking through situations with them. They are not judgmental and want what's best for me, so I can trust what they are saying is from a good place.

What early job was pivotal in your career? Why?

My first coaching job was working at the Roy Williams Basketball Camp at the University of Kansas. Coach Williams' words and actions showed me how a successful program is run. I learned the value of the smallest of things and how to treat everyone in the program in a first-class way. It also afforded me the opportunity to meet many coaches and, because of that, I got my first college assistant job.

Working as a junior college assistant for 11 years was also pivotal. You had to wear so many hats and recruit almost a new team every year. The on-the-job experience and work ethic to be successful was extremely valuable.

What are your first steps when you start a new job? What do you need to figure out, what do you need to get done, who do you need to get to know?

The first thing is understanding the job that you currently have. Understanding the landscape of the university and where you can go to recruit players. You must make sure that you are in alignment with your administration in every way. Alignment is different than being on the same page. Being in alignment means that you have the same values as those in administration, and then are able to create a tactical approach to ensure those values are instilled in everyone associated with the program.

Hiring the right staff is super important. Again, creating alignment within your staff and having people within the organization that will uphold those values.

Getting to know the financial boosters associated with the program is one of the most important things to do early. Creating a relationship with those people is invaluable.

What advice do you have for a college student looking to break into coaching? Who are the best mentors in the world to work for early in your career?

Work as many summer camps and clinics as possible. Volunteering to coach a youth team is a valuable learning tool as the more reps you get at coaching, the better you will become. The more people you can meet in the profession, the better. I always tell young coaches: When you get your first job, treat it like it is the most important job in the world. Nothing is too small for you to do. Obviously, people want to move up in the profession, but you must do it the right way. Working hard and having success at your current job is the best way to move up.

The best mentor is the one who cares about you the most. It doesn't always have to be a famous coach. Find someone who believes in you and wants to help you succeed. Don't worry about name recognition. Find the ones who want to help you.

If you only had two 30-minute sessions a week to train your team, how would you prepare them?

This is a great question! We would compete as hard as we can for 30 minutes. Ultimately, if you do not instill a competitive mindset in your team, then you will not be successful. Strategy, game planning, etc. would not be a part of our 30 minutes. It would be about being as competitive as we can possibly be.

What goes into your decision to leave or stay at a job?

The number one thing is alignment with the administration. If that is strong, then it's hard to leave. If it's not, then you better get out. The other thing would be the ability to recruit good enough players to have success. Money is also important, but not the most important thing.

What do you do to overcome times of struggle, burnout, or overwhelm? Who do you turn to?

My energy-giver is my family. I truly enjoy the time I get to spend with them, and when things are not going well, I spend even more time with them. They are the ones who give you unconditional love and respect. I also get even more into my daily Bible reading and devotions. Learning that God's plan and his timing is way better than mine gives me comfort to be in the moment and not dwell on the future too much. Being balanced is a great way to minimize the times of struggle and burnout.

What do you think about immediately after one of your athletes is injured? What is your mindset in the following week?

How it will affect our team going forward. The mindset better be one of strength and confidence, no matter how you actually feel. The team will pick up on any doubts that the leader has.

How do you approach difficult conversations with athletes, coworkers, or your boss?

Some people really struggle with having difficult conversations. While no one likes to have these encounters, I have never shied away from them. My take is that if things are not going well, then you will have to have a difficult conversation at some point. The sooner the better, so that all parties know where they stand. Being completely honest and transparent is the only way to have these. Anything else and the other individual will see through it and you will lose credibility. Even if the conversation is difficult, being honest and upfront allows you to have mutual respect.

Do you have a "failure" that was critical to your long-term development or success?

I don't have a "failure," but putting my family before my career has perhaps kept me from advancing from a monetary standpoint to some degree. I would not have changed it, however. I trust that God has me right where he wants me and I would rather fail as a coach than as a husband and father.

What traits or skills do your most successful athletes have in common?

I have been fortunate to coach some truly successful players and among those is Damian Lillard, one of the very best in the NBA. I would say that all of them are very secure in who they are as people and have tremendous competitive character. Many players get in their own way because of insecurities, or lack of competitive stamina. The best ones can show up EVERY SINGLE DAY, ready to be their best. It sounds cliché, but it is very difficult to find those that are driven each and every day to be their best.

What books or resources do you most often recommend to coaches?

The Bible—Truths are timeless and knowing the human condition is paramount to being able to lead. The Bible gives insight to the human heart and allows you to understand how and why people react the way they do. Nehemiah is an excellent book on leadership.

The Daily Coach is a leadership newsletter that is a valuable resource for coaches. Very good insight on leadership and team building from some of the industry's most successful people.

Podcasts—I normally stress the importance of finding quality podcasts to listen to while working out, driving, etc. Using your down time to continually feed the mind is much better than just being entertained.

> *"We support the athletes we work with and staffs we work for and we rely greatly on those around us for 'success.' The real success is impacting lives and hopefully helping young athletes reach their goals and dreams but more importantly develop as people. Don't have an ego because your team has 'success.'"*
>
> ## *-Jeremy Anderson*

Jeremy Anderson is entering his sixth year with Creighton University as the Head Coach of Athletic Performance for Men's Basketball. He has helped the Blue Jays achieve consistently high levels of success, including multiple trips to the Sweet Sixteen and one to the Elite Eight, along with a share of the 2019–2020 Big East Regular Season Championship. Anderson worked at Vanderbilt, New Mexico, and Virginia before arriving at Creighton. He helped Baylor Scheierman get drafted in the first round of this past year's 2024 NBA Draft.

Who do you go to when you need advice? Why them?

Mike Curtis—Head S&C for Basketball at Virginia. Mike was my first boss at UVA and critical in my development as both a coach and leader. He set me up to think through the view of systems.

Tony Giovacchini—Ponte Services LLC. Tony is a high-level thinker and consultant in the human performance space and understands the worlds of elite basketball, human performance, and the soft skills of dealing with people.

What early job was pivotal in your career? Why?

My first job at the University of Virginia was the most pivotal in terms of growth and development. I was given freedom to program, run a team, and direct all facets of performance. Mike was an incredible mentor, let me work through mistakes, while also keeping me from making the big mistakes. Learning by doing is the best teacher when you have good guidance.

What are your first steps when you start a new job? What do you need to figure out, what do you need to get done, who do you need to get to know?

Step one is know the job you were hired for. Was the position you took vacant because of success and that person moved on or because of failure? Lack of performance? Injuries and player health? That will answer a lot of what your first steps should be. Organizational alignment is key, so being on the same page as the head coach regarding culture and expectations is huge (has the head coach been there and is bringing you into an existing culture or is the entire staff new?).

After that, get to know the athletes (both as people and as athletes). What do they need? What motivates them? How do they project in their long-term development and how do we get there?

What advice do you have for a college student looking to break into coaching? Who are the best mentors in the world to work for early in your career?

Get experience at the level you want to coach at. Be willing to intern or GA. Apply everywhere. Don't expect to get a job, let alone your dream job, at any level of sport without having a network and experience (as an athlete, intern, or GA) that can recommend you.

If you only had two 30-minute sessions a week to train your team, how would you prepare them?

A loaded question and the best answer is it depends. What phase of season? What's each athlete's training age? When is training occurring (pre-sport or post-sport training)?

Questions like these I view as what provides the best return on time investment or value to the training process to spur on adaptation. The list below is what I've found to be great stimuli in different phases.

- Off-season
  - Short acceleration sprint work.
  - Complex Loaded Movements paired with ballistic or plyometric work.
  - Pushing/Overcoming Isometrics with different durations (0.5–5 seconds).
  - Long duration Isometric holds for tendon work.

- Pre-season
  - High-force, high-velocity work paired with ballistic or plyometric work.
  - Ballistic Isometrics.
- In-season (for high-minute rotation players)
  - Low-volume, high-intensity strength work.
  - Expanded emphasis on soft-tissue work and table (stretching and mobility work).

My sessions would be built around some assortment of the above, depending on the athlete and the phase.

What goes into your decision to leave or stay at a job?

Early on, it was to climb the career ladder. Now it all comes down to the best decision for my family (wife and kids).

What do you do to overcome times of struggle, burnout, or overwhelm? Who do you turn to?

Your purpose has to come from outside of yourself. For me it's a calling and I rely heavily on my relationship with God and Jesus Christ. How can I serve and coach the athletes I work with even in difficult situations in light of everything God has done for me and blessed me with? That is the lens that I try to view coaching in, particularly in difficult times. I feel like I can move forward through difficult situations and times by looking back and seeing all the ways God has provided. Second, I rely or turn to my family and the support they offer. At the end of the day, being able to come home to them is always a huge encouragement.

What do you think about immediately after one of your athletes is injured? What is your mindset in the following week?

I stay process oriented. Audit what happened, try to understand why, and then try to improve in any areas I found that were lacking or deficient. Address the athlete's headspace and psychology and then do everything I can to support them in return to play. Use all performance related metrics they had when healthy to have baseline benchmarks for return to play and utilize them to guide the rehabilitation process.

How do you approach difficult conversations with athletes, coworkers, or your boss?

I always try to approach conflict or difficult conversations as US against the problem, not me vs you. 90% of the time this re-shifts the focus to a solutions oriented approach instead of who is right or wrong.

Do you have a "failure" that was critical to your long-term development or success?

Somewhat early in my career, I was the S&C coach for a staff that was fired for lack of wins. The very next year, I was the director of performance for a staff that won a Power 6 regular season conference championship for the first time in school history and was a top 10 nationally ranked team. While I strive to be a better coach every single year, that entire process helped reinforce the fact that strength coaches never win games. We support the athletes we work with and staffs we work for and we rely greatly on those around us for "success." The real success is impacting lives and hopefully helping young athletes reach their goals and dreams but more importantly develop as people. Don't have an ego because your team has "success."

What traits or skills do your most successful athletes have in common?

Competitive, Self-Motivated, Aware.

What books or resources do you most often recommend to coaches?

Online resources I've found particularly valuable are the ALTIS courses as well as the *Isometric Strength Training Course* by Alex Natera (through Sportsmith). Traditional books pertaining to the field of human performance that I continually go back to are numerous, but some of my favorites are *Supertraining* by Mel Siff, *Special Strength Training Manual for Coaches* by Yuri and Natalia Verkhoshansky, and *High Performance Training for Sport* edited and compiled by Joyce and Lewindon. Outside of the field of human performance, anything by Malcolm Gladwell and *Range* by David Epstein.

> *"How can I be there for them? Injuries can make athletes feel worthless. It's important to empower them during this time."*
>
> ## -Arianna Luther

Arianna Luther is a premier Sports Performance Coach in the Chicago area. Luther previously worked with the Rowing, Swimming and Dive, and Women's Soccer programs as an Assistant Strength and Conditioning Coach at the University of Miami for three years. She joined Miami after serving as the Assistant Director of Strength and Conditioning at the University of Nevada.

Who do you go to when you need advice? Why them?
My mentor, Les Spellman. He believed in me when I didn't.

What early job was pivotal in your career? Why?
Four years of internships working for free taught me that it takes dedication to get where you want to go. Not everything is handed to you.

What are your first steps when you start a new job? What do you need to figure out, what do you need to get done, who do you need to get to know?
Meet with strength staff, medical staff, sport coaches, and athletes immediately. The sooner you build genuine connections, the smoother the transition.

What advice do you have for a college student looking to break into coaching? Who are the best mentors in the world to work for early in your career?
I would tell them to list out all of their priorities: job, salary, location, family, relationships, etc. Do not just take a job to take a job. Make sure your priorities are met.

If you only had two 30-minute sessions a week to train your team, how would you prepare them?
The warm up should not be complex—short and efficient. Setting up the weight room prior to the session also helps. Athletes should have rack assignments and the bars are loaded with warm-up weight so as they enter, the athlete can jump right into the first set.

What goes into your decision to leave or stay at a job?

Do I feel like I'm living out my purpose? Are my basic needs being met? Do I have time outside of work to pour into the things I love? Am I adding value to the organization and are they adding value to me?

What do you do to overcome times of struggle, burnout, or overwhelm? Who do you turn to?

I pray and seek God.

What do you think about immediately after one of your athletes is injured? What is your mindset in the following week?

How can I be there for them? Injuries can make athletes feel worthless. It's important to empower them during this time.

How do you approach difficult conversations with athletes, coworkers, or your boss?

I typically iterate positive feedback about topics related to the conversation first to help de-escalate on the front end. Then, I make sure I use phrases like "I feel as though... What do you think?" Or, "I am noticing... What do you think?" It helps to bring the person into the conversation so that they feel valued, not attacked.

Do you have a "failure" that was critical to your long-term development or success?

I was rejected from seven job interviews before I landed a job at the University of Miami.

What traits or skills do your most successful athletes have in common?
Consistency.

What books or resources do you most often recommend to coaches?
Any of Les Spellman's work, as he has played a pivotal role in my life.

"The second time I immediately recognized them and set out to do the only thing you can do in deep burnout, and that is leave the situation that is causing you to break as a human being. There is no other choice."

-Jorge Carvajal

Jorge Carvajal is a performance coach and consultant that works with elite athletes from both the sports world and the tactical world. He has worked with professional athletes from the NFL, MLB, NBA, NHL, along with surfers from the World Surf League Big Wave Tour. Carvajal has also trained tactical athletes in the fire service, law enforcement SWAT and SRT, and military communities. He gained experience working as a strength and conditioning coach at the University of Florida, the University of Nebraska, and the U.S. Olympic Training Center.

Who do you go to when you need advice? Why them?

I have a very small circle of people, some are coaches, that I turn to for advice in a variety of subjects. The primary reason is that I know they will tell me the truth, are brutally honest, and show me a viewpoint that I may not have considered before.

What early job was pivotal in your career? Why?

GA position at Nebraska. It was essentially ground zero for S&C at the time. I learned to coach a weight room there, and to coach—period!

What are your first steps when you start a new job? What do you need to figure out, what do you need to get done, who do you need to get to know?

For me, it's usually understanding where I stand in the organization and who the other players are. What problems need to be solved? That's followed by figuring out what resources I have at my disposal to solve those problems. I end the day by figuring out if I know others who have been in a similar situation and reach out to them immediately for guidance. Nobody does S&C alone. Nobody!

What advice do you have for a college student looking to break into coaching? Who are the best mentors in the world to work for early in your career?

One of the most important things you can do as you go down the path in S&C is to find a good GA position, preferably with someone who is going to want to be an involved mentor. A lot of GA positions are essentially free help with not a lot of knowledge or coaching experience included. It's important to do your homework and decide not just on a position but a head S&C, that's the piece that most get wrong. The head S&C will make or break your learning experience.

If you only had two 30-minute sessions a week to train your team, how would you prepare them?

- Day 1: Speed Developer/FB Lift push/hip dominant emphasis (Power/Strength/Auxiliary/rotation core)
- Day 2: COD/FB lift pull/hip extension emphasis (Power/Strength/Auxiliary/static core)

What goes into your decision to leave or stay at a job?

How I'm treated. I always recommend Patrick Lencioni's *Three Signs of a Miserable Job* as a resource. Once you start noticing the signs, that's a red flag. Although some of those can be overcome, if you fall into a situation where you have all three, it's time to move on—I speak from experience. The other time I would consider leaving a job is if I feel like I am not making a difference. That could be a you problem or that could be a them problem. If it's a you problem—figure out how you can make yourself more valuable as a coach. If it's a them problem—it may be time to go somewhere else.

What do you do to overcome times of struggle, burnout, or overwhelm? Who do you turn to?

I've been through burnout more than once. The last one was life changing. The first thing to do is to recognize what's happening—awareness is everything. Once again I reference Patrick Lencioni's *Three Signs Of A Miserable Job*. In the first burnout, I didn't recognize the three signs immediately, but I was living them every day, until I was so miserable and suffering from so many physical symptoms that I broke down—mentally, physically and spiritually. I continued in that job, albeit in a very different capacity.

The second time I immediately recognized them and set out to do the only thing you can do in deep burnout, and that is leave the situation that is causing you to break as a human being. There is no other choice. Most will try to restructure their lives, but I can tell you from mentoring and consulting with hundreds of coaches who've gone through burnout, that never works. It's not an easy conclusion to come to, but it's the only solution.

What do you think about immediately after one of your athletes is injured? What is your mindset in the following week?

With injuries, I don't jump to conclusions. I watch a lot of film—that's where I go first. Did a specific movement cause the injury, or was it simply the brutality of the sport? Once we have an understanding of what happened, we switch from performance to "return to play." All the focus then is to get the athlete 1. Healthy 2. Return them to the game in the best possible condition to be successful. We don't follow an "injury prevention program"...it's just simply good programming and smart training.

How do you approach difficult conversations with athletes, coworkers, or your boss?

I've learned that developing trust up front and getting buy in early makes difficult conversations easier later. That goes for athletes, coworkers, and bosses. Establish credibility and integrity and people will see where you're coming from. That doesn't mean you won't have difficult conversations—you will—but as long as people know that you're loyal and will hold space for them during tough times, everyone can vibe out the other end better.

Do you have a "failure" that was critical to your long-term development or success?

Failure is a common part of coaching. It's what you do with that failure that redefines what it means. You're going to make mistakes—count on it. Failure has to be thought of as an opportunity to learn from the experience. What went wrong? What part did I personally play? What can I do better? If I stay in the questions, failure gets transformed into a different experience and you realize it's simply a way toward growth.

What traits or skills do your most successful athletes have in common?

The number one trait I've seen consistently over the last 30 years in successful athletes is self-discipline. They know what needs to get done and they show up consistently and do it. If it's performance training, they're usually the first ones there and they don't miss a session. If they're injured, they don't miss PT sessions, meetings with doctors, or any aspect of rehab. Successful athletes don't have to be cajoled—they carry great self-discipline, which is the impetus to success.

What books or resources do you most often recommend to coaches?

Science and Practice of Strength Training by Vladimir Zatsiorsky. *Conscious Coaching* by Brett Bartholomew. *Creativity Inc* by Ed Catmull. *Three signs of a Miserable Job* by Patrick Lencioni.

> **"There comes a point along the way where you have to start guarding your time and you have to be careful about what you're saying yes to. You don't want to fill up your schedule to the point where you can't say yes to things that really align with you."**
>
> ## -Andrew Coates

Andrew Coates is a leader in the fitness industry and owner of Andrew Coates Fitness. An incredible learner and teacher, he is a fitness writer who has contributed to multiple platforms, including T-Nation, Muscle and Fitness, Men's Health, and many more. Coates has been a featured speaker at numerous events, and is the co-founder of The Evolve Strength - Business and Coaching Conference. He also hosts the *Lift Free and Diet Hard Podcast with Andrew Coates.* **(Coates's responses were transcribed from a Zoom call)**

What early job was pivotal in your career? Why?

I was really good at the skill of school. But when I got thrown out into the world—like so many people who are good at the skill of school and getting good grades—we're not necessarily that adept at navigating the workforce. I worked in call centers, which was terrible. I sold cars for a summer, which had elements of fun, but was in a lot of ways terrible. I worked bar security at different junctures in my mid twenties. There's fun in that, but there's also very dark stuff. I owned a nightclub, and that came with a lot of fun, but a lot of headaches and bulls**t. All of that had me decide I wanted a change of scenery. The first job I fell into was a job at a casino dealing blackjack, dealing poker, and being one of the poker room supervisors.

In a lot of ways, I realized a lot of the s**t that I didn't like and didn't want, and that I hadn't found a career. Now, there is something within the poker realm that was resonant. Most trainers are not equipped to navigate things like dealing with the random crazy s**t that goes on in gyms. There's a spectrum of interpersonal interaction—it's a bell curve. At one end of the bell curve, you're breaking up fights in gyms. On the other end, most of your interactions—and it's an opportunity I think a lot of trainers miss—is the smiling, the engagement, the nods, and the social interaction with the members. From the commercial gym I worked in for the first six years of my career, I have tons of very close friends and old acquaintances that I made because I was so visible on the floor for so many hours. One of my now best friends was a new member, and at the time, we didn't allow gym bags on the floor. I went over, introduced myself, and said, "Hey man, don't worry about it today. Just letting you know, the gym's policy is that we don't allow gym bags on the floor. I figured I'd come over and be nice about it instead of not trusting someone else to be as charitable." We hit it off, and he's one of my best friends to this day.

I'll relate it back to the poker room. You're dealing poker to theoretically 10 people on the table, and every once in a while you end up with what's called a table bully. Some mean, petulant, fragile ego, nasty person, who when they lose, they'll often throw little tantrums, become hostile, or berate other players for playing poorly. Most dealers are afraid of the table bully. They put their head down and they don't A) earn the respect of and be able to keep this person in line, or B) challenge them and put them in their place. The key is if you don't control the table bully, the other nine players don't respect you and don't like being at your table. Some of them quietly, without complaint, leave the poker room and don't come back.

This is true of dealing with the idiots, the egocentric gym bullies, that exist in any commercial gym setting. You need to at least hold their respect and keep their behavior in check, or be willing to confront them and enforce rules—even if often trainers are not empowered to do so. If you don't step up and learn the skill of navigating those tricky situations, then you won't hold the respect of the overwhelming majority of the people that are in there. Be willing to handle it with professionalism, nuance, and skill, and occasionally take a few hits because these types of idiots that you deal with are the sort of people who will run to managers and lie. But if you're very good at your job and people know you for your reputation, good managers will have your back and know that this person is distorting things.

Understand that it's far more valuable to hold the respect of the majority and risk confronting the difficult people you will deal with in everyday life. The relationship side with the broad member base is actually fundamentally crucial. Even the serious lifters who you never would think would be interested in hiring a trainer, if they look at you and see that you're engaged, you're professional and focused on your client, you're not on your phone, you're not sitting down with lazy posture, these people refer people. I've gotten a lot of referrals from people who saw what I was doing and thought that I stood out in terms of that professional demeanor.

What goes into your decision to leave or stay at a job?

If you aren't getting support from management, if you're not truly valued for your work ethic, then there's a problem. I'm a big believer in Seth Godin's philosophy in *Linchpin*. It's about going above and beyond, not thinking I'm only going to give as much effort as I feel I'm being paid for and that my employer is entitled to. When I worked in the casino, and in the gym I worked for, it was always a natural thing to go above and beyond and engage with people. Even though you're playing a long game, the goal wasn't, "I wonder how many of these people might come and train with me."

You'd be shocked after years later, people searching me out and going, "Hey, I remember you from the gym. I want to talk to you about training." It's not transactional. It's not about placing a lot of bets on junk bonds. It's just authentically going about the world because it makes you feel better, because you actually have this abundant mindset. It's the law of attraction. You trust that by putting a lot of good energy out into the world, it pays you back. Unexpectedly, not necessarily consistently, but it's the compound effect of doing this a lot over a long period of time. You end up creating this massive, what I like to call surface area of luck. Luck's always an element, but people use the phrase you create your own luck, which I agree with. By putting yourself in situations, creating positive interactions with people—over time this stuff magnifies for good or for bad.

I've only ever left one gym to go to another, and the reason I left that gym is because there were some good people, but there were also bad people in the organization. Things were swept under the rug and it was a toxic work environment. A friend of mine had opened a gym that allowed for contractors, Evolved Strength, where I am now. My friend who opened that gym, John, now has his eighth location in the works across two provinces in Canada. He's my partner in a conference that we do. It's been an incredible relationship. He knew who I was from the old company, and based on reputation he wanted me involved. When people recognize that you're not transactional they want to involve you in more things. It creates more options and opportunities than you could've dreamt of.

What do you do to overcome times of struggle, burnout, or overwhelm? Who do you turn to?

Number one, if you're feeling burned out, look at what you're doing and realize there's probably more than a little bit that you do not enjoy, that you're not fulfilled by. Get clear on that. Sometimes you have to stop doing something that you don't align with, but you think you're supposed to do because someone else said you're supposed to do it. Early in trainers' careers, a lot of the younger crowd thinks too much in terms of boundaries. You have to be willing to say yes to a lot of things, try them, and then realize, "All right, this isn't for me." Or, "I really love this." See what doors it opens. But there comes a point where you have to start guarding your time and you have to be careful about what you're saying yes to. You don't want to fill up your schedule to the point where you can't say yes to things that really align with you.

Often it's not always doing too much of certain things, it's maybe not enough of the things that rejuvenate you. There are introverts who do too much peopling, and they actually just need some downtime.

Stay connected with the people in your career who are on the same journey or are like-minded and inspire you. Luka Hocevar is my go to for that. Luka and I will get a lot of one on one or group dinners where we share ideas. Sometimes just seeing what Luka's doing, it'll light me up and make me go, "All right, I got more. I can reach into the well a little bit and I can push through." And as you dive deeper in your career, don't lose the foundation of good sleep, good nutrition, and good training.

How do you approach difficult conversations with athletes, coworkers, or your boss?
You can either kick the can down the road and avoid a difficult conversation, or you can rip the band aid off and go have that tough conversation. It is about trying to listen, and not just fake listening, but actually listen with the intent to hear and understand where the other person is coming from. Being charitable in your interpretations of other people's motivations is a really good idea. A good metaphor for this is when you're driving and someone does something stupid. They cut you off and you're swearing at them. If you've heard of fundamental attribution error, we think, "That person's an idiot. They're an asshole." Think about the time when you got pinched off and had to cut in a little bit, or somehow you lost concentration. We've all made mistakes on the road, and we expect people to go, "Hey, it was just a momentary mistake. They're a fundamentally good person." Whereas when someone else does this sort of thing, they're a terrible person. That's fundamental attribution error.

We can apply that to everybody and go, "All right, what motivates this person? What's going on with them? Do they have a bruised ego? What's their goal? What's their agenda?" The reality is, there is going to be a small percentage of people who are genuinely just terrible people. You still have to understand their motivations. If you go in guns blazing, you're not creating an environment of collaboration and discourse. Most people go at it like, "I need to crush my enemies, I need to win, you need to lose." If you really want to get somewhere in life, understand what someone truly values, be willing to make some compromises, and come away from a situation where everybody's won.

Do you have a "failure" that was critical to your long-term development or success?
In my fitness career, the perception from many people is that everything I touch turns to gold. But it's not always necessarily easy. I don't think I've ever had a critical failure. I think the failure was more of a life failure in the wrong direction—owning this bar, getting involved in a party lifestyle—a lot of negative stuff came from that. I became very unhealthy physically and emotionally to the point where I decided I needed to change my environment. I moved across the country and started over, put my head down, took buses for six months, and just showed up to work every day and kind of hid away from the world for a little while.

That was what set the foundation for me to turn around and end up in fitness—because I fell into this. I did not say, "Hey, I want to be a trainer." I got back in the gym, put my head down, and kept showing up after my late night shifts at the casino. I worked out, put music in, just doing it for me. The staff at this gym kept asking me to come work as a trainer, and I kept saying no until I finally was done with the casino. Pretty quickly I did well, and suddenly, I'm really busy. I'm one of the top trainers in the entire company. I'm devoted to education. I'm fulfilled by it. I develop a passion within this career. I keep meeting people, making connections, and people support me. I look around now and I'm like, "I don't know how this happened." It's easy to connect the dots going backwards, but it's surreal.

What books or resources do you most often recommend to coaches?
When it comes to business, Seth Godin's *Linchpin* is a great mindset book. His book *The Practice* is also good for your approach to media content creation. Gary Vaynerchuk's *Crushing It* is a good one on media. I love Joe Polish's book, *What's in it for them?*, on the abundance mindset of being of service to other people versus being transactional. For writing books, *On Writing Well* by William Zinsser and *Everybody Writes* by Ann Handley are the two starting points. If you're struggling with procrastination or imposter syndrome, Stephen Pressfield's *The War of Art* is an easy classic. *The Coaching Habit* by Michael Bungay Stanier is amazing. *Motivational Interviewing in Fitness and Nutrition*

is a must read for everybody. I'll also highlight *Getting Clients and Referrals*—Jonathan Goodman's book.

One danger of making training book recommendations is that coaches will turn around and do nothing but that. You need to know this stuff, but at a certain point, they'll only dive into things they're already good at when you need to be learning business skills. Some other business books that I think are good—the Hormozis' books, *$100M Offers* and *$100M Leads*. Jeb Blount has some sales books—*Sales EQ* and *Fanatical Prospecting* are the two better ones.

Greg McKeown's *Essentialism* is good about getting clear on what matters to you. If you look at my career, I am always pulled in a million directions. It's not what I recommend, because I'm a one man show. But my idea of enjoyment is to work at this stuff. Not everybody's gonna share that. We laugh at the suggestion of work life balance in our careers. For an aspiring fitness professional, it's probably not going to be a thing. With respect to someone starting in this industry with a young family, it's good to be clear on what you're doing so that as you get busier, you can develop boundaries and protect what's important to you. As you get busier, you need to be clear and efficient on your time. At the same time, if you come into this career thinking you're going to work nine to five and then shut off, it doesn't work that way.

As a fitness professional, even if you're an employee somewhere else, you still have to take an entrepreneurial mindset to things. That's what saved me. The foundation of my career is that when I worked for a gym, I still understood that it was my business. The gym was not going to feed me clients, especially if I couldn't renew and sell and get referrals on my own. I put myself in a position where I didn't need to rely on them after the very beginning. I worked very hard at it. I worked very hard at learning. I dove into podcasts early because podcasts are free. Great audiobooks are a really good way as you're driving, cooking, etc. to accelerate getting these ideas in your head.

People will tell you, "You shouldn't read so many books. You need to go deep." No. The book is the resource you could reference at any time. I like sampling and going through a lot of ideas so that they seep into my system. But when I find something I really need, then I go deep. I'll listen to the audiobook and then I might go through the physical copy and give it a deeper look. Or I might go, "Okay, I know this is valuable, but I don't need this now." I put it away, but it's now something I can refer to. This also allows me to become a valuable resource to my network when people are looking for books on specific topics.

> ***"Mentors—people who have not let their need for education, fame, or fortune outweigh their need to invest their lives daily into the people they work with."***

-Kent Johnston

Kent Johnston is a Hall of Fame Strength Coach who currently owns Aruka Health and Wellness in Waco, Texas. Johnston worked in the NFL for over 20 years, winning the Super Bowl in 1997 as the Head Strength Coach with the Green Bay Packers, while being honored as the Strength and Conditioning Coach of the Year by the Professional Strength and Conditioning Coaches Association in 1997. He was also the Head Strength and Conditioning Coach for the Tampa Bay Buccaneers, the Seattle Seahawks, the Cleveland Browns, the San Diego Chargers, and the University of Alabama Football. Johnston's last role in the NFL was as Director of Player Wellness for the Carolina Panthers before retiring from the league in 2022. During his career, he coached notable NFL players Brett Farve, Vinny Testaverde, and Cortez Kennedy. Johnston was inducted into the Strength and Conditioning Hall of Fame in 2005.

Who do you go to when you need advice? Why them?
Al Miller – Al Vermeil – Dan Pfaff – Dr. Mark Lindsey—all mentors in various areas.

What early job was pivotal in your career? Why?
University of Alabama—learned how to multitask efficiently.

What are your first steps when you start a new job? What do you need to figure out, what do you need to get done, who do you need to get to know?
Prove my loyalty and investment into the players. If I can't win their respect they will never trust me. Find who to trust.

What advice do you have for a college student looking to break into coaching? Who are the best mentors in the world to work for early in your career?
Make sure this is really what you want to do and build your tool box—when the economy turns, the people who keep their jobs will be those with the largest tool box.

Mentors—people who have not let their need for education, fame, or fortune outweigh their need to invest their lives daily into the people they work with.

If you only had two 30-minute sessions a week to train your team, how would you prepare them?

With components that always drive athleticism and a balance of compression with decompression methodologies.

What goes into your decision to leave or stay at a job?

The Lord.

What do you do to overcome times of struggle, burnout, or overwhelm? Who do you turn to?

Prayer and meditation. Who do you turn to? Christ.

What do you think about immediately after one of your athletes is injured? What is your mindset in the following week?

What do we need to do to help him?

How do you approach difficult conversations with athletes, coworkers, or your boss?

I make no differentiation—always speak to them one on one.

Do you have a "failure" that was critical to your long-term development or success?

So many I cannot list just one. When I was at Alabama, I almost saw one of our players die from the heat. That was the single most moving event.

What traits or skills do your most successful athletes have in common?

Competitive, hard working, detail to their performance and body.

What books or resources do you most often recommend to coaches?

Sport Mechanics for Coaches – The Charlie Francis Method – Supertraining – Skillfit – Science of Sport Training.

"James Baldwin said, 'Not everything that is faced can be changed, but nothing can be changed until it is faced.' Difficult conversations are a part of life, so if they need to be had then we have to engage."

-Dominick Walker

Dominick Walker is in his third season as the Strength and Conditioning Coach for Men's Basketball at Mississippi State University, where he has helped the program accomplish two 21-win seasons and two appearances in March Madness during his first two seasons in Starkville. He came to Mississippi State after serving as the Assistant Director of Olympic Sports at Northwestern University. Before that, he worked at Texas-Arlington, Louisiana-Lafayette, and the Philadelphia 76ers.

Who do you go to when you need advice? Why them?
I have a small group of friends/coaches that will tell me the good, bad, and ugly. Those are the ones I usually go to.

What early job was pivotal in your career? Why?
Working for the 76ers. It helped improve my soft skills, especially when coaching athletes that make more than you, which is the current climate with NIL.

What are your first steps when you start a new job? What do you need to figure out, what do you need to get done, who do you need to get to know?
Getting to know the athletes, coaches, and environment. Then we begin to master the fundamentals.

What advice do you have for a college student looking to break into coaching? Who are the best mentors in the world to work for early in your career?
Work hard, keep things simple, be yourself, and keep coming back. There are many great mentors out there and the best mentor is the one that is most needed for you at this very moment.

If you only had two 30-minute sessions a week to train your team, how would you prepare them?

Sprint, Jump, Push, Pull, Squat, Hinge, and Carry.

What goes into your decision to leave or stay at a job?

At first it was the motif of "climbing the ladder" but now, as I get older, it's more about what's the best fit for me and my family.

What do you do to overcome times of struggle, burnout, or overwhelm? Who do you turn to?

I turn to those who came before. How did others who lived harder lives deal with their problems? Philosophy and history have helped me a great deal regarding this.

What do you think about immediately after one of your athletes is injured? What is your mindset in the following week?

Injuries are gonna happen, so what's next? How can we get this athlete back to form?

How do you approach difficult conversations with athletes, coworkers, or your boss?

James Baldwin said, "Not everything that is faced can be changed, but nothing can be changed until it is faced." Difficult conversations are a part of life, so if they need to be had then we have to engage. Of course, how I go about them will be different depending on the person, but I tend to have difficult conversations as soon as possible. You don't want that feeling to linger.

Do you have a "failure" that was critical to your long-term development or success?

I've had many failures, and it's those failures that have allowed me to continue to feed my higher nature and get better.

What traits or skills do your most successful athletes have in common?

They have a good attitude, do their very best, treat people well, and are unconditionally grateful, under any circumstances.

What books or resources do you most often recommend to coaches?

Anything by Dan John, *The Alchemist* by Paulo Coelho, and *Meditations* by Marcus Aurelius.

"The trait that most of my successful athlete's share is that they are humble and realize it can all be taken away from them. It's a privilege to play a sport, to work hard, to have the opportunities that they have earned."

-Alex Peña

Alex Peña is the Athletic Director and Director of Strength and Conditioning at Prince of Peace Christian School in Carrollton, Texas. He first started working with POPCS as a strength coach in 2000. Peña continued to grow in his role at POPCS over the years, while also helping to develop one of the top high school strength and conditioning programs in the DFW area. He has also worked with countless high school, collegiate, and professional athletes with his own private business. Peña's impact at POPCS led to him earning the position of Athletic Director in 2022.

Who do you go to when you need advice? Why them?
When I need advice, I reach out to my friend and favorite strength coach in the area, Robbie Cardenas. He's been in the DFW area coaching and training for the same amount as myself and in the same youth to high school setting. We discuss ideas and how to improve (become more efficient) our training programs.

What early job was pivotal in your career? Why?
Right out of college, I started interning and then was hired at Plano Rehabilitation hospital. I was working with a wide range of patients, including youth athletes to post traumatic injuries. This helped me understand the importance of progressive training (rehabilitation at the time) and adapting in different settings. In our field, we must work with what's in front of us. My goal is always to improve human performance and create relationships which builds into confident athletes/humans.

What are your first steps when you start a new job? What do you need to figure out, what do you need to get done, who do you need to get to know?
Let's take POPCS—at the time that I came over there was no athletic developmental program (strength and conditioning). I was new at team/group training and used to training in more one-on-one settings. Even in college, it didn't prepare me for the type

of athletes that I had and the need for youth progressive performance development. I had to adapt, grow, create systems and programs that would work with the athletes that I was training. I had to learn quick how to work in a group setting with different ranges of adolescent athletes. I was also making the mistake of doing too much too soon. Once I learned that LESS and QUALITY were the importance of growth in our athletic program, our athletes were soaring.

What advice do you have for a college student looking to break into coaching? Who are the best mentors in the world to work for early in your career?

We see the glamorous side of strength and conditioning, but don't see the number of sacrifices that these young inspiring coaches have to make. Especially financially, in this field you need to be patient, continue to learn, and grow. I was blessed by many mentors in my career and life. Early in my life was my high school football coach— Coach Rodgers, who inspired me to be a better Christian man. He demonstrated how to be a good Christian husband, father, and coach. He inspired me to chase my dream at the time to play at the collegiate level (football).

My next mentor gave me a chance when our school didn't see a need for strength and conditioning development. He was my Athletic Director—Earl Garland—who helped me create one of the best private school strength and conditioning programs in the area. Especially when that position didn't exist in a private school setting. It all came around when I became the Athletic Director at that same private school and hired him as my mentor the first year.

What goes into your decision to leave or stay at a job?

My three factors for a good work setting:

- Financial Stability / Proper Compensation.

- Job Responsibilities (Are they using me to the BEST of my abilities / Do I feel needed or wanted?)

- Relationships with my co-workers, staff, and athletes.

What do you do to overcome times of struggle, burnout, or overwhelm? Who do you turn to?

The goal is BALANCE, which is very hard in our field. Family is the biggest factor for me at this stage of my life. I've learned that my identity isn't in my work, but in CHRIST. It's being a good husband, father, son, and coach so that I can consistently be the best version of myself. Taking time away from my job (vacation and family time) helps me reconnect with Christ and myself.

What do you think about immediately after one of your athletes is injured? What is your mindset in the following week?

I used to take it personal but over the years I realized that what we do will not prevent ALL injuries. We can't prevent, but we can put our athletes in a better position to reduce those injuries. When one of my athletes goes down, I start thinking of a plan to get them back depending on the extent of the injury. I work closely with our sport medicine team to create a plan and timeline.

How do you approach difficult conversations with athletes, coworkers, or your boss?

First, I pray about that hard conversation. I pray that he/she will receive it in a positive manner. I also approach every meeting by praying with my coach, athlete, and/or staff member. If it's very bad news, like a departure from the position or title, I tell them the news right away but follow up by thanking them for their servant's heart. I keep it short and don't drag it out because it's like beating a dead horse (that sounds harsh, but that's how I would like to be treated in a bad situation).

Do you have a "failure" that was critical to your long-term development or success?

I don't have a "BIG" failure, but many mistakes that I've made in my earlier years of training. But I know things happen for a reason. Those mistakes or failures create a better version of yourself and create growth. If we don't fail, we don't learn. But I'm in this position because of my mistakes/failures and have learned from them.

What traits or skills do your most successful athletes have in common?

The trait that most of my successful athlete's share is that they are humble and realize it can all be taken away from them. It's a privilege to play a sport, to work hard, to have the opportunities that they have earned.

What books or resources do you most often recommend to coaches?

I have quite a few books that I've used or would recommend over the years. Here are my favorite:

- *High-Performance Training for Sports* – David Joyce and Daniel Lewindon
- *Strength and Conditioning for Team Sports* – Paul Gamble
- *The Science and Development of Muscle Hypertrophy* – Brad Schoenfeld

> *"Immerse yourself in your craft. You are one of millions. It is not good enough to be good, you have to hone your skills and set yourself apart."*
>
> ## *-Larry Lumbard*

Larry Lumbard is in his first year as Assistant Strength and Conditioning Coach with the Philadelphia 76ers. Prior to Philly, Lumbard spent three years with the Phoenix Suns—two years as the Assistant Strength Coach and his final year as the Head Strength and Conditioning Coach, working with players including Kevin Durant, Devin Booker, Bradley Beal, Mikal Bridges, and DeAndre Ayton. Lumbard worked as the Assistant Director of Sports Performance at Grambling State and Assistant Strength and Conditioning Coach at Tusculum University before joining the Suns.

What early job was pivotal in your career? Why?

My first job as an assistant at a D2 school where we had over 22 sports and only 2-3 coaches. This job was pivotal for me because as an intern I worked at a university with good resources, and leaving there to go to a D2 with almost no resources was a challenge. However, it was great because I learned to do a lot with a little and I learned that as a coach I will always have to adapt to the environment. It also teaches you that you do not need every bell and whistle—find what works best for your program and your athletes.

What are your first steps when you start a new job? What do you need to figure out, what do you need to get done, who do you need to get to know?

The first step I like to take when starting a new job is to meet everyone I'll be working with or around ASAP. Next, figure out what things worked really well before I arrived or things my athletes like/dislike. Next, check out all training spaces and make sure the equipment is functional and there is no safety risk. Then I build out a training plan based on whatever point in the season or off-season it is.

What advice do you have for a college student looking to break into coaching? Who are the best mentors in the world to work for early in your career?

I would advise any college student to first find a good internship, not so you can get the next job, but to see if you really want to be a strength and conditioning coach.

Second, find a mentor. This is critical. They will help lead and guide you. Third, immerse yourself in your craft. You are one of millions. It is not good enough to be good, you have to hone your skills and set yourself apart. Lastly, Network, Network, Network. Especially in today's social media age, it is easier than ever to reach out to other coaches and build relationships.

If you only had two 30-minute sessions a week to train your team, how would you prepare them?

Depending on the sport, Day 1 would be total body lifting and Day 2 would be sprinting.

What goes into your decision to leave or stay at a job?

Currently, the two most important factors that most affect my decision to leave or stay at a job are: Is this a good situation for me to thrive and grow? Is this a good situation for my family—are they happy?

What do you think about immediately after one of your athletes is injured? What is your mindset in the following week?

First I like to see how, if I was not present (video is always good). Next, I'll talk to the athlete to see how they feel and try to keep them in good spirits. I talk to medical staff about what the injury is and a timeline for recovery. Then, in conjunction with the medical staff, build out the return to play plan. Within that first week, I want to get the athlete back training as soon as it's safe, so that they continue to train and retain qualities, but also so that they're mentally involved. Injuries take a mental toll on athletes and it's hard for them to not be able to play the sport they love.

How do you approach difficult conversations with athletes, coworkers, or your boss?

I approach difficult conversations head on! I have seen people shy away or avoid difficult conversations and that never solves anything. Problems don't just disappear. Facing problems or difficult conversations head on means you go into the conversation with a solution in mind, and always stay respectful and approachable. Be willing to hear out all sides of the issue, and always think before you speak.

What books or resources do you most often recommend to coaches?

Conscious Coaching by Brett Bartholomew, *The Quadrant System* by Daniel Bove, and *Elastic Essentials* by Joel Smith. The last one is an online course, but I think it has great information that is applicable to all sports.

> *"Loyalty is when you give your best to the organization while you are with them. It doesn't mean you will never leave the organization. A coach can be with an organization for a long time and not be loyal because they aren't giving their best."*
>
> ## -Joey Burton

Joey Burton is the owner of Joey Burton Basketball, serving as an NBA player development coach that specializes in shooting development and offensive strategies. He is currently a full-time player development coach for Georges Niang, Ed Sumner, and Trey Lyles. Burton previously spent time as a high school basketball coach at three different schools, while also spending five years as the Director of Operations for Women's Basketball at Mississippi State.

Who do you go to when you need advice? Why them?

I have a board of advisors that I can go to regarding different aspects of life.

- Spiritual/Personal Mentor. Offers advice on all areas of life, but specifically regarding leading my marriage, family, and life difficulties.

- Professional Mentor. This is someone who has a great understanding of the coaching profession because they are in it and do a great job.

- Financial Mentor. This person is someone I can go to regarding any business and financial questions I have.

What early job was pivotal in your career? Why?

I was a painter for 10 years. It provided for me financially while offering the flexibility to coach. It taught me the value of hard work, details, accountability, and leading a team. The other job was being a sophomore head coach at 25. It gave me a glimpse into how hard being a head coach is and revealed blind spots in areas of communication, preparation, teaching, and relationships.

What are your first steps when you start a new job? What do you need to figure out, what do you need to get done, who do you need to get to know?

The first thing I do is make sure I'm not trying to be like the person before me. I must be myself. This doesn't mean I don't have the flexibility to operate in areas that have proven to be successful. If I'm working for a head coach, I first want to gain a complete understanding of how they want things done. This has to be done by over communicating with them, you can't assume. Once understanding is achieved, then it allows for me to implement my ideas and systems. Finally, build relationships with those that will serve under you. Find out their strengths and position them to use their strengths to impact what you are assigned to do.

What advice do you have for a college student looking to break into coaching? Who are the best mentors in the world to work for early in your career?

Be willing to work for free or little compensation. Never say no to an opportunity because you don't know what that opportunity will provide. The goal should be learning early, so research and find coaches you respect and want to learn from and do your best to get in contact with them. I quit a sophomore head coaching job to go volunteer for the all-time winningest coach in Illinois history, and it was the best decision I made early in my career. In one year I learned so much about leading a program.

If you only had two 30-minute sessions a week to train your team, how would you prepare them?

I would focus on skill development and concepts of the system I use. This can be done simultaneously through small sided games. More teaching through live play so we can work on offensive and defensive concepts. I also would put an emphasis on shooting development throughout the two sessions.

What goes into your decision to leave or stay at a job?

First, will staying or leaving benefit my family?

Second is for the opportunity for growth. Will the new job allow me to grow more than I currently am?

Loyalty is often brought up. Here are my thoughts on loyalty. Loyalty is when you give your best to the organization while you are with them. It doesn't mean you will never leave the organization. A coach can be with an organization for a long time and not be loyal because they aren't giving their best.

What do you do to overcome times of struggle, burnout, or overwhelm? Who do you turn to?

My faith in Jesus Christ is who I turn to. I'll read the Bible to find encouragement and allow the Bible to change my focus and attitude. I'll use prayer to overcome struggles and burnout. My wife. My board of advisors.

What do you think about immediately after one of your athletes is injured? What is your mindset in the following week?

I immediately want to address their mental state through encouragement and belief. Second, I want to rely and partner with the sports performance and training staff to devise a plan of attack to get the player back to playing. I believe a strong relationship between the sports performance staff and the coaching staff has a tremendous impact on the athlete. Unfortunately, a strong relationship isn't always the case.

How do you approach difficult conversations with athletes, coworkers, or your boss?

Lead by faith rather than fear. It's so easy to avoid conversations due to fear. Make sure the person is edified, and the conversation is honest and beneficial. Remove emotional connection by staying present and humble.

Do you have a "failure" that was critical to your long-term development or success?

I've made many mistakes. The most critical part of my journey wasn't due to a failure, but it was when I was at rock bottom in the profession after spending five years at Mississippi State on the WBB staff. I was the farthest I've ever been from my professional goals. This was a critical time because it forced me to develop my belief system. It created my foundation and philosophy, and it realigned me with my purpose. Without this season in my life, I wouldn't be where I'm at today with the impact I'm having.

What traits or skills do your most successful athletes have in common?

Growth Mindset, ability to suffer and delay gratification, coachability, smart worker, consistency, willing to sacrifice time and money to develop.

What books or resources do you most often recommend to coaches?

- *The Coach's Guide to Teaching* – Doug Lemov

- *How Good Do You Want to Be?* – Nick Saban

- *First Rule of Mastery* – Michael Gervais

"You have to have a vision for them. That vision has got to sustain their doubts. That vision's got to sustain their failures. It's got to sustain their bad days. It's got to sustain when they don't feel like it...It has to be something that drives you to make them better every day, since you're not afraid to confront them, you're not afraid to be demanding, you're not afraid to hold them accountable, because you truly believe it's in them."

-Tom Crean

Tom Crean works for ESPN as a college basketball studio analyst after serving as the Head Men's Basketball Coach at the University of Georgia, Indiana University, and Marquette University. Crean led Marquette to five appearances in March Madness, including a run to the Final Four in 2003. He then led one of college basketball's greatest rebuilding projects at Indiana, returning the program to an elite level with three Sweet Sixteen appearances and two Big Ten Championships. With over 400 wins as a head coach, Crean has been honored as the Coach of the Year in Conference USA and the Big Ten, while also receiving the AP Coach of the Year and Sporting News Coach of the Year awards. He has coached five Top 10 picks in the NBA draft, including All-NBA players Dwyane Wade, Anthony Edwards, and Victor Oladipo. **(Crean's responses were transcribed from a phone call)**

Who do you go to when you need advice? Why them?

You've got to work at your questions. When you have really good questions and they mean something, people want to help you. People want to help you when they realize you're trying to learn and you're trying to get better, but you're not just trying to get something from them. The people that only keep in touch with people when they think they can help them, or when they think they have a job, and they don't keep in touch the other times—it's real easy not to return their phone call. They're only invested in you to the point that you could help them.

For me, I've been fortunate with mentors across different sports that have been so good to me because either a door was opened from somebody else, we got to know each other because we were in the same line of work, or I had questions and they knew I was thoroughly trying to learn. I wasn't trying to learn something from them that I could go share on the internet or go write and share with everybody else. There was a privacy to it. I wasn't looking for show and tell relationships.

I've been involved with some of the greatest in their sports, and the common denominators are—they want to learn too. You might have information or knowledge of something that they can use.

Great leaders love to share what leadership is all about if they know you're sincere. I say this all the time about sympathy and empathy. Anybody can fake sympathy, and it can look empathetic, but it can be fake. You can't fake empathy. It's real. Empathy is investing in people. It's time. It's putting yourself in their position. It's truly looking at it from their side. That's how you learn. That's how you gain relationships. And not everybody's going to do that because they're not going to make the time for you. That's when the people that make the time for you are that much more valuable, because there's something to it and they see something in you. That's ultimately what you want.

What early job was pivotal in your career? Why?
It goes all the way back to the beginning when I got to coach in Division III at Alma College in Michigan while I was going to school in Central Michigan. I was coaching at my old high school, Mount Pleasant High School, and I actually did both jobs for three years because the two head coaches were best of friends. I got a chance to recruit, make a ton of mistakes, be at a lot of events where other Division I and Division II people were recruiting, and I was on the floor in individual workouts with players. I had so much responsibility at a young age before I ever graduated from college—that was absolutely the difference.

I also think my first boss, Ralph Willard, at Western Kentucky for four years, and for one year at Pittsburgh, was phenomenal. It was very demanding and there were a lot of expectations, but he taught me so well. He gave me so much opportunity to get better and let me live through my mistakes. If I hadn't had those experiences, I don't think I ever would have been as ready to be a head coach when I got my first job at Marquette.

What are your first steps when you start a new job? What do you need to figure out, what do you need to get done, who do you need to get to know?
There's nothing more important, absolutely nothing more important, than who is gonna

be in the key roles on your staff. The full staff is obviously very important—it's your key people. Who will have your back? Who will lay awake at night worrying about your success and how the team is doing, just like you're doing as a head coach? You've got to have people you can really count on basketball wise, that you know are going to be relentless, work really hard, and have a real thirst and desire to be involved in recruiting.

You've got to have somebody that can handle the details, the logistics. It's more than just saying, "I need somebody in operations." No, you need somebody that can help organize your staff when you're not around. You want to hire people that are going to bring energy to you, because if they bring energy to you, then the odds are pretty good that they're going to bring energy to your players. It's so hard when you get people that don't want to be teammates, when you hire people that are more like independent contractors.

That is by far the most important, and then absolutely you want to be able to bring in your own strength coach. But if it's a situation where they're there, you have to get to know them and be on the same page with your strength coach, along with your trainer, your academic advisor, and your compliance director. Those components are absolutely crucial if they impact your program daily. Now you'd want to make sure that you've got a great relationship with the people that run the collective, but overall, those parts, strength coach, trainer, academic advisor, and compliance director— they're part of your cabinet. They have to be part of the main branches of how you run your program.

What advice do you have for a college student looking to break into coaching? Who are the best mentors in the world to work for early in your career?

Get around as many of those collegiate environments as you can to watch practice, to watch workouts, to watch training, and if you're fortunate enough—to get into meetings. The more that you can get immersed—seeing how it's done, seeing how it operates, you're taking notes, you're trying to learn, you're looking at the Xs and Os, you're looking at the teaching—but you're trying to get a feel for it. If you do a good job of that, you're gonna learn a lot, but you're also gonna have a feel on what type of coach you want to be. But also importantly is—could I see myself working for this person? Could I see myself working on this staff? The more you get that the better.

You have to be in as many environments for recruiting and where the players are as possible. Not only so you see how people recruit, not only so you get to know people, but also to practice your own evaluation skills. Events are really important for that. High school, junior college, or prep school practices are really important for that. Film is certainly.

Then you build relationships by trying to get it to a two-way street as quickly as you can. The thing that always turned me off is, "I'm ready for that job...I'm ready to work for you...I just need a chance...I know I'm ready." When you're running a program, you need to win now. It's very hard in this day and age to build a program, and then win. You've got to have people that can come in and bring value. It doesn't mean they've got to be able to do everything, and it doesn't mean they've got to be able to make every player on your team better immediately or recruit the best players in the world. What it does mean is they have to bring something while they're learning. Too many people think they're going to get an opportunity to go in there and learn and be a part of the landscape without trying to find different ways to impact. Sometimes impact is just working really hard. Speaking up when you're asked. Not having an opinion on everything. Work and look for opportunities to make the other coaches and the staff better.

You can't have a great staff if you don't know what every position on that staff should entail to be successful. A lot of times, the way you come up teaches you that. So maybe starting at the bottom is good because you're going to learn a lot about what that job entails. But what you don't know and what you're not doing, you've got to study. Whether it's by watching, reading, or seeing, you've got to study it and get a feel for it.

What goes into your decision to leave or stay at a job?
For Indiana, it was growing up and looking at Indiana as an absolute pinnacle of college basketball. Because of growing up in the Midwest, because of Bob Knight, because of competing against Indiana—that was just such a big deal. There was something so iconic about having a chance to coach there. But I don't think you can pick it that way. You cannot make decisions with your heart. Your heart's gotta be in it, but you've got to make decisions with your head, you've got to make decisions on your instincts, you've got to make decisions based on people that you know you're going to be working with. Are they going to support you in all that they're doing and that you're doing?

I don't think you can get caught up in the hype of a job search. I don't think you can get caught up in the hype of a name, especially in this day and age. You've got to go somewhere where you're able to build some traction, because without traction you have no sustainability. It's harder now, because the teams are changing every year, but there's still got to be core things inside of that school and inside of that organization that you can count on.

Number one far and away is what kind of relationship, what kind of trust, what kind of feeling do you not only have about the athletic director, but about the key people that he or she has in place that are going to be touching your program all the time. Deputy AD, Assistant AD, compliance, marketing—you have to feel good about all those things because they're going to impact your program. The other big thing to me when you decide is—even if they're not winning, is there a tradition in the program that you can build it back up to because it's been done before?

What do you do to overcome times of struggle, burnout, or overwhelm? Who do you turn to?

I started to read devotionals, or I would go to hear a sermon in the morning near our house in Milwaukee, and eventually it got to where I just went into the church to pray. There's this tremendous energy that comes from being in there. Maybe there's other people, maybe there's not, but you're just in there. You're reading the Bible, you're reading a devotional, you're on your knees praying. For me, that gave me great energy. You also need something that literally physically gives you energy too, whether it's lifting weights, whether it's running. You've got to have that.

Staffs energize each other. I say all the time, hire people that bring you energy and hire people you can be around on a three game losing streak. Anybody can be around somebody on a winning streak, anybody can be excited on any given day after a win. When it's not going well and it's hard, that's when you've got to have people that can energize you. My best staffs had that, but I also had some staffs that couldn't do that. I had staffs where I made mistakes and they didn't do that. But when we were building Indiana, we for sure had that. We were able to bring the best out of each other. We read when others were having a bad day, including the head coach.

Ministers have been really important to me. The friendships of coaches in other sports have been really good for me. There's some in your sport that can be good for you to turn to, but once you start competing with them, a lot of times it's not the same, it's just not. For me, where I've always gotten a ton of energy is from film. From studying other film, watching NBA games, watching European basketball, coming up with different things in a game plan. I didn't have to have somebody all the time to lift me up. It might be a book at night, but more often than not, it was film.

There's no question—it always is the Bible. My wife Joani has been incredible in that. At Georgia I had some ministers, but I didn't have enough people around me I could really turn to. I probably didn't do a good enough job seeking some out. But every city we've been in there were ministers, pastors, priests in that town that I could turn to that could be really helpful.

What do you think about immediately after one of your athletes is injured? What is your mindset in the following week?

The immediacy for me is to get them to breathe and try to do something that gets their focus off how bad they feel. Then good, bad, or indifferent, whether they're laying there on the floor, whether they're in a training room, whether they're in a hospital bed, or whether they're on a practice court, I'm going to pray for them. I've done that for a long time. Whether it's right or wrong in somebody's eyes, it's never made any difference to me, because when an injury comes, at that point you are moving from a coaching role immediately into a parental role. You're not the doctor. The doctor is there, the trainers are there. You are in a parental role because—I'm 58 and if I got hurt, I'd want to see my wife. There's no question that if I got hurt, outside of my wife or kids, the first person I would want to see is my mother, right? I know she would be caring. You have to have that role.

Then in the immediacy of that, once you're dealing with the initial injury and that person is out of the game or the next few games, you immediately have to be cognizant of how you look, how you sound. That doesn't mean you're not concerned. I've had to get a team going again, and I had tears in my eyes. That's part of it. You have got to give them a belief that the rest of them can still win, that the rest of them can still do what they have to do, that the player is in a position to be helped because of the medical staff. This is what we have to do. You've got to get them there because they're all concerned too, if they care about the teammate. You have to get them back focused on the task at hand. You have to get through the game, no matter what. Whether it happens in the first minute or the last minute, you've got to get through the game. If it happens in practice, you've got to get to the game and through the game.

After that, now you start making your plans and formulating your goals. There's an old adage—next man up. It's not next man up if the next man's not as good as the one that just went down. That's reality. But the reality is also—you gotta figure it out. That's when a leader should be at their very best. When an adverse situation kicks in like that, you've got to give your team a plan, you've gotta give 'em belief, and you've gotta figure out a way to eliminate your doubts, so you can eliminate their doubts.

How do you approach difficult conversations with athletes, coworkers, or your boss?

You have to see the other person's point of view across the table from you. I was a graduate assistant for Jud Heathcote, the great coach at Michigan State, in 1989–1990. One day during a Christmas break, there was a conversation. Tom Izzo was there, Jim Boylen was there, and he was talking about the media. He said, "Remember this—every person has got a boss, and every person has got a family." I'll never forget where I was sitting. I'll never forget hearing that. It made all the sense in the world to me. It's the same thing when you're dealing with people.

Now, the next part of it is this: if you're afraid of confrontation, or you're afraid of being demanding—I didn't say comfortable, no one is totally comfortable in confrontation, but you can't be afraid. Confrontation and demands, they have to come from a place of care, from a place of knowing that person can be better. From a place of, "We've tried this, we've worked at this, but it's not getting through." There's got to be real substance behind the demands, there's got to be real substance behind the confrontation and the conversation that you're having with somebody. It has to come from a good place in your heart, and it's got to be in a situation where it's helpful. When you're letting somebody go, or somebody who's not playing as much, there's still got to be truth behind it. That doesn't mean they've got to like the truth. That doesn't mean they've got to accept the truth. That doesn't even mean that they've got to believe the truth. It's got to be something that you've thought out, and you truly believe it because of the values that you have and because of the way you do things. It's really hard to be a leader. But if you don't have empathy, if you don't have conviction of what you're doing, if you're not flexible enough to change, if you can't look across the table and see their point of view—it doesn't mean you accept it, but you have to see it. If you can't confront and demand, you will not be a leader for very long.

Do you have a "failure" that was critical to your long-term development or success?

Losing in the first round of the NCAA tournament, year three, in St. Louis to Tulsa. That made me understand how quickly it can go when you get into that tournament. How you've got to take every possible step throughout the season to put yourself in the best position and give yourself the best chance at longevity once you get to that tournament, knowing that there's so many factors in it.

After my third year at Indiana, we hadn't won yet, and I realized that the athletic director wasn't just coming to practice at the end of the year to support me; he was coming to evaluate me. To see if I was still good enough to coach that team and if I still had the team's attention. That crystallized for me that the world of trust in college athletics is only as good as your win-loss record. You better understand that. They can say one thing, but when their actions don't back it up, you've got to adjust. We went out and we started to win, but that affected me big time.

When you've lost your job, there's always a time to learn from that. I look at it every day, even with being on television now with the work I'm doing, the research I'm trying to do, the way I study it, that if I'm trying to get better every day and learn, and really learn, not just check boxes, that you can overcome just about any obstacle you're going to see, as long as you have a mindset of getting better, as long as you have a mindset of making your players better, and as long as you have a mindset of making your teammates better. For me in television, it's the preparation, but it's also being a teammate. It's the same thing in coaching. There's always those moments that you realize, "Boy, this has got to really tighten up. We don't have a big net. There are certain things that we can't budge on that we've got to get better at, and we've got to get that started immediately." There's an urgency that comes from failure that can really help.

What traits or skills do your most successful athletes have in common?

They want to be in the gym. They want to work. They might have to be led in their workout, but they don't have to be led to the gym. I have not coached a great player that did not have a level of empathy in their life. Great people, great players, they do truly have a why. It might be that they were doubted. It might be that they were overlooked. It might be that they want to provide for their family. It might be that they just absolutely want to be a pro. There are a lot of different things that go into that why, and a lot of times you gotta dig in deep to find it, to help them find what it is. What they think it is may not be what it really is. What it is—it's something that sustains you. It's something that wakes you up in the morning. It's something that you look forward to the next day. It's something that you can get to in your worst moments and it can bring you back. You've got to help a player find that, because everybody's got it.

You get somebody that loves the gym, and you have to have a vision for them. That vision has got to sustain their doubts. That vision's got to sustain their failures. It's got to sustain their bad days. It's got to sustain when they don't feel like it. You've got to have a vision that is so strong for them, and I've learned that you've got to see it yourself as a coach. It has to be something that drives you to make them better every day, since you're not afraid to confront them, you're not afraid to be demanding, you're not afraid to hold them accountable, because you truly believe it's in them. Eventually, even when they don't see that early, they learn to see that you're for real and you truly do care about them. You gotta convince them you're not trying to get them great so that you make more money or get famous. Certainly, we're all trying to win, and we all want good contracts. But you're trying to get them to where it's something that they can tap into the rest of their life. You've got to be willing to try to get that. You've got to be willing to fight for that on days that they don't want to do it.

Bonus: In recruiting and for the NBA Draft, how do you project an athlete's ability to develop themselves from where they are now? What are you looking at to see who they can become?

It's harder if you don't know them personally, if you haven't seen them come up. You might call 20 people, and they might have 20 different opinions, but there's gotta be some common denominators to it. It's one thing to evaluate, it's a whole other thing to forecast where somebody's going to be. If you get a person that's got a work ethic, a good heart—that doesn't mean they're mature, it doesn't mean that they're not rough around the edges, it's not that at all. But if you've got somebody that's got some drive, some competitiveness, and you look at their hands, feet, hips, shoulders, you look and see, can they see? What are their eyes like? What are their ears like?

Then you look at the characteristics of what's going to be important for them to be basketball players. What's their shot look like? I study misses as much or more than I study a make. How does the shot look? How does it land? How does it come off? Where does it land? How spacefully aware are they? What is their short space quickness like? How do they change ends? Can they move without the basketball? There's so many things that you can get somebody's skills better in, but you have to understand their awareness or lack thereof, their motor or lack thereof, their competitiveness or lack thereof, and their ability to change direction—North, South, East, West quickly.

What books or resources do you most often recommend to coaches?

I read *The Talent Code* by Daniel Coyle my second year in Indiana, and I wish that it would have been available when I first started coaching. *The Gold Mine Effect: Crack the Secrets of High Performance* by Rasmus Ankersen, it's a lot like *The Talent Code*. *God Loves You* by David Jeremiah was a great book that has a lot of coaching and leadership value in it. *Gridiron Genius* by Michael Lombardi, *One Last Strike* by Tony La Russa, *Patriot Reign* by Michael Holley, *Finding a Way to Win* by Bill Parcells.

"Figure out who's going to be an advocate and who's going to push-back. Run with the advocates and figure out how to engage those who'll resist."

-Lee Taft

Lee Taft is highly respected as one of the top athletic movement specialists in the world, known by many as "The Speed Guy." Over the past 35 years, he has dedicated his time to training athletes of all ages and abilities, while also mentoring performance coaches and teaching his multi-directional speed methods. With the release of *Ground Breaking Athletic Movement* in 2003, Taft revolutionized the fitness industry with his movement techniques for multi-directional speed. He has spoken at multiple global strength and conditioning and sports performance events and consulted or held workshops for numerous high-level teams and organizations.

Who do you go to when you need advice? Why them?
The interesting aspect of this question is I have a Board of Directors of people who do not know they are on it. These are people in business, fitness, therapy, psychology, leadership, learning, financial, etc. that I simply read, listen to, or watch when I need help in a specific area. These guys below are examples of people I would read, listen to, or watch when I need support.

- Simon Sinek—Leadership strategies.
- Gary Gray-Gray Institute-Father of Function—really important principles, strategies, and techniques. Applied Functional Science.
- Carol Dweck—Growth Mindset Strategies.

What early job was pivotal in your career? Why?
When I was young in HS, maybe 9th grade, I worked a basketball clinic as a coach for younger kids. This fit like a glove. I knew I wanted to be a coach/PE teacher from this experience. Of course, having my father and two brothers as coaches and PE teachers, AND sisters that were teachers didn't hurt. I've always been the type of person who enjoys helping others achieve—teaching/coaching was a great outlet to do just that.

What are your first steps when you start a new job? What do you need to figure out, what do you need to get done, who do you need to get to know?

The first thing is to get a bird's-eye view of the job and what it is currently doing and how it has been doing it. Second, figure out who's going to be an advocate and who's going to push-back. Run with the advocates and figure out how to engage those who'll resist. Regardless of the job, you must start a feeder program which teaches the up-and-coming participants the "way it's done."

What advice do you have for a college student looking to break into coaching? Who are the best mentors in the world to work for early in your career?

College students must volunteer as much as possible to get valuable experience. Don't allow money to be the driving force when you are trying to break into a very competitive field of coaching early on—get experience. The best mentors are those who have a positive track record of helping others. Winning isn't always a good marker. But a mentor who spends additional time and energy making sure you get the exposure and experience you need.

If you only had two 30-minute sessions a week to train your team, how would you prepare them?

It would be based on need, of course. If it were offseason I would focus on elevating the areas that are holding us back (speed, strength, agility...). In-season, I would dial in those processes which will help us become successful as the season moves forward. Don't think you can ever go wrong staying strong and staying agile.

What goes into your decision to leave or stay at a job?

Am I making a difference! If not, I have no problem leaving and finding a place that needs to be helped.

What do you do to overcome times of struggle, burnout, or overwhelm? Who do you turn to?

I talk to my brothers. They were 35-year coaches and teachers. They give me the advice that seems to re-energize me and get me back on track.

What do you think about immediately after one of your athletes is injured? What is your mindset in the following week?

Instantly, we go into recovery mode. This doesn't mean sit back and relax. It's about how can we get this athlete's mindset off the injury and into training mode so they feel competitive still and like they are working towards something. We strategize on a way to keep them active around the injury. If this is a player that was a major contributor to the team, we quickly pivot and get the "next man up" mentality and go to work.

How do you approach difficult conversations with athletes, coworkers, or your boss?

Confront it right away. The longer it lingers, the more negative energy you carry around. Deal with it professionally and swiftly.

Do you have a "failure" that was critical to your long-term development or success?

I don't think I have any one failure that did it for me...but a series of failures that caused me to rethink my approach to coaching. Meaning, I was a little too volume based in my early 20's as a coach—I quickly figured out I need to adjust in order to help my program and athletes grow.

What traits or skills do your most successful athletes have in common?

Competitive, high effort, they get over "it" quickly and move on, they don't take many shortcuts, they are very coachable.

What books or resources do you most often recommend to coaches?

I am big on getting back to basics of human movement and areas of track and field, my concepts of the 7-Patterns, and grassroots strength exercises from bilateral to unilateral exercises. I want coaches understanding how we move before they take on a specific methodology. From here, they can build a philosophy that fits their coaching style.

> *"The key is keeping in mind you are dealing with a human being and not a machine. There will be good days and bad days. Constantly reminding the athlete of this is important."*
>
> ## *-Daniel Roose*

Daniel Roose is a recognized Master Strength and Conditioning Coach currently in his second stint as the Director of Sports Performance for Men's Basketball at VCU, having returned in 2019. He rejoined VCU after heading to the University of Texas with Shaka Smart. Roose has been a part of multiple conference championships during his time at VCU, and also helped fuel the program's 2011 run to the NCAA Final Four, a Cinderella story that some call the greatest run to the Final Four ever. Before VCU, he was Director of Strength and Conditioning at UNC–Pembroke, Marshall, and Campbell. Roose has helped develop a number of NBA players, including Mo Bamba, Jarrett Allen, Jaxson Hayes, Troy Daniels, Briante Weber, and Vincent Williams Jr.

Who do you go to when you need advice? Why them?
My circle. A trusted group of friends. This includes strength coaches and sport coaches that I have spent time with over the years. This is not sets and reps talk. Real life Stuff!

What early job was pivotal in your career? Why?
In 2007 I was named the head strength coach at UNC Pembroke. A D2 School with 15 sports. Along with my coaching responsibilities, I was asked to teach two courses, Kinesiology and Biomechanics. I approached this initially with a great deal of apprehension. In retrospect, it made me such a better coach after teaching the science of human movement. I am forever grateful for this step in my career.

What are your first steps when you start a new job? What do you need to figure out, what do you need to get done, who do you need to get to know?
The first year in a new position is critical. The nuts and bolts will always remain the same. Cultivating relationships with staff and players is at the tip of the spear and should be a given. The "other stuff" is the secret sauce. Getting outside of the weight room is critical. Showing your face in the administrative building. Attending other

sporting events outside your scope of practice. Figuring out resources in the area that could be mutually beneficial for your program and the community.

What advice do you have for a college student looking to break into coaching? Who are the best mentors in the world to work for early in your career?

It's not for everybody! If your personality is not a fit for college athletics, it will show itself early on. Be a sponge. Find an established coach that is well regarded in our industry and volunteer. Names that come to mind are Jon Sanderson, Darby Rich, Preston Greene, David Deets, Jason Kabo, Charlie Melton, and Charles Stephenson.

If you only had two 30-minute sessions a week to train your team, how would you prepare them?

- Primal Movements—Run, Crouch, Crawl, Climb, Carry, Throw, and Jump.
- Foundational Movements—Squat, Hinge, Push, Pull, and Loaded Carry.
- Train through the full range of motion and find ways to hit the three cardinal planes of motion.

What goes into your decision to leave or stay at a job?

Fun, Family, and Freedom.

- Fun—Am I having fun? Do I enjoy showing up to my job?
- Family—Is my family in a good place?
- Freedom—Am I the CEO of my area? Am I allowed to use my area of expertise to impact development and winning?

What do you do to overcome times of struggle, burnout, or overwhelm? Who do you turn to?

I am a routine guy. This allows me to have balance in my personal and professional life. The routine can change throughout the year with the schedule we all operate on. There are certain aspects of the routine that never change, regardless of the ups and downs of the job. This is what keeps me grounded.

What do you think about immediately after one of your athletes is injured? What is your mindset in the following week?

Injuries are always devastating to me. I take them more personally than I should. I immediately do an audit of my programs to make sure I am not missing something.

The following week is about having a plan and working your plan. The return to play process never goes exactly according to plan. Adjustments on the fly are necessary. The key is keeping in mind you are dealing with a human being and not a machine. There will be good days and bad days. Constantly reminding the athlete of this is important.

How do you approach difficult conversations with athletes, coworkers, or your boss?

HEAD ON! There is no beating around the bush for me. I take a great deal of pride in the weight room being a place of honesty.

Do you have a "failure" that was critical to your long-term development or success?

In 2015 I took the job as the head strength coach for basketball at Texas. I did not approach it with the level of grace and humility that I should have. There were incredible resources there in the form of some amazing people. I was so locked in to training those 15 basketball players that it was hard to see the forest for the trees. In hindsight, I should have been more open to exploring new ideas and tapping into the resources available to me.

What traits or skills do your most successful athletes have in common?

- Intrinsic Motivation
- Terrific Genetics

What books or resources do you most often recommend to coaches?

Dan John, *Never Let Go.* This is a book I gift to all of my graduate assistants in their first semester with me. It covers the "why" behind the basics of squat, hinge, push, pull, and loaded carries. It is so well written and very entertaining.

"I always tell people—our superpower is in our relationships and the realness and transparency that runs across the board, from top down. Our standards and expectations are super high, but Coach Staley meets each player where they are, truly understands them, and then partners with them to grow throughout that journey of the time that they're here."

-Molly Binetti

Molly Binetti is the Director of Women's Basketball Performance at the University of South Carolina, where she has played a crucial role in sustaining an extraordinary level of success, including four consecutive trips to the Final Four and two National Championship victories, highlighted by an undefeated season in 2023–2024. In just six years at South Carolina, she has helped nine players get drafted into the WNBA. Prior to her remarkable achievements at South Carolina, Binetti worked at Louisville and Purdue. **(Binetti's responses were transcribed from a Zoom call)**

Who do you go to when you need advice? Why them?

I was really lucky to get connected to incredible people early in my career, and I don't even think I knew it at the time. When I was in college, I had no idea what I wanted to do, but I had a class where somebody would come in each week and do a presentation. The head strength coach at Marquette came in, and I was like, "This is awesome." I had no idea what strength and conditioning was, but I ended up interviewing him for a project. I went to the weight room, interviewed him, and he was gracious enough to say, "If you ever want to just come observe or help out, the door is open." I showed up the next day at six in the morning and just kept showing up, having no idea what I was doing. But I think of Todd as somebody super instrumental, giving me the opportunity, knowing that I had no experience. I was this very quiet, pretty insecure and shy person at that point in my life. I will always consider him one of the foundational pieces and people in my career.

Because of him opening his doors to me, that allowed me to apply for different internships and to go out to Athletes Performance, or EXOS, where Brett Bartholomew became a huge mentor of mine when I was 22 years old, and he's been a staple in my life. No matter the time or distance that goes by, he's always somebody that has made himself available to me.

Megan Young is another one. She was one of the first women that I really saw in our field that I put on a pedestal. I saw her present at an NSCA conference, and that was the first person I was like, "That's a female doing what I want to do. That's who I'm trying to be like." I got connected with her super early in my career. Just by putting myself in different experiences, doing different things and saying yes, it's led me to be connected to these people. I've always been told and I always tell people now, it's not about the amount of people that you know in your network, it's about the quality of relationships with those people. The one to three, maybe one to five people that are really going to be the ones in your corner that help you navigate different situations. It's so valuable to not think of it as, "What can this person do for me, or how can they help me get a job?" But how can I help create a relationship with this person where I'm providing value to them too? Nobody gets to where they are without somebody giving them an opportunity or helping them in some way. Nobody is self-made. The most rewarding part of being in these positions now is helping other people figure things out for themselves too and helping them along the way.

What early job was pivotal in your career? Why?

I was at my first job for one year, and it was pivotal for me in that I was thrown into the fire without a lot of direction or guidance. That was an important way for me to learn early on and figure things out. I was 23 years old, working at a Big Ten university, not having any idea what I was doing, and I didn't get much direction from the top down. I learned a lot really fast, and did what was natural to me.

At that time, I craved more mentorship. I wanted more direction and guidance because I wanted to be really good at my job, and I know that requires help. When I went to Louisville, it was a complete 180. Everything I thought I knew about how to do my job suddenly seemed wrong. I got all this structure and a systematic approach to everything, which was a whirlwind, but it also allowed me to understand the process of things much more clearly, and to figure out between those two experiences where I fall with my own beliefs. How I coach and the way that I want to do things. That became instrumental as I took this job at South Carolina and had the chance to run my own show and create the environment that I wanted to.

What are your first steps when you start a new job? What do you need to figure out, what do you need to get done, who do you need to get to know?

Initially when I took this job, I did it the wrong way in that I was so focused on what I had to do, I was so focused on the process and the results, and I put a lot of pressure on myself to get those results. On the front end, you need to take a step back to observe and learn from the people around you. Ask as many questions as possible and take note of everything. I work in college basketball, so I need to spend time around our coaching staff and be clear on what their expectations are. Watch film. What are the things I need to know about how we play? Spend time with our players, getting to know them and asking them questions. Obviously about training, but as people—that's the most important part. I need to get to know the greater performance team, whether it's dietitians, athletic trainers, doctors, academic advisors, administrators—whoever else has touch points with the athletes on a daily basis.

Learn about your environment by just shutting up and observing, asking questions, and just taking it all in. Not trying to do too much at the beginning, just seeing how things operate while taking advice and feedback. "What did the person before me do well that you want to keep doing? What do you like as players, as a coaching staff? What are things that you really like and want to stay consistent? What things do you want to change?" Then figure out those small areas where you can insert yourself and make a change, instead of coming in and being hellbent on doing things your way and trying to change everything at once.

Step back, don't try to do too much too soon, learn from the people around you, ask questions, and then gradually change things as you go.

What advice do you have for a college student looking to break into coaching? Who are the best mentors in the world to work for early in your career?

The best way you can get clear on if you actually want to be a coach is to go observe. Whether that's reaching out to one of the coaches at whatever school that you're in and asking if you can come by and watch, or if you can sit down with them for 10 to 15 minutes. Spend as much time in that environment, because a lot of people think that they want to do it, but they don't know what it actually entails.

I've always gotten the advice to pay attention to who is having success or who's doing what you want to do really well, and then find a way to connect with that person. That might be cold emailing somebody. Within that, it's all about how you structure your email, how you address them, how you are considerate of their time—all these things will factor into whether people are going to give you the time of day. But don't be afraid to put yourself out there in that regard, whether it's social media or email.

What goes into your decision to leave or stay at a job?

I've gotten a lot clearer on what I value most in a work environment. The first is having autonomy. I'm in a situation now where I have full autonomy to do my job the way that I see fit and make decisions. That's really important, not being micromanaged, not working for a head coach that wants to dictate what I do, somebody that fully trusts me and my ability to do my job.

The second thing is being in an environment that's collaborative. Working within a team of people that are all on the same page, willing to be open-minded and at the end of the day, find solutions for whatever we're trying to do, while not letting ego get in the way of working together. To win at this level, you have to have everybody doing their job at the highest level and being willing to keep the main thing the main thing, which is putting our players at the forefront of everything.

The third piece of that is an environment that allows you to grow and gives you resources to grow, whether that's financially to do the things that you want, or being supportive of whatever sort of endeavors that you want to pursue from a professional development standpoint. And at the end of the day, you have to be financially compensated for what your value is. I have never agreed with, "Oh, just be grateful for your position." We don't get paid enough as a whole, so being in a place that values you and pays you accordingly is really important.

What do you do to overcome times of struggle, burnout, or overwhelm? Who do you turn to?

I think by the time I was 28, I had experienced burnout twice already. It's hard because we've normalized this coaching lifestyle, especially if you work at smaller colleges or even in Olympic sports. You work sunup to sundown sometimes, and it's glorified. You're not making a lot of money. Typically you don't have a ton of autonomy. Both times I experienced burnout, I was still figuring out who I was as a person. When you struggle with that and in your identity outside of coaching—often we tie our identity to coaching. Then we become so wrapped up in that, and we carry that stress through every part of our life.

That was the case when I was in that 24 to 28 range. When you really become clear on who you are, you don't tie so much of who you are to your job. You can find ways to have outlets outside of work, even when you are feeling overworked. You're standing on your two feet in a much more solid way than if not. What ultimately helped me was getting really clear on who I was while shifting my perspective on my job and what's important and what isn't.

It sounds cliche, but have hobbies to do outside of work and carve out time. Be willing to set boundaries for yourself—sometimes we fall into that pattern of overworked, overstressed, burnout, and we're doing it to ourselves.

Have a really solid support system, whether it's friends, family, significant others. It's a struggle for a lot of us as we move across the country, away from our family and friends, so finding ways to have community in whatever place you're in is huge. If you're not in physical proximity, be able to pick up the phone and carve out time. Oftentimes, we let those things slide when we're feeling a certain way. We just fall off, we don't keep in contact as much, but we need to be super intentional about those things. That has helped me recharge my batteries, even during the times that I feel overwhelmed or stressed.

What do you think about immediately after one of your athletes is injured? What is your mindset in the following week?

It's obviously a case-by-case basis, but initially our brains want to go to, "Okay, let's find the solution. What do we need to do next? What are the things we need to be thinking about?" In reality, the most important thing in that moment, and even the next few days to a week after, is making sure that athlete is in a good space, while understanding that they're probably not going to be, especially if it's a major injury. Behind the scenes, you should be coming up with a plan of action of, "How are we going to go about this? What are the next steps?" But on a person-to-person basis with an athlete, it can't be about a checklist of the things that they have to do. You have to let the athlete have their time to process and come down from everything.

My approach is always to talk to them like a normal person. Let them say as much or as little as they want—don't try to pry and get more out of them. The most important thing in that moment is not their training. Especially if it's a long-term injury, what you're doing with them in the weight room is not the most important thing. Let them see the doctors, let them grieve it. You need to chill a little bit and let that process play out until you're clear on, "Okay, what are the next steps? When is surgery? Okay we're not having surgery, then let's get back into our routine of things and go from there." It's always gotta be athlete first—not even athlete first, person first. Let them deal with the situation, and then you've got everything that you're organizing behind the scenes.

How do you approach difficult conversations with athletes, coworkers, or your boss?

You have to sit on it for a second. It's easy to make a reactive judgment, but giving yourself time to sit back and let the initial feeling die down gives you an opportunity to approach the situation with more curiosity than blame, passive aggressiveness, or whatever it might be. The most success comes from coming at it by either asking questions to get clarity, or by thinking about the "I" statements. When you come at it like, "You did this," you're putting it on them. Coming at it from, "I perceived this, or I feel like this because..." Coming at it from a place of not blaming them usually ends up being a lot more amicable situation. Our ego gets involved and clouds judgment sometimes, and it's easy to get mad if something's not the way that you want it to be. But just take a deep breath, let it die down, and approach the situation when you're in a better state of mind, coming from a place of curiosity and a place of trying to find the solution to the problem.

Also, come from a place of trying to understand. There's a lot that goes on in people's lives that we know nothing about that influences how we act and why we say things. Those conversations are absolutely crucial. You can't avoid them because then things just build up over time. Let the situation die down for a second, but then you've also got to address it pretty quickly after to make sure that everybody's clear on what's happening and where to go from there.

Do you have a "failure" that was critical to your long-term development or success?

There's two major ones that stick out. When I transitioned from that first job to second, my boss was hard on me, harder on me than anybody else on our staff. It made me feel like everything I did was wrong. That was the first time in my career I was like, "Am I good enough for this? What am I doing?" I was pretty miserable my first couple of years there. But in the back of my mind, I just told myself to stick it out, that in the long term if I can make it through this and navigate it, I'll be fine. But that was really the first time where I was like, "Man, I don't know if I'm cut out for it." That changed my mentality to, "I'm going to prove you wrong. I can do this."

That entire process gave me clarity on the things that I believe in as a coach. What are we doing here that I do believe in and I know I'll continue? What about this experience can I learn from that I don't want to do, or I don't want to be like? Initially, we all just copycat everyone we learned from and mimic what they're doing, so those are formative years when you're trying to figure out who you are.

The second failure would be my first year at South Carolina. I came in trying to be this hard ass, "this is how we're doing things" type of coach. Part of that came from being told that's what needed to happen with the group that we had, but it backfired because I wasn't coaching in a way that was true to who I am. I also neglected putting the people first and learning more before trying to come in and trying to change things. We were getting results in the weight room, but it wasn't enjoyable because of the resistance I had from our athletes. They weren't really bought into what we were doing, and it just didn't feel right. That led me down a deep dive of improving my leadership and coaching abilities, creating a better environment, and diving into the intricacies of psychology, human behavior, motivation—all of those things really changed my perspective and how I approached our players.

What traits or skills do your most successful athletes have in common?

The best ones across the board have a really high skill level in their sport. That is always going to be the most undefeated factor in basketball or any sport. But from a characteristic standpoint, the willingness to be open to learning new things and doing things a different way. Oftentimes we get players that are really stubborn and hellbent on doing things a certain way, just because that's what they've always done. They've been successful to that point. But in order to grow, it requires stepping outside of your comfort zone and doing things a different way. The best ones I've ever been around are open to that, but it's not something that usually happens right off the bat. That's dependent on you as a coach, and how you build that relationship and give them space to grow in some of those areas.

The work ethic has to be there. They have to be disciplined, and discipline is so much different than motivation. We know motivation comes and goes based on how we feel, but the ones that do what they're supposed to do, even when they don't feel like it, and the habits that they create in their daily lives are the ones that separate themselves from everybody else.

Bonus: What is it about the way your program at South Carolina operates, how Coach Staley leads the program, that has allowed such sustained elite success?

Obviously we get really good players, but I also know there have been other teams that have had rosters of highly skilled players too. I always tell people—our superpower is in our relationships and the realness and transparency that runs across the board, from top down. Our standards and expectations are super high, but Coach Staley meets each player where they are, truly understands them, and then partners with them to grow throughout that journey of the time that they're here. While our standards are the same for everybody, how each player navigates their way through our program is different, because every player is very different. Coach Staley's ability to adapt to each player and each team that we have and coach them in the way that they need to be coached, I think is unmatched. That's one thing I can say I do a great job of as well— each one's got to be an individual journey, and it's got to be a partnership.

You can't just do it with talent alone. You've got to be able to develop people along the way. That was probably more evident than anything this past year, losing our entire starting five and everybody's new. Nobody's played significant minutes for us, and we are still able to do what we did. I think that's the best testament to that.

The way that our staff works in collaboration and the open communication, the transparency, the directness, the honesty. It's between staff and players too. You can't grow and you can't get where you want to go unless you're willing to have really hard, truthful conversations. I hear from a lot of people, and this is just not as common as you think it would be. I also think that our staff clearly can develop players at a really high level.

But it comes down to the relationship piece, and the realness of that relationship— knowing Coach Staley is exactly how she appears to be. It's not fake. Whether it's in front of the cameras or behind closed doors, she is who she is at all times. And we allow our players to be who they are and find ways to help them improve in their own way. That seems like common sense, but I don't think it's always executed very well, and I think we execute it better than anybody.

What books or resources do you most often recommend to coaches?

I don't read a lot of strength and conditioning books anymore, but *Conscious Coaching* is one that is so applicable. Actually coaching humans and getting the most out of them is what we are paid to do at the end of the day. Anybody can write a program. It's not rocket science. But the results that you get from training athletes are really dependent on the environment you create, how you coach that person, and what you can get them to do. There are so many nuggets in that book, honestly applicable to all professions.

"Being a high school teacher, then football coach, then principal. Those jobs gave me the experience in dealing with people, providing a challenge, being empathetic, setting and completing goals. It gave me a foundation in how to reach and advance people."

-Deland McCullough

Deland McCullough is currently the Associate Head Coach and Running Backs Coach for the Notre Dame Football team, where in 2023 he helped Audric Estimé become the first running back to become an AP All-American for the Irish since 1998. He came to Notre Dame after serving in the same role with Indiana. Prior to Indiana, McCullough was the Running Backs Coach for the Kansas City Chiefs, advancing to three-straight AFC Championship Games and back to back Super Bowls, winning Super Bowl LIV. He was named the NFL's Running Backs Coach of the Year at the 2020 Combine. Before his time in the NFL, he was the Running Backs Coach and Run Game Coordinator at USC, winning a Pac-12 Championship in his lone year there. He came to USC after his first stint at Indiana as the Running Backs Coach, helping the Hoosiers set 19 different school rushing records and winning the 2014 BTN.com Running Backs Coach of the Year award.

Who do you go to when you need advice? Why them?

I turn to a network of veteran coaches and mentors who have decades of experience. Their diverse perspectives help me navigate challenges. Specifically, I often consult with former head coaches and colleagues who have a deep understanding of the game and have faced similar situations. My dad is usually my biggest resource because he coached running backs in the NFL for over 20yrs.

What early job was pivotal in your career? Why?

Being a high school teacher, then football coach, then principal. Those jobs gave me the experience in dealing with people, providing a challenge, being empathetic, setting and completing goals. It gave me a foundation in how to reach and advance people.

What are your first steps when you start a new job? What do you need to figure out, what do you need to get done, who do you need to get to know?

My first steps include understanding the team's culture, meeting with key stakeholders, and evaluating the current roster and staff. I need to establish trust and open lines of communication with players, assistant coaches, and support staff. Setting clear goals and expectations is also crucial in the initial phase.

What advice do you have for a college student looking to break into coaching? Who are the best mentors in the world to work for early in your career?

Start by gaining as much hands-on experience as possible, even if it means volunteering. Learn from experienced coaches and be open to all aspects of the game. Working under coaches who prioritize player development and have a track record of success, like Nick Saban or Bill Belichick, can provide invaluable learning opportunities.

If you only had two 30-minute sessions a week to train your team, how would you prepare them?

I would focus on high-intensity drills that simulate game conditions, emphasizing fundamentals and situational awareness. One session would focus on offense and defense basics, while the other would be dedicated to special teams and conditioning.

What goes into your decision to leave or stay at a job?

Decisions are based on several factors: the potential for growth, the support from the administration, the quality of life for my family, and whether I can make a significant impact on the program. If I feel that the goals and vision of the organization align with my values and ambitions, I am more likely to stay.

What do you do to overcome times of struggle, burnout, or overwhelm? Who do you turn to?

I focus on self-care, including exercise and hobbies outside of football. I also rely on my support network, including family, close friends, and trusted colleagues. Taking time to reflect and recalibrate is essential to overcoming burnout.

What do you think about immediately after one of your athletes is injured? What is your mindset in the following week?

My immediate concern is the player's health and well-being. Ensuring they receive the best medical care and support is paramount. In the following week, my focus shifts to their recovery plan and how we can adjust the team strategy to accommodate their absence while maintaining team morale.

How do you approach difficult conversations with athletes, coworkers, or your boss?

I approach difficult conversations with honesty, empathy, and a solution-oriented mindset. It's important to listen actively and understand their perspective. Being clear about expectations and providing constructive feedback helps in resolving issues effectively.

Do you have a "failure" that was critical to your long-term development or success?

Yes, I had a player that I recruited that I should have taken more time to develop at Rb rather than look to move him to another position. Not only could he have eventually been a good Rb, but he needed my guidance as a person that his new coach couldn't provide. He ended up leaving the school. I recruited him and even though I didn't coach him, I should've continued to develop him as a man. We are connected now, but I wish I was more impactful during his time with me.

What traits or skills do your most successful athletes have in common?

The most successful athletes I've coached share traits like resilience, a strong work ethic, and the ability to remain coachable. They have a relentless drive to improve and a positive attitude, which not only enhances their performance but also inspires their teammates.

What books or resources do you most often recommend to coaches?

I often recommend *The Talent Code* by Daniel Coyle and *Grit* by Angela Duckworth. Both books delve into the psychology of success and perseverance, which are crucial for both players and coaches. Additionally, I encourage reading John Wooden's *Wooden on Leadership* for insights on building a strong, cohesive team.

"The critical long-term development I learned is that your character and how you approach every situation, even the 'bad ones,' can ultimately impact your career. Courage and humility go a long way in getting to your career goals."

-Luke Lancaster

Luke Lancaster is the Associate AD for Athletic Performance at Abilene Christian University, working directly with the Football program. He came to ACU as an Assistant Strength and Conditioning Coach and worked his way up to Director and then his current position of Associate AD of Athletic Performance. Lancaster arrived at ACU after spending time as a Strength and Conditioning Staff Assistant with the Miami Dolphins. Before Miami, he was an Assistant Strength and Conditioning Coach at Harvard, assisting with football and leading 10 programs of his own.

Who do you go to when you need advice? Why them?

My mentors, who include Ted Rath, Corey Smith, Joe Quinlin, and our current head coach Keith Patterson. They have done it at the highest of levels but have also been great teachers to me. They are one of the main reasons I am where I am today.

What early job was pivotal in your career? Why?

My internship at Harvard University. That was my first introduction to collegiate strength and conditioning and where I learned the most. It led to me getting my first job there at Harvard.

What are your first steps when you start a new job? What do you need to figure out, what do you need to get done, who do you need to get to know?

In month one, I want to learn everyone in the organization's name (players, coaches, support staff, etc.) as well as understand the layout of the university, and develop a needs analysis for my athletes. I try to identify the KPIs and look to improve the movement qualities and reduce commonly injured areas. Finally, understand the city/town that I am in and get fully immersed in it.

What advice do you have for a college student looking to break into coaching? Who are the best mentors in the world to work for early in your career?

Harvard University internship program is a great start for all young students looking to dive in the strength and conditioning field. My advice to them would be to learn as much as possible and to not be afraid to reach out to people they look up to in the field. Find someone who is doing what you want to do, talk to that person, ask questions, shadow them, observe them, and volunteer as much as you can.

If you only had two 30-minute sessions a week to train your team, how would you prepare them?

Both sessions would be total body. One day we would focus on speed and plyometrics and the second day we would do a total body lift.

What goes into your decision to leave or stay at a job?

4 P's—does it improve my Pay, Personal life, Progression in my career, and does it give me a sense of Purpose?

What do you do to overcome times of struggle, burnout, or overwhelm? Who do you turn to?

Remember my why. Going home and spending as much time as I can with my son. Having a set "me" time each day, even if it's a 10-minute walk. Also, read the devotional each morning.

What do you think about immediately after one of your athletes is injured? What is your mindset in the following week?

My first thought is, "Are they okay and how serious is it?" Then immediately after that, I think about how the rest of the group is feeling about the injury and how to redirect their attention to the training. The following week I try to keep in constant communication with the sports medicine staff and work to develop a return-to-play plan for the athlete.

How do you approach difficult conversations with athletes, coworkers, or your boss?

I found that 1-on-1 conversations always work best. I let them tell me their thoughts or side of the story. However, it's also important to preface anything that I say to them with, "This may not be what you want to hear, but it's what you need to hear."

Do you have a "failure" that was critical to your long-term development or success?

I wouldn't necessarily call it a "failure" but getting "fired" the first time. Our football coaching staff got let go at the end of the 2021 football season and a new coach came in. He was allowed to bring in his new strength coach for football only, meaning that I would no longer be in charge of football, the route I wanted to go. I finished that following spring training baseball, before deciding to go over to academics to teach. However, I had built a great relationship with the new strength and conditioning coach as well as the new head coach and was allowed to come back and assist them in the summer of 2022. After a year of assisting, that strength coach left, and I was able to return to my old role as the strength and conditioning coach for football at the same university. I learned that your character and how you approach every situation, even the "bad ones," can ultimately impact your career. Courage and humility go a long way in getting to your career goals.

What traits or skills do your most successful athletes have in common?

The most successful athletes are usually the more successful people. They simplify their lives. They do well academically, they compete every day, they train with intent, and usually are some of the better teammates on the team. It goes to show once again that people who have high character, humility, and discipline in their lives usually succeed in all endeavors in life.

What books or resources do you most often recommend to coaches?

I have always been a podcast fan. *Strength Coach Network, Pacey Performance Podcast,* and *Move The Needle* podcasts are my top favorites for human performance purposes. From a book standpoint, *Peak* by Dr. Marc Bubbs is a fantastic overall resource.

"Something I learned that I needed: a place I can work out outside of the office. I need new walls, new music, new people. It helps me from feeling overwhelmed and helps when I need to get some frustration out."

-Ashleigh Beaver

Ashleigh Beaver was most recently the Associate Strength and Conditioning Coach at the University of Alabama, working with the Women's Basketball program. She arrived at Alabama after serving as the Head Sports Performance Coach for the Women's Basketball program at Duke University for five years. Previously, she also gained experience working with a variety of sports as an Assistant Strength and Conditioning Coach at West Point and as an Assistant Sports Performance Coach in her first stint at Duke University.

Who do you go to when you need advice? Why them?

This one truly depends on what the problem is. I go to my mentor first (Will Stephens) when I need advice. If I ever have any issues, regardless of the nature or the size, he is my sounding board.

If I'm having issues with a new product or new training methodology that I need help working through, I will typically rely on my colleagues whom I know are familiar or at least more familiar than I am in that area. In doing so, I know that person has likely already worked through where my issue would be and can help guide me through. Luckily, I feel like more and more strength coaches are willing to talk shop if you reach out when you need it.

What early job was pivotal in your career? Why?

The first one! I knew nothing about S&C except what I had seen at a National Conference. I learned:

- Networking is important: I got my first internship by meeting people (on my vacation) who took a chance on me because I was interested in their field, conducted myself professionally, and followed up with them a few weeks later.

- The grind is real: I have not seen many people who worked as hard as my first boss (Mike Bewley). He taught me so much, but his hustle was unmatched. There was always time to do more. Finished with workouts—go learn something—finished with reading—go clean this—finished with cleaning—start building a clientele. You can always be doing something.

- Relationships matter: It has been 14 years since I was at Dayton and I still communicate, pass workouts, follow up on life with many of those players and staff. You truly can build amazing relationships with some awesome individuals if you make time for others.

What are your first steps when you start a new job? What do you need to figure out, what do you need to get done, who do you need to get to know?

First, I like to go to the weight room and see what I have, what I need, and what I need to figure out how to use. A mental inventory of everything and anything I might need to help me be successful in my new position.

Second, I like to meet my athletes if possible (might be in the summer so they are gone). It allows me time to get to know them, them to get to know me, and see if they can tell me areas that they'd like to improve. It's not just my decision as to what we do. I like athletes to feel involved in the process and have some autonomy in their development.

Third, I get to know my athletic trainer. There are not two people on staff who are going to spend more time with the student athletes than the two of us. I like to pick their brain, understand their philosophies as well as sharing my own. If we can connect and collaborate as much as possible, I believe that is when athletes have the best experience within the performance arena.

What advice do you have for a college student looking to break into coaching? Who are the best mentors in the world to work for early in your career?

Always try to network. Social media makes it so easy to connect with other coaches these days. If you find someone you appreciate/admire—reach out. Be willing to ask for internships, GA positions, and/or shadowing experiences. There is always a chance of getting a position based on your experiences, but there's a greater chance if you know someone who will attest to you and your abilities.

You want to work for someone you align with early (I'm not saying don't work with people you don't align with—those are some of the best people to learn from because you need to experience all types of coaches/philosophies to grow). I am saying that if you're excited to learn and utilize VBT with athletes, and you work with someone who doesn't use technology and that's your first experience—I don't think you are going to have a great one.

If you only had two 30-minute sessions a week to train your team, how would you prepare them?

I'd do two "total body" days. We'd jump, explode, 1 multi-joint/load, core, and carry.

What goes into your decision to leave or stay at a job?

Is this still a place where I can grow? Am I happy in this location? Am I happy with my situation at work? How is the weather (yes, I was ready to leave after 2.5 years because I could no longer handle three feet of snow in April)? How is my relationship with my staff and athletes? Is this still sustainable for my health and wellbeing?

What do you do to overcome times of struggle, burnout, or overwhelm? Who do you turn to?

Something I learned that I needed: a place I can work out outside of the office. I need new walls, new music, new people. It helps me from feeling overwhelmed and helps when I need to get some frustration out. As for burnout, it happens to all of us. I make sure I plan out a vacation each off-season, spend as much time with my family when I can, and sleep more (this is not a joke).

What do you think about immediately after one of your athletes is injured? What is your mindset in the following week?

Injuries are unavoidable. They are going to happen. First and foremost, I wait until my AT is ready to share the information further with me. Then we usually meet: AT, S&C, and athlete to discuss what actions we'd like to take, but allow the athlete to have a say in their recovery. Again—a little bit of autonomy goes a long way.

How do you approach difficult conversations with athletes, coworkers, or your boss?

I typically talk to someone uninvolved (whom I trust) to get my discussion points ready, precise, and so I have practice. I am a very direct person and sometimes that comes off 'mean' or too insensitive. I try to have a mock conversation with my person before I go into these types of conversations to make sure I'm ready.

Do you have a "failure" that was critical to your long-term development or success?

I have a ton of failures. Any new person to our profession is going to have failures. While most you can recover from, you always have to remember it's how you come back or learn from that failure that defines you—not the failure. Take time to be with yourself and reflect on it. I am sure you will find something to pinpoint and say, "Okay, that is where it went wrong or didn't work," and then change or modify so you don't fail again.

What traits or skills do your most successful athletes have in common?

Most of my most successful athletes are self-motivators. They are the athletes in the gym 4-5 days a week. They come and talk to you about what they want to achieve and how you can help. They are getting in the gym with coaches because they asked. They aren't doing it alone—they bring in other people because they want everyone around them to be better. It is a trait that isn't as prevalent anymore, but you'll know when you see it.

> *"Do not let politics and the ulterior motives of others deter you from doing what is right. Stick to who you are and stand on it."*

> ## -Jonathan Holmes

Jonathan Holmes is in his first year as Assistant Video Coordinator and Assistant Director of Player Development for the New York Knicks. Holmes arrived in New York after working with the basketball programs at both Texas Tech and the University of Texas (his alma mater where he was an All-Big 12 Player).

Who do you go to when you need advice? Why them?

I go to my mom when it comes to advice. She knows me better than anyone and does not always tell me what I want to hear. I know that it is coming from a good place.

What early job was pivotal in your career? Why?

I worked as a mover. I was on call and would go into storage units, houses, and u-hauls and load and unload them. It was hard work in Texas summers, but it instilled in me the importance of hard work.

What are your first steps when you start a new job? What do you need to figure out, what do you need to get done, who do you need to get to know?

I have learned to be careful who you trust and open up to in a new job. Sometimes it is better to say less than you know and not be the loudest person in the room. Make sure to go above and beyond.

What advice do you have for a college student looking to break into coaching? Who are the best mentors in the world to work for early in your career?

Find your why, and if your why is centered around you, then find another career path. Do not let politics and the ulterior motives of others deter you from doing what is right. Stick to who you are and stand on it. One of my mentors is Riley Davis, who is an assistant coach at ECU.

If you only had two 30-minute sessions a week to train your team, how would you prepare them?

I would use the full 30-minutes of one of the training sessions to work on the mental and physical toughness aspect of basketball. The other day would be skill and fundamental training.

What goes into your decision to leave or stay at a job?

If I feel like I am making an impact and I am appreciated for the work and sacrifices I have made. Relationships play a big part in it as well.

What do you do to overcome times of struggle, burnout, or overwhelm? Who do you turn to?

I turn to God and my support system. You are going to have multiple times of burnout and questioning if what you are doing is even worth it throughout the course of the season. Having a steady and consistent support system is key.

What do you think about immediately after one of your athletes is injured? What is your mindset in the following week?

If the player is okay, and what I can do to help. Mentally having to sit out is harder than physically sitting out. Making sure that they are in a good place mentally is important.

How do you approach difficult conversations with athletes, coworkers, or your boss?

Head on. I do not like to tiptoe around hard conversations. The way to get progress is to go through it, not around it.

Do you have a "failure" that was critical to your long-term development or success?

Injuries as a player were failures I could not control, but led me to coaching and trying to be successful in this profession.

What traits or skills do your most successful athletes have in common?

Consistency, work ethic, and positive altitudes.

What books or resources do you most often recommend to coaches?

I don't often recommend books, but a couple that I would recommend to coaches and people in general are *Through the Eyes of a Lion* by Levi Lusko and *I am Number 8* by John Gray.

> ### *"When deciding to leave or stay at a job, I ALWAYS ask myself if I have completed the work that I started at the job."*
>
> ## *-Stephanie Desmarais*

Stephanie Desmarais is in her 11th season as Head Coach of the Girl's Basketball team at Johnson High School in San Antonio, Texas. Under her leadership, the program has achieved notable success, including three district championships, ten bi-district championships, six area championships, and two appearances as regional quarterfinalists. No team in school history had ever accomplished any of the titles mentioned above before Desmarais took over the program. She also serves as the TABC All-State Regional Coordinator, and was selected to coach the TABC All-Star team.

Who do you go to when you need advice? Why them?

I go to my family (husband, mom, and dad) for advice often, because I know they will give me good spiritual advice that meets my inner needs first. I also go to a good friend who is a coach because I respect her for her success as a coach (softball) and her longevity in the field.

What early job was pivotal in your career? Why?

My first coaching job was pivotal because I had the opportunity to teach kids the basics (fundamental skills) and really focus on the little things. I also sat behind coaches that I didn't necessarily agree with (in terms of coaching style, decisions made, etc.), but I learned how to follow their lead and try to find effective ways of communicating my ideas. This experience has been essential in developing me as a head coach (because I know what it's like to follow when I agree and/or disagree with the head coach).

What are your first steps when you start a new job? What do you need to figure out, what do you need to get done, who do you need to get to know?

Observe and ask questions. I need to get an idea of the way things work. I like to know my boundaries and what's expected of me so I can try to do that to the best of my ability. As a head coach, I need to know what my superiors (Athletic Directors, Coordinator, principals) are like and what they expect from me.

What advice do you have for a college student looking to break into coaching? Who are the best mentors in the world to work for early in your career?

The best advice I can give to a new coach is to be observant. Observe coaches and their different styles and note the things you like or dislike. Note the things you would do differently and the things you'd like to emulate. Identify your goals and try to link up with a coach who has achieved similar goals and be a "sponge," learn everything you possibly can from them! Don't be afraid to ask questions.

If you only had two 30-minute sessions a week to train your team, how would you prepare them?

I'd first identify the needs that are specific to that team and then plan accordingly. I would set a vision or goal for the team, then write down the steps necessary to achieve that vision, and then try to make the most of the 30-minute sessions by preparing them. I would take one 30-minute session per month to work on the mental health aspects of the game.

What goes into your decision to leave or stay at a job?

When deciding to leave or stay at a job, I ALWAYS ask myself if I have completed the work that I started at the job. I am led spiritually and truly believe that my footsteps are ordered by God. If I don't feel like I'm finished at a job, I don't leave. I live by the motto "the grass isn't always greener." Meaning, quality of life is more important than quantity of life (how much you make). I will stay at my job as long as I continue to be happy and feel fulfilled.

What do you do to overcome times of struggle, burnout, or overwhelm? Who do you turn to?

As a believer, my first source of comfort and recharge is my relationship with Jesus. If I'm feeling tired or burnt out, I always try to talk to Him about it first. I also am very careful about who I talk with about those things. It's important to me to surround myself with people who are positive and encouraging. I also have reached out to other coaches in my area who I know have just bounced back from a stressful situation or a "not-so-successful" season, and seek some advice about how they got through it or how they turned it around.

What do you think about immediately after one of your athletes is injured? What is your mindset in the following week?

When one of my athletes is injured, I immediately think about them. First, how hurt are they? If it's career changing, I make it a point to continue to reach out to them throughout the season and to help solidify a new role for them on the team. It is important to make sure they still feel like they are a part of the team. They need to feel like they are still wanted and needed on the team. If it's a minor injury, then I try to keep them calm and send them to the trainer immediately. I always follow up with them and check on their status mentally and physically.

How do you approach difficult conversations with athletes, coworkers, or your boss?

I pray about difficult conversations before having them. I also try my best not to have a conversation when my emotions are high, giving it some time before I address it or approach the person (players, bosses, and coaches). Sometimes I make notes (bullet points) of what I want to make sure I address and don't forget to talk about.

Do you have a "failure" that was critical to your long-term development or success?

When I didn't get the job after what I thought was a great interview. It taught me to continue to believe and to "push through" at my current job with a good attitude, no matter what is going on outside of it.

What traits or skills do your most successful athletes have in common?

Successful athletes have these things in common: A vision or goal for their future, a positive attitude, enjoy the game, a great work ethic (hard workers), put in hours outside of practice, and an ability to bounce back from losses or failures.

What books or resources do you most often recommend to coaches?

The resource I would say that I most often recommend to new coaches is the *Coach's Outreach Program*. It is a Christian based, coach led Bible study that meets weekly. It is an organized group that includes weekly worksheets that coincide with the Bible and a central theme for the school year. I recommend this because the Bible study is geared to meet the needs of coaches particularly, and designed to encourage coaches through the daily demands and situations that they may be experiencing or have experienced.

> *"To increase your value in their eyes, you need to increase what they value. After establishing this, you reverse engineer their values and raise them through training."*
>
> ## *-Andrew Nilo*

Andrew Nilo is the Assistant Director of Sports Performance at Oral Roberts University, working directly with the Baseball and Women's Soccer programs. He has helped the ORU Baseball team capture the Summit League Tournament Championship in all three of his years at ORU, along with three NCAA postseason appearances and an incredible run to the 2023 College World Series with a school record 52 wins. Prior to ORU, Nilo worked at Missouri State, TCU, Michael Johnson Performance, and APEC.

Who do you go to when you need advice? Why them?

First, I go to my wife or parents. After this, I seek out people who may have experience in whatever I need advice in. I often try to seek people I believe are smarter than me or have a drastically different perspective on things than I do. Family will always give you advice that is wholehearted. I also believe in surrounding yourself with people that are smarter than you and that look at things through a different lens than you do, allowing you to broaden your thought process.

What early job was pivotal in your career? Why?

The most pivotal job for me was when I interned at TCU. I was surrounded by like-minded people and the staff there was considered elite in their field. This place also skyrocketed my network.

What are your first steps when you start a new job? What do you need to figure out, what do you need to get done, who do you need to get to know?

The first step for me is to introduce myself to the AT. This person is going to be your best friend, they are going to clean up your mess if you ever make one. Odds are they are going to look at training/demands through a different lens than you—their opinion is valuable. After this, understanding what the sport coaches value and how they coach, what do they use to determine if an athlete is progressing in development or not. This determines how you present things to them; to increase your value in their eyes, you need to increase what they value. After establishing this, you reverse engineer their values and raise them through training. However, more importantly building a relationship with the staff and players can take you a long way.

What advice do you have for a college student looking to break into coaching? Who are the best mentors in the world to work for early in your career?

Go somewhere that you are valued and poured into, somewhere that when you leave, you come out with valuable experience and knowledge that is applicable. If you want to be a coach, then coach. A quote that has always stuck with me was from Zach Dechant: "If you aren't coaching it, you're allowing it." To put the importance of coaching into perspective, when I hire anyone, could be Intern, GA, Assistant, the first thing I ask their references is if they can coach and lead a room, everything else is secondary in my opinion. Lastly, be passionate, you can't force passion into someone, they either got it or they don't.

As for mentors, go to someone who has a good track record of producing quality mentees and has a good amount of skin in the game. Like I said earlier, go somewhere that will pour into you. The mentors that helped me get to where I am today are Kade Cole, Kelli Selman, Cortney Davis, Bobby Stroupe, Taylor Nelson-Cook, Mason Hays, Zach Dechant, Michael Wood, and Kevin Rodriguez.

If you only had two 30-minute sessions a week to train your team, how would you prepare them?

I will look at the demands that they are expected to handle in the upcoming days and either shoot above that or below it, depending on the team's collective needs.

What goes into your decision to leave or stay at a job?

Family's quality of life, job security, overall fulfillment, job security, income. Yes, job security is labeled twice. Depending on what sport you work with and what your title is, the college sector tends to be a dog-eat-dog world.

What do you do to overcome times of struggle, burnout, or overwhelm? Who do you turn to?

More often than not, burnout occurs when stress is too high, or boredom occurs. If this is the case, find out what is causing the stress and fix it. If it is boredom, then find another rabbit hole to go down and conquer it. However, in the times of burnout, I just take a break from it and find something else that interests me, or I go to a local driving range and attempt to put golf balls into orbit. As for being overwhelmed, this is usually relative to individuals, just stick with it until it's not overwhelming. However, if I do turn to someone, it's going to be my wife and or family/friends.

What do you think about immediately after one of your athletes is injured? What is your mindset in the following week?

If an athlete gets injured during a training session, the first person I communicate this to is the AT. Following this, I communicate it to the sports coach. Furthermore, if an athlete gets injured, regardless of if it was with me or not, I analyze the previous six weeks of stressors that I track and control leading up to the injury. Doing this allows me to see if there was anything I might have missed in the data that could have mitigated or lead to said injury. Regardless, my mindset stays the same, injuries are going to happen, and the rest of the team must continue to progress.

How do you approach difficult conversations with athletes, coworkers, or your boss?

Say what needs to be said and handle it like a professional, regardless of the outcome.

Do you have a "failure" that was critical to your long-term development or success?

Every year I fail in some sort of capacity, whether it be not getting the athlete where I wanted them in time, or not moving the needle in the direction I had in mind. Whether you look at this as critical/impactful is relative. However, I believe failure is everywhere if you look hard enough and are constantly trying to work on your craft. To answer the question—I do not have a significant failure that was critical to where I am today. I do, however, have a handful of athletes that I have injured and have failed to raise certain qualities within training. I believe this is critical for long-term development, simply because your well thought out program/plan didn't work, forcing you to find out the reason for it not to work.

What traits or skills do your most successful athletes have in common?

They understand the process beyond the skill, they naturally set goals for themselves and have a desire to reach them. To complement this, they seek and accept truthful coaching. Self-confidence and the ability to "send it" come easy to them. With this, they must be optimistic. Personally, I believe this gives the athlete the ability to flow and push the boundaries of problem solving. Regarding the sport and relationship with traits/skills, they usually have adapted to certain compensations/adaptations that have allowed them to succeed in the sport they specialize in. These adaptations vary from sport to sport depending on the demands they require. Furthermore, they will leave clues in how they express output, this will give us a piece of the puzzle of why they are successful in what they do.

What books or resources do you most often recommend to coaches?

Supertraining by Verkhoshansky (just the few pages that talk about Repetition method, Maximal Method, Dynamic Method), *Tier System* by Joe Kenn, *Movement over Maxes* by Zach Dechant, *Triphasic Training* by Cal Dietz. These are your foundation/principle books that all strength coaches should read. After these, the world is full of resources that show you different methods, modalities, and philosophies. However, the better you understand principles and laws of biology, the better you will understand training. The best resource is yourself: read a lot, study a lot, apply it to yourself, track everything, and question everything.

"Be open to a number of opportunities. If I had focused solely on the college level like I had originally intended, I'm not certain I would even still be coaching today. I love coaching at the high school level and all the community outreach that comes with it."

-John Garrish

John Garrish is the Director of Athletic Development & Performance and Head Track and Field Coach at North Broward Preparatory School in Coconut Creek, Florida. He is also the Director of Athletic Performance with the Florida Rugby Union's High Performance Program 7's team, and the Founder and President of South Florida Speed School. He announced in May 2024 the founding of South Florida Preparatory School, where he will be the Head of School and serve grades 6-12. Garrish earned the incredible achievement of being named the National High School Strength Coach of the Year in 2022.

Who do you go to when you need advice? Why them?

There are some staff members here that I admire and go to for advice. Reaching outside the profession helps to gain clarity inside the profession. Some of my greatest mentors are teachers.

What are your first steps when you start a new job? What do you need to figure out, what do you need to get done, who do you need to get to know?

First thing is to consider the adjustments and what you'd be giving up in your current career/position. The grass isn't always greener! However, I believe in pursuing dreams and catching fulfillment. The most important thing to learn is what is the job's expectation of/from you? How will you make sure you fulfill those expectations? I try to under-promise and over-deliver.

What advice do you have for a college student looking to break into coaching? Who are the best mentors in the world to work for early in your career?

Be open to a number of opportunities. If I had focused solely on the college level like I had originally intended, I'm not certain I would even still be coaching today. I love coaching at the high school level and all the community outreach that comes with it.

If you only had two 30-minute sessions a week to train your team, how would you prepare them?

I would start each session with some form of speed, agility, and quickness. Likely a short sprint and/or a multidirectional drill followed by a loaded jump, then an Olympic variation or derivative followed by a strength movement and some hypertrophy work.

What goes into your decision to leave or stay at a job?

Timing is huge. A move could be the right thing, but at the wrong time, the move is no longer the right one. Pay attention to the more important things outside of work.

What do you do to overcome times of struggle, burnout, or overwhelm? Who do you turn to?

Take some time to myself, go to the beach, take a long walk, read a book and/or listen to music.

How do you approach difficult conversations with athletes, coworkers, or your boss?

I've struggled with this early in my life and career. Collect your thoughts and say everything that needs to be said. Perception is out of your hands, so you might as well share all that you're thinking and/or feeling to be understood.

Do you have a "failure" that was critical to your long-term development or success?

I got too wrapped up in my career instead of focusing on the more important things.

What traits or skills do your most successful athletes have in common?

It depends. People blessed with athletic talent depend as well; I've seen great force-driven external rotators and I've seen great speed-driven internal rotators and everywhere in between. Size of course varies, as does the commitment level from each of those athletes and what matters to them. Then there are the select few who aren't as gifted genetically but really want it. Those kids put in immense amounts of work and not only put in effort but also study their craft.

What books or resources do you most often recommend to coaches?

I recommend coaches read something outside of the profession. I like to read for leisure and to get my mind off the hustle, so I encourage coaches to do the same. However, there are many coaches and platforms I admire. Namely ALTIS when coaches ask me for sprinting or track thoughts!

"When I was young, I sacrificed family to climb the ladder at all costs. Becoming a head coach was the only goal I had. After my cancer diagnosis and treatment I had a completely different outlook on life and coaching. It allowed me to enjoy the process but also understand that you don't have to immerse yourself in it 24 hrs/ day."

-Drew Long

Drew Long is the Head Women's Basketball Coach at McMurry University in Abilene, Texas. He was named the 2024 American Southwest Conference Coach of the Year in his third season, leading the War Hawks to 16 wins after only winning three games in his first year. Before coaching at McMurry, Long was the Deputy Director of Athletics for Internal Operations at Abilene Christian University for six years. He spent one year as the Director of Athletics and Head Boys' Basketball Coach at Faith West Academy prior to ACU. Long also served as an assistant coach for the men's basketball programs at the United States Air Force Academy, the University of Colorado, and Southwestern University.

Who do you go to when you need advice? Why them?

I typically seek advice from my dad or my brother. My dad has been in the corporate world for 30+ years and has a tremendous amount of experience in dealing with people and stressful situations. My brother is also in athletics and has worked with some of the best programs and best athletes in the country. It's always good to get their input on certain situations and hear how they would approach certain problems.

What early job was pivotal in your career? Why?

My first coaching job out of college was at the Division III level. Even though I was only there for a year, it taught me a lot about a lot. At that level you don't have a large staff, so you have to do everything. Recruiting, scouting, travel arrangements, expense reports, weight training, on court coaching, part-time academic advisor... you name it, I had to do it. It gave me a crash course in what coaching was all about and really challenged me to get out of my comfort zone.

My second job helped solidify my passion for coaching and gave me the confidence to pursue it as a career. I worked for the University of Colorado and started as their Video Coordinator. I learned a lot about game preparation, scouting, and the importance of film. My boss was phenomenal and gave me the opportunity to speak up in practices and staff meetings. He valued my opinions and gave me the confidence to feel like I belonged in this profession. I went on to become an assistant for him and later worked for a colleague of his as an assistant.

What are your first steps when you start a new job? What do you need to figure out, what do you need to get done, who do you need to get to know?

I start a list of people I need to meet immediately. Those who will have a direct impact on my ability to do my job. I try to create genuine relationships with these people because it's important to build trust with those you will work closely with. I'll also meet with those whom I will supervise. I listen and observe a lot before making any suggestions or implementing any changes. I want them to feel heard and have a chance to take ownership of their role. Lastly, I prioritize my to-do list. What needs to be done immediately, what can wait a few weeks, what can be addressed at a later date.

What advice do you have for a college student looking to break into coaching? Who are the best mentors in the world to work for early in your career?

Be patient, be loyal, be willing to listen and learn. There are a lot of good coaches out there at all levels. Just because someone is not in the pros or Division I doesn't mean they're not a good coach. You can learn a lot if you're willing to show up, be present, be prepared, and take advantage of opportunities that are given to you.

If you only had two 30-minute sessions a week to train your team, how would you prepare them?

This is tough, it depends on the time of the year. Offseason is a lot of basics and fundamentals. In-season would be team oriented drills and concepts and schemes.

What goes into your decision to leave or stay at a job?

Family. Is it a fit for me, my wife, and my kids? Is it worth uprooting my crew to chase the next job?

What do you do to overcome times of struggle, burnout, or overwhelm? Who do you turn to?

I talk to my brother a lot about this—at the Division III level you have more down time built into the schedule because you cannot work your team out in the offseason. It's great as a family man but can be frustrating as a coach. You enjoy the time with your family but you also miss the development time with your own team. Basketball is tough because the kids have eight weeks from the start of school to the first day of practice, then another eight weeks from the end of the season to the end of school. You have to rely on the team to stay engaged and coach each other in the offseason.

What do you think about immediately after one of your athletes is injured? What is your mindset in the following week?

I hurt for them, we recently had a freshman go down with an ACL and it was devastating. She had worked so hard to climb her way into the lineup and was having a great offseason when she went down in a game of pickup. You have to keep them engaged mentally and let them know they are still a part of what you're doing. Challenge them to find ways to improve without being on the floor. Can they modify workouts in the weight room, can they work on form shooting, can they watch more film? As a coach, push them to rehab and continue to check in on them, but you also have to prepare as if you might not have that player for a few weeks or even months.

How do you approach difficult conversations with athletes, coworkers, or your boss?

Be upfront and honest. Tell it like it is but be respectful and thoughtful about how you approach it. Most kids and colleagues will appreciate the truth, even if it's not what they want to hear.

Do you have a "failure" that was critical to your long-term development or success?

I had a medical emergency that took me out of coaching for several years. When I was young, I sacrificed family to climb the ladder at all costs. Becoming a head coach was the only goal I had. After my cancer diagnosis and treatment I had a completely different outlook on life and coaching. It allowed me to enjoy the process but also understand that you don't have to immerse yourself in it 24 hrs/day. I try hard to leave work at the office now and I'll try to arrange my schedule around my family schedule so I can make time to watch my own kids play. Now that my kids are older, they come to practice and games all the time and have become friends with the girls I coach. It's helped me become a better dad and a better coach.

What traits or skills do your most successful athletes have in common?
Super focused, attention to detail, very critical of themselves and their performance, never satisfied with how they played.

What books or resources do you most often recommend to coaches?
I rarely read books on leadership and team building. The most important thing is for coaches to be themselves, be genuine in their approach and how they handle people. It's easy to spot a person who is trying to be someone they are not. If you are sincere, you are knowledgeable and care about people, most of the time they will want to follow you. I watch good coaches, good programs, and try to surround myself with successful people. I ask questions about how they do things and why they do things and then I try to find what works for me and my personality.

"I decided to invest in paying another coach to program for me, and essentially coach me. I've found that when I start getting burnt out or overwhelmed, I sacrifice my own training to try to get more done/keep up and then feel worse. This change for me has been MASSIVE. Making something a priority for YOU, and being consistent with that, helps overcome those moments or feelings."

-Brianne Brown

Brianne Brown is in her third year as the Strength and Conditioning Coach for Women's Basketball at the University of Miami. In 2023, Brown helped the program make a run to the Elite Eight. She came to Miami after spending time in the same position with the University of Pittsburgh. Before Pittsburgh, Brown served as the Director of High Performance for the Racing Louisville FC, the Director of Women's Basketball and Soccer Sports Performance at the University of Houston, a GA at Utah State, and Director of Sports Performance for the Women's Soccer Program at Shattuck-St. Mary's School.

Who do you go to when you need advice? Why them?

My two biggest mentors in my career have been Dave Scholz and Alan Bishop. Coach Scholz is one of the most intelligent practitioners I've been fortunate enough to learn under. He is hands down the individual who has influenced my entire philosophy on training, nutrition, and our role as practitioners, and showed me how those aspects of our job can be done at an elite level. Coach Scholz is extremely knowledgeable in a multitude of areas but has also been successful in the results he's been able to achieve with his athletes and coaching staffs. His continual pursuit of knowledge was something that resonated with me and has stuck with me throughout my career. His opinion and perspective is something that I trust 100%.

Coach Bishop has always been a mentor to me, and I was also extremely fortunate to share a room and work with him as a colleague when I took my first full-time coaching role. Coach Bishop is someone that has an unparalleled level of knowledge about training and nutrition, but was also my biggest advocate. He encouraged me, gave me confidence as a young coach, and also treated me as an equal, even though he was much more accomplished and quite frankly was/is way better than I am (haha). He's someone whose opinion I trust, and trust that he'll always be honest.

What early job was pivotal in your career? Why?

My GA position at Utah State. Without even knowing it, I was learning from some of the best practitioners in this industry on a daily basis: Dave Scholz, Joey Bergles, Brandon Howard, Joe Powell, Derek Owings, and James Blackburn. Not only was being surrounded and learning from an amazing group of coaches pivotal, but I was also on the floor coaching constantly. I worked with every team including Football, and I have not learned as much in a 16-month period as I did as a GA. I developed my coaching voice, my philosophy and I also learned how to Olympic Lift from one of the most respected Olympic Lifting coaches, Richard Borden, during my time at Utah State. That time period is where I developed as a coach, and developed into a coach confident to know that I could do this as a career.

What are your first steps when you start a new job? What do you need to figure out, what do you need to get done, who do you need to get to know?

My first priority is to make sure the training aspect of my job is taken care of. Are we training the way I need us to train, is it organized, is it detailed, is it what my head coach wants? Once the training side is squared away, then I'm moving my focus to how does the team operate—and assessing where I can bring or add value in areas that pertain to performance: recovery, nutrition, return to play, technology, assessments, etc. Making sure you're taking time to get to know your athletic trainer and communicating early with this relationship is extremely important. This relationship on the support staff is probably the second most important outside of your relationship with the head coach. Much like training, I always like to create a needs analysis of the program from MY area: assess, plan, and then execute from there.

What advice do you have for a college student looking to break into coaching? Who are the best mentors in the world to work for early in your career?

Find somewhere where you can start coaching. One of the most undervalued skills is being able to actually coach lifts and having the confidence to do so. The best mentors are the mentors you want to learn from. That is going to look different for everyone.

My advice is to decide what is important to you: do you want to learn how to program the best? Do you want to learn how to use technology the best? Do you want to learn about nutrition and training? Once you answer that question—go out and find who you think does it the best and ask to pay for their time to learn.

If you only had two 30-minute sessions a week to train your team, how would you prepare them?

I'd make sure what I was doing was what they needed, and I'd start with creating my needs analysis for training. Every team, player, coach, situation is going to be different. Don't get caught up on what you saw X Program is doing on twitter, or X coach said you had to do in-season. What is best for your team is what is best for the 12-15 individuals you have standing in front of you. Stick to your principles and coach your face off.

What goes into your decision to leave or stay at a job?

I am a firm believer that the best job you can have is the one that you are currently at. That is the job that you would've killed for one year, three years, five years ago. When I am deciding if I am going to leave a current job, the only question I think about is, "Does this move put me closer to my personal and professional goals?"

What do you do to overcome times of struggle, burnout, or overwhelm? Who do you turn to?

This is an area where I've struggled the last couple of years. I've had periods of being burnt out and being extremely overwhelmed. I want to make sure I say this, because regardless of what position, where you work or what your social media says, it's a real thing and can be felt by anyone. This job has become more demanding in the short period I've been doing this for a career, and even more now as we move into this NIL era.

This past year I made an emphasis to focus on my personal training. I decided to invest in paying another coach to program for me, and essentially coach me. I've found that when I start getting burnt out or overwhelmed, I sacrifice my own training to try to get more done/keep up and then feel worse. This change for me has been MASSIVE. Making something a priority for YOU, and being consistent with that, helps overcome those moments or feelings. I turned to one of my friends for help with that, which is why I pay for his expertise to coach me. I also turn to my circle of coaching I trust to vent, get perspective, and honestly just talk to, which usually helps me realize that we're all dealing with very similar things, just at different places.

What do you think about immediately after one of your athletes is injured? What is your mindset in the following week?

I take training, preparation, and development very personally. Those are areas of my job where I put in a lot of time and thought, and ultimately my standards of execution are extremely high. I also think injuries are multifaceted and you can't control everything in these environments. So, when I have had athletes get injured, I take it personally, but I also use it as a situation to learn.

Depending on the injury, I start connecting with individuals that I know have dealt with this before, and start picking their brains about return to play, exercise progressions, tips, etc. I also use this time to go back and evaluate my program—what was the training goal at this point, what had we been doing up to this point, was there anything I would've wanted to change retrospectively, what should I look to improve moving forward? Every injury is different, every athlete is different. Use it as an opportunity not only for your athletes to get better, but you as a practitioner as well.

How do you approach difficult conversations with athletes, coworkers, or your boss?

Being direct and honest is the best way to go about difficult conversations. Some of the best advice I've been given is to speak to facts, not feelings.

Do you have a "failure" that was critical to your long-term development or success?

My first full-time job at The University of Houston was the hardest but also the most critical "failure" in my long-term development as a coach. That was the first year that the training wheels were off and I was the one in charge of my program. I had difficult conversations with other support staff members, had difficult scenarios and conversations with athletes my first year, and had to try to reset the standard and culture of a team. I would get upset, frustrated, and overthink a lot of conversations and scenarios that at the end of the day didn't matter. But what I did learn was that training and holding a high standard was the most important factor that I could control in my job. My first year at Houston definitely exposed me to situations where I had to TEACH my athletes and INSPIRE them to want to get better. Control what you can control, and attack that with all the enthusiasm and effort that you can!

What traits or skills do your most successful athletes have in common?

An internal drive and motivation—not fueled by parents, trainers, coaches. Great Genetics. Great skill level at their sport.

What books or resources do you most often recommend to coaches?

- *The Poliquin Principles* – Charles Poliquin

- *Strength Deficit* – Tim Caron

- *Your Blood Never Lies* – James LaValle

- *Wheat Belly* – William Davis

- *Stop Overthinking* – Nick Trenton

"This period taught me an incredibly valuable lesson that I can't go into a 'woe is me' mindset when things get hard. Instead, I need to find solutions to the problems I'm encountering."

-Connor Agnew

Connor Agnew is the Director of Basketball Performance at Appalachian State University, serving as the Head Strength Coach for Men's Basketball and Golf. In his second season, Agnew helped the Men's Basketball program win 27 games and the Sun Belt Regular Season Championship. Before coming to App State, he was the Head Strength Coach for Women's Basketball at Texas Tech University. Agnew earned his role at Texas Tech after working at the University of Tennessee on both the Football and Olympic Sports side. On top of his position at App State, Connor is also currently the host for the *Samson Strength Coach Collective* podcast.

Who do you go to when you need advice? Why them?
Dan Wirth - Director of Olympic Strength and Conditioning, University of Tennessee. I go to Dan because he has been my primary mentor throughout my career. Dan gives me advice in a way that is constructive and also forces me to reflect on my own actions in order to get the results I want. I go to Dan because when I listen to his advice, it works.

What early job was pivotal in your career? Why?
Texas Tech Women's Basketball S&C was the biggest time of growth for me as a coach. I was challenged each and every day and it made me better as a coach. This job also taught me to not feel sorry for myself when things aren't going my way and instead focus on ways that I can improve.

What are your first steps when you start a new job? What do you need to figure out, what do you need to get done, who do you need to get to know?
The most important piece is to start building relationships with the athletes I work with. I try to FaceTime them or have one-on-one meetings before my first day. This step is crucial as it sets the tone that I will be a relationship-based coach. The second

piece would be to build a relationship with the staff via the same methods.

What advice do you have for a college student looking to break into coaching? Who are the best mentors in the world to work for early in your career?

Build your network as much as possible. Ask to shadow at every location that is feasible for you to get to. Observe as much as possible to make sure that you are genuinely interested in coaching. Don't be afraid to ask questions and maintain the relationships with those you shadow. Find an internship at a high-quality program. The best type of mentor is one who will be honest with you and hold you accountable. You don't want to work with someone who will not help you improve.

If you only had two 30-minute sessions a week to train your team, how would you prepare them?

Full body sessions. Emphasize efficiency with your team. Super-set or circuit every exercise. Teach them how to warm-up/cooldown on their own so those don't cut into your training time.

What goes into your decision to leave or stay at a job?

The drive to work. If my thoughts are overly negative every morning I drive to work, it's time to find a new job.

What do you do to overcome times of struggle, burnout, or overwhelm? Who do you turn to?

Setting boundaries is the best way to overcome burnout. Learning to say no to things that are unnecessary will benefit you greatly during your career. I also turn to my family. Moving closer to my family has provided me opportunities to see them much more often, stopping me from resenting my career. My fiancée is also a major point of support for me.

What do you think about immediately after one of your athletes is injured? What is your mindset in the following week?

Almost every curse word in existence runs through my head. It's hard for me to not feel like it was my fault when any number of factors could have contributed. My mindset within 24 hours is typically negative. However, within the following week I make sure to remain positive as a negative mindset wouldn't help anybody.

How do you approach difficult conversations with athletes, coworkers, or your boss?

I try to be as empathetic as possible and put myself in the other person's shoes before any conversation. This allows me to remove my personal agenda before the conversation. During the conversations, I also make sure that I reinforce the level of care between myself and that other person. If I'm the one leading the conversation, it's because I care about them. And if the conversation is uncomfortable for me to receive, it's usually because the other person cares about me.

Do you have a "failure" that was critical to your long-term development or success?

My biggest failure would be the pre-season prep for my first full-time team. I didn't understand the level of demand the athlete would need to be prepared for and got upset when the sport coaches expressed that my work was lacking. This period taught me an incredibly valuable lesson that I can't go into a "woe is me" mindset when things get hard. Instead, I need to find solutions to the problems I'm encountering.

What traits or skills do your most successful athletes have in common?

The best athletes I have worked with are driven. They understand that delayed gratification will take them far. They exude confidence but not arrogance. They understand the importance of quality relationships with those they work with.

What books or resources do you most often recommend to coaches?

- *It Takes What It Takes* – Provides valuable insight into how to teach your athletes the concept of "neutral thinking."

- *Rich Dad, Poor Dad* – Great for coaches to learn how to manage their money.

- Resources: Other coaches. The most valuable info I've learned during my career has come from other coaches.

> *"As an assistant, what growth is it going to give you? Am I going to go learn a new system? Am I going to learn a different way of how to run a program? Every time you make a move, you should be able to justify two or three ways that it's going to help you grow as you're preparing to be a head coach."*

-Steve McClain

Steve McClain is an Assistant Coach for the Men's Basketball program at the University of Texas, where he has helped the Longhorns advance to the Elite Eight and win the Phillips 66 Big 12 Championship Title over his first two seasons. Before joining the Longhorns, McClain spent 14 total years as a Division I Head Coach, five years at UIC and nine years at Wyoming, totaling 233 wins. He has also spent time as the Associate Head Coach at Indiana and Colorado, and worked as an assistant for Georgia and TCU. McClain started his career as a JUCO assistant, working his way to become Head Coach at Hutchinson (Kan.) Community College, winning the 1994 NJCAA National Championship, and winning the NABC-Kodak National Coach of the Year in 1994. During his career, he has coached multiple NBA draft picks, including Anthony Edwards, Victor Oladipo, Cody Zeller, Noah Vonleh, and Alec Burks. **(McClain's responses were transcribed from a phone call)**

Who do you go to when you need advice? Why them?

I've been fortunate to have worked for some high-level coaches. When I look back on it, it starts with the guy I worked for in junior college, Dave Farrar, and learning from him. Working in a community college gave me an opportunity to establish an unbelievable network of mentors. Eddie Fogler is another guy that I really learned from early in my career. I always turn back to the people like that, and then the other young coaches that became my friends. Long before I worked for Tom Crean at Indiana, we had become very good friends as young coaches. As you grow as young coaches, you continue to help each other grow, and they become mentors and friendships.

What early job was pivotal in your career? Why?

I started as a JUCO coach, and the greatest thing about that was that I had to learn early to manage programs and to do everything on my own. To be the academic person, to be the strength coach, to get them where they needed to go, and yet also manage the day to day of putting the practice together and how to organize it.

What are your first steps when you start a new job? What do you need to figure out, what do you need to get done, who do you need to get to know?

Whenever you start a new job, you first have to understand—why were you hired? What is your strength? Before you even try to worry about that, figure out how you fit within your staff. Early in your journey, be way more of a listener than you are a talker. Figure out—what can be my niche in this program? What do I bring that this program doesn't have, but they really need? Before you try to show everybody what you can do, learn what the situation needs out of you, and what your strengths can bring to that situation.

What advice do you have for a college student looking to break into coaching? Who are the best mentors in the world to work for early in your career?

Everybody wants to start at the top, but where you start isn't the answer, it's where do you want to finish? What are your goals down the road? For some young coaches, it may be, "I want to be a teacher and a high school coach." Okay, then when you're in college, are you already trying to find the local high school where you could go over and be a volunteer assistant and start learning what it is to be a coach? If I'm at a college, can I go be a manager for the team? Maybe it's not the basketball team, maybe it's the football team—any way I can get in at a young age to start to learn the organizational things. In reality, I am building my mentorship. Most coaches think that if I want to be a basketball coach, my mentors all have to be basketball coaches. That isn't necessarily true. Your mentors can be coaches from other sports, you can learn from any level of coaching. The key is finding mentors that have been successful. Forget about what they coach. Why were they successful?

What goes into your decision to leave or stay at a job?

Let's talk about being an assistant coach first. As an assistant, what growth is it going to give you? Am I going to learn a new system? Am I going to learn a different way of how to run a program? Every time you make a move, you should be able to justify two or three ways that it's going to help you grow as you're preparing to be a head coach.

How is this helping me get to my ultimate goal of being a head coach? What am I going to learn differently in this situation? If I can't answer that question, then I shouldn't be making the move. You never want to make a move just to make a move. It has to be about growth.

When you get opportunities to move as a head coach, you have to measure the same thing. By leaving this head job to take another one, what am I creating for myself and my family? Is it all about money? Too many guys throughout their careers, it becomes about the money, yet it may be a move that ends your career. Even when you make the move as a head coach, is it going to allow me growth? Is it putting me in a situation that I have more than what I had in the other head job? If you can't answer those questions, you shouldn't be making that move to another head job.

What do you do to overcome times of struggle, burnout, or overwhelm? Who do you turn to?

Burnout is a funny word to me. People ask all the time, "How long will you coach?" My answer is always very simple: the day it's not fun, I won't coach. The pressure will eat you up if you can't enjoy pieces of it. Somebody told me this once, and it's very true—in coaching, we don't enjoy the wins, because we're always worried about the next game. If you get to where you can't even enjoy the wins, then it means the job is eating you up. At some point, you've got to sit back and truly enjoy the wins. Enjoy the process of the wins, because it is a process. The more you can do that, then you won't have burnout. You'll walk in everyday excited to do what you do. That may sound too simple, but life's too short. You have to enjoy the process of it.

What do you think about immediately after one of your athletes is injured? What is your mindset in the following week?

I've had players that have had season ending injuries. When you have real relationships with your student-athletes, those decisions become about them understanding that all I want to do is help you make the best decision you can for your career. The disappointment of the injury will be there, but how do we get ready for the future after the surgery? You might be out for four weeks. Okay, we're going to watch film during those four weeks. We're going to keep your mind on growing and treating your body right now. Then the minute they can be back on the court, they might have to sit in a chair to do ball handling. They might have to sit in a chair to shoot. Get their mind back focused on, "I'm going to get this right now," and get them off of the, "Woe is me, I got hurt, now what happens with my career?" We have to get past that. We have to worry about how we are going to get better every day. You try to turn what is a negative situation in the beginning into, "Okay, now we gotta get ready to grow." How are we going to grow and get better from this and not let it become a crutch that holds us back even farther?

How do you approach difficult conversations with athletes, coworkers, or your boss?

Conversations are only difficult if you don't have a relationship with the person you're dealing with. If you have a relationship, difficult conversations aren't difficult. Difficult conversations usually become easy once the other person knows you care about them and you're only trying to help them. If you didn't care, you wouldn't be having a difficult conversation. Most people take every difficult conversation as criticism. It's not criticism, it's trying to help them grow.

Do you have a "failure" that was critical to your long-term development or success?

Whether you get fired, whether you have a bad season, you always have to go back and look at yourself. There are definitely points in your career where you have to evaluate why you failed, and then try to work really hard to make sure that doesn't happen the next time you get an opportunity. Sometimes failure—there's nothing you can do to control it. Yet we all learn in life, you have to control the controllables. That's where you have to go back and look in the mirror.

What traits or skills do your most successful athletes have in common?

They're able to truly do the old statement—look in the mirror. They can evaluate themselves. The network of people they have around them tells them the truth. When they're not good, they tell them the truth. When they're really good, they tell them the truth. The most successful guys I've been around have truth tellers around them, and they understand they need those people around them. The cliché that I could give is that they all worked hard. That's a given. Any high-level athlete works hard. What's the separator? The separator is the kids that have the truth tellers around them that tell them, "No, it's not good enough. No, what you're doing outside basketball or football or baseball, your social life, that isn't going to get you where you want to get." Those are the people that have success.

Bonus: When recruiting athletes, how do you weigh character and talent? And with the condensed recruiting timelines of the transfer portal, how are you uncovering who an athlete really is and making those decisions?

Every kid has a history, and every coach has a history. As you evaluate young people, whether it's a high school kid or someone in the transfer portal, it comes back to intel. It's what you try to tell every kid that dreams of being a pro—everything you're doing on social media, everything you're doing in your personal life, can be found. Even though things move quickly, you still have to do the homework. Every one of us can find something that is out there that opens the door to find more information. We can all make a mistake, but if you're really locked in, then you're going to find the answers you want on anybody you're trying to recruit.

"Just because you can do many things and have your professional plate overflowing doesn't mean you should. The quote/analogy I use for this is, 'If more was better, Golden Corral would be a 5 star restaurant.' I used to be Golden Corral—I did a lot of stuff and my plate was full. I now strive to be the Ruth Chris steak house of strength and conditioning. More isn't better—better is better."

-Greg Goldin

Greg Goldin is in his second season as the Director of Men's Basketball Athletic Performance at Penn State University. He was most recently a Human Performance Manager with the US Navy, and before that the Director of Strength and Conditioning for Men's Basketball at LSU, helping the Tigers earn a trip to the Sweet Sixteen in 2019. Prior to LSU, Goldin was the Director of Men's Basketball Sports Performance at VCU, the Head Men's Basketball Strength and Conditioning Coach at Chattanooga, and the Director of Strength and Conditioning for Men's and Women's Basketball at Murray State.

Who do you go to when you need advice? Why them?

I normally go to my previous mentors or previous coworkers. We all have blind spots in our own lives. The people you have previously worked for or with know things about you that you might not know about yourself, or are aware of things about you that you again aren't aware of. They know how you tick and they most likely know your reactions to things from a previous situation. I will always go to these people first when asking advice so they can lead me through my "blind spots" and make more sense of my reality than even I could.

What early job was pivotal in your career? Why?

My internship when I was first starting out at VCU. It was the summer of my junior going into senior year of college. After applying to every internship on StrengthScoop. com (no joke, it was every single one), I got a call from Daniel Roose at VCU and he asked if I wanted to spend the summer with VCU basketball. I drove down from upstate New York and had little to no idea what I was getting myself into; all I knew was that it was going to be an awesome opportunity. I had a spot to sleep on the video coordinator's floor...until the grasshoppers infested his apartment (most likely too long of a story for this forum).

After that, since we had a locker room in the weight room that wasn't utilized, I made that into my "apartment." I gave tee shirts to the guys that had a sandwich shop in front of Lowe's so I could get a sandwich every day, then it was normally muscle milks and chewy bars for the rest of my diet (which is a combination I still consider a delicacy).

My biggest takeaway was no matter the job you take, no matter what situation you find yourself in, nothing is perfect. You need the ability to "figure it out." This proved to me I can do it no matter the circumstance and to not let the "problems" of a situation stifle the opportunity that is in front of you.

What are your first steps when you start a new job? What do you need to figure out, what do you need to get done, who do you need to get to know?

First steps in my mind are why you got that job in the first place. What was the reason for the coaching change? Did the strength coach leave and for what reasons (you better know those reasons prior to signing your contract)? Did the entire staff leave for a better opportunity? Did the entire staff get fired? That will then set your sights on your next steps. If the entire staff did an awesome job, what is currently going well within the program and how do you build on it? Did the entire staff get fired? If yes, what are the problems programmatically and systematically that you will need to build on?

Historically, my first thing to figure out is the facility. Facilities drive programming. Honestly look at the facility, see the interworking of your weight room, and your program will be driven off this. Train in it immediately, see every in and out of the facility from how strange the J-hooks are, maybe the clips are terrible—you don't know unless you train in it and see how this will hamper or help the logistics of your training sessions.

First and foremost, you need to get to know your team and staff. Each person, get to know them and make a connection with them early. Get to know the person behind the jersey first and see how best you can serve that person. Secondly, find someone who has been attached or a "fly on the wall" of the previous program/someone who will tell you the absolute truth of where your feet find you. All programs have negative things about them, not everything is always sunshine and rainbows—find the person who knows those things and take them to get a coffee as many times as it takes to get the information you need to build on the opportunity which is in front of you.

What advice do you have for a college student looking to break into coaching? Who are the best mentors in the world to work for early in your career?

- Are you sure you want to do this?

- What sport do you eventually want to specialize in?

- Your first job, take the job with the greatest number of teams. Sport is transferable. I am thankful for my years of being with a ton of teams.

- Get to know as many sport coaches as possible. Yes, strength coaches make hires and we all need a network of strength coaches, but at the highest level sport coaches have final decisions. Get to know as many sport coaches as possible who you would eventually want to work with or for.

- I'm glad you know the Krebs cycle, and the insertion point of the teres minor—can you carry on a conversation? What soft skills do you have? Can you drink a beer or have a coffee and not talk about training? Take it seriously, but don't be weird.

- How many retired strength coaches do you know? At the time of writing this I know one. So go be great at your role, and maybe you will be the generation of the retired strength coach. Until that point, you better have transferable qualities to something besides barbells and dumbbells.

- Keep your hobbies—learn the guitar, go to the Brazilian jiu jitsu class, go play golf, and don't stop no matter how "busy" you get.

- If you call yourself a strength and conditioning coach—be strong and in condition. Be able to show things with a high level of skill and strength. Practice what you preach.

- Don't chase money, school names, or the "next step." Chase working for a head coach that cares about you as a person and cares about your development professionally. Chase a coach/program that lets you maintain your hobbies, that allows you to have date nights with your significant other, etc.

Daniel Roose, Ryan Horn, and Tim Kontos: I was EXTREMELY lucky to have worked for this group of guys. They set a great standard. In my eyes, they are still the standard of what a professional strength and conditioning coach is all about. Work for people who know where you are at, love you for where you are at, but also see great potential in you for who you are becoming.

If you only had two 30-minute sessions a week to train your team, how would you prepare them?

Dan John's five basic human movement patterns coupled with an Ethan Reeve's flavor of density training. Keep it simple, keep the session moving.

What goes into your decision to leave or stay at a job?

I love this question. Early on I didn't have a process. I do now thanks to AJ Kerr who introduced me to this; I am lucky to have AJ in my life as a trusted friend and former coworker.

This is the "6 P'S": PLEASE read this and share this with as many people as possible.

Rank the Role—6 P's

- First step is to read the list below and rank them for yourself, or if you are married, rank them with your partner.

  - Purpose—Does what I do matter?

  - People—Am I surrounded by good people?

  - Personal—Do I have enough time to do the things I want to do personally?

  - Professional—Am I getting better professionally?

  - Pay—Can I pay my bills and save some money?

  - Place—Do I like where I live?

If you have a job with 1, 2, or 3, you actively look for a job with 4. If you have 4, you are slowly yet deliberately looking for a job with 5. If you have a job with 5 you are lucky. If you have a job with 6, you never leave. After you rank them, maybe you have 4, but maybe you only have the bottom 4 of your ranking—you will most likely still be unfulfilled. These will also change throughout your life and different seasons of life. I challenge you to do this exercise for where your feet find you right now, see how many "P's" you have, be honest with yourself, make decisions after that.

What do you do to overcome times of struggle, burnout, or overwhelm? Who do you turn to?

I remind myself that all those feelings are a choice I am making of how to look at the situation I find myself in. Sometimes it's as simple as making another emotional choice and re-framing my mindset. I will normally call and check in with former coworkers and friends to seek guidance through the situation.

What do you think about immediately after one of your athletes is injured? What is your mindset in the following week?

My mindset is always how can I in my role best serve the people around me? The mindset doesn't change, modalities do.

How do you approach difficult conversations with athletes, coworkers, or your boss?

- Have the talk—don't wait.
- Run everything that gets said through two filters 1) is it honest? 2) is it good?; If it passes those two filters, say whatever needs to be said.

Do you have a "failure" that was critical to your long-term development or success?

Most of my early failures were thinking that my job was absolutely everything to who I am as a person, and then everything in my life that truly mattered suffered because of this. From a long-term development standpoint professionally, I put a high emphasis on work-life balance (which should be called life-work balance). My no means no, and my yes means yes. As strength and conditioning coaches, we can do a lot of things at a high level. Just because you can do many things and have your professional plate overflowing doesn't mean you should. The quote/analogy I use for this is, "If more was better, Golden Corral would be a 5 star restaurant." I used to be Golden Corral—I did a lot of stuff and my plate was full. I now strive to be the Ruth Chris steak house of strength and conditioning. More isn't better—better is better.

What traits or skills do your most successful athletes have in common?

They always have the best version of themselves in mind. They do the things they don't want to do today in order to have better tomorrows. They realize their limits are for pushing through and not stopping at. They have an invested interest in expanding their own human potential.

What books or resources do you most often recommend to coaches?

Dan John—doesn't matter which one, read everything from him, apply what works for your program. Mike Boyle—read everything and apply what works for your program. Jordan Peterson—*12 Rules for Life: An antidote to chaos.* Everyone with breath in their lungs should read this book, but especially coaches.

"Try to get into situations where you can observe and connect with as many coaches as you can. If you can coach in front of them (like at camps), even better, and then invite feedback."

-Becky Burleigh

Becky Burleigh is a member of the University of Florida Athletics' 2024 Hall of Fame Class, recognized for her foundational role in starting the Women's Soccer program in 1995. She led the Gators for 26 seasons until her retirement. In her fourth season, Burleigh guided the team to victory in the 1998 National Championship. During her tenure, her teams secured 22 NCAA Championship berths, made two NCAA College Cup appearances (1998, 2001), and won 14 SEC Regular Season Titles and 12 SEC Tournament Titles. With 513 total wins, she ranks fourth all-time in NCAA women's soccer history. Burleigh was named the 1998 NSCAA/Adidas National Coach of the Year and received the SEC Coach of the Year award five times. Throughout her career, she coached 37 All-Americans, including the 1998 National Player of the Year, Danielle Fotopoulos. Additionally, she is the co-founder of What Drives Winning, a company that emphasizes character skills, leadership, and the creation of winning cultures.

Who do you go to when you need advice? Why them?

Brett, my business partner, has such a wide view of experiences that other coaches have had to manage. Other coaching/administrative colleagues to help when I have not had that particular experience.

What early job was pivotal in your career? Why?

Becoming a head coach at 21 at Berry College, but with a great support group of coaches and an AD who mentored me was critical.

What are your first steps when you start a new job? What do you need to figure out, what do you need to get done, who do you need to get to know?

Ask a lot of questions and observe to get a good lay of the land before coming in and making big changes.

What advice do you have for a college student looking to break into coaching? Who are the best mentors in the world to work for early in your career?

Try to get into situations where you can observe and connect with as many coaches as you can. If you can coach in front of them (like at camps), even better, and then invite feedback.

If you only had two 30-minute sessions a week to train your team, how would you prepare them?

How are we going to interact and play for one another, and let's have a simple executable strategy that we can all stick to.

What goes into your decision to leave or stay at a job?

Am I still growing? Does the environment give me the chance to work on myself? Does it match my values in a way that I don't have to make compromises?

What do you do to overcome times of struggle, burnout, or overwhelm? Who do you turn to?

Take a step back to determine what's really causing the friction rather than just getting wrapped up in my emotions.

What do you think about immediately after one of your athletes is injured? What is your mindset in the following week?

How can I help support them through what might be a first and quite disturbing to their identity, while still keeping my focus on the team?

Do you have a "failure" that was critical to your long-term development or success?

Every time something doesn't go as I had hoped is a great chance to self-reflect.

What traits or skills do your most successful athletes have in common?

- Empathy: great teammate.
- Curiosity: will always want to be better.

What books or resources do you most often recommend to coaches?

Honestly, it's all of the *What Drives Winning* books. Just such great tools and help that are so specific to what we do every day as coaches. I've also referenced *Fierce Conversations* by Susan Scott for help in having difficult conversations.

"The passion behind coaching is a good thing, but our passions can quickly influence our emotions. When emotions drive your decisions, your clarity for what you want to get out of the conversation becomes muddled."

-Evan VanBecelaere

Evan VanBecelaere is in his third year as the Head Coach for Student-Athlete Performance at Pittsburg State University. He joined Pittsburg State after spending four years as the Director of Men's Basketball Strength and Conditioning at the University of Oregon, where he played a pivotal role in helping the Ducks win two Pac-12 Regular Season Championships, one Conference Tournament Championship, and reach two Sweet Sixteen appearances. Prior to his time at Oregon, VanBecelaere served as an Assistant Strength and Conditioning Coach for the Sacramento Kings and as the Director of Sports Performance at Santa Clara University. He was instrumental in the development of several NBA draft picks, including Bol Bol, Payton Pritchard, and Chris Duarte.

Who do you go to when you need advice? Why them?
Most of the time my Father because I know he is on my side and will tell me things I don't want to hear, but that I need to hear.

What early job was pivotal in your career? Why?
Working for my Dad at his manufacturing plant. It is a line of work that is not sexy or fun by any means and is some of the most blue collar work you'll see. It was about 110 degrees in there from the months of June-August, and you would leave there greased up head to toe. I knew that if I could do that job, I could do anything.

What are your first steps when you start a new job? What do you need to figure out, what do you need to get done, who do you need to get to know?
When I first start a job, my goal year one is to build quality relationships with anyone I will work with (Admin, Coaches, Athletes, Maintenance staff, etc). This is my time to let those around me know I value their working relationship. It is best to find out the strengths and weaknesses of how things operated before to figure out if I can help

accommodate those needs.

What goes into your decision to leave or stay at a job?

· Location of the job.

· Quality of Life with said job.

· Pay.

· The Job itself (will I enjoy it).

If I can only get 1/4 or 2/4 then it is probably not worth chasing unless I am in need of feeding my family. If I can get 3/4 then it is worth considering, and if I can get 4/4 then it's probably a job I could see myself in long-term and maybe even for a lifetime.

What do you do to overcome times of struggle, burnout, or overwhelm? Who do you turn to?

No one likes to answer God anymore, but I am going to say it anyway. The person I turn to is Him. He is the only one I can find true rest in, and He is who I can lay all my burdens on. It doesn't mean I don't still experience struggle and hardship, but it allows me to trust that He will work through those issues.

What do you think about immediately after one of your athletes is injured? What is your mindset in the following week?

Where did I fail that certain individual in not preparing them to handle the demands that were placed on them? Was it the training that wasn't sufficient? Did I do a poor job of communicating with the AT/Coach/Dr.? Did I not speak up enough on training loads? After I have worked through these questions and ultimately come to the understanding that injury happens and is a part of the sport, I can get myself in the mindset of starting that preparation phase for the athlete.

How do you approach difficult conversations with athletes, coworkers, or your boss?

Prior to any difficult conversation, I pray for humility that I do not let my emotions drive the conversation, but that I approach it from a place of sincerity that points more to the objectives that are being addressed. The passion behind coaching is a good thing, but our passions can quickly influence our emotions. When emotions drive your decisions, your clarity for what you want to get out of the conversation becomes muddled.

What traits or skills do your most successful athletes have in common?

Trust and compliance. When athletes can fully surrender themselves to your care, they stop listening to how others prepare and trust that your vision is the only one they need to achieve success. This is not to say that I know more than others, but the more voices that someone listens to, the more complicated the process becomes.

What books or resources do you most often recommend to coaches?

I am not a huge reader, but anytime I try to pick a book it needs to fill 1 of 3 buckets: Spiritual growth, Professional growth, or Emotional growth. Obviously, these can crossover and help fill the buckets of the other, but in my mind I have always found success in trying to approach the book I am reading to help the growth in one of those three areas. Currently the ones that I believe have helped fill those buckets the most are:

- Professional growth: *How to Win Friends and Influence People*

- Spiritual Growth: *He Leadeth Me*

- Emotional Growth: *The Energy Bus* (cheesy, but still one I refer to)

> *"But boy did I want them to feel comfortable in what they did well. We were persistent in trying to put them in those situations. Players will perform for you if there's a trust and a creation to get them to those spots where they're comfortable. Then you let them be who they are."*
>
> ## -Dan Hughes

Dan Hughes was inducted into the Ohio Basketball Hall of Fame in 2024. His head coaching career includes two WNBA Championships, two WNBA Coach of the Year Awards, and 281 career wins (5th all-time). He is an exceptional developer of both players and coaches, demonstrated by the fact that seven of his assistants have become WNBA head coaches. Additionally, several of his former players have had notable coaching careers, including Dawn Staley, Becky Hammon, and Tricia Binford. From 2009 to 2016, he served on the USA Basketball Women's National Team Player Selection Committee. Hughes was then an Assistant Coach for the National Team from 2016 to 2021, contributing to Gold Medal victories in both the 2018 FIBA Women's World Cup and the 2020 Olympic Games. **(Hughes's responses were transcribed from a Zoom call)**

Who do you go to when you need advice? Why them?

I go to my wife more than anybody. It's been a partnership for 40+ years. That's the beginning point for me. After her, I've had various people that I have gone to for advice, and it's really changed. A lot of times it might have to do with where I was. I've gotten advice from players. Somebody who knows you really well might give you the best advice. I probably chased someone who had insight into me and what I was about to decide. As my kids got older, they were also great sounding boards for me. They told me when I was wrong, and rather quickly. You gotta have somebody who can play the role of reflection back to you, and you need someone that you can talk to. Not everything that I said to my wife would I want repeated. Sometimes I was just frustrated, but she would sift through that and then bring it back to me in a way that moved me to the next page.

Bonus: How did you put yourself in a place to learn from your children and your athletes, when many might feel that their role as a coach or parent is just to teach?

I was in Tokyo with USA basketball and Brittany Griner, and we got to the point where we would have conversations with each other after practice. She asked me, "Where do you learn?" I said, "I learn a lot from my players," which she was surprised by, but we had a wonderful conversation. Learning can come at you even in the middle of trying to coach, it can come to you from them. I never cared where I got a good idea. If it's a good idea, it's a good idea.

What early job was pivotal in your career? Why?

The first time you're a head coach is a very critical time. I was 22 years old, and it was critical because when you're a head coach, you own the success of your team and the success of your relationships. It's different as an assistant, but as a head coach you own it, you deal with it, and you find out how badly you really want to be a basketball coach or a person in charge.

What are your first steps when you start a new job? What do you need to figure out, what do you need to get done, who do you need to get to know?

It's totally about culture. I know that's a buzzword that everybody uses, but how you approach the day to day, how you build relationships—and not just with your players, but how you build them with your staff, the people you work with, and your fan base. Your day-to-day walk is gonna tell all those people more about what's important to you than all the words, interviews, or sound bites you put on TV. The majority of my life, I was a builder. I almost always took over programs that were not necessarily good, and I can't think of a position I took where they didn't fire the coach ahead of me. It was about establishing culture and starting those things, because success didn't always come on the doorstep, it came along the way.

Bonus: Would you have approached it differently if you entered situations where the previous head coach left because of success?

No, I wouldn't have. I was heavily influenced by a lot of good coaches, but I never tried to be them. I was okay with who I was, and I was a little different. I tried to come across as a good guy, but people that played with me went through a transition trying to understand what I wanted. I didn't do it like their predecessors. Even if I'd have followed a great coach, I would have tried to create a culture that identified with me. I don't think I would have changed in that way because I do believe there are different ways to win. There are certain players that somebody else might get more out of than me, but I also think there are players I get more out of. I'm fairly good at identifying who's good for me and maybe who's not.

What advice do you have for a college student looking to break into coaching? Who are the best mentors in the world to work for early in your career?

Coaching is a great profession. I obviously would be a proponent that this is a good way to live life. I would alert them that it's a way of life, as opposed to a job. If you're not really into a way of life, then at some point you're going to get tested.

Mentors take all kinds of forms. You need to look right in your life, and it doesn't have to be the biggest name on the page. A great mentor might be somebody who honestly cares, and who honestly will give you a reflection of truth. They probably need to have a common interest with you and have some experience that allows them to do that. You can have great mentors that could be your mother and father, and should be in a lot of cases. My dad was the person who told me about the WNBA, and my dad is not a basketball person, but he read about it in the paper. He knew I wanted to be a head coach, and he said, "This might be your ticket." Sometimes in life, we don't realize who really cares for us, and that might be your best mentor.

If you only had two 30-minute sessions a week to train your team, how would you prepare them?

From a priority standpoint, I would try to accomplish something offensively and defensively so that I was balanced. I would try to accomplish something that had carry over to the times we didn't practice. It was interesting to me, I went to another practice just this past week of a WNBA team and enjoyed it a lot, but what I noticed was there wasn't a lot of individual work before or after, which I think is essential.

I did not practice for long periods of time. I tried to allow them to create some developmental skill work on their own, and then I would try to prioritize what we did together. I'm not saying what this team did was wrong. I'm just saying that for me, the only way that the players could get the work they needed is if they put a lot in themselves, because I didn't attempt to do that. I'm one of the few coaches that probably could say, "Okay, if I got 30 minutes, I got 30 minutes. We'll make it work."

Bonus: Was that extra individual work a result of the players you selected for your teams, or the culture of your team and how you practiced?

To me, it's all about players. I can have a wonderful culture—and I do think it's important. As I told you, it's the first thing that I do. But players are the essential piece. The types of mentality your players bring, the types of talents—I never overestimated what we did as more important than who did it. I do think it's important how you create teams. Who you put together with who really matters. It's not about the 12 best players on a team. People lose sight of that. They even lose sight of that in USA basketball. USA basketball is very successful, but it's not always about putting the 12 most talented players on the court together. There's got to be a positive energy to the role you're going to have, and that doesn't always fit the 12 most talented players.

What goes into your decision to leave or stay at a job?

Most of the times that I left, there were events that led to me moving. A desire to be a head coach, or a team folds. I was in Cleveland, and I could have coached in Cleveland the rest of my life, but Gordon Gund sold the team to Dan Gilbert and we weren't part of the sale. I had to get a new job. But to be honest with you, I turned down a lot of opportunities because it didn't fit my family life. I had a daughter that went all 12 years in one school, which is pretty hard to do as a professional coach. It was the same thing with my son. Those things mattered to me. I didn't want a life where my life impacted them, because they both were Division I athletes, and continuity was important. There were many times when jobs came at me that I just wasn't interested.

What do you do to overcome times of struggle, burnout, or overwhelm? Who do you turn to?

You better have a support system. It helps a lot if you've got a staff that does that, but that's not always the case, just to be blunt. You probably need family, you need friends, and you don't need a lot of 'em, but you better have people you can talk to. It's hard if you're really competitive, and you're used to creating a culture and then finding success with that. You need a gauge as a coach as to, "Am I getting what I should get from a team?" It's twofold. I've had good teams that didn't attain what they should have attained. But I've also had teams that were less than average, who gave me a lot. You need to have a sense of that big picture as a coach and leader, because if they're giving you what they can, and now you are disappointed in that, it's going to undermine what you're trying to do.

What do you think about immediately after one of your athletes is injured? What is your mindset in the following week?

The mindset was to give them a little space. When it's a major injury, you show your concern, but I didn't try to overdo it. I allowed them a little space to process what that meant to them. Then you go about building a relationship that shows that you're involved with them, whether it's eyes on when they're in the training room or when they're working out. But I was never overly active with them. I usually gave them space, and then I would periodically intervene with them, and certainly make them aware that I was aware.

How do you approach difficult conversations with athletes, coworkers, or your boss?

Genuine and direct to the point. I announced what the elephant was in the room immediately. Whatever was there that was causing us to meet, for me to raise concern, I went right to it. After I went right to it, then I showed them I had some depth of understanding, how this might impact them. I didn't bring the problem and just dump it. When I had to cut a player, that's the first thing I said. "We're gonna have to let you go." But then I would talk about maybe how difficult this was and a little about their options. But I always delivered it first and up front.

The Spurs brought me out when Greg Popovich went into the Hall of Fame, and Becky Hammon, one of my players, also went in. I wrote him a nice note just thanking him, he'd been a great friend through the years. He wrote me back, and he said something to me I will always treasure. "Dan, you've always been genuine." And boy, I tried hard for that. It wasn't an act that I put on it, it's just how I roll. But the fact that he recognized that was one of my strengths, that made me feel good. That's where I think you can develop trust with people, and that trust can go a long way as you maneuver landmines of a season or a life.

Do you have a "failure" that was critical to your long-term development or success?

I was a head high school coach for four years, and I had two really good teams in my first job. I took another job, and I had awful teams. We won two games one year, I think three the next. It taught me the essence of how important players are to this process, and that there's gonna be events. I took the job and three of my best players all had events that took them off the court before I ever coached. It taught me you have to be able to deal with failure to have success. I never had jobs where we were already good and we had a culture that carried over into what I did. You've got to have a level of persistence, and you've got to do things in a way that your team, your administration, and your fans—even though you're not winning on the scoreboard—you're winning in relationships, so that they give you time to overcome some of the events that can keep you from being good.

What traits or skills do your most successful athletes have in common?

As I coached them every year, they were talented, but they added something to their game. They have an unquenchable thirst to be better. Even as an older player, I don't think that ends. The other thing that is apparent is that they want the moments that will define success for them and for their team. They wanted that moment. All I needed to do was to get them that opportunity, and then with that opportunity, they created success. That wasn't created by Dan Hughes, it was created because we were just smart enough to put them in that moment and let them be who they are. That really happens with the great ones.

Breanna Stewart is an amazing talent—she was MVP the year I coached her in 2018. We come out of the huddle, and she would just own that moment. I don't know if that moment always looked exactly like all of us thought it would look, but it was owned by her. We'd be in a close game, we'd come in and we'd talk about it, and then all of a sudden—she steps out and nails a three. I remember Suzie McConnell Serio was a great player for me in her last year. We need this win to get into the playoffs, and I had a side out of bounds play. She gets open on the side out of bounds, there was other action for her to evaluate—she was a great decision maker—but the truth was she squared up. She jabbed, stepped back, and just nailed a three and we won. I had all kinds of action for her to make decisions or to create so that they couldn't double team her, but the reality was all she did was jab step, step back, make a three, we're in the playoffs.

Bonus: Do you focus more on enhancing your players' strengths or bringing up their weaknesses?

I'm going to speak tomorrow at a clinic and the ages are fifth to seventh grade, and I'm going to talk to them about working on different skills to improve. But if you're talking about a professional, they're there because we felt they had some sort of skill at the professional level. For them and for us to really be successful, we've got to get them to express that skill. I would hope we're good enough putting together teams that we don't have five people with the same skill. I very much wanted to put them in positions and trust them, and let them feel that a coach trusted them in these areas. Now, I didn't give that to them in some of the areas that they were average or below. I in no way wanted to make them feel comfortable there. But boy did I want them to feel comfortable in what they did well. We were persistent in trying to put them in those situations. Players will perform for you if there's a trust and a creation to get them to those spots where they're comfortable. Then you let them be who they are.

Bonus: You've done an incredible job of mentoring your assistants to become head coaches. How did you empower your staff to grow into those roles?

I was probably a little bit of a one man show at the beginning, and then some events forced me to use my assistants better, like health. I was watching the Minnesota game the other day where the coach got hurt and he couldn't move the sidelines, so he was using an assistant to play call. I went through that. I had achilles tendon surgery and different things. It forced me to use my staff in different ways and be open-minded to get them in their sweet spots.

I became not only a coach of players, I became a coach of coaches. I tried to open the door so that the team was just as interested in what they were going to say as what I was going to say. There was a time that I had a really good staff, but I could tell certain players only really listened to me. They responded more to me. I tried really hard as my career went along to get them the trust that was needed to respond to good coaching, whether it was coming from the head coach or the assistant.

Bonus: If certain coaches on your staff could communicate best with certain players, did you delegate conversations to those coaches when you needed a message delivered?

Absolutely, it was essential to me. I was fortunate that I had a lot of long-term relationships with players. I had players that I coached for 10 years. Not all of them really enjoy you coaching them every day. It's just a fact. I looked at where an individual coach could spend time with them, usually after practice, and help prioritize some things we were doing with that player with a different voice. That player could complain about me. I wanted a relationship where that player had somebody to talk to, to get it off their chest. "I don't understand why Coach Hughes has me doing this. I don't get this." But then they have another voice that is allowing that picture to be created in the player's mind. Not coming from me, I've already tried to do that. Now I had an assistant who could listen, could maybe in some cases understand, but could also help put them in a position as to why this strategy made sense. I had several, and they were VITAL to me. I could not have had those long-term relationships with players without those vehicles of assistants becoming a part of the learning process, separated from me. And having a real relationship with the player where that player wasn't afraid to say, "Hey, Coach Hughes is just wrong." I'm sure they heard that, but before it was over, they'd get them in the right spot to go to the next day. I think people knew that in my league. Almost all of those coaches who formed that went on to head jobs and further success, because I think that became a reputation.

When you're selecting or you're working with coaches or with players, I could put up with people who could complain a little bit. I couldn't put up with people whose actions spoke badly. I had a lot of players I love to death who might say something, but they never took actions I thought were destructive. Never. I didn't have assistants that really went that way, or I didn't bring it out in them, because I think they felt a lot of ownership. If they're feeling that way, there's a pretty good chance they're having to own some of that. You can draw a different kind of loyalty when they feel they have a big part of what you're doing.

What books or resources do you most often recommend to coaches?
Daniel Coyle and *The Talent Code*. It was brought to me by Chip England, the shooting coach for the Oklahoma City Thunder. He was at San Antonio with me when he gave me the book, and man it just knocked me out. I gave it to my wife, I gave it to almost everybody. That's the one. The great thing about *The Talent Code* is it's not all about basketball. It's about people and different walks of life, and it really taught me different learning styles. Without question, I think it's the best thing I've ever read.

"When you build something from scratch and pour your heart and soul into its success, it makes you have so much pride in the end product. It makes you want to do whatever it takes to ensure that it is as impactful as possible to all of your athletes and the community as a whole."

-Heidi Henke

Heidi Henke is in her 23rd year as the Head Volleyball Coach at Prince of Peace Christian School in Carrollton, Texas, where she is the winningest coach in school history with 671 victories. Henke started the Prince of Peace program in 2002, reaching her first state championship match only a few years later in 2007. Since 2007, she has led the program to 14 district championships, 13 state final four appearances, seven state championship appearances, and three state championship victories (2011, 2013, 2019). Henke spent two years as an assistant at Lutheran High North in Houston before starting the Prince of Peace program.

Who do you go to when you need advice? Why them?

My husband—he was a collegiate athlete and has coached and been an athletic director for 25 years. My dad—he was a coach and principal for 40+ years.

I go to them because they are very good at seeing situations for what they are— without filters, emotions, and sugar coating—and they guide me with advice that is helpful and productive and are not afraid to tell me when I'm wrong. They always help me see things from other perspectives so that I can make the best decisions for my program.

What early job was pivotal in your career? Why?

I was the first HS coach at POPCS—this was pivotal for me because I learned how to build and maintain culture in my program. When you build something from scratch and pour your heart and soul into its success, it makes you have so much pride in the end product. It makes you want to do whatever it takes to ensure that it is as impactful as possible to all of your athletes and the community as a whole.

What are your first steps when you start a new job? What do you need to figure out, what do you need to get done, who do you need to get to know?

I've been at Prince of Peace since 2001...and before that I was only an assistant coach for two years at another high school. I haven't started a new job for 23 years—and when I did start at POP, I had to figure out everything on my own because the program didn't exist. But first and foremost, I needed to get to know the athletes so that I could convince them to buy into what I was trying to build. I also needed to get to know the athletic director and principals so that they could see what I was working towards and have them as my biggest supporters.

What advice do you have for a college student looking to break into coaching? Who are the best mentors in the world to work for early in your career?

The most important lesson I learned when I was young...it's not about me. And that was a tough one for me. But when I learned this, my program took off. You have to love and care for the kids as people first, athletes second. You have to be invested in growing them as strong Christian young women and then the volleyball stuff comes after that. I believe my success as a coach is 100% based on me focusing on ministry and relationships first. Winning is a by-product of this. The best mentors to work for are the ones that understand this—it is all about relationships.

If you only had two 30-minute sessions a week to train your team, how would you prepare them?

Fundamentals – mental toughness – the rest is extra fluff.

What goes into your decision to leave or stay at a job?

My situation is different than most. For one, I built this program from scratch...so 23 years of hard work and commitment makes it tough to walk away. Second, my kids—like my own biological children—Prince of Peace is where I want them. Not only are they getting an exemplary education, but they are being built in their spiritual faith by loving teachers and coaches that guide them each day. So, why have I been here so long? Because this place is not only my home, but it's home for the other five members of my immediate family. Prince of Peace isn't just a school, it's a community—and I know that's not how it is most everywhere else. My husband and I have been blessed to be here for 23 years working together every day—with our kids in the same building as well. We know we are blessed to be here and we adapt however we need to in order to keep our family here.

What do you do to overcome times of struggle, burnout, or overwhelm? Who do you turn to?

My husband, my assistant coaches, my athletic director—these are the people in my life that I am closest to. I know this isn't normal, but I'm blessed to have the people in these positions be my best friends.

What do you think about immediately after one of your athletes is injured? What is your mindset in the following week?

My immediate reaction is that we need to get the best treatment possible for the athlete, and I want them on a regimen to get back on the court as quickly as possible. For me, an injury doesn't excuse them from any team responsibilities—they should still be at practices, film sessions, team meetings, going to eat with the team, attending games, etc. But they should also be spending the extra time needed to get themselves healthy as quickly as possible.

How do you approach difficult conversations with athletes, coworkers, or your boss?

I always like to have a third party present for any and all tough conversations. That way, nothing can be misconstrued or misquoted. But I do believe in confronting the individual directly. Many times, I've found that problems can be easily remedied if all parties are on the same page and understand each other's perspectives.

Do you have a "failure" that was critical to your long-term development or success?

I had one season where a good portion of my team's parents wanted me fired. I probably didn't handle the stress very well due to my own stubborn nature, and also the fact that I was pregnant and hormonal at the time. I got through the tough time with the support of my AD, principal, and assistant coaches. But I definitely learned a lot about ministry. I learned to over-communicate with my athletes and parents regarding different situations. I learned a lot about it not being about me, but putting my athletes first. And I learned to be very up front about tough situations—not to avoid the tough conversations, but to have them more often, because when those that are disgruntled know that you care, it changes how they react to your decisions.

What traits or skills do your most successful athletes have in common?

Grit. By far the most important character trait of my successful athletes. The ability to face challenges head on without feeling sorry for themselves or making excuses. Being coachable—my best athletes are those that constantly seek to be coached and never finish learning.

> ***"'You don't need to be an expert at everything, but you do need the experts' phone numbers.' I've since tried to build a network of experts whom I can consult for advice on specific training, coaching, or technique styles."***
>
> ## *-Mike Niklos*

Mike Niklos has served as the Director of Athletic Development at Acceleration Sports Performance in the Greater Chicago area for nearly 15 years. Additionally, he has held the roles of High Performance Manager and Organization Defensive Coordinator for Midwest BOOM Football for almost 12 years. Prior to his current positions, Niklos was the Head Strength and Conditioning Coach at Naperville North High School. He also gained collegiate experience working at Northern Illinois University and Robert Morris University before his tenure at Naperville North.

Who do you go to when you need advice? Why them?

During my internship at RMU, Todd Hamer's advice resonated with me: "You don't need to be an expert at everything, but you do need the experts' phone numbers." I've since tried to build a network of experts whom I can consult for advice on specific training, coaching, or technique styles. This approach has helped me solidify my principles without getting bogged down in methods, as we've experimented with various popular methods but stayed true to our principles. I'm fortunate to have a remarkable wife who, having transitioned from performance to Physical Therapy, ensures that I maintain focus on the essentials of training without overcomplicating things as I tend to do.

What early job was pivotal in your career? Why?

I've tried to take a little piece of knowledge from everywhere I've worked. Working for my dad in high school and pursuing computer engineering helped the concept of reverse engineering and always aiming to improve outcomes. My time at Verizon Wireless further deepened my understanding of a high-performance model, emphasizing collaboration across departments to achieve shared goals. As a server for many years, I learned how to take command of a floor as well as the ability to multitask.

What are your first steps when you start a new job? What do you need to figure out, what do you need to get done, who do you need to get to know?

I've been fortunate to have only one major job in this profession, my current one. Before that, I held various internships, some beneficial and others not so much. However, I see parallels in the private sector when working with new teams and their staff. My initial approach is always to establish expectations with the coaches or those in charge, clarifying what they expect, and laying out my own objectives. Understanding specific KPIs, athlete culture, and any pertinent information beforehand has proven immensely helpful. Setting these expectations and standards upfront makes communication smoother among all parties involved. Early in my career, the lack of such discussions led to misunderstandings and even ended some team collaborations because what they sought from training didn't align with what I provided.

What advice do you have for a college student looking to break into coaching? Who are the best mentors in the world to work for early in your career?

My best advice is to distinguish yourself during your academic journey. This might involve pursuing additional minors, such as data analysis, or gaining practical coaching experience with local teams or through internships. Exercise Science is a broad major, and it can be challenging to navigate without supplementing your studies.

Regarding mentors, while there are numerous practitioners offering valuable resources, the ideal mentor is often a matter of personal preference. For me, my first mentor and current boss is my brother, who instilled in me a commitment to continuous improvement and a mindset of reverse engineering. Tom Myslinski and Todd Hamer were also influential early mentors. While Milo unknowingly served as a mentor by introducing me to the profession, Hamer emphasized the importance of ongoing growth and learning. These mentors not only shaped my coaching style, but also provided the necessary structure for my personal development.

If you only had two 30-minute sessions a week to train your team, how would you prepare them?

To me, this entails two approaches. If athletes already have two 30-minute sessions dedicated to their sport each week, those sessions should prioritize their specific sport training. In such cases, I would focus on integrating sprinting, jumping, or throwing exercises that complement and enhance their performance in their sport without detracting from it.

What goes into your decision to leave or stay at a job?

I'll go with Keir Wenham-Flatt's 4 P's: Personal, Pay, Purpose, and People. If all four aspects are satisfactory, stay. If three out of the four are good, consider leaving only if another opportunity offers all four. If one to two aspects are lacking, leave.

What do you do to overcome times of struggle, burnout, or overwhelm? Who do you turn to?

I believe every coach experiences moments of doubt, and I wish I had a more definitive answer. This profession can feel demanding, often requiring more than it gives. Questioning whether to stay in this field can be challenging. Personally, I try to maintain a balance between my work and family life, which has proven to be the best approach for me. Many times, close friends within the profession have provided support, reminding there is more good than bad in the grand scheme of things. Having a supportive community of friends in this field is crucial; they not only empathize with our struggles but also offer valuable advice on overcoming them.

What do you think about immediately after one of your athletes is injured? What is your mindset in the following week?

I've always thought that an athlete's injury could be the reason I leave this profession. Though the complexity of injuries makes it incredibly difficult to fully prevent and sport will always have injuries, it is hard to not to take them personally. With an injury, I review the past 30 days of training to identify any discrepancies in volume, intensity, or timing, as I believe most injuries stem from these factors. If something is found, I try to understand whether they resulted from my actions or simply a reflection of the month's demands. Once I look objectively, I consider any subjective factors that may have contributed. Ultimately, while we cannot prevent injuries entirely, we can work to minimize them. Learning from each injury is crucial for progress and development in our field.

How do you approach difficult conversations with athletes, coworkers, or your boss?

It's essential to establish trust, respect, and clear standards long before difficult situations arise to handle them effectively. When standards are well-defined, addressing issues becomes more straightforward. When athletes or coworkers trust and respect you, they understand that any conversation comes from a place of care rather than animosity.

Do you have a "failure" that was critical to your long-term development or success?

I consider my failure to be rooted in coaching how I was coached. Growing up during a time when an authoritarian coaching style prevailed, by yelling and screaming, I believed I deserved a certain level of respect simply because I was the coach. However, a time occurred when I raised my voice to an athlete who was having a difficult day, causing them to break down. Hearing that they had come seeking a place to get away, and I had interpreted their behavior as disrespect. This incident prompted me to leave the training group and have a conversation with the athlete. Through that discussion, I realized everyone has their own reasons—their own "why"—for playing sports, training, and reacting the way they do, and it's not always aligned with mine. This completely changed my coaching approach and the personality I bring to coaching sessions. It's been much easier to be a coach that transparently cares than one that is rooted in anger.

What traits or skills do your most successful athletes have in common?

What I've noticed among our most successful athletes is their curiosity—they're constantly asking questions and seeking understanding. They can be challenging to earn respect from initially, as trust is paramount to them. But once they get it, training becomes a true partnership. Additionally, one of the toughest aspects of training them is keeping them out of their own way. The majority of high performers I've experienced tend to want to overtrain and never feel like they've done enough. So ensuring there is proper communication on their expectations as well as what they want helps to build that trust.

What books or resources do you most often recommend to coaches?

The must haves for every performance coach is *Supertraining* by Yuri Verkhoshansky, *The Charlie Francis Training System* by Charlie Francis, *Periodization* by Tudor Bompa, *Ultimate MMA Conditioning* by Joel Jamieson, and *Transfer of Training in Sports* by Anatolii Bondarchuck. Some of the other staples for me have been *The Governing Dynamics of Coaching* and *Applied Sprint Training* by James Smith, *Strength Training Manual* by Mladen Jovanovic, *The Science of Speed The Art of the Sprint* by Tom Tellez/Carl Lewis, *Game Changer/The Process* by Fergus Connolly, and *Reverse Engineering Sport: The 8 Vector System* by Jordan Nieuysma/Nick DiMarco.

Books outside the profession that have helped inside the profession have been *Antifragile* by Nassim Nicholas Taleb, *Poor Charlie's Almanack* by Peter Kaufman, *Why Zebras Don't Get Ulcers* by Robert Sapolsky, and *Thinking in Systems* by Donella Meadows.

"A great mentor is going to let you coach (when you're ready). They're going to let you fail. They're going to invest time into your personal and professional growth. They're going to make you articulate yourself."

-Jason Martinez

Jason Martinez is in his second year as the Head Strength and Conditioning Coach for Men's Basketball and Women's Volleyball at the University of North Texas. Martinez was hired at UNT after partnering with Rick Pitino to guide Iona to a 27-win season, securing both regular-season and tournament conference championships, and earning a spot in March Madness. Before his time at Iona, he worked at East Carolina, Wake Forest, and Lindenwood.

Who do you go to when you need advice? Why them?

You need one person in your circle whose thought process is contrary to yours. These people are important for gaining new perspective and will force you to objectively validate your opinion. The second person in your circle should share a similar outlook as you. This person is beneficial for affirmation, building confidence, and can even add clarity to your situation. The third is someone who lacks extensive knowledge or experience in the matter at hand. After all, expertise is demonstrated by one's ability to teach. It's the "make it make sense to me" approach. I'll run the same idea or situation by all three people, compile the notes, and decipher from there!

What early job was pivotal in your career? Why?

When I was an assistant to Ryan Horn at Wake Forest with the Men's Basketball team, I got a career's worth of knowledge and experience in such a short period of time. Coach Ryan Horn is the best there is. The opportunity to be a sponge next to a coach and human like him every day is something I'm forever grateful for. It changed the trajectory of my career and life in the best possible way.

What are your first steps when you start a new job? What do you need to figure out, what do you need to get done, who do you need to get to know?

Step 1: Have an in-depth conversation with the head coach to discuss expectations (theirs and yours), style of play, KPIs, and scheduling. Not only is this important for getting you rolling with the job itself, but face time with the head coach is an opportunity to forge a personal and professional relationship.

Step 2: Take this conversation and start game planning how to merge their expectations with your style of coaching and training philosophy.

Step 3: Set meetings with each individual athlete to get to know them as people first. Then, and only then, you can create an environment that promotes trust and inclusivity. I always emphasize to them that their personal goals, expectations, injury history, and professional aspirations all hold as much weight (if not more) in their training program as their vertical jump, body composition, and strength numbers do.

Step 4: Take inventory of resources. Space, equipment, and technology is a given. However, I'm also big on taking inventory on what the exercise science department offers. I've had the pleasure of working at universities with elite Exercise Science programs with fully equipped exercise science labs, DEXAS, float tanks, isokinetic machines, you name it! I also like investigating the town to see what is available near the campus. Boxing gyms, yoga studios, CRYO therapy clinics, cooking classes, rope & obstacle courses, whatever! Scope out where the biggest hill in town is (for sprints OF COURSE) and/or where the nearest beach/lake/or pool is.

Step 5: Build relationships and rapport with people outside of your immediate circle. Administration, academics, coaches and support staff of other athletic programs on campus, and donors.

What advice do you have for a college student looking to break into coaching? Who are the best mentors in the world to work for early in your career?
Get involved early and often. I went through my first three years of college "knowing" I wanted to be a strength coach. However, I thought it was a requirement to wait until my senior year practicum course to get intern experience (not the case). When I reached that point, my first internship was a punch in the mouth. I would wake up at 4am to allot enough time to get to the facility and set up for our first group at 6am. Groups would roll in every hour on the hour until I had class at 9am. I would go to class until noon and immediately head back to the facility. Work open hours from 12:30 to 1pm, and right back to training groups hourly until I left for class again at 6pm. Class would let out at 9:30pm, I'd crawl home, microwave ramen noodles, scarf it down and head straight to bed. Wake up the next morning, chug my Monster, and

do it all over again the next day. That experience solidified how much I LOVED it! I couldn't imagine what I would have done if that wasn't the case. I would have gone my entire college career thinking this is what I wanted to be just to find out I hated it. Then what? I would have been lost. All that to say this... get in the trenches as soon as possible. Strength and conditioning isn't for everyone. Find out if it's for you. Fully immerse yourself in it. Get the real-deal experience. Don't shy away from the long hours and hard work. Treat it like a full-time job. That's why the best mentors are the ones that don't shield you from what this thing is. I get that you're working for free but work from 6am to 6pm. A good mentor will keep you there all day (the great mentors will feed you some lunch and give you unlimited access to protein shakes!).

Understand that they're not taking advantage of your free labor, but they're ultimately protecting you from future failure. A great mentor is going to let you coach (when you're ready). They're going to let you fail. They're going to invest time into your personal and professional growth. They're going to make you articulate yourself. When the time comes for you to move on, they're going to hop on the phone and help you land the right opportunity to further assist in your growth.

If you only had two 30-minute sessions a week to train your team, how would you prepare them?

In terms of programming, I find it harder to responsibly occupy an abundance of time (five 1 hour lifts/week) than it is to maximize a minimal amount of time (two 30-minute lifts/week). A majority of what you NEED to get done can be accomplished in a 30-minute time frame, warm up included. 20 minutes of work is a sweet spot. If you can't get your main work done in 20 minutes, you are either doing too much, or you aren't working hard enough. I'd go Monday/Thursday, two total body sessions.

Warm up on Monday would be a Medicine ball warm up. 20-30 different foundational movements done in succession without rest (hinges, squats, slams, Jabs + Rips, slams, core flexion/extension movements, hip lifts, throws, etc.). Single leg quad, Vertical Pull, Bi-lateral hamstring, Horizontal Press.

Warm up on Thursday would be a mini band warm up (ground-based abductor/ adductor work, lateral band walks, monster walks, plyos, jab and drop step series, etc.). Single leg hamstring, Vertical press, Bi-lateral quad, Horizontal Row.

Monday:
A1. Med Ball Warm Up

B1. RFESS (Right)

B2. RFESS (Left)

B3. Weighted Pull Up/Chin Up/LPD

B4. Leg Curl or Reverse Hyper

B5. Weighted Hand Release Push Up

Thursday:

A1. Mini band Circuit

B1. Rear Foot Supported RDL (Right)

B2. Rear Foot Supported RDL (Left)

B3. Z-Press

B4. Heel Elevated Goblet or Zercher Squat

B5. Bent Over Row or Pendlay Row

Let's say each warm up takes 8-10 minutes. We would use time to dictate our main block. Each exercise would be :30 seconds on/ :30 seconds rest, with the goal being 14/15 reps per exercise. What's nice about this is that the intensity can be autoregulated. >14 reps = lower the weight. 14-15 reps = stay at the weight you're at. 16+ reps = increase weight. Complete B1-B5 four times.

What goes into your decision to leave or stay at a job?

I believe you need AT LEAST two years before entertaining the idea of looking for a new job. Year one of a new job is the most hectic and difficult learning curve we experience in our profession. You're learning the dynamics of a new coaching staff. A new system or style of play. Learning the ebbs and flows of practice on a week to week and day by day basis. Going through a full in-season regiment. What does in-season practice look like? How many lifts are you given? What does travel look like? The list goes on and on. Now you take all that information and decipher what worked and what didn't to come up with a better approach to take things to a new level the next season. I'd be curious to see if there's any strength coach in the history of our field who can honestly say their best work was done during their first year at a new job. At this point, you haven't had enough time to make an informed decision about staying or pursuing a different opportunity.

The spring semester going into my second year at ECU, I came into the practice facility to watch one of our guys do his individual workout. Coach did this thing where if you missed two consecutive free throws, you had 10 push-ups. Well, said player missed his two free throws and had to do push-ups...and his form was GARBAGE. More out of laziness than anything else. I got on his case about how everything matters, and he was going to do them again, and do them right. Well, that must have resonated with coach, because after the workout he called me and said, "Let's go get some lunch." From that day forward, we were as close as could be. Up until that point we had a good relationship, but it was more formal than anything. Moral of the story is that relationships take time to foster, and if you don't give them time, you may miss out on an opportunity right where you are at.

Opportunities have always had a funny way of finding me. When one arises, I'll view it through a lens of the personal and professional position in which I currently am in instead of where I ultimately want to end up. Does the job I have still provide room for personal and professional growth? Am I compensated well enough to live the life outside of work that I am striving for right now? How is my relationship with the people I work with? Do I like where I live? These are just a few questions I ask myself when faced with this decision. 99% of the time, the right decision presents itself.

What do you do to overcome times of struggle, burnout, or overwhelm? Who do you turn to?
I'm big on getting on the phone with that network of people that I mentioned before. Chances are they'll all be able to relate because we all go through it at some point and time. When you go through it, it shakes you at your core. To hear that it's not just you and realizing how common it is it seems to ease the symptoms. From there, I just train through it. Training has always been and will always be an outlet for me. I'll start a new training program, or I'll start training for something. One year I learned how to swim because I wanted to do an Iron Man. It helps take the constant focus away from the problem. A healthy coping mechanism or distraction. At the end of the day, "This too shall pass." I heard that from Tom Hanks, and it has stuck with me forever.

What do you think about immediately after one of your athletes is injured? What is your mindset in the following week?
As a practitioner, we take pride in accolades, and rightfully so. When we win championships, we like to think that we played a part in them. When coach comments to the media about how tough your team is or how great of shape they're in, we take that as a compliment to our work. We are notorious for posting body transformation

pictures on Instagram at the end of summer training. Well, if we want to take credit for the good, we must take credit for the bad. Injuries happen, and they are something that can be mitigated through training but cannot be prevented. When they do happen, the first thought in my mind is about the athlete. Give them a big hug, apologize for our shortcomings, and assure them we're going to get through it together.

After that, it's right to the whiteboard. Dissect the mechanism of the injury, the severity, and what we missed in training that could have mitigated its likeliness. Then it's time to take emotions out of it (usually disappointment in myself and sadness for the athlete) and start having meetings with the athletic trainer and physical therapist to establish our role in the recovery/rehabilitation process. With injuries, we shift our focus on what the athlete CAN do and not on what they CAN'T do. Training can be therapeutic for an athlete going through an injury, especially if the injury is causing them to miss time from the sport. So we just have to be creative and get to work!

How do you approach difficult conversations with athletes, coworkers, or your boss?
I try to remain open-minded to what they have to say. It's okay to poke holes in their case to make them articulate their point of view, but always do so unemotionally. Sometimes the hard conversations are just people needing to vent. If that's the case, I just sit back and listen, but I won't involve myself by affirming their thoughts or agreeing. Rather, I like to use motivational interviewing tactics to help them reach their own conclusion.

Do you have a "failure" that was critical to your long-term development or success?
I've had athletes that despite exhausting ALL resources, we failed to get them to gain weight or drastically change KPIs. Each of these cases are critical in professional and personal development if you can take ownership of shortcomings.

What books or resources do you most often recommend to coaches?
Ultimate MMA Conditioning by Joel Jamieson is one of the best (if not THE best) athletic performance books ever written. His ability to describe each individual energy system in a way that a fifth grader could comprehend it is nothing short of amazing. I won't go into too much detail on what that looks like, you'll have to buy the book for yourself and see! (Joel, if you are reading this, I think you may owe me commission for the number of times I've implored coaches to purchase your material). I'll recommend anything from Christian Thibaudeau. *The Concentrated Loading System* has been one of my favorites. *Think Again* by Adam Grant is another one I recommend. Not Strength and Conditioning related, yet super applicable to our field.

> *"My first piece of advice is to get certified and start personal training. The generalist to specialist concept applies to strength coaches as well."*
>
> *-Rachel Hayes*

Rachel Hayes has worked for almost 10 years as the Strength and Conditioning Coordinator at Denton Guyer High School, where she is responsible for the design and implementation of all training aspects for Olympic sports. Her role also includes implementing workouts at the feeder middle schools in Denton ISD. Prior to her current position, Hayes was an Assistant Sports Performance Coach at Stanford University.

What early job was pivotal in your career? Why?

I worked as a personal trainer long before I earned money as a strength coach. Although personal training is technically a different type of career, it's still coaching, and it helped "get my feet wet." I learned how to coach movements and I learned about my individual coaching style. I also think personal training is the best way to bridge textbook to the real world when you're just beginning. Training is presented as ideal within the confines of a classroom or textbook. But when it's time to demonstrate knowledge in the form of coaching, you need to have a clue—and personal training is an ideal way to connect that gap. When college students or anyone looking to get in the field reach out, my first piece of advice is to get certified and start personal training. The generalist to specialist concept applies to strength coaches as well.

If you only had two 30-minute sessions a week to train your team, how would you prepare them?

Training twice a week for 30 minutes is a reality for most high school lifts, so I'm familiar with the challenge. And of course it depends on a lot of factors. However, I can be certain you'd find a hinging variation, a glute bridge or leg curl variation, a lunge that hits one or more planes of motion, and some sort of core stabilization exercise in one or both training days. Of course upper body movements matter, however, these are the things that regardless of sport, or time of year, you would consistently see in my training sessions.

What do you think about immediately after one of your athletes is injured? What is your mindset in the following week?

I want to know in as much detail as possible the mechanism of injury, so I know if it could've been mitigated or avoided. If it's a non-contact injury, I immediately feel the weight of responsibility as my mind sifts through the thoughts and questions of where and when I went wrong, or what piece of training I overlooked. As time moves forward, I reevaluate everything within my control for that team, make changes if deemed necessary, then continue to keep coaching to the best of my ability.

What books or resources do you most often recommend to coaches?

New Functional Training for Sport by Mike Boyle, *5/3/1: The Simplest and Most Effective Training System to Improve Raw Strength* by Jim Wendler, and *Periodization Training for Sports* by Tudor Bompa, PhD.

> *"We just went 27-5 but when you tell someone in the business office they were a part of it, that makes their heart so full and you can see that, which means they greet you with a smile every day!"*
>
> ## -Chad Gatzlaff

Chad Gatzlaff is the Associate Head Coach and Recruiting Coordinator for the Women's Volleyball program at UC Santa Barbara. In 2019, he played a key role in leading the UCSB volleyball team to their first NCAA tournament victory in 15 years. Before joining UCSB, Gatzlaff coached at VCU and the University of Indianapolis, contributing to some of the most successful seasons in each program's history.

Who do you go to when you need advice? Why them?
I go to people that I have worked with that share the same values and beliefs. We have been in the trenches together, we have worked for a common goal together. I know when I was doing that, I was working for their career and they were working for mine. Work is still work at the end of the day unless you love what you do. You won't love what you do if you don't have special people around you that push you, respect you, and love on you every day.

What early job was pivotal in your career? Why?
Going into the real world after college and not coaching. I was working for a Fortune 500 company and had my first salary job. They were expecting me to work 60-hour weeks...and that was normal. I hated the people, I hated the work, and in that job I really started to dream about what I love. If normal was working 60 hours a week, then I wanted my normal to be FUN, EXCITING, and something I wanted to do forever!

What are your first steps when you start a new job? What do you need to figure out, what do you need to get done, who do you need to get to know?
Everyone! I meet with everyone to listen!!! Listening is so important, and kill people with kindness. Very few people hate this (our current strength coach hates this haha). He said I am too happy of a person to be around...I felt like that was the greatest compliment someone could give me. I need to figure out if people are in my corner,

if I can lean on them when times are tough (example: facilities people when I need to have the gym for an extra hour). Thank you's and individual meetings at the end of the year are important as well. We just went 27-5 but when you tell someone in the business office they were a part of it, that makes their heart so full and you can see that, which means they greet you with a smile every day!

If you only had two 30-minute sessions a week to train your team, how would you prepare them?

Interesting, so many rabbit holes to go down with this one...I would take my first meeting as a team to come up with goals in this crazy new rule that we need to follow. After that I would meet individually with every player.

What goes into your decision to leave or stay at a job?

The people, the resources, the weather, my own happiness, work-life balance...and for me money falls somewhere around number 10. I only bring up money because in this life going back to the earlier question...you won't enjoy your money if you don't enjoy your job. Also, if you enjoy your job, you won't feel the need to have money to run away from your job so much.

What do you do to overcome times of struggle, burnout, or overwhelm? Who do you turn to?

I pray. I love Jesus brother...if you can't find what makes you go...you are lost. I was lost before I found him. It's a sad world if you think you were just made to be a volleyball coach and then be dirt.

What do you think about immediately after one of your athletes is injured? What is your mindset in the following week?

Heart drops...wish I could take the rolled ankle or ACL for them. I have gone through shoulder surgery and Achilles, with some minor knee stuff, so I will say I am able to help and talk through all of that with them. I try to go to all doctor's appointments because you never know when it is going to hit them the hardest.

My mindset the following week does not change. I think you are asking if I get tentative with practice or how we coach, no we don't change.

How do you approach difficult conversations with athletes, coworkers, or your boss?

I STINK AT THIS!!!! I am not a direct person. I would avoid this at all costs. I am a big personality index guy. I normally go back to what the other person is and let those books help me and guide the conversation and tone.

What traits or skills do your most successful athletes have in common?

1. They are more athletic than the rest.
2. Hard worker.
3. Good listener.

What books or resources do you most often recommend to coaches?

This changes from year to year. I don't value my opinion enough to reach out to people and give them book recommendations. When I do, it is with close friendships, and that can go anywhere from *Greenlights* with Matthew McConaughey to the book *Outliers* and anything in between.

"Finally, I came to the realization that I had to put myself before others. That by taking care of myself, I could actually push harder and serve more."

-Connor Schoepp

Connor Schoepp recently opened Rebuild Performance & Rehab, his own reconditioning practice in Pittsburgh. Before this, he served as the Director of Applied Sport Performance and Performance Coach for Men's Soccer at Liberty University. Schoepp joined Liberty after working as an Assistant Strength and Conditioning Coach for the Arizona Cardinals. Prior to his time in the NFL, he was a Football Strength and Conditioning Coach at both Mississippi State and the University of Pittsburgh.

Who do you go to when you need advice? Why them?

I have been extraordinarily fortunate to have come by some amazing people throughout my life. In my mind, I have formed a group of people that I consider to be my council. This group is made up of people from different backgrounds, sports, experiences, and personalities. I choose them because I believe in them as people. They are genuine, honest, and have accomplished things I hope to do one day. I know that whenever I come to a crossroads in my life, I can call any one of these people and they can help guide me. I wouldn't be anywhere without them.

What early job was pivotal in your career? Why?

I interned at Mississippi State Football early in my career. At this point I had been interning for several years. I had worked with different coaches, sports, and at a variety of levels. I knew this was what I wanted to do, but I never really felt like I had found what I was looking for. Then I came to Mississippi State, where I felt for the first time I was exactly where I was supposed to be. It was the hardest experience of my life while simultaneously the best. I was working for people who pushed me to be more than I had ever been. They challenged me on so many different levels and showed me what it takes to operate at an elite level. It was also the first time I felt like I had people who were looking out for me and were going to go out of their way to help me reach my goals. This experience became the catalyst for how I hope to help up-and-coming coaches.

What are your first steps when you start a new job? What do you need to figure out, what do you need to get done, who do you need to get to know?

The first and most important aspect of starting any job is establishing relationships. It may sound cliché, but it is for a good reason. No matter how good of a practitioner you are, your work will only succeed to the level of relationships you can develop. In almost every mistake I have made as a coach, it stemmed from a poor relationship. You cannot skip this step.

Clearly defining your role for both you and the people you work with is invaluable. So many issues arise from a lack of communication and transparency on what expectations are. I have seen it happen so many times personally and with others. Leaders hire someone and give vague to no instruction or expectations of what is expected from them. Then people either do what they think is correct or do nothing at all, causing a rift between employer and employee. By clearly defining your role you can take responsibility and ownership of it.

Next is establishing the minimal viable project. This can mean many different things, from a literal project to just your duties. If your primary job is to train your athletes, then start there and dominate it. It may seem obvious, but it is easy to get caught up in the minutia of the role. When starting a new role, keep the main thing the main thing. Once you have established that, you can branch out. You want to always undersell and overdeliver as opposed to oversell and underdeliver.

What advice do you have for a college student looking to break into coaching? Who are the best mentors in the world to work for early in your career?

The first thing I tell undergraduate students is to go experience it so you can figure out if you love it. Because if you don't, get out. It may sound harsh, but this field isn't for everyone. Many people get into coaching because they like training or sports and think it would be a fun career. Then they get there and realize the barrier to entry is high, the work-life balance is poor, compensation is low, and respect amongst peers is often lacking. Coaching can provide a joy and value like no other job in the world. It has brought me more in my life than I could ever pay back. But you need to understand that it does not come without its pitfalls.

Next is to get out and get your hands dirty. Reading, listening to podcasts, degrees, and certifications are necessary and an important aspect of developing as a coach. But nothing can replace getting out and actually doing it. Interning, volunteer coaching, personal training. Whatever it is, there is no replacement for hands-on coaching.

Lastly, make sure you critically evaluate where and who you go work for. At some point you will likely have to intern for free. Many coaches will just use you as a body to clean, set up the room, and take care of the busy work with no intention of investing in you or going out of their way to help you advance in the field. Interning should be a reciprocal relationship. You offer your work to coaches, in return you gain experience, knowledge, and possibly someone that is going to help you get hired elsewhere. Take your time doing your research about who runs a good internship program. Do they treat their interns with respect? Do they invest their own time into you? Do they have a track record of getting people hired?

If you only had two 30-minute sessions a week to train your team, how would you prepare them?

Day 1–

Warm Up:

- · General Movement
- · Mobility
- · Pillar Prep
- · Linear Locomotive Drills
- · Short Accelerations

Lift:

A1. TBDL 3x3 @80-85%

A2. Hip 90/90 W/ Lift Off 3x3ea 0-2-0

A3. Hurdle Hop 3x5

B1. Bench Press 4x3 @80-85%

B2. Alt Dead Bug 3x10ea

B3. Sprinter Calf Raise 2x15ea

C1. SA DB Row 3x8ea

C2. SL Leg Curl 2x6ea

C3. Lying Mini Band Hip Flexor 2x10ea

Day 2-

Warm Up:

- · General Movement
- · Mobility
- · Pillar Prep
- · Multi-Directional Locomotive Drills
- · Short COD's/Reactive Drills

Lift:

A1. DB Ipsilateral Reverse Lunge 3x4ea

A2. Ankle Roll 3x5ea

A3. Staggered Stance Broad Jump 3x3ea

B1. ½ Kneeling Landmine Press 3x8ea

B2. Suitcase Carry 2x40yds

B3. Manual Resisted Anterior Tib Raise 2x10

C1. NG Pull Up 3x8-10 0-2-0

C2. SL 2 DB RDL 2x6ea

C3. Standing Banded Adductions 2x15ea

What goes into your decision to leave or stay at a job?

Does my job fulfill me financially? Does it provide an appropriate work-life balance? Am I developing personally and professionally at my job? Is there room to grow into a new role? Does my job provide me joy? Is the location in an area I want to be? Does this job take me where I ultimately want to be? These are the questions I ask myself when evaluating my current role and the possibilities of others. Each of these aspects plays a role in job selection and retention. The hierarchy of these aspects will be different for everyone. Prioritize what is important to you and then you can identify the role you want. Lastly, simply writing out a list of pros and cons can reveal a lot about what you should do. It may seem simple. But I have come to crossroads with employment several times in my career not knowing what to do. After writing out the pros and cons of each situation, it became clear which path to take.

What do you do to overcome times of struggle, burnout, or overwhelm? Who do you turn to?

This is one that I have faced significant struggle with. I have burned myself out of this field on several occasions. I am just fortunate that I was able to make it back. The most important thing you can do is take care of yourself before you take care of others. It may seem obvious, but it is so easy to lose sight of this when you're in the thick of it. Then set boundaries. This is hard for so many coaches as serving others is in our DNA. If you cannot set boundaries, you are setting yourself up to be taken advantage of. Your job will not be there for you in 20 years. If I left today my role would be filled in weeks. Your health, family, and friends will last much longer than any position.

Make sure you have someone in your life that can keep you accountable to looking after yourself. Nobody is responsible for you but you. However, we do not make it anywhere in life without help. Having a significant other, friend, family member, or mentor to be honest with you is so important.

What do you think about immediately after one of your athletes is injured? What is your mindset in the following week?

What were the driving factors behind this injury? Injuries are complex and much harder to navigate than people want to admit. There are so many factors that go into why an injury could occur. It would be shortsighted to say that it occurred because of one thing. Outside of direct trauma, injuries usually happen when a multitude of variables come together at the wrong time. It is our job to reverse engineer the injury. Identify what may have led to this happening. Then do what we can to support the healing process and mitigate risk of future injury. Far too often, performance coaches fall into guilt that they didn't do enough to prevent it. While building resiliency is a part of our job, it is important to understand that we cannot prevent anything. There are far too many variables outside of our control to take all the blame for them. Critically evaluate the situation and move on.

How do you approach difficult conversations with athletes, coworkers, or your boss?

There is a direct correlation between your success and your ability to have difficult conversations. It's common for people to come off extremely harsh in an effort to be truthful because they let their feelings get in the way. Then blame the other person for being soft for not being able to handle the truth. Honesty never has to be brutal. You can tell someone the truth while still being aware of how it can make them feel.

It is just as disrespectful to beat around the bush and lie to someone about what is happening. While it may not feel that way in the moment, people do appreciate transparency. The most enlightening conversations I have had have been when everyone is transparent about what is happening and how they feel.

Do you have a "failure" that was critical to your long-term development or success?

Very early in my career, I burned myself out. In an effort to make it, I sacrificed my physical and mental health. I put my job before everything else because I was terrified of being a failure. This left me injured, broke, and burnt out. Eventually, I slowly built myself back up before doing it all over again. Over and over again I put others before myself. I made sacrifices I thought were going to help get me to where I wanted to be. Turns out it did the opposite. Finally, I came to the realization that I had to put myself before others. That by taking care of myself, I could actually push harder and serve more. If you are a young coach reading this, please take note. You are serving no one by being a martyr. The idea that being a coach means you can't have a semblance of work life–balance, you have to put your job before everything, and that suffering is a part of the gig, is erroneous. You are so much more than your job.

What traits or skills do your most successful athletes have in common?

The best athletes that I have seen know what level of arousal they need to operate at. If they are a high energy extrovert, then they need to act like it on the field. If they are quiet and introverted, then they need to remain calm and focused. They have an awareness of how much to turn the dial to compete at their own optimal level.

Next, they are extremely competitive. This isn't an outburst of rage when they lose, or simply trying hard. No, they look at everything as an opportunity to win. They have a need to execute whatever is necessary to be the victor. And contrary to what we're told, they hate losing way more than they enjoy winning.

They are submitted to the process. A lot of people are committed. They do what is asked of them. They work pretty hard. They show up on time and don't miss any days. They get better, but deep down they are content with just meeting the standard. Those who are submitted are engulfed by the process. Everything they do is about reaching their goals. It is the first thing they think about when they wake up and the last before bed. They know every decision they make is going to move them closer or farther away from their goal. To the outside world, they have an unhealthy obsession with getting better.

What books or resources do you most often recommend to coaches?

I try to find people I think are experts or provide value in a certain topic and lean into their thoughts. For understanding sport beyond the surface level, Fergus Connolly's book *Game Changer* and James Smith's *Governing Dynamics of Coaching* are fantastic. Many practitioners stay in the same surface level understanding of training and sport for the majority of their career. These two force you to critically think and evaluate what you do on a deeper level.

For return to play Alan Murdoch is someone who is changing the field for the better. Alan is an end stage rehabilitation specialist who reverse engineers' movement better than any practitioner in the game. His intricate but simple system for getting athletes back on the field fast and efficiently is amazing. He has several online resources that I have found extremely valuable.

For speed development, Les Spellman is an elite practitioner and has so many amazing resources. What Les does better than anyone is to take complex issues and create simple solutions that are practical to anyone.

For strength training, there are hundreds of people who have written on this topic, but Dan John's work is timeless. His book *Easy Strength* should be the curriculum for any coach coming into the field. I have used his progressions for years and continue to be amazed by the results. Looking a little deeper into strength, Cal Dietz and Ben Peterson's book *Triphasic Training* is a great resource that digs a little more into the details of strength and some more complex methods.

For agility and change of direction, Jordan Nieuwsma and Nick DiMarco's book *The 8 Vector System* is amazing. It not only covers many foundational principles of training, it also gives you so much insight into how to develop a three-dimensional athlete. Shawn Myzka is another that looks at movement from more of an ecological perspective that can give great insight into multi-directional movement and why athletes move the way they do.

For conditioning, Joel Jamison's *Ultimate MMA Conditioning* is a phenomenal resource. While it is heavily biased towards mixed martial arts, the first several chapters in that book explain the complex topic of energy system development better than anyone. You can extrapolate the lessons in this book and apply them to any sport in the world.

"Putting a student athlete's well-being over the consideration of the team's well-being, which created challenges within the program." (Failure)

-Tricia Binford

Tricia Binford is in her 20th season as the Head Women's Basketball Coach at Montana State University. She has achieved 329 wins at Montana State, ranking first in the university's history and second in Big Sky Conference history. With no losing seasons in the past 17 years, Binford has guided the Bobcats to four Big Sky Conference Regular Season Championships and two Conference Tournament Championships. Before arriving in Bozeman, she served as an Assistant Coach at Utah State and Boise State.

Who do you go to when you need advice? Why them?
Dad-Integrity, Husband-Character, Staff-Knowledge. Dan Hughes-former WNBA Coach, Wisdom/Integrity.

What early job was pivotal in your career? Why?
Assistant Coach—I was eager and thought I was more ready than I was. I had ideas without worrying about consequences. (Helps with mentoring young coaches)

What are your first steps when you start a new job? What do you need to figure out, what do you need to get done, who do you need to get to know?

· Build relationships/Trust with our team/captains.

· Hire Staff.

· Establish Principles/Foundation.

· Recruit.

· Set Out Yearly Calendar/Progression Plan for season.

· Get to Know Other Coaches/Other teams at the School.

What advice do you have for a college student looking to break into coaching? Who are the best mentors in the world to work for early in your career?
Be willing to do "whatever is needed" for the team, coach, and program to be

successful.

Mentors:

- June Daughtery (college head coach) - (value of believing in personnel)
- Dan Hughes (WNBA coach) – (value of teaching the game to be simple)

If you only had two 30-minute sessions a week to train your team, how would you prepare them?

5 min-mental performance/team building, 5 min – vitamins (warm-up drills), 5 min – offense, 5 min – defense, 10 min - strength training/injury prevention.

What goes into your decision to leave or stay at a job?

- Family.
- President/Athletic Director.
- Opportunity to be successful.

What do you do to overcome times of struggle, burnout, or overwhelm? Who do you turn to?

Exercise, family vacations, devotions, hikes. I turn to my family, sister, pastor.

What do you think about immediately after one of your athletes is injured? What is your mindset in the following week?

Make sure they are comforted, and the family is informed. Anything I could have done differently? How do we need to adjust as a team?

How do you approach difficult conversations with athletes, coworkers, or your boss?

Prayer—wisdom for conversation. I might have someone in the room for conversation.

Do you have a "failure" that was critical to your long-term development or success?

Putting a student athlete's well-being over the consideration of the team's well-being which created challenges within the program.

What traits or skills do your most successful athletes have in common?

Consistent, Willing to do Whatever is Needed for Team to Be Successful, Solution Oriented, Competitive, Tough.

What books or resources do you most often recommend to coaches?

Chop Wood Carry Water, Energy Bus, Five Dysfunctions of a Team.

"Any person who can take constructive criticism, by the same definition, will invite accountability from coaches and embrace the opportunity to improve. To resist that notion is to refuse opportunities to improve, which is the antithesis of success."

-Andrew Wright

Andrew Wright is in his second year as the Head Strength and Conditioning Coach for Men's Basketball at Texas Tech University. He arrived in Lubbock after working at the University of North Texas, where he gained experience with the Football and Track and Field programs before leading the Men's Basketball and Volleyball programs. During his tenure at UNT, Wright contributed to the basketball program's high-levels of success, including three Conference USA championships, the program's first March Madness victory over 4th-seed Purdue in 2021, and the 2023 NIT championship.

Who do you go to when you need advice? Why them?
My wife is the first place I go for any advice. A partner is someone who should be in your life because of their significance to you and your trust in them. Why would you go anywhere else first?

What early job was pivotal in your career? Why?
The first full-time position I had following graduation from TCU was as a PE teacher for kindergarten through eighth grade students. It allowed me to find out what being a professional meant. Relative to my future career as a college coach, it was a risk-free time to learn how to manage my life in a way that I could operate as an adult, and my first chance to learn what punctuality, communication, public speaking, and discipline look like.

What are your first steps when you start a new job? What do you need to figure out, what do you need to get done, who do you need to get to know?
Do not rock the boat. Learn. Have humility that your way of doing your new job may not be the only way and it likely was not the way that your predecessor did his job. The

job and your new co-workers likely existed before you arrived and they may be at your place of work after you leave. They matter. Respect them by learning about the place that they hopefully care about before you storm an organization with new, possibly extreme, methods.

What advice do you have for a college student looking to break into coaching? Who are the best mentors in the world to work for early in your career?

I began my career in Strength and Conditioning relatively late. Many coaches seem to begin during their undergraduate time. However, I began my first internship a full year after my graduation. There is no rush. You find coaching when you find it. The effort that you place on your personal growth in this field is what will determine your path. I had a coach tell me that unless I quit my full-time job as a teacher to commit to an internship, I would have significant trouble making headway. Find a job that you volunteer your time for. That will be one that you are most likely to find purpose in.

Mentors are the people who take interest in you as much as you admire them for their work. If either of those components is not present, that person need not be a mentor.

If you only had two 30-minute sessions a week to train your team, how would you prepare them?

With two training sessions per week, my focus would go towards two whole body-structured days. Ideally, these two days would not be consecutive. Preferably, these two sessions would occur with 48-72 hours of lower intensity work between them. Training athletes in this fashion, while superficially may seem underdosing, can be closer to reasonable than one may think. Both days would include speed and plyometrics for 15-20 minutes, followed by a total body strength emphasis. After this point, one could begin to dive into unilateral or multi-planar considerations to provide some more specific components.

What goes into your decision to leave or stay at a job?

3 P's-

- Purpose
    - Every position should provide you with the sense of value in the organization for which you work. Every employee deserves to see that they contribute to the growth of a team or structure. If that purpose is waning, it may be time to

entertain a change.

- Progress

  - Your work should follow an upward trajectory. This may not be "linear," but every position should provide the ability to improve and grow as a professional.

- Pay

  - Simply put, the pay is either an increase, the same, or a decrease. Is the pay worth the level of work? Is the pay worth the time from family?

What do you do to overcome times of struggle, burnout, or overwhelm? Who do you turn to?

Strength and conditioning, and coaching in general, sees quite the turnover rate. Let's not think that this field is unique that way, however. If this occurs, you aren't by yourself. Someone in your office has had moments like this. Find friends or family who you find you relate to. Discuss it. Don't hide from it. Feelings of being overwhelmed or burnout do not individually mean that a job is wrong for you or that you are ill-prepared. It means that the task is unusual or that you need a break. If you are doing a job that matters to you, you will be overwhelmed. If you take a new job that is a step up, you might not feel ready. You wouldn't have the job if someone did not think you could handle it.

What do you think about immediately after one of your athletes is injured? What is your mindset in the following week?

Every coach should have concern when an athlete is injured. If you do not, you are in the wrong business. Once the care factor is established, the logic needs to supersede the emotion. Injuries are as multifactorial as any other situation. It is a simple fix to place blame. However, there is often not any one factor that should be held responsible unless utter negligence has occurred. If a significant injury occurs, the job is to care for the athlete and help him move into the next challenge of recovery. If questions as to "why" the injury occurred, speculation doesn't do anyone any favors in formal conversations. It occurred. It's unfortunate. But, it's part of athletics and, aside from negligence, there is no use in placing responsibility towards anyone.

How do you approach difficult conversations with athletes, coworkers, or your boss?

Difficult conversations are difficult for all parties in many cases. It is never just the "receiving" person or the "delivering" person. With any person, the best method is to find a time that is uninterrupted and contained. Don't let outside factors influence the conversation as distraction. "Do you have a moment this afternoon to talk?" can go a long way to easing the start of these. When the conversation arrives, the more information the better. Visual representations with athletes can be insightful. "We need to improve your lifestyle habits. This track you have been on has not been beneficial. These days show this."

"We" and "Us" always instead of "You." We walk this walk with whomever we speak, if it's a conversation worth having. If we didn't care about them, we likely would not have the conversation to begin with.

Do you have a "failure" that was critical to your long-term development or success?
Everyone has that moment or moments that serve as teachers seared into our memory. The first of mine was an opportunity in which I managed the rest time during a football conditioning drill while I was an intern. Holding this stopwatch and standing side by side with the Head Strength and Conditioning Coach, Zack Womack—who I respect as much as anyone in this field—was like interning for the President. During this drill, I lost myself in the excitement that was involved and neglected to keep track of the rest and consequently when the next rep should begin. Knowing that a drill of its relative magnitude with a large group can be offset by an error as small as time management was a moment that taught me for the rest of my career.

What traits or skills do your most successful athletes have in common?
Athletes who find success, whether in their sport performance or in life pursuing other challenges, all have the willingness to take constructive criticism. Any person who can take constructive criticism, by the same definition, will invite accountability from coaches and embrace the opportunity to improve. To resist that notion is to refuse opportunities to improve, which is the antithesis of success. Successful athletes have humility to remove their pride from thought and appreciate the person who hopes to guide them to improvement.

What books or resources do you most often recommend to coaches?
Read anything that is of interest to you. While I do not claim to be the most avid reader, I do know that I have read more books that have sparked thought than those that have not. Even if you do not agree with a book's particular stance, there is a perspective to take—right or wrong.

"The older I get, the more I realize that we often get tied up in inter-webs of comfort and fear of potential pain. Oftentimes we are sharing those chains in some way, and communicating our problems sets us free."

-Joel Smith

Joel Smith is the owner of Just Fly Sports, where he hosts a highly regarded podcast and offers articles, training programs, and consultations. Smith spent eight years as a strength and conditioning coach at UC Berkeley and four years as a track coach at Wilmington College. He is a significant contributor to the field of sports performance, not only through the *Just Fly Performance Podcast* but also with his educational courses (*Elastic Essentials, Sprint Acceleration Essentials*), seminars, and books, including *Speed Strength, Vertical Foundations, Mechanics and Development of Single Leg Vertical Jumping,* and *10 Essentials for Training Power Athletes.*

Who do you go to when you need advice? Why them?

It depends on the advice, as I have different coaches I look for guidance on in different areas. For years, Adarian Barr has been a go to for anything movement related. Sending him various sprint and jump videos and getting his feedback has been massive for me in deepening my understanding of human movement and function. With neurology-oriented questions, I go to Jeff Moyer of DC Sports Training. For questions on instinctive human movement and strength training, I have gotten great insight in conversations with Tommy John. For basic play and human movement ideas from a philosophical standpoint, I love chatting with Aaron Cantor. Anything related to youth athletic development, Jeremy Frisch is a go to. For anything speed and power related, Piotr Maruszewski is a Polish coach with a wealth of knowledge. For things related to physiology, biomarkers, and adaptation, Mark McLaughlin of Performance Training Center has given me helpful insight. Each of these individuals has a lifetime of honing their craft, and I highly respect the wisdom they have to offer.

What early job was pivotal in your career? Why?

Getting an assistant coaching job at Wilmington college was a breakthrough for me. Prior to that point, I had simply assumed that getting a master's degree and volunteer assistant coaching experience at a successful NCAA D3 school (UW-LaCrosse) would be a ticket to a paid coaching job (you may be thinking this as well). I had applied to a dozen jobs at the end of my time in grad school, and didn't get a single email back. Depression began to sink in at that point, and I had planned on volunteering another year at UW-L, in hopes of trying again for a paid job the next year. Before I kicked off the next coaching season there, a key event (the interim head coach working to give away my events to the graduate assistant coach) led me to one last effort in finding a paid college coaching position.

As fate would have it, there was an opening at Wilmington College, which was only 30 minutes away from the place I did my undergraduate (Cedarville University). Each coaching job is going to easily get over 100 applicants, and the head coach at Wilmington had remembered me from being a successful high jumper at Cedarville. With that familiarity at my aid, I ended up getting the Wilmington job, and it spearheaded my subsequent coaching journey. It was also the perfect place for me at that point in my coaching development (still very inexperienced and immature), and I learned a massive amount on many levels of coaching, administration, and life in general in my time there.

What are your first steps when you start a new job? What do you need to figure out, what do you need to get done, who do you need to get to know?

I can't say I'm much of an expert at this, as I've only held full-time coaching positions at two different colleges, and I am currently self-employed. If I were to start again at a place of employment, I would work to get to know the expectations and backgrounds of those I was working with as well as possible. I would put extra effort in to ask questions, get regular feedback, and get to know people on a more personal level. I'd also work hard at making peers, co-workers, and administrators regularly feel appreciated. This is my own journey however, as my lone-wolf and competitive aspects of my personality have given me different weaknesses to address, where social and professional aspects will come more easily to others.

What advice do you have for a college student looking to break into coaching? Who are the best mentors in the world to work for early in your career?

I wouldn't say there is any one mentor or guru who will transform anyone. In life, I believe the right help will come at the right time, as long as we are looking for it. The mentors who appeared in my life, such as Adarian Barr, did so at the time that was right for me. As the saying goes, "When the student is ready, the master shall appear." In the world we live in, I would generally advise students to find mentors who can help them in both their strengths and their weaknesses. This means a student who loves strength training should seek some form of mentorship from those who are experts in human movement, motor learning and sport skill, martial arts, dance and parkour. We work in a field where things can get very one sided quickly, instead of becoming more integrated.

If you only had two 30-minute sessions a week to train your team, how would you prepare them?

It depends on the team (it likely drives people nuts to hear that), but if it is a very general situation, with a team playing and practicing full-time outside of the weight room, it would look something like this with each session:

- 10-15 minutes of bodyweight-oriented movement, crawls, climbs, hangs, lunges, partner-based strength (partner carries, etc.), and dynamic mobility-oriented work.

- 5-10 minutes of a few key lifts (but only one set = 1x10-20 reps of each).

- 10 minutes of bodyweight iso holds, or working key auxiliary muscles (i.e. feet, hip flexors, etc.).

- I know a lot of people would put some sort of sprint or depth jump in this grouping, but that would be something I would add if I had more time. As I see it, these are the basics that can optimally complement the speed and power athletes are already displaying in their sport itself.

What goes into your decision to leave or stay at a job?

As I mentioned, I've only been in two paid full-time positions. I left the first job due to a lack of pay and difficulty in the recruiting quota aspects. A nail in the coffin was a phone conversation with a female athlete who had run a time in the 200-meter dash in a time slower than what seven-year-old Kharisma Watkins ran a few years back, and was being given an athletic scholarship to a competing school. Seeing how desperate small Ohio schools were to fill their rosters amidst a small pool of athletes was disheartening, to say the least. We were fielding track teams with athletes who wouldn't even be on the varsity team of many high schools, to have athletes on a roster, paying school tuition.

The second job I left from both a level of boredom (coaching lifts, more than sport skills, to the same sports, year over year) and then the sustainability of family life in the area, largely due to living expenses. For me personally, I have a large need for autonomy and self-expression, and although it was a risk to leave Cal (which was a fantastic place to work, with amazing people), it was definitely worth it for me.

What do you do to overcome times of struggle, burnout, or overwhelm? Who do you turn to?

My wife has always been very helpful and is a calming presence and personality. Walks in nature and getting outside is highly therapeutic. I do breath-work in the morning, along with gratitude journaling. Faith in a greater purpose has been key, as well as working on the willingness of my ego to be dismantled by life if need be (i.e. "surrender"). I also reflect on the importance of difficult life situations to increase our strength in a way that goes far beyond the gym. Recently, I've had the good fortune to have neighbors I do cold plunges with in the morning, and sauna with in the evening. Doing so has had tremendous benefits for me mentally and socially.

What do you think about immediately after one of your athletes is injured? What is your mindset in the following week?

I look at injuries as opportunities. Often, it's an opportunity for the athlete in the fact that they simply needed to rest and were burning the candle too hard. It's also an opportunity to see the body in a new way, and to work much more "inwardly" for a period of time. It's also a period of reflection, as per all of the movement (my training included) that athlete has been engaged in during recent months and even years.

How do you approach difficult conversations with athletes, coworkers, or your boss?

The older I get, the more I realize that we often get tied up in inter-webs of comfort and fear of potential pain. Oftentimes we are sharing those chains in some way, and communicating our problems sets us free. So often, the difficult conversation is a gateway to leveling up a relationship, as well as one's own abilities and belonging in the workplace.

Do you have a "failure" that was critical to your long-term development or success?

I generally failed as a recruiter at Wilmington College in my first three years. This led to a lot of stress and difficulty with my job security there, and motivated me to start the Just Fly Sports brand. If not for the failure, I very well may have stayed in the NCAA track coaching circuit, which on a level would have been enjoyable, but ultimately was not my highest calling. Funny enough, I had good success in recruiting my 4th and final year at the school, when I was also working on building the Just Fly Sports website. In looking back, that burst of motivation and autonomy likely had an impact on my professional duties with the school as well.

What traits or skills do your most successful athletes have in common?
After working with Olympic swimmers in particular, I've found that they are obsessive with their craft, and highly detail oriented. This comes in different forms, but across the board I saw this as a general staple. We talk about training as being in body, mind, and spirit. Training the body is pretty straightforward. I view the "detailed" nature of those successful athletes as a product of the mind, and then the obsessive desire for success as a portion of their spirit. You could also liken that obsessiveness to the desire of the heart, and having a love for something that carries the weight of being greater than one's self. When an athlete has this, they don't have to "spend willpower" to pour themselves into training; it just happens.

There is a pure motivation that we all have access to that is driven from a higher purpose. I also saw what happened to high-level athletes when "their heart wasn't in it" anymore, which is an instant and substantial decrease in one's physical performances, regardless of the exact nature of the physical, and even mental, training strategies.

What books or resources do you most often recommend to coaches?
There's a lot out there with the basic sciences and fundamentals of progressive overload and exercise selection. Most of the common literature and reading material is based on simple, scalable methods to run larger groups of athletes through resistance training, jump, throw, and sprint progressions. With the rise of data-based systems and artificial intelligence, creative coaching and the development of one's intuition are becoming even more important. This is not only for the sake of improving one's "employability" but also is a critical aspect of improving the athlete experience and ultimately their performance ceiling. In this regard, we have both creativity and intuition on the levels of understanding human movement, and then creative coaching application.

To explore movement, I'd start with Adarian Barr and Jenn Pilotti's book *Let Me Introduce You.* Adarian Barr is my movement mentor, and his well of mechanics runs deeper there than any existing system. Regarding creativity, we actually are served to go back in time and look at training that came out of the 1970s to 1990s. The works of Gilles Cometti and Tadeusz Starzynski are a good place to start. Jumps training books like *The Jumps: Conditioning and Technical Training* by Derek Boosey, or *The Triple Jump Encyclopedia* by Ernie Bullard, are great primers on building balanced and effective power training. These are particularly helpful, because they came at a time where physical education carries more value, and existed before the barbell-dominated arm of athletic performance was ushered in later on.

"My first job in 1961 in Canton, Ohio, as an Elementary Physical Education Teacher and Junior High School Football, Basketball, and Track Coach with only volunteers for help. I had to do it all—no assistants, very little administrative help, and plenty of mistakes—but working to learn and adjust every day on the job was invaluable. I would recommend this path to all."

-Jack Harbaugh

Jack Harbaugh has made a significant impact on the football world throughout his coaching career. He served as the Head Football Coach at Western Michigan University and Western Kentucky University, winning the NCAA I-AA National Championship and the American Coaches Association National Coach of the Year Award in 2002 during his final year at Western Kentucky. In the 2023-2024 college football season, he came out of retirement to become the Assistant Head Coach at the University of Michigan, helping his son, Jim Harbaugh, secure the 2024 College Football Playoff National Championship. Throughout his career, Harbaugh held various assistant coaching positions and also served as the Associate Athletics Director for two years at Marquette University. His initial head coaching opportunities were at Eaton High School and Xenia High School.

Who do you go to when you need advice? Why them?
Family, Good Friends, and Trusted Allies.

What early job was pivotal in your career? Why?
My first job in 1961 in Canton, Ohio, as an Elementary Physical Education Teacher and Junior High School Football, Basketball, and Track Coach with only volunteers for help. I had to do it all—no assistants, very little administrative help, and plenty of mistakes—but working to learn and adjust every day on the job was invaluable. I would recommend this path to all. Many today choose the Graduate Assistant route.

What are your first steps when you start a new job? What do you need to figure out, what do you need to get done, who do you need to get to know?

Take your time to find your way, learn the landscape, the pecking order, and the office procedure and personalities. Much of what may have been told to you may not be in place. Listen—a mistake is made when you want to impress with your knowledge too early. Some in the room appreciate silence until you earn your place through hard work.

What advice do you have for a college student looking to break into coaching? Who are the best mentors in the world to work for early in your career?

Find a Job! Everyone wants to start as a college or pro coach. Go to clinics, visit high school and junior high school practices, get to know coaches, ask how you might help, do the jobs others avoid, come early, stay late. Amazingly good things happen. Find someone who is studying video, learn the technology, watch tape with him, and listen and ask good questions.

If you only had two 30-minute sessions a week to train your team, how would you prepare them?

30 minutes is not a lot of time. I would break it down:

  5- Stretch.

  7 – Individual – blocking, tackling, fundamentals that relate to a position.

  8 – Group – 9 on 7, 7 on 7.

  10- Team – Team Drill.

  Special Teams find time before or after practice.

What goes into your decision to leave or stay at a job?

Does this move put my family at an inconvenience? Don't take it. Does this job put me in a better position to achieve family goals? Take it, if comfortable with the new environment. I have never taken a job based only on money. In fact, I never inquired about salary unless brought up in conversation.

What do you do to overcome times of struggle, burnout, or overwhelm? Who do you turn to?

I turn to myself and put a plan together that will allow a chance for success. The Lord helps those who help themselves.

What do you think about immediately after one of your athletes is injured? What is your mindset in the following week?

I'm always concerned for the health of our athletes. Then allow those qualified to attend to the injured athlete and make all decisions as to what is best for him. All decisions as to his return to playing or practice are given to those who are medically qualified to make those decisions.

How do you approach difficult conversations with athletes, coworkers, or your boss?

I have always described myself as a "confrontational problem solver!" When faced with a problem, move forward in a timely fashion and get it solved. Get together with those who are involved in the problem (TOGETHER!) Talk it out, listen, get all to voice thoughts, then, make a decision in a timely fashion.

Dragging issues out creates a lack of leadership. If a decision doesn't work out, admit the decision was not the best and move forward. That is called vulnerability and is essential in good leadership.

Do you have a "failure" that was critical to your long-term development or success?

I was fired from my first head coaching job. In my second head coaching job, I was told by our President that he had the votes to drop football. When he didn't have the votes, ten years later, we won a National Championship.

What traits or skills do your most successful athletes have in common?

I describe success as having a great experience in his or her time with you. We make a Great mistake when success is starting, earning a scholarship, winning a championship, etc. How will he answer this question twenty years down the road, "I am glad I played football for Jack Harbaugh, I am a better man for that experience."

What books or resources do you most often recommend to coaches?

Five Dysfunctions of a Team—Patrick Lencioni.

"I actually never think of things as failures. I have always just assessed an outcome and tried to do better the next time I face that situation. I 100% believe in lesson learned more than game lost."

-Kevin Eastman

Kevin Eastman is regarded as one of the best teachers in basketball, with over 40 years of experience in both college and professional coaching. Known as a thought leader, he is now an engaging speaker who inspires sports teams and diverse corporate groups alike. Eastman coached in two NBA Finals (2008, 2010) with the Boston Celtics, winning the NBA Championship in 2008. He also served as an Assistant Coach and VP of Basketball Operations for the Los Angeles Clippers and spent 11 years as a College Head Coach, 11 years as a College Assistant, and four years as a College Director of Athletics. Additionally, Eastman worked with Nike as the Director of Nike Skills Academies, collaborating with the company's elite college and high school players. Throughout his career, he has worked with and coached numerous NBA All-Stars, including LeBron James, Kobe Bryant, Chris Paul, Blake Griffin, Paul Pierce, Kevin Garnett, Anthony Davis, and Ray Allen. Eastman has been inducted into the Hall of Fame at the University of Richmond, Haddonfield Memorial High School, and South Jersey Basketball. He also received the University of Richmond's Spider Athletics Alumni Achievement Award in 2020.

Who do you go to when you need advice? Why them?

George Raveling—former D1 Head Coach and Director of Basketball at Nike. He is a deep thinker with great wisdom. Also Lawrence Frank—President of Basketball Operations with LA Clippers and Dave Wohl—former NBA coach and executive. My wife Wendy, as she is one of my truth tellers and sees things differently than I do and I feel this is important.

I go to them because I trust them. I know they have wisdom to share, and they see things I may not see but need to see.

What early job was pivotal in your career? Why?

Graduate Assistant at the University of Richmond (my alma mater). It was entry level where I got to understand the amount of work that goes into being a coach. As a player, you never have a clue about how much coaches do to prepare a team and run a program. I was fortunate that the Head Coach allowed me to be in on everything, even if I did not have the responsibility or authority in a given area of the program.

What are your first steps when you start a new job? What do you need to figure out, what do you need to get done, who do you need to get to know?

- Totally understand my role and expectations.
- Meet the people and build genuine relationships with those that will impact my success.
- Know how my boss best receives information (good or bad).
- What is most pressing—get those done—make the main thing the main thing.

What advice do you have for a college student looking to break into coaching? Who are the best mentors in the world to work for early in your career?

- Start close to home where you can drive to places that do what you hope to do for your career. Visit local programs or pro teams to observe and meet people.
- Begin to study the game at a deeper level.
- Research YouTube, articles, books about the field.
- Meet people so that you can begin to develop relationships.
- Work at summer camps so they can see your effort and knowledge—offer to do the little jobs that no one else may want to do.
- Start to develop a niche—mine was skill development—everyone who applies for a job will say they work hard and are loyal—so what separates you? Skill development? Analytics?

If you only had two 30-minute sessions a week to train your team, how would you prepare them?

- This would depend on the strengths I believe that team possesses. I would need to determine how this group can win games and make sure we are very good in that area.
- I would encourage them to work on their individual skills like shooting and

dribbling on their own, as we would likely have to spend our 30-minutes on team growth and improvement.

- I would try to meet individually off the court to watch film with them and talk to them about their role and how they are doing (as well as making sure I have a read on how they are doing off the court).

What goes into your decision to leave or stay at a job?

For me it's pretty simple. If I feel I cannot give everything I have to a job, if I have lost a little of the juice you have when you wake up every day, if you feel you are no longer contributing to the level the job requires, or if you have a greater desire to do something else—those for me would be signs.

What do you do to overcome times of struggle, burnout, or overwhelm? Who do you turn to?

- Try to be very aware that I am struggling.

- Put thought to why I am feeling this way.

- Talk to people I trust who will give me the truth and help me work my way out of it.

- Understand that I have to do the work to get out of these challenges.

- With burnout, I simply get away from it mentally and physically for a while (or as long as I can relative to the demands of the job at that point in time).

- I also always try to remember why I wanted so badly to enter this field and ask myself—do I still have this feeling?

What do you think about immediately after one of your athletes is injured? What is your mindset in the following week?

- What is the injury and how bad is it?

- What can we do to help the athlete recover from this?

- Have we properly prepared the "next man" and who is that?

- From the time they are injured to the time of their recovery, I want to make sure they stay involved with and feel a true member of the team, and make sure they understand the power of the rehab program to their recovery.

How do you approach difficult conversations with athletes, coworkers, or your boss?

With total honesty...Period. The key becomes how you deliver this message.

Do you have a "failure" that was critical to your long-term development or success?

I actually never think of things as failures. I have always just assessed an outcome and tried to do better the next time I face that situation. I 100% believe in lesson learned more than game lost.

If I had to point to one—we did not win as much as I wanted to at Washington State University—nor to the level that I thought it should be so I decided it was best for the school and the returning players that our AD bring in a new voice. I talked it over with our AD and decided it was best for everyone that I resign. It was a great decision for me.

What traits or skills do your most successful athletes have in common?

There are many, but these are most important in my mind:

- A burning desire to continue to improve.
- A disciplined focus.
- A willingness to be coached—an open mind to learn more.
- Resilience to fight through hard times.
- They are true competitors.
- They understand they cannot do it alone—there must be a team focus as well—they know they need their teammates and coaches.

What books or resources do you most often recommend to coaches?

I first talk about the person going out on their own to find great books in their areas of interest or the areas they want to grow in. I have found that when you put the work in is when you earn the right to get the results. I also recommend they search for YouTube videos and articles as it is not always books that have the best information. I know you will get a lot of books, but I strongly believe it is the work you put in to find them yourself that returns the best information.

> *"He said, 'I think one of these days you're going to amount to something.' That changed my whole attitude. Now here's a guy who had no reason to care, but cared. I used that story for almost every kid that came into college, that you need somebody to show you the direction to go, and help you get to where you wanna be."*
>
> ## -Bill Brogden

Bill Brogden is a Hall of Fame Men's Golf Coach who led programs at LSU, Oral Roberts University, and the University of Tulsa, winning a total of 16 conference championships. At ORU, Brogden guided the program to four national top-10 finishes, including a third-place finish in the NCAA National Championships in 1980 and a national runner-up finish in 1981. He was inducted into the ORU Athletics Hall of Fame in 2011 and again in 2024 as part of the 1981 team, the first team in ORU athletics history to be inducted into the Hall of Fame. Throughout his career, Brogden coached numerous All-Americans and players who went on to compete on the PGA Tour. **(Brogden's responses were transcribed from a phone call)**

Who do you go to when you need advice? Why them?

I went to my dad growing up. Then I went to somebody I trust. I've gotta have faith in them, and I have to know that they've been successful before I can listen to them. They have done what I want to do, because you're trying to learn from somebody that's already done it.

What early job was pivotal in your career? Why?

I went to high school first for two years—did not like it at all. I didn't like the teaching aspect of it. I was in Durham, North Carolina, and I went to Duke and asked the head basketball coach for a job. I said, "I wanna work for somebody I can learn from." My dad was very successful as a high school coach, and he got me my first job I'm sure. It was good, but I wanted to learn more, so I just went and I asked for a job.

He told me, "I don't have a job, but I have a graduate assistant position." He gave me all types of opportunities. He had me teach golf classes, coach the freshmen team, go on the road and recruit for three weeks, and work as a football trainer. He helped me become a coach. I went there, and there were two guys at Duke at the time as assistant coaches—one was Chuck Daly and the other one was Hubie Brown. They were the most powerful people I'd ever met. Scared me. I'm a little 'ole North Carolina boy, and these guys were somewhere between eight and twelve years older than I was, so I was pretty rookie. I took notes every day—what I liked at practice and what I didn't like, what they did say and what they didn't say. I had a suitcase full of notes from every day for a year and a half.

What are your first steps when you start a new job? What do you need to figure out, what do you need to get done, who do you need to get to know?
The first thing I'd wanna know is who are the good guys and who are the bad guys. You have to be careful because you may get a bad guy to start with that you think is a good guy and you get all messed up. But as long as I did my job, kept quiet, did what I was supposed to do, I could figure out eventually who the good guys are and who is important and who is successful. And those guys that are successful are usually the good guys. That way you figure out what you need to do, what you can't do, what you should do, who you can bark at, who you can't bark at.

You need to know who the good guys are—who's gonna take care of you, who's gonna be interested in you, and who's not. From there, as long as I did my job, I didn't worry about anybody else. I wanted to have an X amount of money, and budget, and all that stuff to do what I needed to do, but other than that I'd pretty much stay to myself. My dad said something to me one time, "You know, you've never been fired after about 30-40 years of coaching." If I do my job, why am I going to get fired? If I try to take care of people and we all do what's right, then I'm not worried about getting fired.

What advice do you have for a college student looking to break into coaching? Who are the best mentors in the world to work for early in your career?
Some coaches make coaching look easy. It's not that easy. Successful coaches spend a lot of time and energy in coaching. It's one of the neatest jobs that allows you to get close to guys and help them become who they want to become. All these athletes that think they can do it on their own—they can't. But they don't know that. They have to have someone in order to help them. I had guys that helped me along the way.

I was a basketball player in college—I'm just having a great time, not going to class very often, and doing all kinds of things that most athletes do. The AD said, "I'm going to call your dad." Being the smart ass guy I was, I go, "It's none of your business." He kind of ticked me off. A couple of weeks later, he called me back in his office. He goes, "You know why I called you in?" I said, "No, I'm none of your business." He responded, "I think one of these days you're going to amount to something." That changed my whole attitude. Now here's a guy who had no reason to care, but cared. I used that story for almost every kid that came into college, that you need somebody to show you the direction to go, and help you get to where you wanna be. We're not telling you what to do, we're just trying to help you get to where you want to be.

To get into coaching, it takes a special person, because it's not easy. I was very lucky when I started coaching; I happened to run around with the best college coaches there were. I learned from the best from the very beginning. I didn't know what I was doing, but why wouldn't you want to associate with successful people? Why would you want to associate with a guy that's not very successful?

If you only had two 30-minute sessions a week to train your team, how would you prepare them?
I would spend at least one of them on mental, self-belief, trusting, being able to know that I can do what I need to do. The other one trying to do the physical skills. But if I know I can do something, I can do it. In golf, we spend way too much time working on the swing rather than how to mentally play the game of golf.

What goes into your decision to leave or stay at a job?
If I'm happy at a job, and happy is I have what I need to be successful. Money is not everything. I was at LSU, which was in the top ten programs in golf, and then I came to Oral Roberts and they did not have a program. Oral made it worthwhile for me to be here, not financially as much, but he was going to give me a budget and I didn't have to teach classes. I could be the golf coach and he just wanted a successful team. With his support, we went out and recruited the best players in the country. And Oral Roberts, nobody knew about that program. We were very good the next year. We were very good, but that was because of the support of Oral Roberts. People ask me who was the best athletic director I ever had—Oral Roberts. He could do things. If he wanted to have a good program, he'd have a good program. If he wanted to spend money on it, he'd spend money on it. If he wanted to show support, he did it. I was very fortunate

to be associated with him.

If I'm happy I'm gonna stay. Like I said, money's not everything. The area you live in is important. I don't want to be up north, I'm not a cold bodied guy, so I'm gonna stay south. If you've got what you need to be successful, then do your job and be successful.

What do you do to overcome times of struggle, burnout, or overwhelm? Who do you turn to?

I try to talk to older coaches that have been through it. They can tell you how to handle situations. You learn by your own experiences, but you also need advice from people that are successful, because everybody goes through burnout, everybody goes through struggles. You just have to ask people what they do. I had a kid one time that I couldn't stand being around, but a great player. I'd ask coaches, "What do you do when you got a guy like this?" They said, "You can do one of two things: you can cut him, or you can ignore him and play him." So being a younger coach, you feel like you've got to have every player, particularly a good player because he's going to determine whether you win or lose, blah blah blah...So I just put up with him, I didn't talk to him, I just stayed away from him.

Something happened and the kid left. The team absolutely flipped and became twice as good after he left. They go, "Coach, this guy pissed us off every day." I said, "Why didn't you tell me, cause he pissed me off every day!" We were way better off without him. That's the experience that you go through that you've got to understand your team and what's gonna make them better and why they work the way they do. I'd always ask older coaches that had been around a long time whenever I had a problem. I used to have two or three guys once I got older that called me the godfather. They'd call me and say, "Godfather, I've got a problem."

What do you think about immediately after one of your athletes is injured? What is your mindset in the following week?

I'm back to the one guy doesn't make a team. I feel sorry for him being hurt and that he can't play, and we try to get him ready and all that kind of stuff that you do. But it's not going to distract the team from being a team. You gotta have more than one player on a team.

How do you approach difficult conversations with athletes, coworkers, or your boss?

I got a master's degree in counseling because I didn't want any more physical education. I wanted to learn how to deal with people. That's what I enjoyed the most about coaching, that I could sit down with a kid, a player, or a coworker, and I'd try to understand what they're thinking along with what I'm thinking. That's the interesting part, learning your players. I spent a lot of time with my players individually to sit down with them and understand them and why they act like they do. There is always a reason why someone acts the way they do. In counseling sessions, I'd take the worst kid in high school in the 10th grade, 11th grade, 12th grade, and I'd sit down and interview them. I'd say, "Why do you act like you do?" (Grumble in response). Then all of a sudden, they'd go, "Well, you know my mom or my dad..." Okay, now we have a reason why you act the way you do. Now we can help you. If you sit down with a person long enough, they'll tell you everything. That's the beauty of doing it. "I have a girlfriend problem." Okay, that's why you're not playing good golf. That's why your grades aren't good. There's always a reason that person acts the way they do.

With my boss, that's a little more difficult, because you will never get to know your boss like you would like to in most cases. He's going to be standoffish enough to keep you from getting too close. A coach may get that way also with a player, but I try not to get that way. I always try to get close enough to them, but not too close where we got to be buddy buddy. I wanted their respect, and they had my respect.

Do you have a "failure" that was critical to your long-term development or success?

I never called it failure. I called it tough times, and good guys get through tough times. I thought I was a good guy and tough guy for most situations. I felt that if I was doing my job, then I'd get through it and everything would be alright. It's never as bad as you think it is. Somebody always has it worse than you do. You're not an extreme, you're not an example. Most of the time it's just a tough situation, whatever that might be. I feel like I was blessed, because I never really thought of it as a failure. We didn't succeed when we probably should have, but there was always next year, and I always had a job, so I never looked at it as a failure. We finished second in the NCAA one year and lost by two shots. Was that a failure? No, that wasn't a failure. Were we ranked number one in the country? Yes. Should we have won? Should, could, whatever, but I don't look at it as a failure. I look at it as a very successful period of time.

What traits or skills do your most successful athletes have in common?

They all have a desire. They all have a willpower. I think willpower has been lost somewhere in the years past. I don't know why exactly. You need a desire and a work ethic, and you have to ask questions, you have to learn as much as you can possibly learn. Most great athletes have a knowledge of what to do. Then it's an execution of doing the job. They all have something they are shooting for, something that drives them.

Most of the successful athletes are successful because they can execute when they need to execute. When they have to perform, they perform. They are few and far between. There are a lot of great players, but there are very few superstars that can perform, you know your Michael Jordans, your Tiger Woods, your Tom Bradys. When it's time to perform, they perform. They're exceptional.

The best players I've ever had always ask questions because they want to get better. The mediocre or average player, I ask them, "Why don't you ask questions? You don't want me to know that you don't know, that's why you don't ask questions. I already know you don't know!"

> *"Learn the names of all of your athletes and staff—use roster pictures and literally study their faces. Being able to call someone by their name goes a long way in building relationships."*
>
> ## -Alex Dee

Alex Dee is the Assistant Director of Sports Performance at Wichita State University, where he works directly with the Baseball and Men's and Women's Tennis programs. In his first season at Wichita State, he helped the Baseball program reach the AAC Tournament Championship. Dee previously held the same role at Oral Roberts University, where he worked with Women's Basketball, Volleyball, and Men's Tennis.

Who do you go to when you need advice? Why them?

Professionally: Previous directors/more experienced coaches I've worked with—I trust them and value their opinion and know they will tell me things straight. Also, other coaches my age or in the same sport that I work with—I value sharing experiences with people in the same stage of life as me.

What early job was pivotal in your career? Why?

- University of Denver internship—took practical knowledge and applied it to coaching, gave me the responsibility of actually leading groups.

- First full-time job at Oral Roberts University—no hand holding anymore. Go out and coach and learn from your mistakes, assist in every session possible to learn from other coaches.

What are your first steps when you start a new job? What do you need to figure out, what do you need to get done, who do you need to get to know?

Learn the names of all of your athletes and staff—use roster pictures and literally study their faces. Being able to call someone by their name goes a long way in building relationships. Meet with the athletic trainers for your sports—going to be a major relationship. Immerse yourself in everything your teams do—go out of your way to be involved in meetings and practices and other things that will give you time with everyone. Probably part of the interview, but ask questions about expectations and what the last coach did well and things they could have done better.

What advice do you have for a college student looking to break into coaching? Who are the best mentors in the world to work for early in your career?

Go coach! Train yourself and your friends. Ask to intern/volunteer with the athletic department at the school you go to, learn from them and then use their connections to find other opportunities. Don't be swayed by a coach just because they have a big logo, ask around and find out who is actually good.

If you only had two 30-minute sessions a week to train your team, how would you prepare them?

Both Sessions I would sprint and jump and fill the rest of the time with lifting.

- Sprint—have different starts and compete.

- Jump—find a new jump "problem" for them to solve.

- Squat—Tons of different variations (SL or DL).

- Row—some sort of upper pull daily.

- Core—Flex, Bend, Rotate-change it up.

What goes into your decision to leave or stay at a job?

Happiness—do I enjoy going into work? Do I like the athletes and coaches I work with? What about my coworkers?

Room for growth—am I improving as a coach? Can I get a raise, be promoted, or gain responsibilities?

What do you do to overcome times of struggle, burnout, or overwhelm? Who do you turn to?

I turn to God. I make more time in my day to sit with Him. I have a morning routine that sets me up for the day. Find something that takes your mind completely off the job or challenges you in a different way. Could be a book, mindless tv, golf, or your family. I recently started running a couple miles per week because it's new to me and it sucks.

What do you think about immediately after one of your athletes is injured? What is your mindset in the following week?

The natural reaction is to figure out, "What could we have done differently?" That could be a reasonable response if someone got hurt from something preventable like exercise set up. If someone pulls a hamstring or something, then we have to focus on what we can do now to help that athlete. The injury already happened, so beating yourself up or feeling sorry for yourself over something you could or couldn't have prevented isn't worth going crazy over. Figure out what you can do now to get that athlete back quicker. After that, then you can look into what we can change next time.

How do you approach difficult conversations with athletes, coworkers, or your boss?

Work on building a strong relationship first. If that is established, then the difficult conversation becomes less difficult. The sooner you build relationships, the better off you'll be. Just pull the band aid off and be direct.

Do you have a "failure" that was critical to your long-term development or success?

- I got denied from a few jobs—figure out why, get better at those things.
- Train yourself—if you don't get better then you can make modifications for your athletes.

What traits or skills do your most successful athletes have in common?

Most successful in the weight room:

- Hard working - gives good effort and wants to do more.
- Body awareness - control body in space.
- Adaptable - can solve movement problems with multiple strategies.

Most successful on field/court:

- Be really good at the skill and tactics of your sport.

What books or resources do you most often recommend to coaches?

Internships—go watch someone coach and ask them questions about their why. Podcasts/social media—follow coaches that interest you, then dive deeper into the methods they talk about—use that as a direction to find resources.

"It isn't just my program; it is OUR program. Each person has a percentage of the program that is theirs, and I can't run the show without them."

-Stephanie Mock Grubbs

Stephanie Mock Grubbs is the Assistant Athletic Director for Sports Performance at the University of Pittsburgh. She oversees the strength and conditioning and sports science department for 19 teams, while directly leading the Pitt Volleyball program that is currently ranked No. 1 in the nation at the time of this writing. Grubbs also helped lead the team to three straight Final Four appearances and two straight ACC Championships. Before starting at Pitt, she spent three years at Mississippi State as Director of Olympic Sports Strength and Conditioning, directly overseeing the Softball and Volleyball programs. Grubbs previously worked at Clemson as the Assistant Director of Olympic Sports Strength and Conditioning prior to Mississippi State.

What early job was pivotal in your career? Why?

I was surrounded by amazing leaders early in my career, and I never take that for granted. When I think about leadership, I think of all the people that invested into me as a young professional, and it is now my job to pass that along. Leadership is about being selfless, making the hard decisions, and doing whatever is best for the team no matter what role you are in. Leading people is a great opportunity daily, and you should never take it for granted.

What advice do you have for a college student looking to break into coaching? Who are the best mentors in the world to work for early in your career?

It's important to know your own "Why" before leading others. Mine is "get comfortable being uncomfortable." Surround yourself with people that have similar core values as you and a similar mission. I can't surround myself with just ordinary people when my goal is to be extraordinary. I have been trained to have a "want to" versus "have to" mentality from mentors that developed me early in my career and still do to this day. I am constantly wanting to grow and learn no matter what step I am in within my career.

Some other core values I have lived by originate from the book *Wins, Losses, and Lessons* by Lou Holtz. I could immediately apply these keys to success as an educator into how I not only get the most out of my staff, but more importantly, my student–athletes.

Keys to success as an educator or coach:

· To get people to buy in, it takes enthusiasm and passion.

· Have to know the X's and O's inside and out.

· Show how much you care.

· Present and communicate information in a manner that relates to them.

I've found that these four keys to success have allowed me to stay grounded and never lose my identity as a leader, no matter how crazy things get around me. People will follow you if you show great passion in your position, but also if you are truly invested in them as a person and professional.

Bonus: Can you share insight into your process of building a team/department?
When building a team, it is most important to have the RIGHT people on your team. I have always valued hiring people with the following: Character, Loyalty, and a Strong Work Ethic. Those three initial characteristics will get you in the door. To stay on the team, you need to have a relentless pursuit of knowledge and be willing to always push yourself CONSISTENTLY. I have been extremely grateful to have the opportunity to hire great staffs. When going on the interview, administration will always look for you as a leader to have a clear and concise plan of what the first 90 days will look like, as well as a 3–5 year plan for goals for the department.

Be **clear and direct** with your staff members through the hiring process about roles and expectations for the position. Once hired, be explicit with staff expectations and leave no stone unturned. This allows you to hold people accountable and drive a tight ship with roles and expectations because you have created the grounds to do so.

I truly believe when building your team, it is critical to **lead not manage.** It's always important to set an example in terms of work ethic for the staff to truly buy into what you are building. It is also important to develop leadership within the staff. In order to develop future directors, I want to give my staff members areas of responsibility that will develop their leadership skills. It is my job to develop and prepare my staff to be the leaders of tomorrow.

It is not only important to talk about building the team, but also how I keep my team together and don't let people pluck off my talented staff. This comes down to creating a unique work environment that makes people feel respected and that they are constantly being challenged or growing. One area I know my staff appreciates is the fact that I am **organized** and respect their time. Have an agenda and create structure for your staff. Always communicate ahead of time about staff meetings and professional development sessions. Not only are you respecting your staff's time, but they also know to do the same with my time because I set that expectation from the start.

Have a vision to share with your staff that they can always go back to regarding who we are. I have always put my staff first, and building trust with your team is the foundation of where we start. You can build trust by being vulnerable with your staff and owning up to your strengths and weaknesses. As the head person, you are not perfect. You must hire a great staff around you to complement your weak points.

Bonus: How do you try to empower your staff members?
As a leader, I am constantly looking to not only get the most out of my potential, but the ones around me as well. "Leadership isn't one person leading a team. It is a group of leaders working together, up and down the chain of command, to lead." (Book: *Extreme Ownership*)

I constantly tell my staff that language is important. It isn't just my program; it is OUR program. Each person has a percentage of the program that is theirs, and I can't run the show without them. It is powerful to give each staff member full autonomy of their responsibilities and let them run with it. No one enjoys being micromanaged, and it is key to create opportunities for people to take on new responsibilities that fit their skill set and personality while making it theirs.

It is my job as a leader to inspire, challenge, and show direction for the program and allow the talented people around me to give constructive criticism to make the vision OURS.

How do you approach difficult conversations with athletes, coworkers, or your boss?
An area I am always looking to cultivate with my staff is having healthy conflict and constructive debate. You never want to have a group of "yes" men or women around you because your program will become stagnant. This is necessary to get the most out

of meetings and create an environment for unfiltered and passionate debate of ideas, allowing the program to consistently grow and be the best in the country.

What books or resources do you most often recommend to coaches?

We are always staying on the cutting edge and creating the best training environment for our student-athletes. From James Clear's book *Atomic Habits*, "Every action you take is a vote for the type of person you wish to become." One of our staff goals is to have a relentless pursuit of knowledge, and we build it into our crazy work weeks to create an environment for growth. I look to hire lifelong learners and people that challenge me. That's what will make our program the best in the country and develop the next generation to do the same.

"After every season, I watch film of our close losses and watch the decision making that went into each possession. What players were on the court, what offensive plays did I call, what defense were we in? What can I learn from each of these games to take into the following year and get better from?"

-Beth O'Boyle

Beth O'Boyle is in her 11th year as the Head Women's Basketball Coach at Virginia Commonwealth University, where she currently holds the record for the most career wins in school history. O'Boyle led the 2023-2024 team to a program record of 26 regular season wins. Additionally, the team set an NCAA record for the largest one-year turnaround, progressing from a 7-22 record to 26-6. She guided the Rams to their second-ever NCAA Tournament appearance in 2021, accompanied by the A-10 Conference Tournament Championship. O'Boyle was named A-10 Coach of the Year in 2019 after leading VCU to the program's first Conference Championship. She earned her position at VCU after elevating the program at Stony Brook and gained experience as the Associate Head Coach at Canisius and as the Head Coach at Montclair State University.

Who do you go to when you need advice? Why them?

Who is on your train? Who are the group of people that you trust with your career, with your team, and whose advice you know will both be supportive and challenging at times? I have a former athletic director and highly successful coach (not basketball) who I rely on. In addition, I have two other college basketball coaches, and a college friend who runs her own business, that I constantly run situations by. Be open to what those who know you the best have to say, and then trust yourself on how to take the advice and apply it.

What early job was pivotal in your career? Why?

I was the assistant at the University of Rochester with Head Coach Jim Scheible. I learned how to build a program and take one that had been traditionally unsuccessful to the highest level in Division III. It was a great opportunity to learn how to recruit, how to build confidence, and to learn all aspects of the game.

What are your first steps when you start a new job? What do you need to figure out, what do you need to get done, who do you need to get to know?

Get to know your current players. Why did they choose the school, why do they play, all the things that have nothing to do with the court, getting to know them as people first. Second, put together a staff that believes in the way you want to coach your players and the experience that you want to create. In the first couple of weeks, it's helpful to talk with other sport coaches in the department and ask lots of questions. How do you sell the university, what places do you take recruits, what challenges have you faced, what have been the best parts? Be a sponge and take it all in.

What advice do you have for a college student looking to break into coaching? Who are the best mentors in the world to work for early in your career?

One of the most important pieces to breaking into coaching is doing a great job where you are. If you are a current player and are about to graduate, getting a great recommendation from your current head coach or assistants is very helpful. Joining the WBCA and going to the Final Four is an excellent way to network. Following coaches on social media is a good way to stay up to date on job postings.

If you only had two 30-minute sessions a week to train your team, how would you prepare them?

One of the best drills to do over the summer is to play one on one. It forces you to play all parts of the game—defensive, offensive, works on your handle, rebounding, and it's competitive. 30 minutes is a great workout time—if all drills are done at game pace. I like utilizing goals and the clock to help push the pace.

What goes into your decision to leave or stay at a job?

When I took my first college coaching job, my college soccer coach gave me great advice—"Who are the people you are going to be working with?" It wasn't about the salary, the part of the country, or the division. It was about if being a part of this program was going to help me prepare to be a successful college coach.

What do you do to overcome times of struggle, burnout, or overwhelm? Who do you turn to?

Burnout is very difficult these days for both coaches and players. There are so many pressures and demands on your time. My family and my friends are all important pieces for me to stay present and find joy in everyday life.

What do you think about immediately after one of your athletes is injured? What is your mindset in the following week?

Injuries can be really hard on players, both mentally and physically. First piece is checking in and asking how they feel, what they need, and trying to stay very in the moment with them. Not on to the next part of practice or the game—in that moment, really listen and show care.

How do you approach difficult conversations with athletes, coworkers, or your boss?

I start with—what is in the best interest of the program? How am I communicating? Where is the meeting taking place?

Do you have a "failure" that was critical to your long-term development or success?

After every season, I watch film of our close losses and watch the decision making that went into each possession. What players were on the court, what offensive plays did I call, what defense were we in? What can I learn from each of these games to take into the following year and get better from?

What traits or skills do your most successful athletes have in common?

The highest performers I have coached all have a Consistency. They have an incredible work ethic on the court, in the weight room, on the track, and in the classroom. It just never turns off, they constantly work like a pro.

What books or resources do you most often recommend to coaches?

It's really important for coaches to keep learning. I am a huge advocate of joining our coach's association and attending our convention. It's great to listen and watch coaches go through drills and talk about their experiences. There are a ton of great books, videos, and podcasts about coaching, but what I think matters the most is being open to really learning.

> *"A lot of people see the big logo. Do you actually want to coach athletes, or are you a fan? You can find that out real quick by what you're doing in your spare time."*

> ## *-Zack Zillner*

Zack Zillner is in his eighth season as the Head Sports Performance Coach for Women's Basketball at the University of Texas, where he has helped the team win three consecutive Big 12 Championships and reach the Elite Eight three times in four years. Before arriving in Austin, Zillner worked at the University of Kansas, the University of Illinois, and Southern Miss. He has coached numerous players who have gone on to have professional careers, including Charli Collier, the number one pick in the 2021 WNBA Draft. Additionally, Zack is the co-host of the *Coach Em Up Podcast* with Tim Riley.

Who do you go to when you need advice? Why them?
Andrea Hudy—I've seen her do it at such a high level for so long, this is what pushes me to keep going—she's won more national championships and conference championships in basketball than anyone—and she's going back to school to get her doctorate. Someone like that could easily run her same program from 2008 and just rest on her accomplishments of, "We won 9 Natty's, this is what we did, rinse and repeat." But the fact that she is still pushing the needle to get smarter and find that one percent—she could retire tomorrow, but instead she's breaking her back over a dissertation. If she's doing that, then why are you so good with what you're doing at 34 or 40 that you think your program's fine? The lack of complacency on her part is so cool.

    Cory Schlesinger—We were friends forever and then recently got to work together at Texas. What I admire about Cory is that he's a forward thinker and isn't afraid to put his ideas out there. He's a brilliant dude, and thinks about movement beyond the confines of the weight room. His ability to take what he's seen on the court at all levels and translate it to sports performance is a thing of beauty. He's not afraid to put himself out there and try new things. Whether it's business, personal life, training—he's very comfortable with who he is and is not afraid to put his opinions out there. I really admire him for that.

Luke Bradford at Kansas was probably my biggest influence as an intern coming up because of how closely I worked with him, Joe Staub, and Glen Cain. The fact that they would include me in all parts of sports performance, from the X's and O's of training, to bringing me into team meetings that would help prepare me for the day where I would be running my own program. **Danny Foley,** he's in the private sector; he does a lot with fascia training and he's a high-level person with the human body, physiology, and integrating movement patterns with return to play.

Tim Riley from Kollective—I do the podcast with him. Tim's got an unbelievable story, and talk about a guy that can just figure it out. That's Tim, he's super savvy. Obviously if you're in the private sector, you have to be good at business. Otherwise it doesn't matter how good of a coach you are. I bounce ideas off of him all the time. Not to mention just a great human to hang out with.

Adam Fletcher, Brady Welsh, Jena Ready, Molly Binetti, and Kelly Dormandy are other coaches that inspire me as well.

What early job was pivotal in your career? Why?

I lucked out with my first internship at the University of Kansas. I had no idea who was a good strength coach, who was a bad strength coach. The fact that I was there with Andrea Hudy, who is arguably the best basketball strength coach in the world... that's insane. I was so fortunate to work for her for seven years. While I was there, the assistants Kansas had were unbelievable. I didn't know that when I was younger, I was like, "Oh, this is cool. This is how coaches interact." We had a lot of group meetings, and she would include me in everything. In a lot of internships, the real coaches have the meetings and you just set up and clean up. That was my main responsibility, but she would include us in the staff meetings and take us to meetings with head coaches, assistant coaches, and she'd assign us to a different coach every semester so we'd learn different methodologies.

You hear horror stories from other coaches, and that was so foreign to me. It's been great and bad in the fact of the standard that she set there—I thought that's how every weight room should be.... Things like edited music, school issued gear on when training, every athlete is doing things at the standard of excellence that's required, and if you don't—there's the door, there was no wiggle room for any nonsense. Everything was validated by results. If you couldn't prove that whatever you were doing actually moved the needle for performance, why was it in the program?

I'll keep tooting her horn, I think she does a great job of empowering her staff.

She never once referred to any of us interns as interns. She referred to us as her assistants. Little language stuff like that makes people more invested because they do feel like they are part of the bigger picture of everything. If you call someone an intern, that puts you in a box. "I'm just an intern." Why does it matter what I do? But if they're making the statement, "No, this is my assistant," and value your opinion, it makes it a joy to come to work every day. Seeing those coaches, being observant and almost like a chameleon of—how does she handle different situations? I use that to this day with how to deal with tough coaches and tough athletes. If I didn't have that Kansas internship, I don't know where I'd be right now, probably selling insurance or something.

What are your first steps when you start a new job? What do you need to figure out, what do you need to get done, who do you need to get to know?

I always talk to the head coach first; figure out what they want. Then I need to figure out the staff. Who's the assistant coach that has the head coach's ear the most? Head coaches are busy with recruiting, administrators, parents, scouts, all this other stuff; I'm not going to get as much one-on-one time with the head coach as I may hope for. Especially if the head coach doesn't get what I'm trying to accomplish in the weight room, it's up to me to find whoever has his or her ear the most. That needs to be where I put all my time and energy, and put it into grabbing coffee, getting breakfast, anything to build that relationship. A lot of coaches say what they want and then they do something totally different. It's my job to talk to all the other assistants to figure out—the coach before me, what did you really like about them? What did you not like about them? I always try to figure out what's the culture of that team and that head coach. Work backwards from there.

Then I try to meet all the other people that will make my life easier; ops people, the athletic trainers, and different administrators. Navigate the landscape of wanting to come in and make a big change, but I also don't want to step on people's toes who've been there.

I'd also say to spend as much time in your first year at the facility. You should be in there all the time. It shouldn't be a situation where they don't know where you are or what you're doing. Then it's establishing a relationship with the athletes, as far as your standards and how you can help them get results.

As young coaches, we're always concerned about being liked. It's really easy to be relatable and likable when you're 25 and the athlete is 22, but the older you get, chances are you're not going to dress like them or listen to the same kind of music. I've found that you want to be the coach that can get results. If these athletes know they're going to get better with you and can make a solid training culture, you're going to have immediate buy-in right there. Just know there's growing pains with any new job and stay the course. Document everything, cross your fingers, and let it rip.

What advice do you have for a college student looking to break into coaching? Who are the best mentors in the world to work for early in your career?

You have to figure out whether you're a coach or a fan. A lot of people see the Texas logo, or any big name school logo, and they're like, "Wow, that's so cool." It's this fake fame. Do you actually want to coach athletes, or are you a fan of the whole lifestyle? You can find out real quick by what you're doing in your spare time. If you're done working all day in the weight room and you find yourself on YouTube and Google, reading different articles about sports performance, listening to podcasts about sports performance, doing all that type of training yourself—basically you're obsessed with it—then I think it's a good career path. If you leave work, shut it off, do other hobbies, that's fine, but I don't think you're fully obsessed with it enough to put in the time that's required to be a really good coach. I would find myself getting home and not doing my homework to look at a new T-Nation article. It sounds ridiculous, but when I was growing up with other coaches who had other hobbies, it was nice for them, but they're not in the field anymore. I don't think they were obsessed. You have to find that obsession.

There's no way around it, you'll have to make sacrifices. Just like I tell my athletes; if you want to be the best, you're going to have to come early, stay late. I don't want to romanticize guarding your desk all day or "the grind", but when you're in an internship, there are usually three or four interns. If one job comes up in the spring, who's the director going to recommend? They can't recommend all three of you. You're in a competition every day of not only doing a good job, but also how you treat people.

Find someone who's been doing this a long time. I always discourage people from interning for me. I'm only 35; look for someone who's in their 40s, or an older coach who's had success at a high level for years and years. Find someone who's constantly pushing the field forward with innovation and research, not just that they're in a certain spot because they've been there for a while. I'd ask around, there are good coaches everywhere. I'd shoot for the best, and then if you don't get those, eventually get down to someone like me.

What goes into your decision to leave or stay at a job?

I had a conversation with one of our assistants today, and you need to have five things that are important to you. It's family, location, money, the sport you're working with, and then whatever X factor you want (Friends/Institution/ability to grow), and then rank everything in order of importance.

I was talking to this assistant, and family and location were the most important to them, but they wanted to be a Division I strength coach, and all their family is in Austin.

"Okay, you want to be a women's collegiate basketball strength coach, but your family is really important to you, and the city is really important to you, which is Austin, Texas... and I'm probably not going anywhere. So, are you willing to move or be away from your family?"

If being within driving distance to your family is super important, it narrows down where you're able to go. They came to the conclusion a private sector job would be better suited for them. Now they are crushing it on and off the weight room floor.

Find out what's important to you, and then build a life around that. For me, I just wanted to be a power five basketball strength coach. That was my number one priority. Every decision went off that. I didn't care if I had to live in some small town or big city, or Timbuktu. But I think different things have to come into play if you're at that point in your life where you have a spouse or kids—do you want to be a mom or dad that's home and around to see your kid take their first steps, go to tee ball practice, pick them up from school? Or is that not important to you, and you'd rather chase the career? I believe you can do both with the right situation.

Figure out what the most important factors are for you, and then when a job comes up, you can look and think, "Location's important, but I really want to be a collegiate basketball strength coach. Maybe for a few years I'm going to have to be in a less desirable city and then go from there."

Figure out what's actually important to you versus what you think is important to the outside world. When you're young, you think the coolest thing ever would be to be sitting in my shoes. For me, I have to experience something before I can say, "Nah...Or somebody's right, it's bigger than that." But if you're not happy, you can't be a good coach. The better you can make your outside life, the more conducive it is for you to be successful inside your job. A lot of people are burnt out because they're in a city they don't like, not making the money that they want to make, and their job is not meeting their expectations because their outside life isn't how they pictured. It all bleeds into one another.

What do you do to overcome times of struggle, burnout, or overwhelm? Who do you turn to?

Everyone needs at least a core group of friends or a family member that you can call. We should have someone in our phone book that when things go wrong, you need to take off the mask of everything's alright, you can call and be like, "Yo, this sucks." Life is super hard if you don't have at least one person like that. Find a really good friend whose opinion and advice you trust, and then don't be afraid to reach out if you're feeling like, "I'm struggling right now, this isn't what I thought it would be." If they are a good friend worth their weight, they're going to help you talk yourself off the cliff and realize what's important to you. "Your Achilles isn't going to be torn forever...If you want to leave this town, you could leave it tomorrow and go somewhere else." Having that close network of friends or family that you can call—that's the best thing in the world.

What do you think about immediately after one of your athletes is injured? What is your mindset in the following week?

The biggest thing is I think a lot of strength coaches wear it. The second anyone gets hurt, if it's not a collision or something crazy, you open up Twitter and it's, "Fire the strength coach, what is the strength coach not doing, blah blah blah." We wear it, even though we know an injury is so multifactorial and that it's not our fault. We take pride in preparing these athletes for the demands of sport, and then in a chaotic environment like a game or practice, when somebody gets hurt—we wear that. It's a time to go over what could have changed, but you can't dwell on that for too long because it's not gonna fix the ACL overnight.

Then it's up to you to go to the drawing board and have a plan. If you're the injured athlete, nothing would be better than the person that's helping you get back already having a plan ready to roll for you. For me, I tore my Achilles a year and a half ago. My whole identity is being active. Run, lift, I'm always doing something. For that to be taken away, it was like a part of me was gone. I'm like, "Dude, you're 33 and you're struggling with this, like my life's over for the next eight weeks." Hopefully I'm more emotionally mature than an 18 or 19-year-old with an actual pro future ahead of them. I think we dismiss the mental side of things with athletes getting hurt, and they think their whole livelihood and career is done. Getting on the same page of, "This is a little step back, but what things can we do to come back better than before?" You need to find those small wins with the athlete. It's a great time and opportunity for you to work on your relationship with the athlete and keep the train moving forward.

How do you approach difficult conversations with athletes, coworkers, or your boss?

You can't listen to tone or attitude. You need to figure out—what is your goal with the conversation? As a head coach, I know you're ticked off that a player isn't tough on the court, but what does that mean for you? How are we judging it? How do you see me best helping you solve the problem? A lot of the time, strength coaches are just a catchall for all the problems on a team. When I was younger, I used to be defensive, but coaches don't care. They just want to vent to you about why so and so isn't tough or out of shape. It's up to you to communicate that to the athlete and get them to start performing at the level they need to be.

I don't think there's enough clear communication of what people want. It's usually a roundabout way of saying it. When you get in a fight with your girlfriend, it's usually not the dishes that's the issue. It's you not caring enough to do the dishes. You have to dive deeper. When an athlete isn't doing something you want them to do, I come at them in a more vulnerable way. I learned this from Hudy—"Hey, I know you want to go to the NBA and I know you're not this defiant not to do said activity. What is the reason you don't feel like you need to complete this?" If you lay it down like that, and, "Just so you know, this is how I make money. This is how I put food on my table for myself. How can I better help you get done what coach needs you to get done?" Come at it that way, instead of bullying people and trying to out alpha people. If you approach it with, "Hey, I know you're not enjoying this and you're not putting forth the effort that we need. What is the reason? Are you out of shape? Do you not believe in what we're doing?" If you come at a human with a human, empathetic element, you're going to get a better result than trying to fight fire with fire.

Do you have a "failure" that was critical to your long-term development or success?

When I got my first job at Southern Miss, I wanted to move up the rankings so quickly to prove to everyone that, "I am a freaking good coach," because if you're at this school at this stage, that means you're a good coach. Now looking back, it's just kind of luck. At my first job, I was so impatient to leave and go to a big name school. I left nine months in to go to Illinois. When I went there, it was in a location I didn't like, and the teams I worked with weren't super competitive.

I was doing great at my job, but I'd come home and I'd be like, "I have no friends. It's negative 10 degrees outside. I live in this gross apartment." I almost got out of strength and conditioning. It helped put to the top of my attention that having a good group of friends and location were super important to me. I know moving forward, if friends, or at least a few people that I can hang out with, aren't pretty close, I don't know if I'm going to take that job. I don't know something till I touch the stove and I burn myself. Everything was going good at work, but outside of work, I dreaded going home. It showed me that if the outside of work sucks, it's going to bleed into work and I'm just going to be miserable.

What traits or skills do your most successful athletes have in common?
At the highest level in collegiate athletics, who's willing to put in the extra time and become a pro sooner? I always tell these athletes, on the most basic level, if you want to be a good basketball player, you need to be in shape. You can't play basketball out of shape. Do you want to get in shape in June or do you want to wait until October to do that? We always talk about—do your actions align with your goals? Athletes say all the time, "I want to be an All-American." I'm like, "Cool, I've worked with plenty of All-Americans. Here's what they did. Here's what you need to do. You need to come before practice and shoot. You need to come do a little extra weight lifting. You need to make sure to stay on your recovery and eat like an adult." They'll do that for a couple of days, and the next week they don't come to shoot anymore in the morning, and then they're missing their extra weights session. "Hey, let's change your goal. You don't want to be an All-American because you're not doing these things All-Americans do. Let's be an All-Conference player. That's fine. All-Conference players do X, Y, Z." They say, "No, I still want to be an All American!"

Don't talk about something that you're not fully invested in. I hate when people just throw up goals that aren't something they truly believe in. We've all worked with a team that finishes second to last in conference, and they break down a huddle to "Conference champs on three, ONE TWO THREE CONFERENCE CHAMPS!" You guys all know you're not going to do this, why are we making that the goal? Maybe our goal is to finish in the top half of the conference. That's fine. But if your actions are different from your goals, you need to change one of them. The best athletes, they lean into that kind of professionalism sooner than later, and it's hard. You have to give up certain things to achieve what you want to achieve. Everyone, whether you're playing sports, in business, whatever—for you to cut out some stuff, it's addition by subtraction.

We had this talk a couple of weeks ago. All the teams had an off day on Wednesday, except for women's basketball, and on Wednesday it was an optional lift. I had half the team come, half didn't. I'm like, "Guys, you say you want to win a national championship. I know the bottom half of you guys didn't come because football's off, basketball's off. You probably went out last night. When going out and being a college student interferes with your bigger goals, then you've got to cut it out. Have fun, be a college student. I get it. I did it. But when that outside stuff interferes with what you say you want to do, you have to cut it out." There's some athletes that can juggle both, but more often than not you're going to have to pick not going to a Thursday night party because you have practice Friday morning. Actions have to reflect your goals. The sooner you realize that, the better you're going to be, but being good at anything is all about reps. If one athlete's getting more reps than you, they're probably going to eventually beat you. Find out what's important and then work backwards.

What books or resources do you most often recommend to coaches?

I honestly haven't been recommending any strength and conditioning books. I think if you have a strength and conditioning question, it's easy enough now to figure out who's the foremost expert, and listen to three or four podcasts, or make a call, send a DM, or even go visit them. What people are doing now in the weight room, by the time you see it in a book, it's probably done and evolved already. You can learn a lot in a book, but if someone writes a really good book and then you follow up with them after you've read it, they'll probably give you some more nuanced stuff that they've learned since writing that book.

The big thing I've been diving into lately is anyone that does stuff at a high level. Business, entrepreneurs, musicians, doctors—read those types of books. Building a business is very similar to building a strong team. In the business world, you either make money or lose money, and it's not because you have a more talented player or got lucky with a good recruiting class. You have to consistently make these decisions to bring yourself forward in the business world. I think that's the true marker to success. We've all seen or worked with teams where the athletes had horrible attitudes, didn't do anything extra, and still won in spite of everything. But in the business world, it's really hard to be successful if you don't have positive cash flow. *The Almanack of Naval Ravikant* is a really good book.

Then get a basic understanding of finance. The biggest issue we run into with burnout is that you're putting in all these hours and you're getting compensated for what you think is not enough. That's why people get out of it. They're like, "I'm working one-hundred-hour weeks and making $40,000 a year, this doesn't make sense." Okay, you have a couple options. You can quit and get a sales job and triple that. Or if you want to coach, you need to be savvy with how you save your money and invest your money. What can I do on the side? There's too much of a pity party with strength and conditioning. "We're underpaid and overworked and blah, blah, blah." If you have a better understanding of how the world works outside of the weight room, you're going to go a lot farther than spending all your time reading about what's better, a back squat or a front squat.

> *"When you only seek the advice of a few people instead of a council, and you close yourself off to those of varying backgrounds and levels of expertise, you subsequently limit your perspective. Diversify. Diversify. Diversify."*

-Brett Bartholomew

Brett Bartholomew is a performance coach, the author of the best-selling book *Conscious Coaching*, a globally recognized keynote speaker, and the founder of the leadership development company Art of Coaching™. The principles outlined in his book and courses have been applied and adopted by world-class athletes, members of the United States Special Forces, Fortune 500 companies, non-profit organizations, and universities nationwide. His expertise has been featured in numerous local and global media outlets, including ESPN, FOX Sports, Inc. Magazine, and Outside. As a performance coach, Bartholomew has worked with a diverse range of athletes across 23 sports worldwide, including those competing in the NFL, NBA, MLB, UFC, MLS, and the Olympics.

Who do you go to when you need advice? Why them?

This is a very broad question as it depends on the nature of advice. I don't have 1-2 "sages" that I go to for everything. Instead, I recommend that coaches build robust social capital and have a diverse range of people with varying levels of expertise, and also ensure they get around people from a wide range of professions. When you only seek the advice of a few people instead of a council, and you close yourself off to those of varying backgrounds and levels of expertise, you subsequently limit your perspective. Diversify. Diversify. Diversify.

What early job was pivotal in your career? Why?

Waiting tables. Hands down. In coaching, nothing is more important than learning how to deal with people and how to communicate across a wide range of constraint-based scenarios.

What are your first steps when you start a new job? What do you need to figure out, what do you need to get done, who do you need to get to know?

I want to emphasize once again how important it is to not think about things like this in a one-size-fits-all manner. When we think in absolutes or try to mimic the models/ approaches of others without considering the context and other mediating variables, we are asking for trouble. The tendency for coaches to debate about "the best way" is what has gotten many in trouble in their careers. Leadership, coaching, and guiding others are riddled in complexity; it is not formulaic. So follow principles instead. The first of which should always be to LISTEN and OBSERVE. Try to avoid starting a new job with the mentality of "kicking the doors down and making an immediate impact." It's not about you. Get to know others, read the room, and understand your audience. If not, you're not going to accomplish anything other than alienating the very people you are trying to help.

What advice do you have for a college student looking to break into coaching? Who are the best mentors in the world to work for early in your career?

The "best" will always be contextual. What are your deficiencies, what's your experience level, how do you learn best, what setting are you operating in? What are your core competencies? A better thing to focus on is what traits or behaviors do great mentors possess? That's the real question. Here are some things I think are critical for a mentor to possess:

- They should be excellent communicators.
- They should possess a love of learning.
- They should make you put skin in the game and not spoon-feed you.
- They should know their limitations.
- They should be someone who receives coaching of their own. Any coach without a coach is engaging in a certain level of hypocrisy. You can't say you're a "lifelong learner" if you don't have someone pushing you as well.
- They should encourage you to take risks.
- They should share their own failures, not just their successes.

If you only had two 30-minute sessions a week to train your team, how would you prepare them?

By taking a first principles approach. What's the team? Sport? Training age? What do I have available to me equipment-wise? What time of year is it? Start with the basics. Then make sure your program is focused on ground-based, multi-joint movements that are multi-planar. Build around the fundamentals, not fluff.

What goes into your decision to leave or stay at a job?

Deciding to leave an organization is a nuanced decision influenced by personal and professional factors. In my journey, after contributing years to a company I loved, I recognized the need for growth beyond what was offered.

Understanding the types of commitment I discuss in my course *Valu(ED)*, which is my most in-depth take of how to manage various points in your career and the mistakes coaches need to avoid. Ultimately—it's critical to consider whether you are staying at a job because you fully align with the mission and have a deep sense of personal fulfillment, if you are doing it out of necessity because you're stuck, or if you are staying in the job out of guilt or a misplaced sense of moral obligation.

I had clear goals for furthering my career, including mentoring, gaining freedom, and learning about business to secure my family's future. You're supposed to evolve.

All of this said, no job should be left hastily or without considering ethical implications. If you are constantly skipping around every couple of years, you're asking for trouble. Of course this doesn't apply if you are speaking about internships, graduate assistantships, etc.

What do you do to overcome times of struggle, burnout, or overwhelm? Who do you turn to?

I turn to things I cannot turn into work. I get outside, sit in a hot tub, spend time with my son, and turn off my phone.

Do you have a "failure" that was critical to your long-term development or success?

Absolutely. Nearly losing my life at a young age due to a combination of poor medical care and my own bad choices in managing my own emotions was pivotal. This was something I spoke about in great detail within my book *Conscious Coaching.* Ultimately, it's these dark moments where we get to know ourselves the best. Spending a year in the hospital was one of the best things that happened to me as I had to learn to deal with my own demons.

What traits or skills do your most successful athletes have in common?

There's far too many to list exhaustively here, so I'll try to provide a handful of some that I think are often underappreciated below. Of course, most will list things like accountability, resilience, and consistency, which are incredibly important but also already oft-cited, so those go without saying:

- Creativity and Innovation

  - Great athletes often exhibit a high level of creativity in their approach to their sport. They're not just following the playbook; they're rewriting it. This creativity enables them to see and execute plays that others might not even consider possible, setting new standards and changing the game in the process.

- Emotional Intelligence

  - The ability to understand and manage one's own emotions, as well as the emotions of others, is pivotal. Emotional intelligence allows athletes to handle pressure, overcome setbacks, and maintain focus on their goals, even in the most intense moments.

- Instinctual Decision-Making

  - Rather than relying solely on pre-planned strategies, the most successful athletes often trust their instincts. This gut-driven decision-making allows for spontaneous and often unpredictable plays that can turn the tide in their favor.

- Passionate Pursuit of Personal Bests**

  - A defining trait is the relentless pursuit of personal improvement, beyond external validations like medals or records. Their true competition is with themselves, always striving to push beyond their perceived limits.

- Adaptability and Learning

  - The willingness to learn from every situation, adapt to changes, and apply lessons learned to future challenges is crucial. This includes adapting to opponents, overcoming new obstacles, and constantly refining their approach to their sport.

- Non-Conformity
  - Many of the greatest athletes do not fit into the conventional mold. They challenge norms, question established methods, and often take unorthodox paths to their achievements. Their careers are testaments to the power of following one's own path, rather than conforming to the expected route.

What books or resources do you most often recommend to coaches?

Most coaches would benefit from reading more broadly in general. This includes both nonfiction and fiction. The more varied your reading, the better you become at finding relatable points of reference to everyone you interact with.

> *"Understanding where you are in the organization and what is needed out of your role will allow you to survive and thrive...While I stay true to my principles of honesty, loyalty, training, and working extremely hard, how I serve and impact each team I've been a part of is different. Being able to make these small changes is key for durability in this field/profession."*
>
> ## *-Preston Greene*

Preston Greene is in his second year as the Director of Basketball Strength and Conditioning at Clemson University, where in 2023-2024 he helped the Tigers win 24 games and reach the Elite Eight for the first time since 1980. Before returning to Clemson, Greene spent one year at the University of Miami, where he contributed to the Hurricanes' journey to the 2023 Final Four. Prior to Miami, he worked with Men's Basketball at the University of Florida for 11 seasons, advancing to four Elite Eights and achieving a Final Four appearance in 2014 during the program's 36-3 (18-0 SEC) season. Greene has also spent time at Stanford, Charlotte, and Arizona. As one of the most respected professionals in the field, he has been featured in multiple publications and on ESPN's *Gymratts* show. Greene has helped numerous players reach the NBA, including Bradley Beal and Dorian Finney-Smith.

Who do you go to when you need advice? Why them?

My family is what keeps me grounded when I need advice. My love for them drives me each and every day to put them first and to give my best effort. I am fortunate enough to have a deep network of coaches and former assistants that I can reach out to that can challenge my thoughts and push me to grow season after season.

What early job was pivotal in your career? Why?

Moving to Charlotte in 2003 and becoming a director at 25 years old was a big step in my career. I was fortunate enough that at my stops before this at Clemson, Minnesota, and Arizona that I was surrounded by great mentors that educated me and pushed me forward. Being able to apply this knowledge and run a department was crucial for me, as I was able to develop my own coaching and leadership style.

What are your first steps when you start a new job? What do you need to figure out, what do you need to get done, who do you need to get to know?

Whenever starting a new job, I first meet with the head coach and get an understanding of his team and his vision for the strength coach role. Meeting with the AT is extremely crucial to understand injury history and common areas of concern with the players' bodies in the past. Meeting with each player and understanding their goals and their previous experiences is critical, and it takes time to develop these relationships. Assistant coaches, operations, video coordinators, etc. can all play a role giving insight to the team and its culture.

What advice do you have for a college student looking to break into coaching? Who are the best mentors in the world to work for early in your career?

Begin in the weight room as an intern and get on the floor practicing coaching. There are no shortcuts to becoming a better coach. Show up early, pickup things quickly, clean, serve, put others and the program first. The best mentors in the world are coaches who will hold you accountable and push you to become a better coach. It is not about the logo of the school or the team that they work with. You can take and learn something from everyone.

If you only had two 30-minute sessions a week to train your team, how would you prepare them?

Eccentrics. Training the brakes of the body and lifting using prescribed tempo will ensure the fastest and highest quality results. Two sessions a week would use a full body split including combining upper and lower movements paired in supersets. Squat paired with chin-up or a deadlift paired with a press, i.e. For long-term success, you will need a proper offseason with multiple training sessions each week.

What goes into your decision to leave or stay at a job?

Ultimately this decision comes down to your family and what is best/works best. I have been fortunate to be a part of many winning teams and cultures, and working for a head coach that has a great track record of winning and constant stable success is what I value when looking at working for a head coach. Competing in Final Fours, developing NBA players, and teaching these players values that will allow them to succeed in life is what motivates me.

What do you do to overcome times of struggle, burnout, or overwhelm? Who do you turn to?

Constantly train and take pride in your nutrition. Training every week my entire career and never being satisfied or complacent has pushed me through difficult times. My family has kept me grounded and stable while I have pursued this career. Taking pride in taking my strength program to the next level and adding layers on how to impact the team and organization causes me to be hungry and to continue to pursue excellence. Thoroughly enjoying what I do for work and knowing how I can impact my players' lives allows me to continue to move forward 29 years later.

What do you think about immediately after one of your athletes is injured? What is your mindset in the following week?

Injuries are a complex problem that can drive strength coaches and sport coaches crazy. Very simple tools such as sleep, diet, and proper training can be the biggest drivers in preventing these situations. Every year I look over my program and think to myself how I can improve or slightly alter my coaching and exercise selection to make the most results. I immediately think what can I do/help to get my player back to the court as soon as possible. You are one injury away from being fired and making sure these players are living well-rounded lives is extremely important to this picture of health.

How do you approach difficult conversations with athletes, coworkers, or your boss?

Direct, honest conversations always work much better in the long run. Trying to dance around hard topics or issues won't result in long-term success. The best organizations and teams out there speak directly, honestly, and frequently. Letting a player know that their effort is not good enough is a high level of accountability. Utilizing these conversations in private and then rewarding effort and not results are the keys to these difficult conversations. I want my players and strength staff to put their best foot forward every day and to enjoy the process of getting better.

Do you have a "failure" that was critical to your long-term development or success?

As a student strength coach at Clemson in 1999, I was in charge of six teams, including Women's Volleyball. I read that utilizing clusters would help peak the team for the conference tournament. Using the method, I fried the entire team, made them neurally fatigued, and they performed poorly. This failure taught me an important lesson to never give an athlete a workout that I had not done myself and to understand that everything that is written in a textbook might not be optimal for the sport and the practical application. Learning to think, adjust, and form my own thoughts was key to my growth in the field.

What traits or skills do your most successful athletes have in common?

Ability to adapt. Playing on different teams, being a part of different organizations all demand a different role from the player. Understanding where you are in the organization and what is needed out of your role will allow you to survive and thrive. No two setups, coaches, teams, or organizations are the same, and being able to adjust and fit in is key. While I stay true to my principles of honesty, loyalty, and training and working extremely hard, how I serve and impact each team I've been a part of is different. Being able to make these small changes is key for durability in this field/ profession.

What books or resources do you most often recommend to coaches?

The Poliquin Principles is my go-to for the science of training, exercise selection, and program design. Charles Poliquin was one of my mentors and his impact on strength and conditioning can be felt all over the world. *Cracking the Metabolic Code* by James LaValle is another great book I recommend that looks at the overall impact of health and how our body metabolically responds to our surroundings. *Tools of Titans* is a book that combines some of the top thinkers in every field from around the world. I try to be widespread in my thoughts and have an understanding of a multitude of topics.

"In those moments, that's where I love being a coach. I enjoy being there for them and picking them up. Helping a player get from A to B, helping them improve, helping them gain confidence and overcome tough times in their careers. From tough losses, to setbacks, to even injuries, that's where I thrive in lifting them up and being there for them."

-Philip Farmer

Philip Farmer is a highly regarded professional tennis coach on the ATP tour, currently coaching Austin Krajicek and Hans Hach Verdugo. He has coached three different players who achieved a career-high ranking of No. 1 in doubles, including Krajicek and the legendary duo of Bob and Mike Bryan—the Bryan brothers—whom Farmer helped lead to four Grand Slam titles and three additional Finals. Farmer also coached American singles players John Isner and Sam Querrey, both of whom reached the top 20 in the world rankings. He was named the USPTA Touring Coach of the Year - Texas and National in 2013, and was featured in Greg Levine's book *Mental Toughness 101.* **(Farmer's responses were transcribed from a phone call)**

Who do you go to when you need advice? Why them?

My main coach since I was 13, Keith Christman. He's really cerebral and sees things through a unique lens—letting your eyes dictate what those moments look like in a competitive situation and what those athletes need to do to perform better under pressure. He's also big on playing with freedom and competing with a relaxation about yourself, and I try to coach that way as well. The three Cs: Calm, Composed, and Confident—learning to play with freedom and relaxation so the magic can come out.

Another coach on tour that worked with Hubert Hurkacz from Poland is a good friend of mine named Craig Boynton. He's had a lot of success over the years with many singles and doubles players. He has a calm demeanor, but he's very competitive and intense internally like me. It's healthy to have a balance of being really competitive and to have a certain intensity about your coaching style, but also one that's balanced with a calmness and composure.

What early job was pivotal in your career? Why?

I started dating a girl that had just turned pro and was a very good player. Her name was Tara Snyder, and she was a new hope for American women tennis. I brought her to work with my coach, a big mentor of mine to this day, named Keith Christman. A lot of my coaching, thinking outside the box, and learning how to deal with different personalities and motivate each person I learned from him. We worked together in coaching Tara because he was the main coach, but he was running a club in Houston and couldn't travel. I became the traveling coach, speaking his voice on the road. I learned so much from him and Tara, and from the experience of seeing her compete and improve to a career high of 33 in the world. Keith was also coaching a guy named Tommy Ho. He was making a comeback from an injury but was just a phenomenal young talent, and I learned a lot from him as well in Houston. Those experiences helped springboard me into my coaching career while fulfilling the competitive spirit and passion that I got from playing.

The other time was when I was coaching a doubles player named Graydon Oliver in early 2003, and then I helped Bob Bryan in singles at a Challenger in Joplin, Missouri. Graydon won the doubles and Bob won the singles. Bob and I really connected that week at the Challenger tournament, and he went back home to his brother Mike with excitement and told him they needed to hire me as their coach. Months later, now I'm coaching the Bryan brothers, and we all win our first Grand Slam together at the 2003 French Open, becoming number one in the world. They got asked to play for the first time on the Davis Cup team, which were their three main goals: win a slam, become number one, and make the United States' Davis Cup team. Helping them accomplish those kinds of career goals was pretty special, and that really helped me feel like I belonged and could coach somebody of that caliber.

What advice do you have for a college student looking to break into coaching? Who are the best mentors in the world to work for early in your career?

To be a good quality coach, you have to be able to look through different lenses. You have to look through your own coaching lens, but it's also important to step outside yourself and look through your player's lens. See it through their lens as well as the corrective coaching lens we're always looking through. Also, continue to listen. As coaches, we think we always need to fix and talk and solve. We forget to listen to our players, but also listen to other coaches that we respect, other mentors. The ability to think outside the box is really important. As you get to higher levels of the competitor you're coaching, they've been told a lot of stuff in their development and throughout their competitive life. Sometimes the things we're trying to accomplish with them they might have heard several thousand times. A lot of times, it's being creative with the information that you're trying to get across. Be open-minded and think outside the box, whether it's communicative or visual, but getting the lesson to them with a more creative solution that makes them think and view it differently so that it clicks. Every player you're coaching is so unique in their DNA, their culture, their development, and their maturity. It's important to look through a different lens, be open-minded, be a good listener, but to also trust your information, trust your coaching, and also trust your player. They'll feel that confidence that you trust them. Teach them the perspective that you don't have to be perfect, you just have to be efficient and perseverant.

For a mentor, somebody who's going to be honest with you, somebody who's going to push you, somebody who's going to be supportive and passionate. Somebody that trusts your opinion, trusts your eyes, and trusts your judgment. Somebody that's going to tell you if you're headed down the wrong path, and then guide you down the right path while keeping you motivated at the same time.

Bonus: How do you teach them that perspective that they don't have to be perfect, they just have to be efficient and perseverant?

What's your equal sign to success? In other words, what equals success? A lot of times their definition is not realistic. I might get an answer, "It's when I don't make mistakes." That's not realistic because you're going to make mistakes, have errors, and miss in sports. In tennis, you're gonna miss serves, forehands, backhands, etc. In basketball, you're gonna miss free throws. In baseball, you're gonna get struck out. Sport is not perfection. First, let's define a more realistic equal sign of what success means to us, so that when you get out there you're not let down. When your equal sign is more realistic, you will handle stress and frustration better, therefore making success more attainable.

Number two, let's not get caught up when we don't achieve that. There's so many ways that can lead you to success, but there's also so many ways that can lead to you being frustrated and things not working. Have a good perspective of those mistakes, and help them realize that mistakes are a part of sports. Let's stay calm and figure out ways to resolve those issues in that moment and turn it around. Stay calm and have the ability to have a realistic equal sign of what success is, and know that it's something within your reach. When mistakes creep in, it's part of it. Let's not allow that to overshadow what we're trying to accomplish. We're still playing our game, playing to win. Fear, errors, and frustration are all a part of it, so we're going to accept it. We have a game plan for it and that's part of the competition. When you know that and you're prepared for it, you handle it better. Federer, Djokovic, Nadal—they know they're going to lose 45% of the points, but their equal sign is, "I just have to get to around 55% to win the majority of my matches. I don't have to be at 80%. I don't have to be perfect at 100% to compete at the highest level and dominate."

Another example I may give an athlete is that Steph Curry is one of the greatest three point shooters we've ever seen. His career three point percentage floats around 38%. That's less than four out of 10. That means the majority of the time, he's actually missing. His equal sign is very realistic. "I only really need to make three or four out of 10 to be successful and help my team win." When he does encounter struggle and frustration, he doesn't panic. He still lets it fly and trusts it because he knows that his percentage to be highly successful needs to just be around three or four. It doesn't matter that he missed the first five, and he doesn't think about it in that moment. "I've missed five. I should stop shooting. I'm not very good." In fact, he does the opposite. "I'm going to keep shooting because I know I'll eventually find my range, and I know that my equal sign is three or four out of 10." You try to portray that to your athlete to help them deal with the fact that they're human and that part of sports is failure. Making those little mistakes along the way is a part of sports. They are a part of business. They're a part of life! It comes down to how you deal with it and how you stay focused on knowing what your equal sign is to achieve success.

What do you think about immediately after one of your athletes is injured? What is your mindset in the following week?

Injuries are a part of sports, but in professional sports it's even more highlighted because it's their income and profession. The beautiful part, the blessing and gift of being a coach, is helping others. I've got my own goals and I'm very competitive, but I'm very much about my player. I look through their lens and what they're going through, and let them know I'm there for them. I'm making sure they feel the support more than ever during those times, because those are tough moments when athletes go through injuries. Some are career ending. Sometimes they're out for a while and it's a loss of income and opportunity. There's a lot of heartache and sadness that comes with that.

In those moments, that's where I love being a coach. I enjoy being there for them and picking them up. Helping a player get from A to B, helping them improve, helping them gain confidence and overcome tough times in their careers. From tough losses, to setbacks, to even injuries, that's where I thrive in lifting them up and being there for them. Keeping them upbeat and positive while looking at the big picture of where we're going. Let's find a solution to the problem. Let's come up with some new goals and let's stay positive. I love that part about coaching.

Do you have a "failure" that was critical to your long-term development or success?
Coaching Tara when I first started out, I could have been more mature and a better listener. But some of those disappointing and tougher times probably helped me become the coach I am today. I was very fortunate to be a part of a great team with Tara and Keith, and I found my avenue of being able to vent my competitive juices, and use each experience to get wiser and better every year.

This tennis business is extremely volatile because you're hired by the individual that you're supposed to be telling what to do. If you take Greg Popovich or Bill Belichick, some of these coaches can coach these players, teams, and superstars with less of a filter. They're able to get the work that they need out of them without worrying about upsetting them and being fired. Those guys aren't writing their checks at the end of the day. The owner is. Tennis is a tricky sport because you're with these players one on one, almost more than married couples because you travel with them up to 30-40 weeks each year. You're with them at breakfast, lunch, and dinner. You're on the road with them, on the flight with them, on the buses, every meal, every practice, every match. That makes it challenging because the person writing your checks is also the person you're trying to keep in line and get the results to help them achieve their goals, sometimes by having some tough love and constructive criticism. It makes it challenging, but it's shaped me and made me better.

Next would be some of the Grand Slam losses. I've been fortunate to win five Grand Slams between the Bryan brothers and Austin, but I've lost another five finals. Although those five are really sweet, the losses in the finals of those grand slams that I've experienced—going through those moments with them after the match are tough. Especially the 2022 French Open final with Austin, in his first grand slam he and his partner had three match points and lost. That sure was a tough pill to swallow, but we stayed mentally strong. We used it to ignite us, fuel our fire, make us better and hungrier, and sharpen our tools as coach and player. We came back the next year and won the French Open pretty convincingly in the final. The losses motivate me to push through tough times in tennis, in coaching, and definitely in life—to stay passionate, stay happy, stay motivated, stay hungry, stay faithful, and keep trusting my craft.

All those tough moments and emotional times, you share that with one or two players in my world, so it's a very intimate group. That can be difficult because in those really low times together, to pull each other through, you're relying on one another in a small group. But the upside when you achieve the goals, it is just as motivating and powerful. That shows you the tough side of the business that I'm in, but also the beautiful part of the tennis industry.

Bonus: With the unique dynamic of you being hired by the individual player, how do you still build the relationship to be an honest truth teller in their life?
You have to do your job, and your job is to make them better. Sometimes in making them better you have to tell the harsh truth and call them out, and those aren't easy moments. Hopefully the player is open-minded knowing that you have their best interest in trying to make them better. Trust yourself, trust your player, trust the craft that you love and that you're going to eventually make them better on and off the court.

Part of it too is the art of how you get that message across. Everybody's different. I have my moments where I can be tough on them, but I'm also a big believer of saying it in a positive light that paints it in a way that motivates them. I find that most athletes, especially in individual sports like tennis and golf where it's one on one, are pretty tough on themselves anyway. Most elite champions are their own toughest critics. You try to build them up when they're down, and sometimes you have to bring some tough love to it, but you also have to learn to balance it with positivity and good energy to build them up.

What traits or skills do your most successful athletes have in common?
What sticks out to me is the ability to execute under pressure. That "it" factor. The ability to handle the stressful and emotional moments that sports can bring, especially as tennis is such an individual sport. Being able to handle the variety of emotions and still learn to compete. The ability to trust your shots, go for your shots, and trust your

game.

The other one is learning how to deal with, as I call them, the "little no's" or the "little disappointments" along the way. In tennis, you lose a lot of points. Federer, Djokovic, Nadal, they can lose 45% of points, but all they need is 55% to win a match. Losing 45% of points every match you play, that's a lot of points to lose and still remain confident, unbroken, and composed. That's a really important trait to be able to deal with the misses, the losses, and the errors that you make while not letting it affect your confidence. Not letting it detour you from playing your game with confidence and freedom. The ability to bounce back—not letting a loss, blowing a lead, or an injury that you're coming back from deteriorate the core of your confidence and your belief in all the work that you've put in. The same is true in other businesses, such as a car salesman or a real estate agent. They go through their workdays and are often told no by potential customers/clients in their sales process. However, like an athlete, it's extremely important to deal with these "little no's" that can be frequent in many businesses as you are trying to achieve success. You must learn to stay calm and patient, and have the perspective that you only need a few yeses to equal success. In the example of the car salesman or the real estate agent, they may get told no several times in a month but in reality only need a few yeses to achieve their goals and be successful in those industries. By dealing with these "little losses" and "little no's" along the way, these athletes and business professionals can alleviate frustration and disappointment while remaining composed and confident.

Lastly, keeping the excitement and the passion. As you go through each week, each competition, and then each year, you do it over and over again. It can weigh you down. There's a lot of stress to it. Some pertains to travel. There's a physical and emotional toll it can take. Having the overall awareness to hit the reset button, stay fresh, stay hungry, stay passionate, and stay motivated is a key component. A lot of times it's flushing it, hitting the reset button, and moving forward. Or if you had a big tournament win, letting that motivate you to hit the practice courts and work even harder. Hard work is key, but I don't think it's everything, because there's other components that are important. But the ability to get back on the horse, hit the practice court, set your new goals, and be excited for another opportunity to excel and accomplish your goals is critical.

Bonus: If you're working with an athlete that doesn't have the ability to deal with those "little no's," how do you try and help them build that mental ability?

In a way, it's like training the physical parts of tennis. If your forehands off, then we're gonna work on the technique or preparation. You'll do a bunch of repetition on it, watch some film, and compare it to how you were hitting when it felt good. That's very similar to training the mind. I use a lot of different sayings, different motivational or educational videos, or things that I've found that can help connect the player to seeing where they can mentally be better with their emotional control. A lot of that stuff you can train just like you would the physical parts of the game. You build in some of those formulas of, "Hey, here's what we're trying to think in these moments. Here's what we're trying to avoid that can get us off track." Basically coming up with different things to do during those critical moments, or things they can say to themselves that take away the fear and keep them in a relaxed, comfortable, fluid and free state.

Then you've got to know your player and how they operate. What method works best for them? It's a series of communication and conversations and being open and accepting that you're getting tight, nervous, or losing emotional control. Once we can accept it, let's talk about some ways that you as the individual might alleviate some of that. But you also let them know that we're not trying to get rid of the fear or the nerves, because realistically you can't just get rid of it. "We're gonna work on these things so that you never get nervous again, or so you never lose emotional control or get frustrated." That's just impossible. You're human and it's competition at the highest level. So you work on within those scenarios when this does happen, here's how we're going to alleviate some of those feelings so you can get back to a free, relaxed, neutral state of competing.

Bonus: As their coach, how do you try to help them keep the excitement and passion through the monotony and stress of the year?

Scheduling is really important, making sure that they have off weeks. So many players don't realize that less will a lot of times give you more. They're so driven on "hard work leads to success," and that's true. But you have to learn to rest your body and you have to learn to rest your soul, mind, and emotional track. It's a long year with very little downtime and off-season, so scheduling and rest time becomes really important. The other thing is keeping things fun, keeping things fresh. New hitting partners, working on new things, and keeping things fresh in practice. On and off the court, try to keep the player relaxed so they don't lose sight of, "Yes, it's your career and you're trying to compete at the highest level and it's very intense, rigorous, and brutal—but you're playing a sport that you love. It is a game and you have to still go out there with a smile and enjoy it." That's the best way to achieve your goals because you're more relaxed and playing free and confident.

Bonus: How do you keep that excitement and passion for yourself as the coach through the monotony and stress of the year?

Everybody's a little bit different, but you need to have your outlets. I'm a social person, so being with family and friends, going out to dinners, going to concerts, laughing and having fun—those kinds of moments and getting away from the day-to-day grind of tennis keep me fresh, hungry, and motivated. Find your outlet and what helps you disconnect—not only physically, but also mentally and emotionally from what you're doing day in and day out. This can give you a break and help you escape, keeping the excitement and passion in your craft.

> *"Fail forward and seek feedback. Have a continuous growth mindset, ask questions, work your @$$ off."*
>
> ## -Quadrian Banks

Quadrian Banks is in his eighth season at Ohio State as the Assistant Director of Strength and Conditioning for Men's Basketball, where he has helped the program win at least 20 games in five seasons. Before joining the Buckeyes, Banks worked in the NFL for both the Indianapolis Colts and the Philadelphia Eagles. He transitioned to the NFL after serving as the Director of Athletic Performance at Gardner-Webb and as an Assistant Strength and Conditioning Coach at Ole Miss, Richmond, and Hampton, as well as the Head Strength and Conditioning Coach at Prairie View A&M. While at Ohio State, he has contributed to the development of Keita Bates-Diop, E.J. Liddell, Malaki Branham, and Brice Sensabaugh, all of whom became NBA draft picks.

Who do you go to when you need advice? Why them?
It depends on the nature of the question. Administrative resource for those relevant questions, practitioners in the professional space, etc.

What early job was pivotal in your career? Why?
Selling books door to door. I had to learn how to take rejection and persevere.

What are your first steps when you start a new job? What do you need to figure out, what do you need to get done, who do you need to get to know?
Get to know the landscape of where to go and what resources are at play.

What advice do you have for a college student looking to break into coaching? Who are the best mentors in the world to work for early in your career?
Fail forward and seek feedback. Have a continuous growth mindset, ask questions, work your @$$ off. The best mentors are the ones who genuinely invest in your short and long-term development.

If you only had two 30-minute sessions a week to train your team, how would you prepare them?
I would have the room set up to be as efficient and effective as possible. Have the team learn and execute the warm up on their own. Have help. Be efficient and effective.

What goes into your decision to leave or stay at a job?

Family. The people I work with. Pay. Opportunity for growth.

What do you do to overcome times of struggle, burnout, or overwhelm? Who do you turn to?

Pray, focus, and believe in myself. Turn to the Lord, Jesus Christ, and the Bible.

What do you think about immediately after one of your athletes is injured? What is your mindset in the following week?

Re-evaluate everything leading up to injury. What could have been done better?

How do you approach difficult conversations with athletes, coworkers, or your boss?

Rip the band-aid off and have the conversation. No need to dance around. Hopefully the existing relationship is positive.

Do you have a "failure" that was critical to your long-term development or success?

Anytime you get a reality check that you are not as good as you think, it serves me to re-evaluate and come back more focused and working smarter and harder.

What traits or skills do your most successful athletes have in common?

Growth mindset, consistency, and uncommon confidence.

What books or resources do you most often recommend to coaches?

Strength Training for Basketball, Perfect Practice, Wooden on Leadership

> *"Nothing you do in the seconds immediately following injury will heal them, but how you respond will affect how they see you after."*

> *-Kendall Crisp*

Kendall Crisp is in her second year as the Head Women's Volleyball Coach at Hardin Simmons University. In her first year as Head Coach, she led the Cowgirls to a win in the first round of the ASC Tournament. Before becoming the Head Coach of the program, Crisp spent two seasons as an assistant at Hardin Simmons. She also gained experience working with the Texas Tech Volleyball program and with Key City Volleyball Club.

Who do you go to when you need advice? Why them?

I have a mentor at a much larger university who is older, wiser, and someone that I trust in all thing's volleyball. She took me under her wing early in my career and I am so thankful to have her as a friend and resource. I have two friends who are in very similar life/career situations I go to for practical advice about how to balance work/family. Being a new mom and new head coach definitely has come with its fair share of challenges, but being able to share these experiences with people who are walking through some of the same struggles has been invaluable.

I have someone who I trust at my school to help me navigate my work life. She has been at my school for a long time and has found great success in her sport, so being able to turn to her for advice for camps, recruiting, managing people, and just knowing the ins and outs of our school has been so helpful. Also, having a coach that I am close to within our conference has proven to be valuable. Again, he has been at his school and in our conference for much longer than I have, so guidance from him is appreciated.

What early job was pivotal in your career? Why?

Volunteering at Texas Tech. I met some incredible people and learned a whole lot about volleyball, yes, but a lot more about who I wanted to be as a coach and role model to young women. The year I spent at Tech was unpaid and what I learned was completely up to me. I was welcome to join in most meetings (excluding HC top secret meetings ya know), participate in practice planning, and aid in the behind the scenes of recruiting. If I had questions, it was up to me to go to the coaches and ask or put my head down and figure it out the hard way. It made me realize how important it is to continue to learn and grow in your sport.

What are your first steps when you start a new job? What do you need to figure out, what do you need to get done, who do you need to get to know?

Gosh, that's hard and I am still figuring it out a year into the job. I would recommend starting with documenting EVERYTHING you do, when you do it, and staying on top of being organized on the administrative side of things. I am not this way by nature, and this has been the biggest struggle I have run into. I always think that I will remember what I am doing or what I need to do, but that's rarely the case. I have a task list for me, my assistant, and GA that I add to daily, so we are all on the same page about what needs to get done that day/week. Additionally, organizing a program calendar and way of communicating that is online (we use Outlook Calendar and GroupMe) is really nice also. Planning ahead is huge. Having an idea about what your program needs over the next few years is just as important as knowing what you need in the next few weeks.

Make friends with the coaches around you! You work with them everyday so you might as well have a good time when you're around them—even better if they become a mentor and they can help you get to know the school better!

What advice do you have for a college student looking to break into coaching? Who are the best mentors in the world to work for early in your career?

Go be the little guy at a big program. Be underpaid and under rested for a short period of time. Learn all you can, take what you know, then spread your wings somewhere else.

What do you do to overcome times of struggle, burnout, or overwhelm? Who do you turn to?

I try to spend quality time with my family. Less technology when I get home. Less working at home. Spending the time that I do have with my family recharges me to be the best I can be for them and for my athletes. Take a break from working (hard when you're in season) and spend the weekend or day off really relaxing and regrouping. I try to be 100% at work or 100% at home. The less I try to mix those areas of my life, the more balance and endurance I find to keep on keeping on.

What do you think about immediately after one of your athletes is injured? What is your mindset in the following week?

Deal with the here and now. Nothing you do in the seconds immediately following injury will heal them, but how you respond will affect how they see you after. I had a kid get concussed for the third time in her life during practice. Somewhere in her athletic journey, she was told that after you have a third concussion, you are done playing sports (inaccurate, but that is all she could think of when it happened). Instead of focusing on what this might mean for the future of her career, we focused on breathing, getting comfortable, and talking about what she was physically feeling so that the trainer would have all the information she needed once she got to the player.

How do you approach difficult conversations with athletes, coworkers, or your boss?

I need your answers on this. I hate confrontation. I know you have to be honest and clear, even if it's hard and uncomfortable.

Do you have a "failure" that was critical to your long-term development or success?

Still early and still will fail!

What traits or skills do your most successful athletes have in common?

They are excellent in more areas than one. Being great requires discipline and if they lack that (bad grades, bad reputation, bad choices being made), chances are they will fail in their athletic career long term.

> *"I was a school teacher for seven years prior to becoming a college coach, and I've viewed myself my entire collegiate career as a teacher. Everything that I do in basketball always comes from a teacher's perspective—whether it's watching film, teaching a drill, or scouting reports."*
>
> ## -Chuck Martin

Chuck Martin is in his first season as an Assistant Coach and Recruiting Coordinator with the Men's Basketball program at the University of Arkansas, after holding the same position at the University of Kentucky. He has been recognized as one of the top 50 most impactful high-major assistants in men's college basketball. Previously, Martin served as the head coach at Marist from 2008-2013 and has held assistant coaching positions at Oregon, South Carolina, Indiana, Memphis, St. John's, Drexel, UMass, and Manhattan. Throughout his career, he has helped coach multiple NBA draft selections, including top 10 draft picks Derrick Rose, Reed Sheppard, and Rob Dillingham. **(Martin's responses were transcribed from a Zoom call)**

Who do you go to when you need advice? Why them?

It depends, what is it that I'm looking for? What advice, what arena, what route, who is it, what's the topic? I'll give an example. If I'm trying to figure something out that is catered to a demographic of 18-30, I'll ask my kids. I'll say, "What do you think of that? When you see this right here, what do you see? When I say this, what do you hear? When I show you this, what do you see?" That's their world. I don't have one particular person who I go to for everything.

What early job was pivotal in your career? Why?

I was a school teacher for seven years prior to becoming a college coach, and I've viewed myself my entire collegiate career as a teacher. Everything that I do in basketball always comes from a teacher's perspective—whether it's watching film, teaching a drill, or scouting reports. The film room is essentially my classroom. It allowed me to effortlessly transition from the classroom to the court. I still viewed myself as a teacher. I still do today, although the title is coach.

What are your first steps when you start a new job? What do you need to figure out, what do you need to get done, who do you need to get to know?

The biggest thing for me is immersing myself in the community. The players, the staff, support staff, and then I work my way out. Team, kids, their parents, support system, their families, secretaries, athletic directors, assistant athletic directors, and then the local lady at the dining hall security. I just work my way out from there.

What advice do you have for a college student looking to break into coaching? Who are the best mentors in the world to work for early in your career?

Understand the craft itself. What is it that you're teaching? What is it that you're trying to emphasize? Really invest in the craft itself, and then try as best you can to find your voice as you do that. Which is really hard, because you're trying to find "how do you teach this?" You can't teach it the way Pat Riley teaches it. Work on your craft, and then every day start to figure out what is your style. This is my style of coaching— start developing that.

For mentors, find people who have succeeded in the past, but how have they done it? People who are smart and have grit. If you're smart and you're intelligent, but you've never faced adversity, you never know how they'll react to it. So looking at mentors, it's "Man, I got a really smart guy, and he stumbled a few times, but he was able to wipe himself off and get back up and double down." Let me learn from that guy. He's really smart. He's really good at what he does, but he did fall. He was able to get back up from that. How does he do that?

If you're looking for a mentor, who's the guy that can touch people? Everyone interacts with someone. Whether it's 10 minutes or 10 years or 30 years—did they leave that person's situation better off? Who's that guy? That guy's really smart. He's good at his craft. He stumbled and was able to recover, and he's got grit. And then in his journey, when things were going well, did he impact someone and make him better? Along that journey, when things were not going well and he was trying to fix it, did he still have the ability to leave it better and impact people in a positive way?

What goes into your decision to leave or stay at a job?

The first thing for me is, will the job, and the people at the job, add value to me? Would taking that job immediately add value to me? Will I become better? Whatever it is that you're good at, when you join that staff, that organization, am I going to be better for it? The last one for me is to take the job that will mean greater opportunities.

So take the job that adds value. Okay, that's pretty good. If I take the job, am I going to become better? Yes, you'll be better for it. Okay, if I take the job, will it create greater opportunities for me? Yes, it will. Great. Take the job.

What do you do to overcome times of struggle, burnout, or overwhelm? Who do you turn to?

For me, it was you have to go to what you're good at, which is teaching. Go back to what I feel most comfortable doing. When I struggled at Marist, and I was frustrated and just couldn't win the game, I went back to teaching. I'm gonna teach spacing, I'm gonna teach offensive concepts, I'm gonna teach defense, I'm gonna teach rotations. Now it doesn't mean that you're gonna win. It doesn't mean you're gonna get the outcome, but go back to what you feel confident in that's been proven you're good at. Now what happens is you're struggling, but you're confident that you're going to do this. They feel that energy from you. They know that, "Hey, we're struggling, but coach seems pretty confident speaking to us about this. He seems pretty prepared." So for me, it was go back to what you're good at, which is teaching.

What do you think about immediately after one of your athletes is injured? What is your mindset in the following week?

My thing is leadership, because that kid now needs help. He has no direction. He doesn't know what the future is. He needs leadership and guidance. I'm thinking as a parent, "What would I want that coach to do for my kids?"

How do you approach difficult conversations with athletes, coworkers, or your boss?

What I've learned as I've gotten older is to have a conversation with myself. What is it I'm trying to get out of the conversation? I'll write that down. Am I trying to make that person better? Okay, then gear the conversation to make them better and to telling them the truth. Am I trying to make them aware of a situation they're unaware of? Okay, then I go into that conversation and I want to make y'all aware of A, B, and C. When it comes to critical conversations, before you speak, you've got to ask yourself, "What are you trying to get out of this?"

If you don't, you may go in with good intentions to tell the truth to help, but really you may crush his spirit by telling the truth because you don't have any direction with it. "You stink, you're absolutely awful. You don't work." I'm being truthful, but man, you just crushed that kid's spirit. What am I trying to get out of it? I want to make them better. "Look, you struggled last week. Here are the two things that I think you can get better at tomorrow, so I'm going to help you with these two things." I've already gone into that conversation understanding what I want to get out of it. I want to make him better, so I'm going to have a difficult conversation and tell him the truth, but ultimately I want to get him better. Once I've determined what I want to get out of it, that dictates what direction and how I do it.

Do you have a "failure" that was critical to your long-term development or success?

I'm a better coach today after being a head coach and struggling. I'm a more impactful leader. After struggling as a first time head coach, I'm just a better version today. Me today, after that experience, would dominate myself before that experience. It taught me you have to trust your instincts. If things don't go your way, you can't view it as a failure. You made a decision—it worked, great. You made a decision—it didn't work, stop, correct it. I made a decision to become the head coach at Marist. It didn't work. I can't view it like it's a failure. You made a decision. You took the job. It didn't work. Stop. Learn from it. Move on.

What traits or skills do your most successful athletes have in common?

They're super competitive. They're willing to learn. If you can teach them something, they'll listen. If you can't teach them anything, they'll ignore you. They're going to have a motor and internal fire. They want to learn, and they want you to help them get to that next level.

Bonus: With the major roster turnover in college basketball and condensed recruiting timelines for transfers, how are you trying to still identify those qualities and understand who a recruit is beyond the surface level info?

I spent one year with the Oklahoma City Thunder in 2013. One thing I learned from that organization, they would say over and over—"Draft good people, who are good players." In our case, recruit good people who are good players. You already know they can play. Are they good people? Man, that's the guy to recruit because regardless of the circumstances, difficult times, challenges, the good people are going to stick with you. They're going to rally with you. They're all going to row in the same direction. They're going to do it because they are innately good people who happen to be good players.

Bonus: What are you looking at to see if they are good people? Especially when they know the answers to the test, how do you get underneath the surface to find who they are going to be in those moments of stress and struggle?

It's hard, but you try to pay attention and watch how they behave around people that they know can't help them. Whether it's holding a door for someone or saying thank you, you can tell that's not rehearsed. That kid held the door for that lady. That kid, after the waiter or waitress came by, he said thank you. You're walking, and there's an elderly gentleman or lady behind you or in front of you. They go around the person to make it easier for them. You can see it. My man went out of his way to make sure that this couple was comfortable. Pay close attention—sometimes it's not as obvious. How does he react when you're around people that can't help him, that can't give him anything?

What books or resources do you most often recommend to coaches?

There's a simple book. It's an easy read, the title is *Two Chairs* by Bob Beaudine. It's a simple conversation between you and God. It's called *Two Chairs* because there is an exercise where you pull up a chair, and you sit in front of that chair, and you welcome him into a conversation the way I would with you right now.

"Finding mentorship is pivotal. It will likely be a trial-and-error process, one must expose themselves to as many professionals as possible and attempt to be critical at finding an appropriate fit."

-Jason Hettler

Jason Hettler is the Speed and Agility Coach at IMG Academy in Bradenton, Florida, where he also serves as the Head of Strength and Conditioning for IMG Academy Tennis. Before joining IMG, Hettler worked at ALTIS for over six years as the Performance and Innovation Manager. In that role, he was the lead for a group of sprinters, consulted with professional organizations, developed educational content, and coordinated the internship program.

Who do you go to when you need advice? Why them?

I have a large network of people to go to for various topics, but the commonalities between these individuals are a growth mindset with great critical thinking abilities. They are curious, lifelong learners.

What early job was pivotal in your career? Why?

Working at ALTIS with Dan Pfaff, Stu McMillan, and the rest of the staff was crucial to my development as a coach. It was a professional environment with an emphasis on learning and mentorship.

What advice do you have for a college student looking to break into coaching? Who are the best mentors in the world to work for early in your career?

Finding mentorship is pivotal. It will likely be a trial-and-error process, one must expose themselves to as many professionals as possible and attempt to be critical at finding an appropriate fit.

If you only had two 30-minute sessions a week to train your team, how would you prepare them?

Speed kills! I would focus on speed development and plyometrics. I feel there is no better stimulus than a well-coordinated, high-intensity sprint.

What goes into your decision to leave or stay at a job?

Am I challenged? Am I valued?

What do you do to overcome times of struggle, burnout, or overwhelm? Who do you turn to?

Nature and childhood friends!

What do you think about immediately after one of your athletes is injured? What is your mindset in the following week?

What could/should I have done differently over the last couple of hours, days, weeks, months? It is a problem-solving mindset alongside trying to get back to performance levels as quickly and efficiently as possible.

How do you approach difficult conversations with athletes, coworkers, or your boss?

Directly and in a timely manner—anything else is inadequate.

What traits or skills do your most successful athletes have in common?

Unwavering focus and drive with a big-picture perspective.

What books or resources do you most often recommend to coaches?

Peak by Dr. Marc Bubbs, *Science and Practice of Strength Training* by Zatsiorsky, and *The Coach's Guide to Teaching* by Doug Lemov.

"Is this a place where I can continuously be challenged? Is it an environment for continuity and collaboration? Do I have a voice, and can I make an impact within the organization/franchise outside of my department?"

-Cliff Spiller

Cliff Spiller is the Director of Strength and Conditioning for Men's Basketball at the University of Oregon, where he played a key role in helping the program win the Pac-12 Conference Tournament Championship in 2024. Before joining the Ducks, Spiller had multiple stops in the NBA and G-League, most recently serving as the Assistant Strength and Conditioning Coach for the Utah Jazz. He also held positions as the Head Strength and Conditioning Coach for both the Phoenix Suns G-League team and the Philadelphia 76ers G-League team.

Who do you go to when you need advice? Why them?

When I encounter difficulties in my professional life, I have two valuable sources of support—my family and my mentors. My family always stands by my side, offering unconditional love and support while helping me make the best decisions for my career. My mentors have faced and overcome many of the same challenges I face, and they can provide me with valuable advice and guidance based on their own experiences. I learn best from real-life examples, and my mentors are always willing to share their stories with me. With the support and knowledge provided by my family and mentors, I can surmount obstacles and realize my objectives.

What early job was pivotal in your career? Why?

I am grateful for the chance to have worked with the Philadelphia 76ers. It was my first professional job and was crucial in developing the right training philosophy and habits to succeed. I learned the importance of effective communication, punctuality, collaboration with other departments and team members, and adaptability and flexibility.

What are your first steps when you start a new job? What do you need to figure out, what do you need to get done, who do you need to get to know?

To establish a strong bond with the athletes—getting familiar with their personalities, goals, and interactions with other athletes and staff members is essential. The same applies to the coaching staff and front office/administration. Understanding the daily operations, training philosophies, rehabilitation methods, and systems in a new setting is crucial to start on the right foot.

What advice do you have for a college student looking to break into coaching? Who are the best mentors in the world to work for early in your career?

To pursue a career in coaching, I recommend you major in Exercise Science, Physical Education, or Kinesiology. It's essential to gain relevant experience as soon as possible. You can start interning with the Olympic Sports Department during your undergraduate studies. Additionally, having great mentors can be very impactful in shaping your training philosophy. Todd Wright, Jesse Wright, and Christian Allen were some of the best mentors who helped me early in my coaching career.

If you only had two 30-minute sessions a week to train your team, how would you prepare them?

I suggest focusing on total-body workout sessions incorporating functionally dense exercises. These exercises simultaneously address mobility, flexibility, stability, strength, and power. Loaded movement training is an efficient way to get the most out of your workout. I would suggest programming upper body push/pull, lower body squat, hinge, and lunge exercises in three different planes of motion. It's also good to mix in some integrated core strength and stability exercises.

What goes into your decision to leave or stay at a job?

Is this a place where I can continuously be challenged? Is it an environment for continuity and collaboration? Do I have a voice, and can I make an impact within the organization/franchise outside of my department? Do I receive feedback to help me improve?

What do you do to overcome times of struggle, burnout, or overwhelm? Who do you turn to?

I prioritize being a part of a community and having hobbies outside of work. I often visit my local mosque for prayer and to socialize with others. I enjoy playing chess and try to find local chess clubs to attend. I believe separating work and leisure time is important to prevent burnout.

What do you think about immediately after one of your athletes is injured? What is your mindset in the following week?

If an athlete gets injured, I often wonder if there was anything more I could have done to help prevent it. Injuries are complex and caused by several factors. I try not to blame myself for it. Instead, I focus on creating a plan for the athlete's recovery. This involves meeting with the athlete, coaching staff, and medical staff to discuss the timeline for their return and provide the necessary support for a successful return to play.

How do you approach difficult conversations with athletes, coworkers, or your boss?

If I need to have a difficult discussion with someone within my organization, I usually approach them directly. If I feel like I may have offended them, I would ask, "Did I do something to upset you? I want to make things right and work well with you." If it's a situation where I need an outsider's perspective or a different strategy to approach something, I discuss it with people I trust outside and gain their perspective.

Do you have a "failure" that was critical to your long-term development or success?

Failure to me is a lesson in disguise. In strength and conditioning, like most occupations, you'll have your ebbs and flows, highs and lows, whatever you want. The most important thing to long-term success is your ability to adapt and consistency.

What traits or skills do your most successful athletes have in common?

The most successful athletes I've been around share a common trait: they are the hardest workers in their organization. They arrive early and stay late, always working to improve their craft. Above all, they are fiercely competitive and hate losing. Winning is their ultimate goal, and they approach everything with a mindset to beat their opponents.

What books or resources do you most often recommend to coaches?

When it comes to taking courses related to fitness, I highly recommend the courses offered by the Gray Institute. Their ideology lays the foundation for functional training by emphasizing the importance of three-dimensional movement and viewing the human body as an integrated unit. I suggest *Supertraining* as a great resource and refer to it a lot. Any college-level textbook related to anatomy, physiology, and biomechanics has helped me tremendously.

> *"Experience is the most valuable paycheck a young coach can receive, and you need to put some in the bank."*

-Colton Rosseau

Colton Rosseau is in his second year as the Assistant Director of Sports Performance at Oral Roberts University, where he leads all aspects of sports performance for the Volleyball and Men's and Women's Golf programs, while also assisting with the Men's Basketball program. Rosseau joined ORU after serving as the Director of Olympic Sports and Interim Director of Strength and Conditioning at Hardin Simmons University. Prior to that, he worked as a teacher and coach of multiple sports within Abilene Wylie ISD. Additionally, he has experience at two private training facilities in Abilene: D1 Sports Training and The Forge Training Facility.

Who do you go to when you need advice? Why them?

The two men I seek coaching advice from most are Hagen Little and Kent Johnston. Coach Little is a friend I coached with to start my career, and he has taught me so many valuable lessons about impacting athletes, programming, and not losing sight of the big picture. He is so effective at developing relationships with his teams and has shown me how to do the same.

Coach Johnston is a long-time mentor and has a wealth of experience, understanding, and wisdom that I hope to have a fraction of by the end of my career. He has always been patient with me, taken time to answer my questions, and humbly explains complex subjects about human health and development in refreshingly simple ways.

What early job was pivotal in your career? Why?

The summer after my freshman year in college, I waited tables at a local restaurant. This is certainly not my favorite job I've ever had, but it was instrumental in developing my standards of professionalism that I would later carry into coaching. I was introverted growing up, and at first very uncomfortable with approaching customers at tables and making conversation. I quickly grew out of that and realized that my only essential role at the restaurant was to serve people well, regardless if I was comfortable with it or not. This realization gave me more confidence to simply try and make every customer feel welcomed, cared about, and leave wanting to come back again. My focus shifted from me to them. I still think about that summer, and hope that any athlete who comes to train with me feels welcomed, cared about, and looks forward to the next session.

What are your first steps when you start a new job? What do you need to figure out, what do you need to get done, who do you need to get to know?

Before I start a new job, my first priority is to know the people I will work most with are of high moral character. Proverbs 13:20 states, "Whoever walks with the wise becomes wise, but the companion of fools will suffer harm." I want to ensure the people I spend between forty and sixty hours per week with will have a positive impact on me.

Once I am actually in a new place, I want to meet the athletes as quickly as possible. I need to know where they are from, what they are studying, their career aspirations, and what their experience with strength and conditioning has been like. It is almost impossible to impact athletes you do not know personally.

What advice do you have for a college student looking to break into coaching? Who are the best mentors in the world to work for early in your career?

Find a volunteer opportunity. Experience is the most valuable paycheck a young coach can receive, and you need to put some in the bank. It is highly likely you will work long hours, do tedious work, and be unappreciated, but you will learn much more than you ever could in a classroom. The best mentor you can look for is an experienced coach who is willing to teach you, and when they do teach you something, keep your mouth shut and just listen. You'll be amazed how far you can take your career when you listen to people who know more than you.

If you only had two 30-minute sessions a week to train your team, how would you prepare them?

I actually have a scenario exactly like this with my in-season volleyball team right now. With their practice schedule and how frequently they are traveling, my opportunities to work with them are limited. The two sessions I have with them look almost polar opposite from one another. The first day is focused on training density, with the goal of maintaining player health throughout the season. The goal on the second training day is to achieve high intensity to maintain or even improve athletic performance.

In the first training session, I set up a submaximal strength circuit (typically including unilateral RDLs, sled pulls/drags, various upper body pulls/rows, balance training, auxiliary shoulder work, hip mobility, and isometric trunk exercises). These days require very little warm-up, so we spend about twenty-five of our thirty minutes in this circuit.

On the second training day, I want to sprint, jump, and lift at near-maximal capacities. The warm-up on this day requires more time and energy, so I spend twelve minutes preparing the team to sprint and jump with a dynamic warm-up and technical drill work, six minutes on competitive accelerations (5-7 yards) and measured countermovement jumps (approximately thirty seconds of actual work is done in this period; recovery times are high). The final twelve minutes will include a very low-volume (less than 10 total reps), high-intensity (80-90% 1RM est.) squat variation and some auxiliary trunk, shoulder, and ankle exercises. There are weeks in which I reduce the intensity of this day, based on the players' level of fatigue.

What goes into your decision to leave or stay at a job?

I am still fairly young in my coaching career, so growth is important to me. I want my knowledge, my influence, and my salary to continue to grow. Once I feel my potential for growth in these areas is limited, I know it is time for me to consider other options.

What do you do to overcome times of struggle, burnout, or overwhelm? Who do you turn to?

Although I regrettably always take too long to recognize burnout in myself, I lean on my faith in God more during the times that coaching feels especially draining. I learned several years ago that the areas of life that cause the most anxiety are often the areas least prayed about. I frequently forget this truth and find myself struggling for far too long with issues that seem to dissipate when I bring them to the Lord in prayer. I am often reminded during these times that I have been guilty of idolizing my job, and need to refocus my priorities.

Another practical step I try to take is simply to spend a little less time at work. Sometimes I will step outside for a few minutes during lunch and walk half a mile, and sometimes I will recognize when a certain project or task can wait until the next day and I will go home an hour early. Many coaches, myself included, are guilty of constantly trying to out-work our competition, often at the expense of our own rest and well-being. We know this type of behavior is detrimental to our athletes' performance, yet we fail to recognize when we exhaust ourselves into being less effective in our role.

What do you think about immediately after one of your athletes is injured? What is your mindset in the following week?

While I know injuries will always exist in competitive athletics, it is hard for me not to feel personally responsible for every injury to one of the athletes I coach. I immediately question my training program when one of my athletes sustains an injury. I re-examine the volume, intensity, and exercise selection I have prescribed, as well as my teaching of movement skills for that athlete. I sometimes also have a peer assess my program and ask for their input on any potential blind spots I may have. After that re-examination, I will try to rationally determine if a change in volume, intensity, or exercise selection is necessary. I will either make an adjustment to the program the following week, or monitor the condition of the team as a whole more closely.

How do you approach difficult conversations with athletes, coworkers, or your boss?

Conflict management is a critical part of every work environment, but is especially important in competitive athletics. Stress and emotion are often high in an athletic setting, which is why I try to approach conflicts with athletes, coworkers, and superiors very slowly. I have had many unproductive conversations with an athlete or coworker because I simply did not take time to think before speaking, and instead spoke out of emotion. This adds fuel to the fire and leads to conversations that can be very divisive and counterproductive.

I am improving in my ability to be patient when I face conflict, and consider how to calmly and clearly communicate to the other person involved without causing them to feel defensive. Having a one-on-one conversation with an athlete instead of a public shouting match will virtually always lead to a more positive outcome. It is the athletes who suffer most when conflicts within an athletic department remain unresolved.

Do you have a "failure" that was critical to your long-term development or success?

When I was coaching football at the beginning of my career, I remember a specific play in which one of my middle school wide receivers got a holding penalty on the back side of a 70-yard touchdown run which negated the play. I pulled him out of the game and proceeded to lose my temper at him for such a costly and unnecessary mistake. He was one of my most respectful, hard-working athletes, and also a good player for our team. I moved on from that night and forgot all about the exchange until the following semester, when that receiver informed the staff that he would not be coming out for the football team the next year because "it just wasn't fun."

I was left wondering how much his perception of football was influenced by how I handled that single instance. When I am in a situation now in which an athlete needs correction, I am often reminded of that middle school football game, and my need to exercise patience and thoughtfulness when I correct an athlete.

What traits or skills do your most successful athletes have in common?
The most successful athletes I have worked with are all very driven. They are intrinsically motivated to be the best, and prioritize their training, sleep, and nutrition better than their peers. They are also successful outside of athletics, and are not dependent on their athletic talent as their only opportunity to positively impact their community.

What books or resources do you most often recommend to coaches?
One of my all-time favorite coaching books is John Wooden's *They Call Me Coach*. Wooden's humility and desire to develop young men are so impressive to me, given his tremendous longevity and coaching success.

> *"My first step is to build a relationship with the head coach or coaches. They determine how my work life is going to go and so I need them to trust me asap."*

> *-Will Graham*

Will Graham is the Director of Performance for Women's Basketball at Liberty University and also serves as the Performance Coach for Softball and Women's Soccer. He has played a significant role in elevating the Women's Basketball program, tying the program record with 28 wins in the 2021-2022 season and securing back-to-back WNIT appearances in 2022 and 2023. Since joining Liberty in July 2019, Graham has also worked with the Men's and Women's Tennis, Swimming and Diving, Men's Soccer, and Golf teams. During his first full year (2020-21), five of the six teams he coached captured conference titles. Prior to his time at Liberty, Graham spent four years as a Sport Performance Specialist at APEC in Fort Worth and Tyler, Texas, where he worked with high-level athletes, including NFL MVP Patrick Mahomes, and served as the Director of Adaptive Training at APEC Fort Worth. He also spent two years as the Men's Basketball Strength and Conditioning Coach at LeTourneau University.

Who do you go to when you need advice? Why them?
Henry Barrera—I know he cares about me as a person and my career. Also my new boss Robb Hornett—I know he has a ton of experience and is very smart.

What early job was pivotal in your career? Why?
I actually did youth ministry in college. That was probably the most important job for me because it made me lead and come out of my comfort zone.

What are your first steps when you start a new job? What do you need to figure out, what do you need to get done, who do you need to get to know?
My first step is to build a relationship with the head coach or coaches. They determine how my work life is going to go and so I need them to trust me asap.

What advice do you have for a college student looking to break into coaching? Who are the best mentors in the world to work for early in your career?
Take initiative. Don't wait for someone to tell you to do something. The best mentor

is someone that cares about you and is competent.

If you only had two 30-minute sessions a week to train your team, how would you prepare them?

I would analyze their training age, time of year, sport, and do a needs analysis. We are going to hit the aspects of training that they are needing/missing. (Also sprint)

What goes into your decision to leave or stay at a job?

Who I am working with/for. And how much money I am making.

What do you do to overcome times of struggle, burnout, or overwhelm? Who do you turn to?

I turn to my wife; she is my best friend. I think it's the insecurity in me, but I would rather not show weakness to my peers.

What do you think about immediately after one of your athletes is injured? What is your mindset in the following week?

I do an analysis that considers volume and intensities from all aspects of their week, including school, practice, training, lifts, etc. I want to be there for the athlete the best I can in the following weeks afterwards.

How do you approach difficult conversations with athletes, coworkers, or your boss?

Definitely in person. Try to make it seem like we are in this together.

Do you have a "failure" that was critical to your long-term development or success?

Last summer I was in a depression/funk and really wasn't paying attention to detail on my programming and was ignoring what my boss wanted paperwork wise. I got my ass chewed out, and that was what I needed to restart my drive to be the best I can be.

What traits or skills do your most successful athletes have in common?

Consistency. Ability to learn skills quickly. A personal drive to be successful.

What books or resources do you most often recommend to coaches?

ALTIS *Need for Speed*. It's a course that is so crucial for any coach on how to think about athletic development in general, not just team sport speed. *Game Changer* by Fergus Connolly. *Burn your Goals* by Joshua Medcalf.

> *"Every failure, no matter how big or small, has been vital to any success that I've had thus far. The question has only ever been, was I too proud to recognize it and learn from it?"*
>
> *-Ethan Gold*

Ethan Gold is the Return to Football Coach for the Houston Texans. He joined Houston after serving as an Assistant Strength and Conditioning Coach for the Jacksonville Jaguars. Prior to his time in the NFL, Gold was at the University of North Texas, primarily working with the Mean Green football team. His collegiate experience also includes positions at SMU, Arkansas State, Ole Miss, and East Central University.

Who do you go to when you need advice? Why them?

I am fortunate to have many people in my life that in some way, shape, or form have been mentors to me. The key takeaway here is not necessarily WHO, it's WHY. Surrounding yourself with good people who work hard creates an environment that elevates those around them. I have been in those environments with those people, and they have rubbed off on me. As much as I would love to say that I figured it all out on my own, the fact is that I didn't. The mentors and people I seek advice from are not only highly respected from an X's and O's standpoint, but they relate to people the best. They are leaders, and they are empowering. I find my best advice coming from these individuals, and I hope to be that for anyone that I can be when appropriate.

What early job was pivotal in your career? Why?

My internship at Ole Miss in 2016 was one of the most pivotal points for me in my career. Being under Coach Paul Jackson and his staff set the foundation for all of my jobs and experiences I was afforded in my career thus far.

What are your first steps when you start a new job? What do you need to figure out, what do you need to get done, who do you need to get to know?

People and tempo. Who are the people that I'm working with and what tempo are we operating at? First thing at a new job is not to prove my value, but to add value

386

to what is already being done. A "how can I help" mentality. Obviously, job roles and responsibilities differ as those positions differ, but foundationally this is how I approach any new setting. There will be time to implement the longer I am there, however if I can't work well with those around me, how helpful am I in the long run? This sounds cliché and out of a motivational book, but I have lived this and it's very prominent in every place I have been. Teamwork is simple, but not necessarily easy.

What advice do you have for a college student looking to break into coaching? Who are the best mentors in the world to work for early in your career?

Apply for everything, be willing to work for little, and question everything out of curiosity and with an eagerness to learn. Talk to people, seek them out. If it takes 1,000 emails to coaches and only three answer, then those three are the ones you want to follow at that time. Take visits, and don't be afraid to reach out and explain your position. I feel today we are paralyzed by having simple conversations and showing a bit of vulnerability that it shuts down what could be a great conversation and a potential opportunity.

If you only had two 30-minute sessions a week to train your team, how would you prepare them?

Loaded question, they probably wouldn't be prepared. A sport/position specific field session / a comprehensive weight room session.

What goes into your decision to leave or stay at a job?

If I feel God has led me to this place, or is this on my own accord? Does it support my family goals geographically/monetarily? Who are the people that I will work with?

What do you do to overcome times of struggle, burnout, or overwhelm? Who do you turn to?

I turn to God and my wife and family. I pray, I seek help when needed, and I do my best to self-audit my priorities and perspective on my current situation. Things often are not as bad or as good as they seem. If it was not for prayer in God's word and my wife and family, I would not have the perspective and peace that carries me through pretty much everything this world has to offer.

What do you think about immediately after one of your athletes is injured? What is your mindset in the following week?

What could I have done better? Did I miss something? How can I help NOW? My mentality is support.

How do you approach difficult conversations with athletes, coworkers, or your boss?

The art/science of communication is so vast that pinpointing and utilizing one strategy will only get you so far. Do the best you can to build a relationship and get to know who you are really talking to. Do your homework. Ask around, "How is this athlete/coach/coworker viewed? Who do they hangout with?" Understand that listening and paying attention to the ones you're trying to communicate with is pivotal to the success of any hard conversation. There are instances where people are afforded clout off the jump, either due to status or rumors. This changes the power dynamic, and as a result, the available options to your approach.

Do you have a "failure" that was critical to your long-term development or success?

Every failure, no matter how big or small, has been vital to any success that I've had thus far. The question has only ever been, was I too proud to recognize it and learn from it?

What traits or skills do your most successful athletes have in common?

They have a good attitude, do their very best, treat people well, and are unconditionally grateful, under any circumstances.

What books or resources do you most often recommend to coaches?

Speedworks has been my go-to resource in this space among a few others as far as movement quality/expression in a field-based context. As "new school" as it may sound, social media is a great resource for picking up new ideas and following top notch coaches who are at the top of their game at their respected craft.

"That was a big learning moment for me—these are someone else's kids. This is someone's child. I was only 25 or 26 at the time, and you don't think about it at the moment, but two years down the line when I was at Harvard, those are the things you look back on. Was that really my best that I could have done?"

-Sean Hayes

Sean Hayes is a recognized Master Strength and Conditioning Coach, currently in his fifteenth year at the University of Georgia. He serves as the Director of Athletic Performance for Volleyball, Men's Tennis, and Men's Swimming. For his first 12 years at Georgia, Hayes also led the Men's Basketball program. Prior to his time in Athens, he spent four years with the Buffalo Bills. His collegiate experience includes roles at Clemson, Harvard, and Tulsa, where he became Harvard's first full-time Director of Strength and Conditioning, overseeing all 41 varsity sports. **(Hayes's responses were transcribed from a Zoom call)**

Who do you go to when you need advice? Why them?

It changes as you get older. When I was younger, I called Mike Boyle. When I was at my first job, I called J.T. Allaire. But now I've been married for almost 24 years and I go to my wife. My wife tells me the truth. She tells me if I'm being too emotional about something or I'm not thinking it through. At work, I go to my boss. She has a few more years of experience and she's been here for 20 years. I also talk to the young kids. I love our young assistant, Brandon Hummer. I sit down, I slap my program in front of him and say, "Tell me what you think." I don't have an ego. I don't think I'm the smartest man in the room. I'm humble about it and I want help.

You need to have a village. A village makes people successful. Put your ego down. Everybody helps each other. Everybody doesn't do everything great. I want to find out what everybody is the best at, and then I'm going to pick their brain. With our GA Jared, I've slapped down my program. He's a young kid, but I want to know what he's thinking to help him out, but it also helps me out. When he asks questions, it makes me have to defend what I'm doing, give reasons, and it keeps me sharp.

What early job was pivotal in your career? Why?

My first experience was pivotal for me. After playing college lacrosse, I went to grad school thinking I wanted to be a lacrosse coach. After the first semester, I started thinking, "I don't want to travel. I don't want to do recruiting. Especially at a Division III school, you're covering seven, eight, nine states, and just spreading yourself out." I approached the department head, and I got a GA in strength and conditioning. What got me there was that I previously had done an internship with Mike Boyle when he was still at Boston University.

I partied that summer, working lacrosse camps, and traveling around the whole Northeast eating, drinking, and having a good time with all of my former teammates while playing in summer tournaments. I went into this internship way out of shape, 15 pounds heavier than I needed to be. Mike is such a great guy and has such worldly experience, but he's very straightforward with you. He looks at me, puts his arm around me, and goes, "Until you start looking like a strength coach, no one's ever going to listen to you." You could say things back then, this is '95, and he says, "You're fat." I was like, "Damn!" That kind of hits you a little bit, right? My girlfriend didn't call me fat. That was pivotal because after the shock wore off and we sat there and laughed, he goes, "It was not to be mean, it was to say if you're going to require your athletes to do things, you better be able to demonstrate them really well and be able to do them yourself."

That started a second phase in my life of self-discipline. It was my next level of, "Okay, I have to get back into things and refocus. If this is what I want to do, this is what I got to do." I was still wavering about going to grad school a year after, but that experience of working for Mike, having such a good time, and him being open and sharing everything drove me to want to be a strength coach.

The second biggest part would be my first full-time job at the University of Tulsa. It was an unbelievable moment for my family. Moving halfway across the country and living on your own, having the experience of not always relying on someone else and saying, "Hey mom, I need 50 bucks to pay my bills." It was just myself and my wife. J.T. Allaire also taught me the understanding of how to be a strength coach at a Division I level.

What are your first steps when you start a new job? What do you need to figure out, what do you need to get done, who do you need to get to know?

Ingrain yourself in the school's community. When I got here 15 years ago, I made sure that I got to know all the coaches, support staff, and everybody that was around each sport as well as I could. At the end of the day, you're a servant leader. You're there to serve and help these teams. The more you get to know everybody, the better you're going to be at your job and the better you're going to help everybody. I haven't worked basketball going on three years, but there are a few managers left over that to this day, we stop each other and talk in the hallway. In basketball, there's a bunch of managers, and the more you get to know those guys, the more fun the atmosphere is, the better travel is, the better practice is.

They always make fun of me around here because I smile and say hi to everybody. I don't care who it is because I don't think we're better than anybody. The janitors, the people that come in and paint, the bug people, I'm always talking to everybody. I'm smiling and saying, "Hi, how you doing?" You don't know whose day you're going to affect and make better. I'm also a big manifestation person. If you're smiling and giving off positive vibes, people are going to give it back to you. It creates such a nice work environment. So the answer is you've got to get to know everybody. There's not one or two people—except for your direct boss or head coaches, they do make your life a little easier if you have a better relationship—but it's the assistant coaches, the director of operations, the janitors, the secretaries, administrative assistants. When you get to know them really well, they're the ones that tell the head coach, "You seen Sean today? He said hi to me." That means a lot to people when you're willing to stop and carve out even a minute of your day. It's easy to do.

Everybody matters. There was an ex-janitor who was in charge of our building—Jonathan. He hasn't worked in our building for five years, but I still text him. I know that during fall festivals his church sets up little booths, and I always go over and find him. Get to know everybody. It's good for your soul.

What advice do you have for a college student looking to break into coaching? Who are the best mentors in the world to work for early in your career?
I'm going to ask, "Why do you want to do it?" It's a hard field. Everybody gets caught up on what they see on Instagram. They all expect to be on the sidelines and to be the "rah rah" guy. That is such a small segment and portion of what we do. People only video the best reps. No one's videoing the strength coach banging their head against the wall because they've taught the same kid a hang clean for 12 weeks and he still is not hip hinging correctly. No one sees that. These young kids that think, "I'm going to make hundreds of thousands of dollars because these football strength coaches

make hundreds of thousands of dollars," I tell them to do their research and make sure this is what they want to do. It's a phenomenal field. The bonds that you make, the camaraderie, the culture, all those things that you have on a staff and a team, they are unmatched in any other job in this world. There's something different about this, the environment that keeps you young and happy. Make sure you're doing it for the right reasons and because you want to help young kids.

I got into this field because I want to help young kids grow and to see them flourish. Almost every basketball and volleyball player I ever coached, I still keep in touch with to some level. If you want to impact someone's life in more ways than one, become a coach, because you can have a phenomenal effect on someone's life. I told this to our volleyball team today. I became a coach to see everybody succeed, but I want to make sure that I'm setting these ladies up for success beyond college volleyball. We have one lady who will make a lot of money playing pro. The other ladies are, like that commercial says, "going pro in something else." If I've helped them get ready for life, that's why you become a coach. You're helping kids get ready for life.

Look for places that post and boast about where they've put their interns—places that are successful placing their interns, because that means they invest into their interns. That means they're investing in their education, helping them get certifications, and helping them prepare for the rigors. Ask questions to people that have worked for them. "Hey, how was it working for Sean Hayes? Was he a complete jerk, or did he care?" As long as you feel that you're going to work for people that are going to care and invest in you, in and out of work, then you're going to find yourself a good place.

What goes into your decision to leave or stay at a job?
This is my 15th year here. I've been very blessed. It's hard to stay at one job, no matter what level, for five years. For me, being 50 years old, 27 years into my career, it is all about what's going to make my family life better. I'm not looking for more vacation time or for kickbacks, but it has to be a financial advantage. I have a house and a mortgage. I have two daughters that play college soccer, both in the state of Georgia. Back in 2017, I had an opportunity to go back to the NFL. In my mind and my wife's mind, we were prepared. We were mentally packing the house and preparing the kids. But when it came down to it, the money changed at the last minute. All of a sudden, moving from Georgia, a low cost of living, to Minnesota, a higher cost of living, that money didn't make it easier to pay the bills. It has to be a situation where it can make my family life

better financially, because I know my routine. I can go see my daughters play a couple times a month, I can be involved in their life. If I'm going to take a job that has more responsibility, changes my location, and doesn't make it better for paying bills and out-of-state tuition now, that just doesn't work. It has to be a significant impact.

I'm also not a big believer in taking lateral jobs, unless it's a major financial impact. You just find yourself in the same things that you're doing now, but it makes it harder because it's a new place. It needs to advance your career title wise or position wise. When I took this job, for my first 12 years I had basketball, volleyball, and golf. Then I had basketball and volleyball because someone else did golf. A job at another SEC school where it was just basketball only is a better job because then you have less responsibility. But a job that was basketball and volleyball and another sport wouldn't be for me. You don't want to take an advance that puts more stress on doing your job.

What do you do to overcome times of struggle, burnout, or overwhelm? Who do you turn to?

The first nine years of my time at Georgia, I had Mark Fox as the basketball coach, and then Coach Crean came in. Naturally, after nine years, you get comfortable with what your system is. Coach Fox liked to lift four days a week, and he liked to do things on certain days. Coach Crean wanted a different up style tempo, all different things. Making that transition late in my life and career, that was a tough time. Not a bad time, it was a tough time. As a human being, we all get comfortable. Coach Crean said, "Hey, I'm gonna challenge you. I want you to come up with solutions." He challenged me to become a better coach. He made me understand that there are other ways to do things in the way that he needs it done for his program and his success. You can't be offended by it.

As a human being at 46 years old, I realized this is a major challenge in my career, because the golf coach doesn't give you that hard of a time. Those weren't the challenges. But at 46 years old, I had to change some of my coaching style, some of my uptempo stuff. I had to pull on those football experiences, because he liked that kind of intensity. I walked across the street and I talked to Coach Sinclair. He helped me get back in that mindset. The people around you are important, but I also think some of the people that are challenging you are important to talk to, because no one's challenging you because they want you to fail. People challenge you because they want you to be successful. That was part of it too, learning to communicate better with Coach Crean, learning to understand what he needed more out of me, going up and having those difficult conversations with him. Sometimes they were tough, but that made me better. That made me more resilient. That made me tougher. All those things happen for a reason in your life and career. Asking the people that tell you the truth and help you out the right way, confronting what that challenge is, helps get over that challenge. Don't run from it.

What do you think about immediately after one of your athletes is injured? What is your mindset in the following week?

Different levels of injuries cause different feelings. A good example was in the spring, our starting libero sprained her MCL, grade four. I said, "Hey Jubilee (Athletic Trainer), was there something that we were missing?" She said, "No, it was a slip the way her leg went out. There's nothing you can do. Because of what we're doing, I think that helped mitigate that to not become a tear." When we talk to recruits as coaches, our first thing is always, "We're going to prevent injuries..." We can only do our best to prevent injuries. We have to know the sport, and we have to know the risk-reward with exercise selection. If we do our homework, we're on the same page with the trainers, we're doing the right things, your first reaction doesn't have to be negative and dark. When it's a contact injury, there's nothing you can do. When someone steps on someone's foot and rolls their ankle, there's nothing you can do. It's those non-contact ones, the demon ones that I don't even like to talk about for the lower body, that's when you have to reflect and really think, "Are we doing everything we need to do?" That's when you have a conversation with your trainer. How do we make adjustments to reduce the risk as much as possible?

I try not to blame myself, but I think as strength coaches, we all go to that spot. But if you start blaming yourself, getting negative, and overthinking it—you're doing your team a disservice. If you start over-correcting, your athletes are smart. They'll be like, "What is this guy doing?" Have a little self-reflection. Talk to the medical staff, talk to the trainer. Having a great relationship with your athletic trainer is key to having success at the college level because they can be your advocate, they can be a positive voice for you, and they can give you important insight. People get defensive, and "you do your job and I'll do my job." If we just all put our guard down, then we can do the best for that athlete and team.

How do you approach difficult conversations with athletes, coworkers, or your boss?

The hard conversations are the ones that make you grow the most. Not confrontational.

We've all had confrontational stuff, and that gets you nowhere. Everybody gets defensive and walls go up. The biggest thing I found is that if you don't have that conversation and you avoid it, there is a bomb waiting around the corner. Be direct, honest, open to listen, and open to ideas—on both sides. I'm only seeing it through my lens, but that person is seeing it through their lens. If I go in and attack, I fully expect that person to have their defenses go up. Now we're not getting anywhere and there's no solution. I love trying to be as direct, honest, and understanding as possible so I can resolve a situation. Not having solutions causes more problems and will eventually blow up in your face down the road.

I'm not always saying I've done that. I've failed more times than being successful. But every time I fail, I try to learn from that and try to be more successful the next time I have that conversation. A couple of the best people that I bounce stuff off of in those kinds of difficult conversations are athletic trainers, because they are used to having a lot of difficult conversations. Our volleyball trainer is phenomenal at this—Jubilee. She has a lot of difficult conversations with female athletes, so I get to learn from that.

Do you have a "failure" that was critical to your long-term development or success?
I look back at Tulsa, that was back in the days of strength and conditioning that I call the Wild West, because there were no NCAA regulations. Everything was mandatory, you could punish kids, and it was "keep going until you get hurt." What really made me start thinking is when we had a new coaching staff come in and they're like, "We're changing the culture. The old staff didn't win." They pushed us into that pressure where at the end of the day, it's their team, they're hired and they're fired, and the administration is backing them. We had guys' backs getting blown out on back squats, while we were just getting hammered because they weren't strong enough...and that's why we were losing.

Naturally as a coach, "Alright, load it, you can do it, you can do it." But they couldn't do it. That was a big learning moment for me—these are someone else's kids. This is someone's child. I was only 25 or 26 at the time, and you don't think about it at the moment, but two years down the line when I was at Harvard, those are the things you look back on. "Was that really my best that I could have done?" I always reflect back. Remembering those times makes me better now. These kids ask today, "How different is it now? How different are you?" I'm different because it's a different mentality. If you squat 405 or 410, is that really making a difference in someone's career? Is that making a difference in someone's risk of injury? I look back and I remember this kid named Mike Mallory. Never forget his name. Big, tall, defensive end, 6'6 kid. That poor kid, his career was over. He was such a good guy, but how's Mike Mallory? Does he still have issues because we hurt his back in 2000? Those are the things I reflect on, like risk-reward, and that's changed my attitude of being safe, making sure a kid can be successful, and not trying to end someone's season.

What traits or skills do your most successful athletes have in common?

One is self-discipline. It is unreal. One that sticks out in my mind was in Buffalo. In the in-season, you have to work out twice a week or you get fined. There was a defensive back named Nate Clements. He was an All-Pro special teams kick returner, and that dude lifted every day. His self-discipline—it was the same time, his routine was his routine, and it was unreal. That's what separates people. People think they work hard in their own way, but truly those cliché lines are what separate people. His self-discipline, his leadership skills, all those things were unreal. Our big hitting days were Wednesday and Thursday with full pads, and he'd come in and do extra cardio every Wednesday.

At the college level, it's the same thing. Talent is talent. Anthony Edwards, his talent was unbelievable. His work ethic though—it was unmatched. You can see it now. They still tweet about him shooting in the gym by himself after the USA stuff, probably 12 o'clock at night. He'd be here until one, two o'clock in the morning shooting—it's unbelievable. The best have the self-discipline, the best are the leaders, and they want people to follow them.

What books or resources do you most often recommend to coaches?

The two books that I always have my interns read are *Advances in Functional Training* and *New Functional Training for Sports* by Mike Boyle. If I went and said, *Supertraining*, or one of the other older books, those are hard for young kids to understand. But Mike's books are made to understand and learn at an easy level so they can broaden their horizons. Once they've read those two books, then we can take our next step. But those are my go to books for any young strength coach to read, because I think he does the best job making it easy to read and absorb. He makes it easy to understand what you need to get in, and the reasons why. He gets slammed sometimes because of his lack of back squatting, but that's fine. You don't have to back squat to be successful. I don't back squat our volleyball team and we're successful. These books provide information that can grow the confidence of a young strength coach to then program, read the next book, and grow and ask more questions.

"Try to expose yourself to different styles of coaches when you find a program. Learn from the winners, losers, bookworms, and free spirits. They will all have something valuable to teach you."

-Damian De Santiago

Damian De Santiago is in his first year as the Strength and Conditioning Coach at Spearman ISD. He joined Spearman after two seasons as the Director of Men's Basketball Strength and Conditioning at Abilene Christian University. Before ACU, De Santiago served as the Assistant Strength and Conditioning Coach for Texas Tech Men's Basketball. Prior to his time at Texas Tech, he was the Director of Strength and Conditioning and Nutrition for both Men's and Women's Basketball at Weber State.

Who do you go to when you need advice? Why them?
Some of my mentors that include Darby Rich, Tory Stephens, Jason Wooding. Also former colleagues like Connor Agnew, Scott Ramsey, and Justin Irwin. My mentors keep me grounded. I can come to them with any issue I'm dealing with and they more often than not have a reasonable solution. The other three keep me sharp and challenge my way of thinking on a regular basis.

What early job was pivotal in your career? Why?
Bartending. Communication and multi-tasking skills were developed there. Helped me refine my soft skills in the coaching field.

What are your first steps when you start a new job? What do you need to figure out, what do you need to get done, who do you need to get to know?
Meet and introduce myself to every staff member and athlete. Figure out layout of facilities and other resources. It's also a good idea to introduce yourself to administrative staff. They are clutch in directing you to the right people to talk to.

What advice do you have for a college student looking to break into coaching? Who are the best mentors in the world to work for early in your career?
Start early and be about it. You'll have to spend time grinding and working for free. Be humble in how you approach this field and ask good questions. Try to expose yourself

to different styles of coaches when you find a program. Learn from the winners, losers, bookworms, and free spirits. They will all have something valuable to teach you.

If you only had two 30-minute sessions a week to train your team, how would you prepare them?

Two total body splits. Probably some form of the Tier System, and depending on what time of the year, it may be linear or undulating periodization. Plyometrics and speed work as a primer, simple rep and set scheme (3x5, 4x3, 5x2) on main lifts, accessories specific to sport. Ideally, this would be right before practice and can also aid as a warm-up for practice.

What goes into your decision to leave or stay at a job?

Will this put me in a better position to support myself and my family? Does a coach align with my values? Quality of Life. Location. Salary.

What do you do to overcome times of struggle, burnout, or overwhelm? Who do you turn to?

Outlets outside of work such as leisure or family time, BJJ, night life, etc. Important to keep balance outside of work. All work and no play makes Jack a sad and single man.

What do you think about immediately after one of your athletes is injured? What is your mindset in the following week?

It used to be, "What could I have done better to prevent this?" But now it's just part of the continuous process of development. Be positive, supportive, and understanding of the athlete's mental as you go through the process. BE CONSISTENT.

How do you approach difficult conversations with athletes, coworkers, or your boss?

Peel the bandage off and don't beat around the bush. Always be direct but respectful and never act out of emotion.

Do you have a "failure" that was critical to your long-term development or success?

Corny, but I don't really see anything as a "failure." All just learning experiences. Having that mindset has done more for my development than anything else.

What traits or skills do your most successful athletes have in common?

Desire to be great. Bottom line. It's apparent who wants it and who doesn't. You never have to bargain or negotiate their effort.

"In my interview I'll ask, 'What do you need from my position that will get us closer to reaching X goal?' From there, I can better assess what matters, what the staff feels the team is lacking, and how to better communicate when those factors are being met or hindered."

-Victoria Saucedo

Victoria Saucedo is in her first year as the Associate Sports Performance Coach for Women's Basketball at Stanford University. Prior to Stanford, she served as the Director of Sports Performance for Women's Basketball at VCU, where she helped the 2023-2024 team set a program record with 26 regular-season wins. Her team also achieved an NCAA record for the largest one-year turnaround, improving from 7-22 to 26-6. Before her time at VCU, Saucedo held a similar role at Wake Forest University as the Director of Women's Basketball Sports Performance. She also gained experience at Saint Louis University and Northern Arizona University before joining Wake Forest.

Who do you go to when you need advice? Why them?

My partner and my family. They bring a refreshing perspective to the situations I am in. They have my best interest in mind, know me better than I know myself at times, and help me see the bigger picture. Aside from them, I usually turn to my mentors. Those who are older and have been in similar shoes, learning from mistakes, successes, forgotten considerations, what matters, what doesn't.

What early job was pivotal in your career? Why?

I'd say a tie between Northern Arizona University (NAU) and Saint Louis University. NAU was where I completed my graduate assistantship. I grew a lot as a strength coach because of how uncomfortable I was. I say that because I had never worked football before and I was going to be assisting with them. So, for my first start, I would be yelling at 80-100 young men and assuming they would listen to me. I was the only female on staff, so when I yelled out times, reps, sets, directions, I really had to dig deep.

It was my first experience working with a sport coach who wanted to program for their own team—a lot of conversations, back and forth, compromising, being confident in myself, and trusting in what I knew. It was also where I was able to start up a nutrition station and create a budget to feed the student athletes. I had to work with administration on the vision of the university along with sport coaches. A whole lot of new, being comfortable with uncomfortability, and staying confident in myself.

At Saint Louis, this was my first full-time position, growing into who I want to be as a coach, branching out, and getting more confident. I worked under the guidance of Robb Hornett, who gave me a lot of perspective into screenings, return to play, administrative duties, managing people, etc.

What are your first steps when you start a new job? What do you need to figure out, what do you need to get done, who do you need to get to know?

Understand the staff and what they need. Usually in my interview I'll ask, "What do you need from my position that will get us closer to reaching X goal?" From there, I can better assess what matters, what the staff feels the team is lacking, and how to better communicate when those factors are being met or hindered. When I step foot on campus I hit my Big 3. First, passive and active "movement screen" to see how, where, and what they compensate. Any restrictions that will lead to issues down the road or identify the compensations that may be what causes them to be an elite level athlete. Second, get KPIs that I think are beneficial. Third, a sit down with the athletes on sports performance. Getting to know their perception of it, what they want to get better at for their sport within my field, and it's also a way for the athletes to get to know me outside of me yelling reps and sets.

If you only had two 30-minute sessions a week to train your team, how would you prepare them?

Pending what they need, I would hammer the heck out of that. I'd keep it simple, so no more than four exercises each day, 2 upper, 2 lower. 8-10 mins for warm-ups, use that as any plyometric work or primer for the lift. Make sure there is flow to the lift so there are no jams or waiting. Also utilizing the warm-ups for the sport as part of S&C prep.

What do you do to overcome times of struggle, burnout, or overwhelm? Who do you turn to?

Take a vacation, get away for a week or so, and/or go to an exciting/thought provoking continuing education event to re-energize me. I turn to family or friends to get me away from the environment I am usually in.

What do you think about immediately after one of your athletes is injured? What is your mindset in the following week?

My thought process varies pending the injury. Understanding contact vs non-contact, mechanism of injury, and predispositions are the first few thoughts that pop into my mind. Is this the first athlete to have this type of injury, or is it a trend? When I feel like it's a trend or similar injury, I look into my programming—what have we missed, or are we over exposing the athletes? We have GPS, take grips, RPE scores, force plates, so I look into those as well to see if there was something missed or overlooked to help paint a clearer picture. I also work super close with our Athletic Trainer. We sit down, I get his point of view/thoughts on it, and collaborate on what we can do better.

How do you approach difficult conversations with athletes, coworkers, or your boss?

Difficult conversations happen...a lot. Having them is somewhat easier when you develop a relationship. Not saying you have to be best buds, but a mutual understanding of having the student-athletes' performance and well-being in your best interest along with respect for one another. If that's there, the conversation will probably go a lot smoother (not saying the conversation will end with what you want). After that, make sure you are prepared for what you need to talk about. Running through how you are going to approach it, all your facts/points are clear and concise, and be ready for any questions/comments/concerns that may follow. Understanding a compromise will most likely need to happen, so unless it's a hill you want to die on, don't be too stubborn.

What books or resources do you most often recommend to coaches?

- *Science and Practice of Strength Training* – Vladimir Zatsiorsky
- *Almanack Of Naval Ravikant* – Eric Jorgenson
- *Ultimate MMA Conditioning* – Joel Jamieson

> *"Be very cognizant that you're either going to leave a job before people want you to or after people want you to. And you don't want it to be the latter."*
>
> ## -Debbie Hill

Debbie Hill was inducted into the William & Mary Athletics Hall of Fame in 2014 following her incredible tenure as Head Volleyball Coach for over 30 years. In 2022, she was honored as one of the "Godmothers of Volleyball" by the AVCA for her impact in growing the sport. Hill finished her career with 587 wins, a victory total that put her at 23rd all-time in Division I at the time of her retirement. Included in those 587 wins were seven straight CAA championships from 1985-1991, eight conference championships in total, a 56-match conference winning streak, and five CAA Coach of the Year awards. **(Hill's responses were transcribed from a Zoom call)**

Who do you go to when you need advice? Why them?

You have to have a cadre of people that you completely trust. You may be lucky enough that it might be your boss. It could be a fellow coach you trust to share stories with. For me, I was fortunate enough to have a mentor who was not a volleyball person, but my athletic director. I was 24 and green behind the ears, head coach of two programs, I didn't know what I was doing, and she was amazing. You have to have somebody you can trust.

Then you take generic advice from your family, if it's your parents or a brother, in my case, my wife. I also spent a lot of time with our sports psychologist asking her for advice. She would never have broken confidentiality, but she knew if certain things we were doing weren't received well. So a sports psychologist is always a good asset and former athletes can be good sounding boards too. For me, our senior woman administrator was amazing. She was the one who hired me and she was my boss. I consulted with her often and with other longtime coaches in the athletic department as well.

What early job was pivotal in your career? Why?

I went to school at the University of Houston, got a master's at UNC Greensboro, and then came to William & Mary in 1976 as a 24-year-old. In my generation, everyone coached two sports and taught Physical Education classes as part of their job. I'd been at William & Mary for six years when women's sports were governed by the Association for Intercollegiate Athletics for Women. In 1982, the W&M women's athletic department began transitioning to an NCAA Division I athletic department. I loved my job. We were successful at the equivalent of a Division III program. I wanted to upgrade my knowledge of the game so I took a leave of absence from William & Mary and became a graduate assistant at a very successful SEC program.

This university had a top-20 program in Division I. They had unlimited funding and everything they needed to be successful. I intended to upgrade my knowledge of the game and move on from W&M. I had attracted the attention of a couple of big programs and I thought I was ready for a "big-time" coaching job. As soon as I arrived at my new job, I realized that it was the epitome of everything I thought was wrong about athletics at the time. There were few NCAA regulations about the length of practices and very low academic requirements. I supervised the players lifting weights from six to eight AM, and then they had four hours of on-court practice in the afternoon. The athletes were told what classes they could take. They were told what they could eat and drink. There was an athletes-only dorm and athletes-only dining room. This was in the early 1980s, long before most of the current NCAA regulations concerning student-athlete wellness and academic progress were in place. I soon realized that everything about that athletic program was the polar opposite of everything that I believed in. Academics were completely tangential to anything to the athlete's first job, which was to win. I learned a lot that year. We were a very successful program, but it was at great cost to the student-athletes. It was a one-year part-time job, but it was pivotal to my career because I probably would have moved on and moved up, and then changed jobs every five years to go to the next job and become firmly ensconced in a rat race.

Instead, I returned to William & Mary the following year, having learned many things to be avoided in an athletic program. I retired from here after 32 great years. That year away caused me to think a lot about who I wanted to be as a coach, who I wanted to be as a human being, and what I wanted athletes to experience through sport. I had to experience a job that, almost right away, I realized was not a fit for me and what my values were. It certainly was a defining moment.

What are your first steps when you start a new job? What do you need to figure out, what do you need to get done, who do you need to get to know?

It is important to befriend the facilities staff. Introduce yourself to the folks who set up the court and clean the floors. About once a month I'd buy pizza for the whole crew that mow the fields and cleaned the facilities. Make friends with all of those people. Then meet with your athletic trainer, your sports information person, and the sports psychologist.

Of course, at the beginning of each season, it is important to have individual meetings with every team member. The thing is to look into your athletes hearts and minds and find out—"I know we've been through the recruiting process, but you're here now. Really, why are you here? What's in your heart? What speaks to you about what we're about to try to accomplish? What goals do you have that I might not be aware of? Academic, fitness, nutrition, strength, all of those things. What are your goals I may not have heard about yet?" As a coach, we know what our program needs, but we don't know everything from our athletes yet. Coaches try to be thorough in the recruiting process, but what might we have missed? Often the family is involved in the recruiting process and later you find out, "Actually my parents are getting divorced. It has been difficult, and I only have the support of my dad, not my mom, or vice versa." You can never spend too much time getting to know your support staff and your players.

What advice do you have for a college student looking to break into coaching? Who are the best mentors in the world to work for early in your career?
You have to know yourself very well and many young coaches don't have the bandwidth for that yet. I certainly didn't. Be introspective about what kind of a coach you want to be. You have to match your career goals with the person that you want to work for. Then you just have to start at the bottom. For many people, that means to go coach club at a really high level, rather than going directly into college coaching. The entry to college coaching now is director of operations or volunteer coach. You start at the bottom. Unless you're in a power five program, you're probably not going to be paid for these jobs. You're going to be a volunteer for a year or so, and then you'll maybe be the 2nd assistant for several years. You have to be ready to pay your dues. In most of volleyball, there are not a lot of places that as an entry level coach, you're going to be making six figures. You might have to be willing to take a lot of pride in starting at the bottom of a pyramid and work your way up. At some point in volleyball, I do think it can be helpful to work in the club system, and probably the same thing in basketball.

If you only had two 30-minute sessions a week to train your team, how would you prepare them?

Before those two sessions, I would make sure they had been in the training room and in the weight room. I would make sure they had in writing ahead of time what that 30 minute block was going to be. I would want them to be mentally prepared for what every minute of that 30 minutes was going to be. Physically and mentally to know what they were going to be in for.

What goes into your decision to leave or stay at a job?

My wife is a very smart woman—she's a surgeon. She used to say that a surgeon usually retires a little too soon or a little too late. They retire before people want them to or after people wish they had. The same is true in coaching. For me, thirty-two years in one place was a long time. I just knew that my time of complete and total absorption in my job was nearing an end. Be very cognizant that you're either going to leave a job before people want you to or after they want you to. And you don't want it to be the latter.

What do you do to overcome times of struggle, burnout, or overwhelm? Who do you turn to?

Of course your family. After my wife and I got together, she was the rock. Also, I used to go out for a run or a workout. I used to get away from the desk and that always helped me clear my mind. I also had good coaching friends that I could call up and run things by them.

What do you think about immediately after one of your athletes is injured? What is your mindset in the following week?

I'm a very compassionate coach and it was always so painful when one of my players was injured. You have to walk this fine balance of, "I'll be there for you to do whatever I can to support you, but you have to do your rehab." I made a mistake early in my career that taught me an invaluable lesson. One of my athletes tore her ACL, and the surgery didn't go well. As time went on she just drifted away from the team. There were no scholarships, and she decided not to try out the next year. She was in the hospital, and the team wasn't allowed to go to the hospital, but I put them all in a van and we stood up in front of her hospital window. We waved and we sent cards to her and I thought we did what was needed. But then I just lost track of her. I would call her and things like that, but here's the thing—she remembered none of that.

Years later, I reconnected with her. I reached out to her and wanted to meet her for coffee and talk about her experience, and she said it might be a hard conversation. I said I want to have it, I want to know why I lost track of you. She said she felt abandoned and that it was very painful for her emotionally and physically. It is now forty years later. We are Facebook friends, but she still feels the pain of her time on the team. That was a learning experience for me. I thought I had done what she needed. I did not. Now, of course, there would be assistant coaches and there would be athletic trainers to help keep injured players engaged. Now there would be help with that. But I would say that you cannot err on the side of too much comfort care. You can't be too careful taking care of the injured athlete's emotional AND physical needs.

How do you approach difficult conversations with athletes, coworkers, or your boss?
Early in my career, I was very conflict-averse, but I got better at advocating for myself and our program. I also learned to document conversations and research the information I needed to back up my positions. You have to learn to be direct, but respectful when the respect is earned.

Do you have a "failure" that was critical to your long-term development or success?
The two things that I come back to are the two stories I've already told you, the athlete that I didn't take care of, I considered to be a failure. The other was the time that I spent at the SEC school early in my career — it was a failure that led to a huge success. I say this all the time: you always win or you learn. You learn much more from a loss than you do from a win, because you learn where you need to go, what you need to work on, and your vulnerabilities. That job for me was a failure, but it was a win because it taught me what I wanted in a job. The second was the experience of the athlete who didn't feel seen after an injury.

What traits or skills do your most successful athletes have in common?
Resiliency and commitment paired with passion are so important. If you've got resiliency, especially at a university like William & Mary where the academics are so intense, you will be more successful. Our athletes have to be passionate about the game, but they have to be resilient too. You're not going to win every match. You might get injured. How will you handle those moments? I always said when I was recruiting people, I had three characteristics that I looked for. The first was what kind of person is this athlete? Secondly, what kind of student is this player? And lastly, what kind of an athlete is this player?

"The best mentors are ones that will help you but not give you answers, challenge your thought process but understand where you are in your development. If you are working directly under them, giving you autonomy and a chance to fail."

-Hunter Eisenhower

Hunter Eisenhower is the Associate Head Coach of Sports Performance for the Men's Basketball Program at Arizona State University. He is also the co-founder of Move the Needle Human Performance, where he co-hosts a podcast, organizes a symposium, and provides online training programs. Eisenhower is well known for developing the Force System. Prior to his role at Arizona State, he served as a Sports Performance Coach and Sports Scientist for the Sacramento and Stockton Kings. His collegiate experience includes positions at UC Davis, Southeastern Louisiana, and Minnesota State Mankato before joining the Kings.

Who do you go to when you need advice? Why them?

I've been fortunate to develop an intelligent, helpful, honest, and accessible network of mentors and colleagues. These are people that are always willing to help and are as passionate about this field as I am. They are extremely helpful, but they are not an echo chamber of "yes men." They may give answers/advice I don't agree with, but it's more beneficial for me even if I don't accept it in the moment.

What early job was pivotal in your career? Why?

UC Davis. Because I played college basketball, I was enamored by the novelty of training within college football. I was also training Men's Basketball at the time, and because of the incredible experience I had with the guys on the team and basketball coaching staff, it brought me to knowing I wanted to be within basketball long term. It's what is most natural to me and what I know best. That has led to a job in the G-League, NBA, and now Arizona State.

What are your first steps when you start a new job? What do you need to figure out, what do you need to get done, who do you need to get to know?

Individual meetings with everybody within the program are extremely impactful. You get an idea of what the true culture is, not what one or two individuals tell you it is. You get an idea where you can make the biggest impact in terms of development, culture, etc.

What advice do you have for a college student looking to break into coaching? Who are the best mentors in the world to work for early in your career?

Be curious, be passionate, and be productive. It is so easy in this world to be complacent, fall into the dangerous trap of "we've always done it this way," and be consumed with wasting time on social media or tv. Be a lifelong learner that challenges tradition. It's okay to be wrong and venture off the path of squat, hinge, push, pull. That's not to say don't learn the basics. But I'd rather have 30 different years in this field than the same year 30 times.

The best mentors are ones that will help you but not give you answers, challenge your thought process but understand where you are in your development. If you are working directly under them, giving you autonomy and a chance to fail. They need to be invested in your career, not just in the need of somebody to sweep the floors and refill the fridge.

If you only had two 30-minute sessions a week to train your team, how would you prepare them?

I would sprint, do depth drops, and focus on LTP (Local Tissue Prep). More about all this can be found on my Instagram.

What goes into your decision to leave or stay at a job?

Am I being valued? Do I feel as though I'm able to make an impact? Am I giving up more time with my family than I deem as worth it? (Minimal money = better have a lot of time with family/A lot of money = willing to give up slightly more within reason. There is an ultimate breaking point in my opinion though, regardless of how much you are compensated)

What do you do to overcome times of struggle, burnout, or overwhelm? Who do you turn to?

Take time away. It's easy to be consumed by this field, thinking about your program, your current read, research, etc. Sometimes you just need to turn your brain off and fully invest in other hobbies or material. I tell myself every night that I get home that I am turning off "coach mode" and turning on "husband and dad mode." Am I perfect at it? Not a chance, but the short breaks from material are very helpful to avoid burnout.

Staying in positions too long will inevitably lead to burnout. Working 12–15 hour days for minimum wage is not sustainable no matter how much you love your career and athletes.

What do you think about immediately after one of your athletes is injured? What is your mindset in the following week?

That it's my fault. That's not the right way to think. Injuries are nobody's fault, but I've always heard, "Strength coaches prevent injuries." In some situations, we can negate the likelihood, but it's impossible to prevent. Early after an injury, it's more important to take care of the athlete's psychology than their physiology. It takes time to process an injury, and shoving your RTP plan down their throat might set you back more than you know from a trust and buy in perspective. Take time to care about the person and then that will give you more access to rehab the injury.

How do you approach difficult conversations with athletes, coworkers, or your boss?

Honesty and transparency. Say what you think, even if the other person doesn't want to hear it.

Do you have a "failure" that was critical to your long-term development or success?

My "failure" is consistently feeling like I'm falling short as a husband, dad, and coach. I don't want this to come off the wrong way. I think I am good at all those areas, but I always strive to be better. It's the lack of complacency that I consistently try to keep. There is always room to improve.

What traits or skills do your most successful athletes have in common?

Passionate, competitive, talented, genetically gifted, hardworking, intentional.

What books or resources do you most often recommend to coaches?

Force and *Biomechanics of Sprinting* by Dan Cleather. The best course I've ever taken is *Elastic Essentials* by Joel Smith.

> *"Being a middle school coach forced me to learn how to be creative...you are limited in equipment, space, and time. At the same time, you are working with athletes that are at different points in their stages of development. Every day was a new day."*
>
> ## -Kyle Keese

Kyle Keese is the Director of Strength and Conditioning at Denton Guyer High School, where he has played a pivotal role in helping the football program achieve consistently high levels of success, including back-to-back state championships in 2012 and 2013. In 2019, Keese was honored as the National High School Strength Coaches Association Southwest Region Coach of the Year. During his tenure at Guyer, he has been instrumental in the development of numerous athletes who have gone on to play at the collegiate level, including Jackson Arnold, the former Gatorade National Football Player of the Year.

Who do you go to when you need advice? Why them?

I reach out to Bryan Kegans and Monte Sparkman because they have an unbelievable amount of knowledge in our field and because I know they have a tremendous amount of experience working with all athletes in all situations. I want to hear and learn from coaches who are, or who have been, in my shoes before.

What early job was pivotal in your career? Why?

Being a middle school coach forced me to learn how to be creative. As a middle school coach, you are limited in equipment, space, and time. At the same time, you are working with athletes that are at different points in their stages of development. Every day was a new day. I had to find ways to keep things simple in order to teach a kid how to squat, jump, and sprint. This has helped me learn how to adapt on the go.

What are your first steps when you start a new job? What do you need to figure out, what do you need to get done, who do you need to get to know?

It is extremely important that coaches do less talking and more work. Too many coaches step into a job and believe they should be respected because of their job title.

You must earn respect from your fellow coaches and your athletes. Not many people can argue with you if they see you come in every day and give your heart and soul into everything you do.

Don't wait for someone to tell you to do something. If there is something you see that needs to be done, do it. If someone has to constantly tell you to do things, then it may be time for a career change or to move back in with your parents.

Get to know your athletes first. The more you buy into your athletes, the more they will buy into you. There's a lot more to our profession than just trying to win games. You never know if the impact you have on an athlete may change their life forever. It is also important that you get to know everyone in your culture. The head coach and the athletic director are not the only people that you need to invest in. You need to get to know your colleagues, the maintenance people, the equipment managers, the athletic trainers, and the janitors. All these people have an impact on the culture.

If you only had two 30-minute sessions a week to train your team, how would you prepare them?

You can check a lot of boxes starting with speed and power. With speed needing to be tapped into every 3-7 days, it would take priority. Every session would begin with a sprint based warm up followed by some variation of sprinting or agility. That would be immediately followed by a total body emphasis strength training session.

What goes into your decision to leave or stay at a job?

I must ask myself these questions. Do I love getting up every day and going to work? Can I financially support my family? Are the people above me doing right and fighting for the same fight I am in? Does my family love where we are? If you struggle to say yes to these questions, then it might be time to leave. Every job has its struggles, but the grass is not always greener on the other side.

What do you do to overcome times of struggle, burnout, or overwhelm? Who do you turn to?

Prayer goes a long way. That has solved a lot of problems in my past. Something I have had to learn as I have gotten older is that it's okay to take a break from your job. "Grinding" will grind you into the ground eventually. Life is too short. As a coach, you need to go on vacation, you need to take time every day to spend time with your kids, it is important to make time to take your wife out for a date, and it's okay to get up a little earlier in the morning to sit back and enjoy that cup of coffee. Work will always be there. Your family and your health are way more important.

What do you think about immediately after one of your athletes is injured? What is your mindset in the following week?

Is there anything that I could have done to prevent this? I also know we can't control everything. I will always look back on our training to see if there was any way we could have reduced the chances of this happening.

Following an injury, I want to get the athlete back into the normal routine as fast as I can. If I can modify training and keep the athlete "busy," then I know they will be better off psychologically. As long as we are finding a way for athletes to progress, then I know we can keep them engaged.

How do you approach difficult conversations with athletes, coworkers, or your boss?

Before having difficult conversations, it's important to take a step back and evaluate the whole situation and see all perspectives of those involved. Second, I want to make sure I have done everything on my end to help the other parties be successful. Once I realize conversations must happen, I will approach it with a calm manner. There's nothing worse than making a tough situation even tougher by escalating the issues with anger. I've seen a lot of those issues resolved by clearly defining the expectation before it gets to that point. If you clearly define the expectations, then people know where you stand. A lack of communication will cause a lot of problems.

What traits or skills do your most successful athletes have in common?

Besides the obvious physical abilities that make them stand out, the good ones have a great work ethic, competitive drive, and a love for the game they play. The ones that have the competitive drive are the ones that are different. There will always be those types of athletes that you come in contact with that have the physical ability to be something great but there is a disconnect upstairs. Those types of athletes will always run faster, jump higher, and be stronger, but when competition hits, they are nowhere to be found.

The love they have for the game keeps them from getting complacent. In order to continue to stay on the field and play the game they love, they understand they have to bring it every single day.

What books or resources do you most often recommend to coaches?

As far as strength training goes, I recommend every strength coach to start out with *Science and Practice of Strength Training* by Zatsiorsky, Kraemer, and Fry. This book covers everything from programming to daily practical procedures that every coach should follow. *The Coach's Strength Training Playbook* by Joe Kenn offers great insight into Coach Kenn's tier system. He thoroughly explains how he sets up his program and how to periodize throughout an annual plan. *Strength Training Manual: The Agile Periodization Approach* by Mladen Jovanovic is another great book that will really open a coach's eye to other methods and strategies for programming. *Game Changer: The Art of Sports Science* is a great book to learn how to train an athlete from every aspect. It covers everything from training and preparation for games to the art of coaching. *Speed Strength* by Joel Smith is my go-to resource for everything speed training.

"Have the conversation as soon as possible and move forward. Give people the benefit of doubt and don't jump to conclusions. Listen, hear all sides, be transparent on what you're wanting to get accomplished, and be honest."

-Tory Stephens

Tory Stephens is a recognized Master Strength and Conditioning Coach with 20 years of experience at Texas Tech University. He currently serves as the Assistant Athletic Director and Director of Strength and Conditioning, having initially joined the program as the Associate Head Strength Coach and Director of Sports Nutrition. As the strength coach for Baseball, Stephens has contributed to the team's success in winning three Big 12 titles and advancing to the College World Series four times. He has also played a key role in helping several Red Raiders become MLB draft picks, including Josh Jung, who was selected as the No. 8 pick in 2019.

Who do you go to when you need advice? Why them?
I go to the Bible and my parents for any advice 99/100 times. I was blessed to be raised by great parents that I look up to and respect, and the Bible will guide the choices you make in any situation.

What early job was pivotal in your career? Why?
My high school days were very influential in me wanting to become a strength coach. I had a great relationship with my coaches and trained with them outside of team workouts. They inspired me to fall in love with the training aspect of sports. The pivotal job decision that set my career where it is today was when I was offered the football job at the University of Houston by Coach Art Briles. I was young, eager, and willing to go, but Texas Tech countered and offered me the Director position. I stayed at Texas Tech and am now Asst. AD and Director of S&C and have been here for 27 years total. I am very fortunate to coach at one school my entire career.

What are your first steps when you start a new job? What do you need to figure out, what do you need to get done, who do you need to get to know?

First, get the weight room in order. Organize, add/subtract equipment that doesn't align with my training. Set up meetings with all your coaches to talk plan/agendas for your program, leave no stones unturned! Next, get to know your athletes on a personal level. Find out everything you can about them that will influence how you coach them individually. Finally, meet and visit with the administration, especially those you'll be working alongside daily. Get your budget laid out, prioritized, and list any needs you'll have to get your job done at the highest level. Invite them in for a workout, they'll appreciate it.

What advice do you have for a college student looking to break into coaching? Who are the best mentors in the world to work for early in your career?

You must get face-to-face time with strength coaches when you are just getting started. Don't just send an email saying you are interested in becoming a strength coach or volunteering at their school. Drop in, set up a meeting, and visit in person with them. It makes a big difference! Lift and train yourself before even considering coaching. If that isn't already a priority in your day, then you'll have a hard time being a strength coach. Any mentor will bring experience, some good, some bad, but it's all invaluable experience.

If you only had two 30-minute sessions a week to train your team, how would you prepare them?

Include the basic fundamental movements in both sessions or you'll have gaps in your program. Push, Pull, Hinge, Squat, and carry heavy things!

What goes into your decision to leave or stay at a job?

The decisions to stay or leave a job changes the older and more established you get. Spouse, kids, parents, etc. Don't leave a job to make a lateral move. Sometimes you won't realize how good you have it until you leave. If you are happy, you like your coaches, you like the school/town, then work your ass off and you'll get promoted.

What do you do to overcome times of struggle, burnout, or overwhelm? Who do you turn to?

Hobbies outside of your job are an absolute must. I love fishing, for example. I take my travel rods and bag everywhere I go when I travel with teams. Any down time I get, I go find some water and wet a line. Work/life balance is very important to me and for my staff to have. Go to your kids' games, take them to school or pick them up when you can. We are all replaceable in our jobs, but we are not replaceable as husbands, fathers, etc.

What do you think about immediately after one of your athletes is injured? What is your mindset in the following week?

It is never pleasant when your athlete goes down with an injury; I take it personally every single time. It is part of sports and you need to remember that. As long as I can honestly say I did all I could for them and it's backed with data then I can sleep at night.

How do you approach difficult conversations with athletes, coworkers, or your boss?

Don't beat around the bush and avoid conversations thinking it will get resolved on its own. It'll only get worse. Have the conversation as soon as possible and move forward. Give people the benefit of the doubt and don't jump to conclusions. Listen, hear all sides, be transparent on what you're wanting to get accomplished, and be honest. They will appreciate and respect that.

Do you have a "failure" that was critical to your long-term development or success?

Failure is a part of life, and I have failed miserably at times. From programming to reacting to things too quickly, there will be things you won't do again. That is what experience is and why experience is so invaluable.

What traits or skills do your most successful athletes have in common?

The most successful athletes and people all have this one trait: they are all obsessed with what they are doing. They have OCD when it comes to their sport or their job. If you aren't obsessed with it, there is no long-term success or long-term opportunities.

> *"The athletes that have the most success over time are the ones who can appreciate the small incremental improvements that turn into significant improvements over time when they begin to stack."*

> ## -Jon McDowell

Jon McDowell is the Co-Owner and Coach at VIVE Personal Training in Dallas, Texas, which he opened in 2016. At VIVE, he provides high-level training to both athletes and general population clients. Drawing on his background as a Division I All-American Track and Field athlete and his experience qualifying for the Olympic trials, McDowell delivers exceptional results in sprint training for both track and team sport athletes. Additionally, he is a member of the Designs For Sport sports advisory board.

Who do you go to when you need advice? Why them?

When I need advice, I always confer with peers in the industry. Every case is unique and leveraging the knowledge of peers can help provide solutions to individual cases!

What early job was pivotal in your career? Why?

Being a part of the Athletic Lab and being able to learn and observe under Dr. Mike Young was pivotal in my learning. Many aspects of what I learned from business to training were discovered in that first training experience.

What are your first steps when you start a new job? What do you need to figure out, what do you need to get done, who do you need to get to know?

Internships are invaluable. Ideally, you can intern or volunteer where you would like to work. This gives you immediate insight into the inner workings, the demands of the company, the operational expectations of the positions, and daily workflow.

What advice do you have for a college student looking to break into coaching? Who are the best mentors in the world to work for early in your career?

For college students, I would do internships each summer. I would work in all fields, personal training and coaching; this will provide deep insight into which direction you want to go. Full-time coaching, personal training, and coaching, etc. For the best mentors in the world, seek the people in the area you are most passionate about and learn from them. For example, in track, Dan Pfaff is one of the most knowledgeable coaches. I took the ALTIS one week internship three times to learn from him. I did the same with coach Charles Poliquin in strength and conditioning. Finding individuals who have had real-world success in an area you are passionate about is vital!

If you only had two 30-minute sessions a week to train your team, how would you prepare them?

Depending on the sport—for example track athletes, and depending on the time of year—GPP, SPP, Championship. We would cover the big rocks for injury prevention and maintenance of power. Both sessions would be full body.

- A series would be a power exercise - Trap bar jumps, Olympic lift variations.
- B Series, we would cover assistance exercises - Presses, Vertical Pull, Split squats, Lunges, Rows.
- C Series, we would train remedial exercises - Hip extension, knee flexion, knee extension, external rotation, etc.

What goes into your decision to leave or stay at a job?

Growth. I was at a corporate gym and I did very well there, but the education and growth opportunities capped off after three years. To keep improving, it was time for me to go on my own to continue learning and growing as a coach.

What do you do to overcome times of struggle, burnout, or overwhelm? Who do you turn to?

I had the fortune to work with coaches like Brooks Johnson, who was coaching in his 70s, and Dr. Mike Young, who would work 90-100hr weeks at times. This really sets the bar for the effort that is possible. Also, I always enjoyed the learning process, so it was never like I dreaded going to work. This is why it is critical to intern and work with different sports, personal training, kids, high school, and college, and see what demographics you enjoy working with. The time requirement to be successful in any field will always be there, but if you enjoy what you do, you will stay energized! I have worked about 363 days a year for the past few years! It still never gets dull or monotonous. I genuinely enjoy getting to help individuals achieve their goals!

What do you think about immediately after one of your athletes is injured? What is your mindset in the following week?

Assuming it is a soft tissue injury, or even stress fracture, and an area is immobilized—

immediately we go into recovery mode. Here in Dallas we have access to Curewave laser. It is a very efficient localized laser treatment. It dramatically accelerates healing, so they do that about 3x a week. We also have a Theralight 360 bed in our gym, so athletes are in that as well 2-3x a week after they train. We train whatever the athlete can without using the injured site; we work alongside Chiro/Physical therapist during this time so athletes can still come to the gym, be around peers, and help the mental mindset during the recovery period.

How do you approach difficult conversations with athletes, coworkers, or your boss?
The best way to have difficult conversations is to address them head-on, as soon as it happens. The worst can be when things build up over time, then someone explodes and the entire situation unfolds badly. I like to address any issues immediately and be in a culture and environment where everyone is on the same page and working towards a common goal!

Do you have a "failure" that was critical to your long-term development or success?
There is a famous quote: "If you have never failed, you have never tried anything new!" I think the track was a great teacher because you can't always be the fastest person, but you can always improve yourself. It teaches us to control our controllables; and our efforts are all we can control. It gave me a growth mindset to focus on myself, self-improvement, and not worry about where anyone else was in their journey!

What traits or skills do your most successful athletes have in common?
Growth mindset. "He who says he can, and he who says he can't are both usually right." The athletes that have the most success over time are the ones who can appreciate the small incremental improvements that turn into significant improvements over time when they begin to stack. The most successful athletes I've had took years to develop, and it is the grit, determination, and will to continue working on the craft that expresses itself in significant performance improvements over time!

What books or resources do you most often recommend to coaches?
A few great books I recommend are:

- *Transfer of Training in Sports* – Anatoliy Bondarchuk
- *The Sprint and Hurdle Bible* – Ralph Mann
- *66 Strategies to Program Design* – Stephane Cazeault

ALTIS website is a great resource as well for speed development.

"It's human nature to keep things the same when everything is going well and you are winning, when in reality constant evaluating is a must, win or lose. Unfortunately, there have been times in my career where it took a loss for me to get better."

-Jordan Johnson

Jordan Johnson most recently served as the Director of Strength and Conditioning at Owasso High School in Oklahoma. Prior to his role at Owasso, he held the same position at Jenks High School. Johnson began his career at the collegiate level, with experience at Texas Tech, Arkansas, Ole Miss, UTEP, and Tulsa.

Who do you go to when you need advice? Why them?

I usually lean on people much smarter than I am. Bennie Wylie at USC has been a mentor to me for the last 20 years. Bryan Kegans, Kyle Keese, and Jason Wilfawn are also my go to guys. I am blessed at Owasso to work with coaches that have been coaching for 40 plus years like Bill Blankenship (football) and Larry Turner (baseball) and their wisdom is priceless! I choose these people because many of them are in the same situation I am in and they are extremely successful in what they do.

What early job was pivotal in your career? Why?

The first would be my first job at Texas Tech back in 2004. Bennie Wylie helped me get my foot in the door and I owe him for all the jobs I have been able to get. From a coaching standpoint, my job at UTEP, in charge of seven teams, challenged me to be the coach that I am today!

What are your first steps when you start a new job? What do you need to figure out, what do you need to get done, who do you need to get to know?

Step number one is meeting with the administration and sport coaches. The relationships you create with administration and the coaches you work with every day will make or break your job. Step number two is your staff. Do you get a staff? If so, are they retained staff or do you get to hire staff? If retained staff is the only option, creating a relationship with them built on trust is key. Step number three is inventory of the facilities, equipment, etc. Knowing what you have to work with and what you need to get is important for programming and growing your strength and conditioning department. Step number four is player meetings. Sitting down and getting to know the players you will work with every day is a must to gain their trust and learn about their life. Every athlete has a different story and knowing their story helps me understand what they are going through daily and allows me to help them reach their potential.

What advice do you have for a college student looking to break into coaching? Who are the best mentors in the world to work for early in your career?
Do an internship and soak up as much knowledge as you can. Work your butt off and set yourself apart from the other interns. Gain the trust of the head strength coach and go above and beyond in helping that program. Network as much as possible!

The best mentors to work for are those that genuinely care about you and helping you be the best coach you can be. Mentors that view you as a part of their coaching tree are the ones that will take the most pride in you being successful.

If you only had two 30-minute sessions a week to train your team, how would you prepare them?
The first session would be sprinting. No matter what sport it is, I believe that would give you the best bang for your buck. The second session would be core, Olympic movement, and single leg movements.

What goes into your decision to leave or stay at a job?
It all comes down to leadership in Administration. Great leadership in that area equals a great job, bad leadership in that area equals time to leave.

What do you do to overcome times of struggle, burnout, or overwhelm? Who do you turn to?
For me, it is always spending time with my wife and kids.

What do you think about immediately after one of your athletes is injured? What is your mindset in the following week?
No matter how perfect I think the programing is, I always look to see what I could have done to prevent it. There are so many factors outside of my control when it comes to injuries, but I still take it personally. Sometimes I find something to tweak, sometimes I don't, but regardless, I still train the team as I normally would and keep

moving forward and evaluating as I go.

How do you approach difficult conversations with athletes, coworkers, or your boss?

I always approach those types of meetings with an open mind. Sometimes I feel like I have all the answers, but it is always important to listen and keep my mouth shut. Nine times out of 10 when I do that, I learn something from them I did not know and end up coming to a peaceful resolution.

Do you have a "failure" that was critical to your long-term development or success?

The best "failures" I have had in my career are quite simply losing. With every loss with sports teams over my career, I get better and learn. It's human nature to just keep things the same when everything is going good and you are winning, when in reality constant evaluating is a must, win or lose. Unfortunately, there have been times in my career where it took a loss for me to get better.

What traits or skills do your most successful athletes have in common?

- Coachable
- Unbelievable work ethic
- The ultimate competitors

What books or resources do you most often recommend to coaches?

From a leadership standpoint I always recommend books like *Legacy, Extreme Ownership, Purpose Driven Life,* and *Above the Line.* From a strength and conditioning standpoint I direct coaches to Simplifaster, Westside Barbell, Brian Mann, and Cal Dietz.

"Try to make yourself irreplaceable or highly missed. Get to a point where you provide so much value that it's an incredibly difficult decision for you to be let go, or if you are let go, the loss is felt far and wide throughout the organization."

-Jordan Forget

Jordan Forget is in his fourth year as an Assistant Strength and Conditioning Coach with the Dallas Mavericks, where he played a key role in helping the organization win the 2024 Western Conference Championship and reach the NBA Finals. Additionally, he serves as the Executive Assistant to the National Basketball Strength and Conditioning Coaches Association (NBSCA). In 2022, Forget was the Head Strength and Conditioning Coach for the Chinese National Team.

Who do you go to when you need advice? Why them?

The journey to my current job has been filled with obstacles, tough decisions, and lots of "no's." I've relied on mentors, friends, and family to help me along the way, and I've always been the type of person to communicate with those closest to me so that I can gather all the information and perspectives to help generate my own opinion. I'm in the role I am today because of the support I've received from those around me.

Build a support team around you to help guide you along your journey. Some people are better suited to advise on certain things than others, but it can always be helpful to gain an outside perspective. Let your support team be a variety of people; a family member, a supervisor, a role model, anyone who has your best interest in mind. Building a support team will help silence some of the noise when tough decisions need to be made or when bias may steer you in a particular direction. Sometimes you'll need to relocate, take a step backwards, or pivot entirely, but having people around you that can see past the obstacles will help you stay focused and on your path to success.

What early job was pivotal in your career? Why?

Until my third year of undergrad, I had no real sense of what I wanted to do after graduation. I did a few internships in various fields within health and performance, but lacked clarity on what I was passionate about professionally. I had played basketball nearly my entire life, often leaning heavily on it for the structure it provided me during rough periods of my childhood. It created a passion in me that made me adamant about working in basketball in some capacity. I had also begun resistance training in high school and carried that into college. Having played basketball for so long, I appreciated what training did for my athleticism and ability to avoid injuries. After taking time to consider how both areas impacted my life, I decided I was going to reach out to the strength and conditioning coach at my school about interning for the basketball team the upcoming semester.

The strength coach, Rich Casella, had a graduate assistant that was leaving but did not have an internship program. After going back and forth via email, some in-person conversations, and a touch of persistence, he gave me the opportunity to intern. At the time, I would equivocate that with winning the lottery. It was the first real step toward a field I thought could be my future. After day one of my internship, I knew I was exactly where I was supposed to be. Having always wanted to play collegiate basketball but not being skilled enough to do so, the opportunity to be a part of a team doing something I enjoyed filled that void. The energy was electric, the culture was rich, and the atmosphere just felt comforting; I was absolutely hooked.

After a few weeks, I realized I wanted my future to be in strength and conditioning, and I now had my first real exposure to what that looks like at a Division I level. However, I knew this opportunity alone wouldn't be enough to make me a great strength coach, and I wanted to be great! Rich had quickly become a mentor, and he also wanted me to be great. He was on me from day one about learning in any way possible. He didn't care if I followed hundreds of strength coaches on social media, watched lectures for hours, listened to podcasts, or just locked myself in the library— he wanted me to do whatever I needed to learn, no matter the means or obstacles.

I took his advice. I started searching online for strength coaches and trainers whose methods caught my eye and reading books and research articles he would recommend. He'd ask me to answer strength and conditioning related questions and back up my answers with research. After being thrown into the fire of learning strength and conditioning, my passion grew stronger, as did my skills as a coach.

I can clearly think back to this first internship experience and confidently say that this opportunity made me who I am today. Rich gave me an opportunity, identified my "superpower" of being persistent and eager, and shaped me as a young coach.

It was this opportunity that lit the fire in me to keep pushing forward despite the obstacles along the way. It is because of this opportunity that I'm nearing my dream job of becoming a Head Strength and Conditioning Coach in the NBA.

What are your first steps when you start a new job? What do you need to figure out, what do you need to get done, who do you need to get to know?

It's always best to be observant the first few weeks. There's a lot of value and information that can be gained simply by watching and listening to how others around you operate. How your co-workers behave, how they treat and interact with each other, and how they treat you, are all valuable pieces of information that can help you understand your role, the work environment, and how to be successful in your new role. I also like to begin an open chain of communication with my supervisors. This allows for expectations, constructive criticism, and feedback to flow freely and more quickly, thus allowing you the opportunity to be more successful.

One thing I try to figure out as early as possible is how I can best serve the team I'm working with and where my skills can best be directed, while still staying within the scope of my role. One of the best pieces of advice I've gotten is to try to make yourself irreplaceable or highly missed. Get to a point where you provide so much value that it's an incredibly difficult decision for you to be let go, or if you are let go, the loss is felt far and wide throughout the organization.

It's certainly important to get to know your supervisors and individuals in your department, but it's also valuable to get to know everyone in your workplace. If you're working for a team, everyone has the same goals: keep the athlete's best interests in mind and win games. With all these people around you working to achieve the same goals, it can only be beneficial to build relationships so that a collaborative environment comes naturally.

What advice do you have for a college student looking to break into coaching? Who are the best mentors in the world to work for early in your career?

Since I was a high school student, I've been helping friends and family members with their training. Creating free workouts and suggestions, trying to help others achieve their goals. I wasn't credentialed and therefore may not have had any business doing what I was doing, but that is exactly how many coaches start off. You don't wait until you sit for your certification to start coaching. All that to say, start coaching as soon as possible. Find individuals who trust your opinion, are receptive to the information you're sharing, and coach them! You of course need to make sure that you're not harming anyone due to ignorance or negligence. As you continue to learn and acquire the appropriate credentials, your opinions and suggestions can become recommendations and prescriptions. Along this journey, keep in mind that the relationships you build with the individuals should be the priority. Coaching is all about building relationships that allow those whom you work with to look to you for guidance and leadership.

The idea of finding the best mentors can be a bit misleading. The best practitioner in a particular space may not be the best mentor for everyone. Some of the best mentors I've had are individuals who were incredible at creating meaningful, impactful, and genuine relationships with people. They were well educated and highly skilled at strength and conditioning, but the personal relationships they had with their athletes always mattered most. Find mentors that can provide you with wisdom in relationship building, but in a way that is specific and relevant to you. With the number of resources so readily available, access to the science and hard skills of strength and conditioning will always be there. Find individuals whose athletes have nothing but great things to say about them, who respect them, and whose relationships extend past just the weight room or the practice space.

If you only had two 30-minute sessions a week to train your team, how would you prepare them?

In the early stages of learning strength and conditioning, we learn endless ways to create these complex 3, 4, or 5-day programs that span weeks, months, and sometimes years. What's often overlooked is the reality that often in sports we are left with minimal training availability and it's up to us coaches to adapt. With my experience in professional sports, sometimes during the season we may only get two actual team lifts in each week.

My first thought is to see what other opportunities I have in a given day or week to fit in more work. There are various things to consider, the priority of the work, the time of season, the accumulation of stress (internal & external) and so on. The point isn't to add in as much work as possible, but to prioritize specific things and find out where you can fit them in. Once you've done that, then you can see what you'd like to do during those two short training sessions. Referencing my experience at the professional level, we usually get about 15-20 minutes before every game to prepare the athletes. Depending on context, I may use these times for mobility, correctives, tendon loading, or even actual lifts.

Let's say there are no other opportunities to get supplemental work in, and I only have two 30-minute sessions a week to train the athletes. I would still take time to consider many variables, time of season, training age of the athletes, some variation of an acute to chronic workload, injuries, and so on. I would then choose my focus areas for those two sessions, the adaptations or traits I want most for those athletes. The respective adaptations would then help dictate the direction of that session. If the context of the situation demands the athletes to be powerful, quick and explosive, but well rested, like in the playoffs, then those sessions would reflect those goals.

What goes into your decision to leave or stay at a job?

This is one of the most important questions in this book to ask yourself. As you go through your career, you'll most likely go through multiple stops, supervisors, and employers. It's important you know the things that drive you to stay or leave a particular job. For some people, it's a financial decision, maybe a matter of being valued, or perhaps just a matter of work-life balance. Sometimes it will be easy to make these decisions, and sometimes it won't. At this point in my career, I've learned some things that I value regarding these types of decisions:

- Pay – While it's not ALL about money, the amount a position pays often is in line with value, financial freedom, and security. I enjoy working somewhere where the organization supports their value in me by investing in my role. Having an amount of money that you're happy with can often provide financial freedom for things you want or would like to do, whether it's experiences, possessions, or security for the future.

- Value, Respect and Culture – I've learned to appreciate the feeling and the importance I place on being valued for my personality and my skills. It's a normal human instinct to want to be valued. You want to feel like the work you do matters. I also value being respected. Whether that's from the organization, the players I work with, or my coworkers, I want to feel like we're all respected and working towards a similar goal. Lastly, the culture within an organization is highly important. At the professional level, the people you work with are the people you'll spend much of your time with, traveling on late flights, working early mornings or late nights, through wins and losses. It's important that not only do the people I work with get along, but that we enjoy being around each other and working together.

Each person and each scenario may be different, but it's important when you start your coaching career to take the time to learn what it is you value in a workplace. Coaching will force you to make tough decisions. Having clarity on your values will drastically help you navigate through those decisions.

What do you do to overcome times of struggle, burnout, or overwhelm? Who do you turn to?

Regardless of the situation, the way I've always coped with these types of negative emotions has been to communicate and vent with those closest to me. I lean on my support group during difficult times to help me get through. If I'm struggling with something or feeling burnout, I seek advice from different people, which in return has always helped me get back on track. It's not always immediate or that simple, but it has helped guide me. Sometimes action will need to be taken to continue progressing back on track. If it's a matter of feeling overwhelmed and burnout, sometimes I discuss it with my fiancée, and we unwind by going to a nice dinner or taking a small vacation. If it's an issue I'm struggling with at work, sometimes I'll go to my supervisor/mentor or a friend at work to get advice, but will then have to make a correction or adjustment to resolve the issue. Ultimately, the same two themes that I do to cope with challenging situations or emotions are to talk it out, then act.

What do you think about immediately after one of your athletes is injured? What is your mindset in the following week?

The unfortunate but undeniable fact about sports is that injuries are not preventable. Even though I know this to be true, any time one of the athletes I work with gets injured, I can't help but think about what I could have done better to prevent it from happening. Did we do too much work? Was that exercise not a good fit? Should we have done more? Could I have done something different?

All completely fair questions to ask, but with the complexity of sports paired with the even greater degree of complexity of the human body, there is no way to narrow down the source of injury to a specific action or inaction. That doesn't mean that things may not have been done optimally, but rather that those involved need to learn from the incident to work to reduce the likelihood of another injury. The mindset moving forward is exactly that: how do we reduce the likelihood of this athlete getting injured again? As many of us know, the biggest risk factor for injury is a previous injury. The focus must be on being even better and making sure each participant involved with that athlete is on the same page.

How do you approach difficult conversations with athletes, coworkers, or your boss?
There will always be times where you need to have difficult conversations with either the athletes or the individuals you work with. The thing I've always leaned on is the relationships. The relationships you have with your athletes or coworkers will have a huge impact on the outcome of the conversation. If a player is struggling to comply with certain requirements or requests, I can lean on the relationship I have with that athlete to find a resolution, because I know that there is mutual respect and genuine interest for one another's success. The same applies for coworkers. The resolution has always been to approach difficult situations with an open and honest conversation, and again, if the relationship between all parties is strong, usually a resolution can be found. However, if a relationship hasn't been established, the approach is still important. Having open conversation where both parties can share their respective concerns and interests allows for an outcome that can be mutually beneficial.

Do you have a "failure" that was critical to your long-term development or success?
Each time I have "failed," it's provided a learning opportunity that has shaped my future. The first of such failures was just after I finished college. My goal was to obtain a graduate assistant position, get my master's degree, and continue my journey as a strength coach. I had been accepted to the school but was turned down from the graduate assistantship, as they felt I did not yet have enough experience. It felt like a huge blow and that perhaps I'd never be able to reach my goal of becoming an NBA Strength Coach.

After that point, the focus was to keep my head above water. I needed to get a job, but also to get more experience so that when I applied to another position, I'd be more qualified. I ultimately landed a job as a personal trainer at a high-end gym. That proved to be a very beneficial opportunity as it taught me a lot about working with all types of people, from children, to disabled elderly, to professional athletes. It taught me a lot about marketing myself and my skills.

During my time at that gym, I gained experience from interning for a local Division I school, shadowing a strength coach for the local NBA team, and above all, building valuable relationships. After a few years of being a personal trainer, COVID-19 had arrived and spread. While the world was essentially shut down, I pursued an online master's degree and doubled down on networking with individuals at the NBA level.

I knew that with my current circumstance, I had to make a concerted effort to build relationships with people who either have or had the type of job I wanted to have one day. After finishing my master's degree, one coach I connected with offered me a short-term opportunity that catapulted me into an NBA strength and conditioning internship.

The important thing about this story is that the first "failure" is what tested my desire to be a strength coach and taught me that this journey would not be easy. Without that "no," I don't know if I am where I am today. My advice is to find ways to turn your losses into wins. Find ways to learn from every "failure." If you do that, you will succeed.

What traits or skills do your most successful athletes have in common?

I've been able to work with athletes from middle school to the professional level and the one thing I've found that most successful athletes do is take care of their body. Not all of them are like that from day one. Some athletes enter their highest level based primarily on just pure skill, but eventually there comes a time where they realize the importance of making sure their body is taken care of at a high level. Many of you have heard that famous line that Lebron James spends $1.5 million on his body every year. While this may come as a surprise to some, many professional athletes have a team of people who help make sure their body is performing and recovering at the highest level possible.

What books or resources do you most often recommend to coaches?

For some, learning comes easy. For myself, I had to gain a solid understanding of what methods are best suited for me. Each coach should take the time to understand what type of learner they are and THEN what they want to learn. After you've figured out what type of learner you are, take time to list out topics you are most passionate about and/or where you feel you are weakest. Some coaches thrive off of developing their weak points while some may simply have better compliance and retention with material that they're most interested in.

Those two steps have gotten me to a point where I've now become highly motivated and invested in my professional development. As an example of practicing what I preach, I started first with focusing on material I was most interested in. As I became more interested in overall learning and growth, I was able to shift focus as needed to areas I was weakest.

"For myself, during down time I lean into things that help me unplug and get away (books, hikes with wife and dog), while also recognizing that any time you start to feel overwhelmed at work is when you most likely need to lean in. The best way to relieve anxiety about a task or project is to complete it."

-Joel Reinhardt

Joel Reinhardt is an Assistant Athletic Performance Coach and Sports Science Coordinator for the San Jose State University Football team. He also oversees sports performance for the Women's Indoor and Beach Volleyball programs. Prior to joining San Jose State, Reinhardt served as the Assistant Sports Performance Coach and Sports Science Coordinator for the Stanford Football program. He has also worked as the Assistant Director of Sports Performance at UMass and as the Assistant Strength and Conditioning Coach at Nicholls State.

Who do you go to when you need advice? Why them?
Matt Shadeed. He always provides me with level-headed advice that pushes me to make the right decision.

What early job was pivotal in your career? Why?
Nicholls State with Greg Carrasquillo and UMass with Matt Shadeed. In both spots I was a young assistant, but both of my bosses trusted me with a lot of programming and autonomy that helped boost me forward into subsequent jobs.

What are your first steps when you start a new job? What do you need to figure out, what do you need to get done, who do you need to get to know?
The urgency of certain tasks will depend on the time of year (joining a college football team in August versus January), but the most important thing to do is listen and ask as many questions as you need to feel aligned with what the organizational goals are for your team.

What advice do you have for a college student looking to break into coaching? Who are the best mentors in the world to work for early in your career?

Go out and get experience. If you're hoping to get a GA after undergrad, it's useful to have a couple internships under your belt. Make it a priority. I would go back to Greg Carrasquillo and Matt Shadeed because of how they helped me grow by handing me responsibility at a time when they didn't need to.

What goes into your decision to leave or stay at a job?

This one depends on your time in life big time. When I was finishing my GA, I was looking for a job that would be under a mentor who would help me truly learn and grow. I wasn't worried about pay, location, etc. Now I'm weighing all sorts of factors like proximity to family, professional responsibility, the people I'd be working around, the compensation. When in doubt, using Keir's 4Ps is a great place to start (Pay, Purpose, Personal Life, Professional Growth).

What do you do to overcome times of struggle, burnout, or overwhelm? Who do you turn to?

For myself, during down time I lean into things that help me unplug and get away (books, hikes with wife and dog), while also recognizing that any time you start to feel overwhelmed at work is when you most likely need to lean in. The best way to relieve anxiety about a task or project is to complete it.

What do you think about immediately after one of your athletes is injured? What is your mindset in the following week?

In the immediate, it's to support the athlete and their well-being physically and mentally. From there, it's important to break down the factors that went into the injury occurring to mitigate risk in the future.

How do you approach difficult conversations with athletes, coworkers, or your boss?

Full honesty and a calm demeanor.

What books or resources do you most often recommend to coaches?

- *Governing Dynamics of Coaching* – James Smith
- *Strength Training Manual* – Mladen Jovanovic

"You need to provide so much value that the person at the top CHOOSES to be a great mentor to you. If you are lazy, even the best mentor in the world won't invest in you. So get an opportunity and MAXIMIZE it."

-Jim Kiritsy

Jim Kiritsy is the Head Football Strength and Conditioning Coach at the Naval Academy. He was hired at Navy after serving as the Associate Athletic Director for Sports Performance and the Director of Football Strength and Conditioning at Kennesaw State. During his time at Kennesaw, Kiritsy played a key role in the program's transition from its inaugural season of football to winning multiple conference championships and achieving FCS playoff victories within just a few years. Prior to his role at Kennesaw State, Kiritsy served as the Associate Director for Strength and Conditioning at The Citadel and as an Assistant Strength and Conditioning Coach at Vermont.

Who do you go to when you need advice? Why them?

1) Bring problems/difficulties to current staff—don't skip this step unless you have to. This can help build trust and create buy in/ownership with staff.

2) Trusted mentors (Donnell Boucher for me)—they know you and can relate to your struggle. Also, their influence is strong on you so the way they think can connect to the way you think, which means you trust them and they trust you.

3) Online/Social Media profiles that do things that seem to have an expertise in your area of struggle (sift through the BS!).

4) Buy books/online courses and try to learn.

What early job was pivotal in your career? Why?

University of Vermont as a Coaching Assistant. I coached all day with all kinds of athletes. You learn to appreciate different sports and different personalities. I had to work side jobs to pay rent—it was critical to learning how to coach and if I wanted to keep coaching.

The Citadel (2nd job). I got my first real mentor and completely changed how I viewed S&C. Prior to working with Coach Boucher, I had no concept of organization, management, staff cohesion/development, or outside the box thinking. I owe so much to that time.

Kennesaw State (first director job). "Assistants make recommendations, Directors make decisions." A lot changes when it's your name on the line for the results of a program. This job also got me involved with sport coaches and all the layers of team sport organization. Class schedules, practice times, budgets, CARA hours, field sign ups, travel, etc. There is so much more than just the S&C part of athletics.

What are your first steps when you start a new job? What do you need to figure out, what do you need to get done, who do you need to get to know?

Get to know your direct supervisors' expectations of you. Make sure you are focusing on doing the job they are hiring you for. As you prove your worth, you can branch out and expand into other areas that will bring value to the program outside of your first job responsibility.

What advice do you have for a college student looking to break into coaching? Who are the best mentors in the world to work for early in your career?

There are good and bad mentors out there, but you might not have control of who you work for. You need to go where the opportunity is. As such, you need to provide so much value that the person at the top CHOOSES to be a great mentor to you. If you are lazy, even the best mentor in the world won't invest in you. So get an opportunity and MAXIMIZE it. Setup, break down, clean. Be early, stay late, ask great questions. Be responsible, be mature, be dependable, bring great positive energy.

If you only had two 30-minute sessions a week to train your team, how would you prepare them?

Day 1: Super active warm up, build up to 1-3 FAST SPRINTS over 12-30 yds over 10-15 minutes.

- Go to weight room – Hang Clean 4x3 (light and fast) paired w/ Jumps.
- Vert Push/Vert Pull/Core 3-4 sets.
- Nordic Ham Curls and Neck/cuff/arms 2-3 sets.

Day 2: Super Active Warm Up, build up to 3-5 FAST ACCELERATIONS (1min rest).

- Go to weight Room – Front/Back Squat 4x3-5 (ascend to 1 heavy set).
- Bench Press (BB or DB) paired w/ Horizontal Pull.
- RDL (BB or DB) paired w/ Neck/cuff/arms.

What goes into your decision to leave or stay at a job?

Family (does spouse want to go? Are kids in school/daycare?) Finances (does it improve your quality of life or ability to set yourself up for the future?) Opportunity (does it excite you? Or your ego?) Do you really love/hate your current job?

What do you do to overcome times of struggle, burnout, or overwhelm? Who do you turn to?

Remember that you GET to do this, and that most people would kill to have a job filled with as much purpose as yours, and that you get to be a part of a TEAM with an OBJECTIVE that you CARE ABOUT. That is so rare. You are working in an area around your passion. You still need to create professional borders where you say "NO" to things. If you don't fight for yourself, nobody else will. Have a hobby that you can find joy in outside of work (cooking, hiking, BJJ, reading, woodworking, etc.), and find a community of people outside of work (dating, social recreation groups, family, etc.).

What do you think about immediately after one of your athletes is injured? What is your mindset in the following week?

- Is the kid okay? Do they need immediate attention?
- Was that something that could have been avoided? (logistics, equipment, rest interval, etc.)
- Was the outcome worth the risk? (ex: kids need to sprint; did they get hurt sprinting?) If so, did you warm them up/progress them appropriately? If so, then it is what it is. Sometimes we have bad luck. Did they get hurt on a 1RM back squat? Did you need a 1RM squat with that athlete? (If no, then you probably shouldn't have been maxing out with that population)
- Don't forget about that kid. Go out of your way to include them in everything in some way. When they get back to training full speed, remember they are behind everyone else, so make smart decisions to avoid re-injury (The first week back, they shouldn't test a sprint if they got hurt sprinting. If they were hurt squatting,

go back through a full squat progression and remind them it takes time to return to where they were).

How do you approach difficult conversations with athletes, coworkers, or your boss?

Prepare your questions/statements and think about how they will answer them. Do your best to play Devil's Advocate against yourself so you can prepare to answer their questions. Always leave with an action plan so that something productive comes directly from the conversation.

Do you have a "failure" that was critical to your long-term development or success?

A lot of them! We fail every day! The goal is to not make LAZY mistakes. When you make a mistake because you were wrong, it's okay, because you will go back and find a way to be better. If you make a mistake because you were lazy, that is irresponsible of you and you owe the victims of your mistake an apology. Always be critical of your decisions and be looking for ways to improve.

What traits or skills do your most successful athletes have in common?

They are super competitive. Most of them are also very engaged in PROCESS and believe that preparation and practice will make them better. The "gamers" are few and far between, and usually (but not always) will end up becoming great students of the game by the time they are seniors/5th years. Great players invest in their craft and work on their game constantly. The best of the best have all of those positive traits and are extremely coachable.

What books or resources do you most often recommend to coaches?

Strength & Conditioning Books

- *Advances in Functional Training* by Mike Boyle
- *Triphasic Training* (original) by Cal Dietz
- *Ultimate MMA Conditioning* by Joel Jamieson

Leadership Books

- *The Five Dysfunctions of a Team* by Patrick Lencioni
- *Good to Great* by Jim Collins
- *Sum It Up* by Pat Summit

"I had mentors that encouraged us to interview in the off-season. Many times you come back with a fresh perspective or new ideas based off the questions you were asked in an interview...This allows you to come back and continue to develop and mold your own philosophy."

-Steven Greek

Steven Greek is in his first year with the Frisco Heritage Football program after serving as the Head Football Coach and Athletic Director for the Ferris Yellowjackets for three years. Before Ferris, Greek was the Head Football Coach and Athletic Director at Argyle Liberty Christian, where he led the program to the State Semifinals in 2018. He served as the Assistant Head Coach and Offensive Coordinator at Plano Prestonwood Christian for 9.5 years, winning four State Championships during his tenure.

Who do you go to when you need advice? Why them?

When I need advice, I talk to my family. My wife is my source of strength, comfort, and encouragement. She knows me best, and helps me look through a different perspective. We have gotten to a stage in our marriage where I can vent to her about things I'm going through, and she has become a safe place and a soundboard for me. Sometimes I have to tell her I just need to talk and let it out. Other times I ask her to please tell me how she really feels about a situation, because I genuinely want her opinion. Even though she may not know all the ins and outs of what I'm going through, she knows my personality and my priorities, and because of this, she can either reinforce what I'm already thinking, or remind me of who I am and what's important.

I also go to my father and mother for advice. I am blessed with amazing parents who have always been there for me throughout life's greatest challenges. They simply listen and reassure me they are praying for us. That alone is priceless. My wife and I have three sons. Two of them are young adults, and they have reached the age where I can talk to them about challenges or ideas. I even ask their advice about things because they have a perspective that I may not have.

Professionally, I have several coaching friends and mentors that I call when I have to make a critical decision. These are all people that I admire and respect because they are successful in the profession and in the things that matter most in life. There are some coaches I would never call for advice, because while they may be successful on the field or court, they have failed in areas that matter. We all need forgiveness. We all make mistakes. And we all can choose who we go to for advice. I have found that there is wisdom in council, and there are many people in this profession who have gone through many things. Build a relationship with at least 5-10 veteran coaches outside of your circle of influence and get to know them. Ask questions, share stories, and learn to listen. Take mental notes and give honor to those who have gone through the fire. Many of these friendships and relationships are my most valued.

What early job was pivotal in your career? Why?

I would say that my most pivotal job was my first one. I had a great mentor-teacher and coach who wanted me to have a good experience. They saw something special in me and helped us navigate joining a school, having mentor-teachers, and becoming part of a coaching staff to impact kids. This experience allowed me to learn and grow rapidly while being surrounded by caring people who were willing to mentor me and help me onboard into the profession.

Understand that relationships matter. Connections matter. I had to learn how to meet people and connect with people. Believe in yourself and where you want to go. When you do a great job at where you are at, it will open up more doors down the road. Don't burn any bridges or act unprofessional, because you never know when you may cross paths again or will need a recommendation or reference. I truly believe that my first job led to my second job, which led to my third job, fourth, and fifth job. When you seek to do a great job where you are at, be where your feet are, and make a significant impact—more opportunities seem to come your way.

What are your first steps when you start a new job? What do you need to figure out, what do you need to get done, who do you need to get to know?

Come in and learn about the people, culture, and community. Observe, listen, ask questions, watch, take notes, and try to find out what the heartbeat of the community is. That is the big picture understanding that leaders desire to understand. This process takes time. The big picture is developed by small touches, casual conversations, and one-on-one meetings with teachers, coaches, principals, community members, alumni, and anyone else that has an interest in making a difference in the lives of kids.

Some people speed this process up by conducting questionnaires or online surveys. These can help. Nothing works as well as talking to people and asking questions to better understand what they want, what drives them, what inspires them, and what motivates them to bring their best every day.

Every place has expectations and priorities. It is important to understand the expectations. Familiarize yourself with the core values, and find out from veteran teachers—what is a priority in the community and what is not that important? Every place I've been there has been "sacred cows." There are just some battles you don't want to fight or get in the middle of. These issues and conflicts may have been around for generations, long before you arrived, and they very well could be around long after you move on to your next assignment.

Ask questions after meetings or on the side to mentor-coaches who are willing to help. Get to know your leadership and your staff. Some leaders don't mind questions in a group setting, and others do not want interruptions or meetings to drag out with comments or questions. Get to know the styles and preferences of your leaders as well as the staff you are on.

What advice do you have for a college student looking to break into coaching? Who are the best mentors in the world to work for early in your career?

If you want to market yourself and stand out against the competition for better jobs at better schools, it may serve you well to get certified in areas that are in high demand, such as math, science, English, and special education. Coaches who are certified in these areas can usually find jobs in areas they desire to live in, and can also receive pay incentives and bonuses in the district they work in.

Mentors are important in the teaching and coaching profession. Many times, a young coach will gravitate toward another younger coach that appears to be cool, hip, and popular on the staff. Sometimes this is OK, and sometimes this may not be a great formula for professional development. Who on your staff is professional, knowledgeable, and steady? Who treats people right? Who builds people up on staff? Who is available to answer questions about processes, systems, and schemes? Often these are the best mentor teachers and coaches, because they are accessible, humble, and willing to help. If you find yourself on a staff and you are feeling alone, learn to reach out and ask for help. Mentors are everywhere.

We just have to make sure that we are seeking advice from the right leaders with the right energy. Never seek advice from anyone that is disloyal, unprofessional, or slanders coworkers or the boss. This will come back to hurt you and poison you. Many young coaches will chase after bigger paychecks, and while it is important to be well compensated, it is very important to be in a place with good people, good leaders, good kids, and a great culture. I recommend getting a job on a staff that is successful and has a track record of producing high-quality young people and staff members moving on to get head coaching jobs.

What goes into your decision to leave or stay at a job?

Sometimes you get to go when you want to go, and sometimes you get to go when God opens up a new opportunity. This may or may not be on your timeline. I encourage coaches to interview in the off-season for coordinator or head coaching jobs. I had mentors that encouraged us to interview in the off-season. Many times you come back with a fresh perspective or new ideas based off the questions you were asked in an interview. You also hear things that are important to a community in these interviews. This allows you to come back and continue to develop and mold your own philosophy.

Some leaders do not want their staff to interview with other schools or opportunities because they feel like it is disloyal and shows they want to leave their current job. If jobs have toxic environments, losing is commonplace and accepted, or people are not appreciative of the value you bring, it may be time to look at other options. We also have to understand that there is no perfect place to work because there are no perfect people. Every institution has things it does well and areas that may be less efficient. Focus on the good and bloom where you are planted. Make every situation better because you are involved, turn a problem into an opportunity, do not complain. Bring solutions to the table and help make where you work the greatest place on the planet to work. Be so good at doing your job that other people around you are sharpened by your work ethic, attitude, and expertise. What happens over time is your reputation is being built, and people will speak on your behalf and recommend you to others when job opportunities open up. Success breeds success. Get on a staff where you can be a sponge and learn. Then take what you learn and go make other places better...And change lives.

What do you do to overcome times of struggle, burnout, or overwhelm? Who do you turn to?

In times of struggle, adversity, and burnout, remember who you are and why you do what you do. Have friends and mentors outside of the profession. There are people who will see what you do and appreciate you. These people will check on you and remind you of the difference you make in the lives of adults and kids. It is important to have a group of encouragers outside of the coaching profession. Have a church family that will pray with you and encourage you during tough seasons of life. When things are going well, give thanks and appreciate them. When there are times of struggle and disappointment, understand with a mature perspective that it will pass, the sun will come up tomorrow, and the opportunity to go change one life will be right in front of you through this profession.

When we are going through tough times, sometimes we just need to look around and realize there are people who are going through tougher situations. Learn to have an attitude of gratitude and give thanks for the blessings of life in the areas that matter most. Some people like to journal or write down prayers to remind themselves of seasons of life they have walked through when things get so overwhelming. It is good and healthy to pause and reflect. It may mean that a change of scenery is needed. It may mean that a vacation is in order. It may mean that it is time to put more time into your personal faith, your marriage, relationships with your loved ones and children. Sometimes it means getting more sleep. Sometimes it means eating better and exercising. Sometimes it means praying more and worrying less.

I believe that so much of life is learning to let go and let God have control of our lives. Sacrificing your family, marriage, physical, spiritual, and mental health for a job is meaningless—because we are all replaceable at work. We are not replaceable at home. When facing doubt and discouragement, find one of your favorite Bible promises or quotes, and take it to heart every day. Believe that good things are about to happen, and keep the faith!

What do you think about immediately after one of your athletes is injured? What is your mindset in the following week?

I want to bring a calm, steady voice to the situation. I asked our coaches and training staff to model this as well. It is important to not overreact, but also to respond with a sense of urgency and genuine care. Always take potential injuries seriously. Don't allow staff to belittle or diminish possible injuries. In 2021, my son hurt his knee in a game. I walked out there calmly to check on him with our trainer. He was not getting up. As a coach's kid, this is not acceptable. However, because he did not get up, I knew it was serious. We helped him up and he attempted to walk off the field on his own strength, but could not.

Ultimately, he had torn his ACL and would need surgery and 11 months of intense rehab to be ready for his senior year. I remember that moment well. As a coach, it was awful. As a dad, it was terrible. To see the pain my son was in physically was challenging. The emotional energy and mental toughness of going through rehab and physical therapy for almost a year was taxing on my son, my wife, and the family. I share this to say it is important to check on your athletes when they are injured and make sure there are good plans in place to take care of them with larger injuries. It is equally important, if not more important, to have mentors in their life who can help check on them and walk them through the long road to recovery.

How do you approach difficult conversations with athletes, coworkers, or your boss?
What I have found over the years is to remind myself and my staff that we all have different perspectives. Sometimes we don't see eye to eye in areas or situations that arise because there is a misunderstanding or a gap in communication. It is important not to communicate when one or both parties are angry or upset or emotional. We have a 24-hour rule in our program that encourages athletes, parents, coaches, and leaders to get a good night's sleep, gather their thoughts, and set up a time to visit in person or by phone to share what is on their heart. This has helped many of us have productive conversations and meetings to work through misunderstandings or challenges that happen in the world and arena of competitive sports.

We also encourage our leaders and coaches to be great listeners. Understand that a coach's job is to put the team first and a parent's job is to put their child first. Neither of them are wrong. Helping parents to understand that as a coach, it is our job to put the team first, this means that the individual wants and needs of the athlete may or may not always be met. This does not mean that we do not love them or care for them greatly, however, it means that we have to learn to love and support all our kids and make sure that they know their role and feel loved and valued as a member of the team.

The same is true with coaches on a staff. Different coaches serve in different roles. Sometimes egos get involved and people get their feelings hurt. Sometimes we have to get in a room and respectfully and calmly clear the air, ask for forgiveness, talk through ways we can make the situation better, and be agreeable and professional to work with one another. Very rarely have we found people who will not work on themselves to make a situation better. Most of the time, if we humble ourselves and model the type of behaviors we want to see, others will follow. It is important to create an atmosphere of unity and encouragement because the profession can be challenging.

Do you have a "failure" that was critical to your long-term development or success?
We fail forward. One reason leaders may possess experience and wisdom is because

they have gone through hard times and tough stuff. I have failed in many areas, and I know my weaknesses. This is why I have always tried to surround myself with great people who have strengths in areas where I am weak. This is how you build a team and this is how you build a program and a coaching staff. Insecure leaders are fear based and power hungry. Secure leaders empower and enable individuals to serve and utilize their gifts and talents to make everyone around them better. I believe this with all my heart.

What traits or skills do your most successful athletes have in common?

The best athletes are dependable. They show up every day ready to work and get better. They are steady and reliable. Sometimes they are the most talented, many times they are average, below average, or slightly above average. What happens overtime is an average athlete can become good, and even great, because they have learned to separate themselves and do the work that champions must do.

Our society is filled with a microwave mentality. People want instant success. They want to show up a few times, microwave it, post it on social media, talk about the grind, and then expect the results. Champions fall in love with the process. It is more like a slow cooker mentality. Let it bake, let it marinate, let it cook long and slow. Understanding the big picture, it is about the daily work. This won't get you tons of followers on Instagram, but it will get the long-term results you're looking for. The student athletes we love and rely upon are the ones that show up every day with a great attitude, starving to get better, to make everyone around them better, and have fun competing against themselves to become the best version of themselves possible.

What books or resources do you most often recommend to coaches?

I recommend books that strengthen your character, area of focus and expertise, and personal development. I love books by John Maxwell, Jon Gordon, and authors who help strengthen my spiritual life, like Max Lucado. The coaching profession is very rewarding and demanding, especially of time and commitment. This can carry over into your personal life and family time. I highly recommend books, audiobooks, and podcasts that help us prioritize our faith and our family life. The coaching profession can be challenging, but for those of us that are married, you can find strength and encouragement in your spouse. It is important to surround yourself with information that helps strengthen your marriage as well as tools and strategies for parents. I highly recommend spending time in the Bible every single day. The wisdom and encouragement found in God's word will keep you grounded and encouraged with perspective on the things that matter most.

> *"I have felt struggle and being overwhelmed, in fact I constantly do. But I like that, as I feel it's pushing me to my edges and making me grow and adapt."*

-Michael Zweifel

Michael Zweifel is the Co-Defensive Coordinator, Special Teams Coordinator, and Defensive Backs Coach for the UW-La Crosse Football team. Before taking on his current role, he served as the Wide Receiver Coach at the University of Dubuque. Prior to coaching college football, Zweifel was the owner of the Building Better Athletes performance center in Dubuque, Iowa. He is also a member of the movement education group "Emergence."

Who do you go to when you need advice? Why them?
My dad, he's been a coach for 50 years and always has a good perspective. He also knows me, so he knows when to be a sounding board and when to step back and just let me vent.

What early job was pivotal in your career? Why?
Two things stand out—first was that I coached a lot of camps when I was in HS and College. My dad was a college football coach and I would coach youth camps while in HS and then MS and HS camps when I was in college. I got to get my hands dirty at a young age and get a lot of exposure to coaching various levels of athletes at a young age.

The second would be working on a hobby farm. Every day was a new job/project on this farm, and I learned a ton of new skills and problem solving. It was usually just me and another guy, so we had to figure out creative solutions, as we rarely had the manpower for certain jobs. Farming is similar to coaching in many ways. You are trying to create the best environment for your plants to grow, so you have to be observant and sensitive to their environment and constantly fine tune their environment to help them grow.

What are your first steps when you start a new job? What do you need to figure out, what do you need to get done, who do you need to get to know?
Try to learn what was successful with the previous coach. Too often coaches come

in and try to change everything, but the reality is every job has things that went well before you showed up. I want to keep as many things as similar as I can. I'd much rather have me adapt to a few things (language, structure, timing, etc.) than have all the athletes have to adapt to me.

Also, the cultural piece is important to figure out. Every new job has nuances in the culture of the program. In a simplistic example of working at a program in a rural community vs a program in a big city, there will be differences in the values and beliefs of each program. That example is pretty obvious, but there will be small details like that in every job that are important to figure out.

What advice do you have for a college student looking to break into coaching? Who are the best mentors in the world to work for early in your career?
Depends on a couple of things—first what type of coaching is the student looking to get into? If one is looking to coach at the college level, then intern or GA at the college level. College coaching is definitely still a Who You Know business, and interning or GA'ing at a bigger university gives you a big advantage.

If you're looking to just get coaching experience or don't care what level you coach at—then I'd recommend finding an internship at a private facility or HS or smaller college. While an internship or GA at a Power 5 looks great and gives you better connections, you really won't get the chance to actually coach or program. At a private facility, HS, or small college, you'll get an opportunity to get hands-on coaching and probably some programming as well. You'll also work with more "normal" populations that are much more common. Power 5, professional is great, but the reality is those athletes are most often outliers. HS, MS, small college often aren't as gifted or natural movers and learners.

If you only had two 30-minute sessions a week to train your team, how would you prepare them?
Not in a weight room. In their sporting environment. Sport is a stress, find ways to add load (physical, cognitive).

What goes into your decision to leave or stay at a job?
I left the S&C world because I don't feel S&C has a major impact on a team's performance. Went into sport coaching because that is the only way to affect on field performance.

What do you do to overcome times of struggle, burnout, or overwhelm? Who do you turn to?

I have never felt burnout. I have felt out of place or not doing exactly what I wanted, but haven't experienced burnout.

I have felt struggle and being overwhelmed, in fact I constantly do. But I like that, as I feel it's pushing me to my edges and making me grow and adapt.

A solid sounding board, quiet time to reflect, meditation, sleep, or vacation are all good remedies for me.

What do you think about immediately after one of your athletes is injured? What is your mindset in the following week?

I think about what I could have done differently to prevent it. I review all the factors I control and see if there is anything I can do better.

Mindset the following week is to make adjustments to anything I have found that may have influenced the injury and to make sure I stay engaged and connect to the injured athlete. Injured athletes often struggle mentally the most as they feel disengaged and disconnected from the team, so I try to make sure they still feel a part of it and we are thinking about them.

How do you approach difficult conversations with athletes, coworkers, or your boss?

Open and honest. Should be coming from a shared perspective and goal, so just be open and honest.

Do you have a "failure" that was critical to your long-term development or success?

I fail all the time. Every week I fail at something that makes me reevaluate, rethink, and meditate over things. Nothing singular over my career stands out, but trying new things, pushing boundaries, being open to learn and change has led me to fail a ton.

What traits or skills do your most successful athletes have in common?

- Ownership – They want ownership. They want some control, some agency over what they are doing.

- Failure – They aren't afraid to fail or look stupid. They respond to failure positively.

- Competitive – They are ultra-competitive. They love to be challenged and compete.

- Self-Learners – The best coach an athlete will ever have is themselves. The best athletes I've worked with were their own worst critics, were really adaptive during practice and games, and relied on themselves for making adjustments.

- Open/Receptive – They were open to coaching, feedback and criticism, but also knew when to trust their instincts and didn't rely on it.

What books or resources do you most often recommend to coaches?

- *Learning to Optimize Movement* – Rob Gray

- *The Constraints-Led Approach* – Renshaw, Davids, Newcombe, Roberts

- *Do Hard Things* – Steve Magness

"My natural inclination has always been to take a 'I can make it work' approach...I have had to actively work on being better at making my stance clear and direct, no matter how difficult the situation."

-Natosha Gottlieb

Natosha Gottlieb is in her first year as the Director of Sports Performance for Women's Basketball at the University of Cincinnati. She spent the previous four years as the Strength and Conditioning Coordinator for Women's Basketball and Women's Tennis at the University of Florida. Before her time in Florida, Gottlieb served as the Associate Director of Strength and Conditioning at Florida State, where she trained Women's Cross Country, Volleyball, and Beach Volleyball. During her tenure at Florida State, she won two conference championships with the Beach Volleyball team and contributed to back-to-back regional championship titles in Women's Cross Country.

Who do you go to when you need advice? Why them?

I typically go to one of my former supervisors (Elisa Angeles, Melissa Moore) or one of my close colleagues in the industry (Mike Chatman, Ashleigh Beaver, among many). I find no matter what the situation, someone has gone through it before and more than likely has a perspective on it you are not seeing. I go to those people because their breadth of experience reassures me that I am getting advice from someone who has had success navigating similar challenges to get to where they are.

What early job was pivotal in your career? Why?

My first full-time position at Florida State University was pivotal to my growth as a coach. I trained Cheer, Dance, certain events of Track and Field, and Cross Country to begin with before moving to Volleyball and Beach Volleyball. Due to training a varied group of athletes, it helps inform the decisions I make with the type of athletes I work with now. There are not many mobility issues, restrictions, or modifications I haven't seen because of the experience of training a diverse group of people with different training ages and needs. This also helps in understanding that not everyone responds the same way to a particular type of coaching.

What are your first steps when you start a new job? What do you need to figure out, what do you need to get done, who do you need to get to know?

- Get to know the facility you will primarily work with inside and out. What do you have available to you? How many?

- I find that the person most important to get on the same page with as soon as possible is the Athletic Trainer. The two of you need to get on the same page regarding the day-to-day operation of player health and performance, communication with the coaches and each other, who's handling prehab, previous injury history, and general philosophies.

- Meet with the Head Coach.

- Communicating with the players in the way that the head coach wants when you start out is super important to getting off on the right foot.

- Be present at as many things regarding your new teams as possible.

- Whether it be practices, team dinners, or other team functions—establishing yourself as part of a greater team culture and organizational structure as opposed to just the weight room person. While this can be time consuming to begin with, it helps create invaluable buy in with athletes and coaches.

What advice do you have for a college student looking to break into coaching? Who are the best mentors in the world to work for early in your career?

Be as proactive in your development as possible. Read, reach out to people, and observe as much as possible from as many people as possible. The more diverse your knowledge and experience, the further ahead you will be.

What goes into your decision to leave or stay at a job?

The biggest factors are happiness/fit and growth potential. Ambition is a trait most strength coaches have, so knowing that there is a potential to move into bigger roles and a higher earning potential has to be a big factor. Being happy (working with good people in a healthy, happy environment) is going to outweigh any amount of money or growth potential. Can't put a price on happy.

What do you do to overcome times of struggle, burnout, or overwhelm? Who do you turn to?

I like to read, play video games, go to the beach, or hang with friends in order to escape from work and thoughts of work. When I start to feel overwhelmed or burned out, I try to make a consistent schedule so that I have a set time when I am no longer working on work related things. The computer or programs get put away and then my focus goes elsewhere. I find when I'm the most exhausted is when my mind is never off of work, whether it be at home or elsewhere. I start to feel better when I leave work at work and do something else when done with work such as yoga, working out, etc.

What do you think about immediately after one of your athletes is injured? What is your mindset in the following week?

The first thing I typically think about is, "Was this possibly avoidable?" While it's impossible to prevent all injuries, I'm a big believer that consistent training done intentionally can have a huge mitigating effect on that. My mindset the next week is figuring out how to best keep that athlete involved with the team until we know a final diagnosis and go from there. I would like to think I would have a comfort level with the quality of our training and development that my first action wouldn't be to question what could have been done differently, but instead to figure out a path forward.

How do you approach difficult conversations with athletes, coworkers, or your boss?

I try to approach in a direct, clear way. I try as much as possible not to address it through email or even phone call if I can help it, but face to face. So much context can get lost in other types of communication. The hope would be that I have enough touch points with the coach, athlete, or coworker that doing this does not seem like an attack but instead another conversation among ones we regularly have, where we can both be clear. This was my greatest weakness as a younger coach and still something I work on now. My natural inclination has always been to take a "I can make it work" approach, even if I know there is a better solution that can be directly addressed. I have had to actively work on being better at making my stance clear and direct, no matter how difficult the situation.

What traits or skills do your most successful athletes have in common?

Most successful athletes have a dedication to discipline that others who are less successful do not. They have the ability to consistently do what is necessary, even when not convenient, and conceptualize that as a part of what they need to do to be successful as opposed to a burden or punishment.

"A quality Mentorship is personal, something that lasts a lifetime. You can have multiple Mentors in a period of time that all help develop specific skills that are unique to that Mentor."

-Anthony Cockrill

Anthony Cockrill is the Assistant Director of Olympic Sports Performance at SMU, where he primarily works with the volleyball program. He played a key role in leading the 2023 SMU Volleyball team to win the AAC conference title, secure an NCAA tournament victory, and achieve the program's best end-of-year RPI in history at 24. Cockrill joined SMU after serving as the Assistant Director of Sports Performance at UMBC, where he contributed to multiple conference championship-winning teams. Before his time at UMBC, he worked as a Sports Performance Assistant at the University of Houston.

Who do you go to when you need advice? Why them?

Bri Brown (University of Miami). I would consider Bri to be my Mentor. I was lucky enough to work under her for about 10 months at the University of Houston. The experience I gained through watching, listening, and replicating is invaluable. She helped mold me into the Coach I am today, so any big or small decisions I have she is the first person I ask. I find us to be extremely similar but also so different, so there definitely is some confirmation bias. But most times she's there to keep me on track if I steer too far off.

Alan Bishop (University of Houston). Bishop is what I would consider a "Master." Again, lucky enough to observe and listen for 10 months at the University of Houston. When I am in a situation that requires some intense thought processing or decision making, my initial way to navigate a situation is to think how Bishop would handle the situation. I find him to be extremely cerebral in how he quantifies decision making, so for me it's more so how can I mimic those thought processes based on my experiences with Bishop. Like Bri, there are a lot of confirmation biases for sure, but when it comes to decisions that can shape my career, he is one of the first people I ask for advice.

Vinnie Calautti (SMU). Vinnie and I have been working together every day for the past two years here at SMU. I would consider Vinnie to be a great friend and mentor. Usually, Vinnie is the first person I go to for advice with any situation in the Microcosm of SMU. There are always these micro-interactions in the day-to-day environment that in the grand scheme of things do not have much adherence, but do give shape to the environment we work in. Because Vinnie is in it with me every day, his point-of-view is extremely valuable on how I may handle these micro-decisions.

What early job was pivotal in your career? Why?

My first Internship at Midwestern State University while I was an Undergrad. MSU was a small Division II School with only one Full-Time Strength Coach. Jake Landon was the Director of Strength and Conditioning, while Nathan Morris, Cody Ballard, and McKenzie Smith were all Graduate Assistants. I was an intern for three semesters and one summer, and it was the best time of my life. I worked with every sport from 5am-5pm and loved every minute of it. Jake, to this day, is the reason I do what I do. He was such a great mentor and human. His values, open-mindedness, and love for his people are what I try to replicate on a day-to-day basis. The GAs were so intelligent and hilarious; they welcomed me with open arms. I never once felt like an intern. I was leading groups like I had been doing it for years, purely off the confidence they instilled in me so early. Working with that Football program from 2016-2017 was the best group of people I have ever worked with and am still in contact with some individuals to this day. If it wasn't for the environment cultivated by Jake, the GAs, and all the athletes of MSU, I would not be a Coach today.

What are your first steps when you start a new job? What do you need to figure out, what do you need to get done, who do you need to get to know?

The universal step one should be to learn every single person's name and begin creating relationships. If you don't already know a Head Coach's values and philosophy (you should), the next step would be to identify those things. The next few steps become relative to the individuals' personal values and beliefs. For me, it is establishing quality nutrition. Establishing what I believe training tables should be, ordering supplements and setting up the locker-room with food. Reaching out to local restaurants and companies in hopes of creating a relationship in which they can provide us a service. Utilize the honeymoon phase to work with administration and coaches on any major purchases. Early on with administration, establish a future outlook for the position/department over the next few years. What the hopes for the position/department are, establishing goals and the possibility of expanding roles. It is all about adding value outside of the room. For me, nutrition is an easy avenue to begin with early on. My hope is to expand more administratively with decision making and managing people, so planting that seed as early as possible and watering it over time with the right people.

What advice do you have for a college student looking to break into coaching? Who are the best mentors in the world to work for early in your career?

Before you succumb yourself to the world of Coaching, you must really evaluate if this is truly your life's purpose. I am not sure quite how to quantify what that means. I feel like as you weigh the idea by reading, watching, and listening to Coaches, you will have a sense of direction whether or not to pursue Coaching. If you are to pursue a life of Coaching, I believe the most important thing is the Mentorship. A quality Mentorship is not a 3-Month Summer Internship with a group of 12 Interns where the primary responsibility is to set-up and break-down rooms. You need an environment that values learning and developing the skills that excite you. Skills that you will use 10 years down the road to create something unique to you and not a regurgitation of your Mentor.

A quality Mentorship is personal, something that lasts a lifetime. You can have multiple Mentors in a period of time that all help develop specific skills that are unique to that Mentor. Over the course of five years, I would say I had about seven different people I could consider Mentors. Four of the seven being a more traditional Mentor-Mentee relationship and the other three being more indirect where I could take qualities subconsciously and apply them currently. It is nearly impossible for me to say who are the best Mentors because I believe the skills and qualities necessary for each Mentee is unique, so the Mentor necessary would be unique to that individual as well. Purely off personal bias and what I see/hear:

- Bri Brown – University of Miami
- Alan Bishop – University of Houston
- Dave Scholz – Louisiana Tech University
- Zach Dechant – Texas Christian University
- Nick DiMarco – Elon University
- Tim Caron – Allegiate

If you only had two 30-minute sessions a week to train your team, how would you prepare them?

To create some more individualized insight to this question, I am going to be referencing my answers as if I were talking about our volleyball team who I have been training for two years.

To make it more relatable, we are going to start with us being in the beginning of the season in September following the Pre-Season. I don't think it would be wrong to assume two 30-minute sessions in-season is pretty common. I believe this is one of the two highest stress times of the year with school just starting, travel, match density, pressure to perform, and various lifestyle factors. The overarching goals for us in-season are #1 Health, #2 to be PRing jumps going into the NCAA tournament. With that in mind, we never have the mindset to "Maintain" qualities in-season, but rather to continue developing. The in-season is the longest training block of the year; you must maximize that time.

With all this in mind, during this time of year I will tend to gravitate towards the ideas of a "Generalist." We would perform about 3-4 total training movements in the weight-room. Only movements I feel we would get the Biggest Bang For Your Buck: Full Range Of Motion Squatting, Chin-Ups, and Overhead Pressing. Total Body exposure each day with an emphasis on Upper Body on Day 1 and Lower Body on Day 2. Early In-Season we put an emphasis on Extended Pauses in End-Range. Anecdotally, I feel when the external stress is high, Extended Pauses allow us to organically limit any additional high neural stress by the low ceiling external loading. For example, all volleyball players are weakest in the bottom of a Squat with a 6 second pause where you are limited by your Concentric ability, so naturally the weight on the bar is low. Especially in a sport that is reliant on the Stretch-Shortening Cycle like volleyball. We tend to utilize some version of Contrast Training with the Squat and Chin-Up. The method depends on the emphasis of contraction type. In this period where we are putting an emphasis on the Concentric contraction and eliminating the SSC, our contrasted movement will replicate that. For example, Front Squat with a 6 Second Pause is paired with a Non-Counter Movement Jump. Where both movements eliminate the use of the SCC, but the velocity of how each movement is performed is vastly different.

A 2-Day session outline may look like this:

Day 1 – Total 1 – Upper Emphasis
Gymnastics: Back Bridges, Tumbling
    A1) Chin-Ups x1-2 26X0
    A2) OH MB Slam x3 06X0
    B1) CG RDL x3 24X0
    B2) NG Push-Ups x2-4 24X0

Day 2 – Total 2 – Lower Emphasis
Gymnastics – Hand Stands, Cart-Wheels
    A1) Back Squat x1-2 26X0
    A2) NCMJ x3 06X0
    B1) BB OH Press x3 24X0
    B2) Triple Jumper Step-Up x3 24X0

What goes into your decision to leave or stay at a job?

Pretty cliché, but it's all about people. People cultivate an environment that will either be positive or negative, relative to how you perceive it, but I view this pretty straight forward.

Support and/or the value of the position. This is controllable by you based on how much value you bring to the table. At the end of the day, every Coach and Administrator has their own values. If Strength and Conditioning is not one, it can get quite tough.

Growth Potential, which is a broad idea but the idea on Growth Potential was a driving factor in my move to SMU. Dallas is one of the fastest growing cities in the country, SMU is heavily invested in Athletics, for as long as I remember had been rumored to be possibly moving to a P5 conference (now happening), and what seems like the best donor support in the country. If you view these moves like investing in companies, SMU at the time was early 2000s Amazon. Obvious risk, but the potential reward outweighs the risk.

Sport Coaching Staff. As I get deeper into the weeds of this profession, the more I value a quality Coaching Staff. This seems obvious, but personally, there are a few qualities I hold higher than others. The first is how personable they are as people, pretty simple Human First idea. It is impossible to cultivate a positive environment without an emotional investment in the people. The second is how progressive they are, complacency is a dangerous mindset. I am a big advocate of pushing the ceiling for various things in our profession, so it is a great feeling when you are surrounded by people that have and support that same progressive mindset. The third and probably most important would be how cerebral they are. Similar to a progressive mindset but more so the application. How they quantify their actions with logical thought-out processes, or the ability to apply different methods of teaching based on the scenario. In a simple explanation, it's having awareness. The social awareness to know how to interact with different individuals. The self-awareness to self-evaluate and hold oneself accountable.

What do you do to overcome times of struggle, burnout, or overwhelm? Who do you turn to?

Honestly, anytime I feel a negative emotion in this context I tell myself, "Keep Going, You're Doing Good." Shout out Larry June, Bay Area legend. But in all reality, I have learned to disconnect myself from anything that can be perceived as negative and really self-evaluate the long-term effects of it. I always ask myself, "Does it affect where you want to be five years down the road?" If the answer is no, it becomes easier to brush off. In the case of some real struggle, I believe you need to talk it out. For me that is talking to my Fiancée or asking my mentors for advice. I used to have a bad habit of holding these things in and overtime letting it snowball. It's 2024, it's okay to talk to someone and embrace those emotions.

What do you think about immediately after one of your athletes is injured? What is your mindset in the following week?

My initial reaction is always a feeling of empathy for the athlete. Understand that more often than not, sport is the driving force in their current life. Serious injury is a life-altering event for any human, but it is magnified as an athlete. Then I probably, like most other Coaches, am going to evaluate the injury and work backwards to find what got us to the point of injury. Number one is injury history; the leading cause of injury is a previous injury. Number two—evaluating lifestyle factors: nutrition, sleep, school, major life events, etc. Number three is training history. This includes sport practice, games, and strength and conditioning. After we think we have evaluated all facets that led up to an injury, it becomes what can we change on our end to make sure we never get to that point again?

How do you approach difficult conversations with athletes, coworkers, or your boss?

We can all agree that we need conflict. It is how you solve problems and can stimulate change on important issues. The approach depends on the conflict type. More often than not, it is probably going to be task, value, or relationship oriented. The initial reaction to any conflict should be to disconnect one's self from the situation to evaluate from an external point of view rather than having an internal bias. Simply put, if you can remove bias and evaluate each side of a situation, it becomes easier to come to a resolution.

Do you have a "failure" that was critical to your long-term development or success?

I think I have been lucky enough to say I have not had a major, life altering failure to reference. But I have and will continue to have micro-failures that I use as a chance to develop in an area I may have not been aware of at the time.

What traits or skills do your most successful athletes have in common?

Not taking into account Sport Skill, I believe Kinesthetic Awareness is the greatest trait to have as an Athlete. The general ability to control your body in space is so valuable in almost every sport scenario. A volleyball Middle Blocker being able to react to a hitter in a split second to make a powerful block move. But not just the action happening, but how visually "smooth" and natural the movements look while also expressing maximal outputs of forces. We have all seen athletes perform various skills, and it looks like a baby giraffe learning to walk. That's not just a lack of obvious skill but the Kinesthetic Awareness to express the skill. This is definitely a trainable quality. Gymnasts have the best Kinesthetic Awareness in the world. So, applying remedial Gymnastic methods can be beneficial when looking to improve Kinesthetic Awareness.

What books or resources do you most often recommend to coaches?

- *Mastery* – Robert Greene
- *Grays Anatomy* – Henry Gray
- *The Psychology of Money* – Morgan Housel
- *Strength Deficit* – Tim Caron

> *"Everything is an opportunity to learn or grow. I see lessons all around me."*
>
> ## -Velaida Harris

Velaida Harris is currently the Associate Head Coach for the Utah State Women's Basketball program after holding the same role at UMKC. Prior to UMKC, Harris led the Weber State program as Head Coach from 2018-2023. She made history as the first Black woman to earn a Division I head coaching position in the state of Utah. Harris has also worked as an assistant coach at Rhode Island, the University of Utah, and the University of Oregon. Before entering collegiate coaching, she achieved significant success as a high school coach at Lake Oswego and Lincoln Senior High, as well as serving as the program director and coach for the Nike-sponsored Portland Elite Basketball Organization.

Who do you go to when you need advice? Why them?

For advice, I speak with friends and colleagues in the business. I seek out people I respect; those who have been in the business for some time. I am also a BIG Inky Johnson listener.

What early job was pivotal in your career? Why?

My job as an assistant coach at Oregon. I was able to see that this is a BUSINESS to many and not simply about basketball and student-athletes. There are a lot of people touching each program in their own way. Many times it is Ws or bust, even if you are effectively leading all the other aspects of the program.

What are your first steps when you start a new job? What do you need to figure out, what do you need to get done, who do you need to get to know?

- Clarify expectations with your Direct Supervisor.
- Understand what type of resources you have or do not have at your disposal.
- Reach out to the lead in every department that touches your program.
- Become familiar with anyone who touches your program daily/trainer, strength and conditioning coach, facilities/maintenance people.
- Donors-Potential Donors, Alumni.
- Meet with each of the players 1v1.

What advice do you have for a college student looking to break into coaching? Who are the best mentors in the world to work for early in your career?

My advice would be to work hard and exceed expectations. Don't be too proud to do the work behind the scenes. Show your worth. Do your best to shadow those above you so you understand the importance of the work you do.

- Network.

- Attend clinics, Final Four & WBCA events.

If you only had two 30-minute sessions a week to train your team, how would you prepare them?

Session 1:

- 15 mins – Individual skill development/teaching that they could work on alone or with a teammate throughout the week.

- 15 mins – Team work at an increased rate of speed.

Session 2:

- 10 mins – Up tempo / team drills or small group competitions.

- 20 mins – Opponent Prep (in season).

    Or

- 20 mins – Team teaching concepts/breakdowns (out of season).

What goes into your decision to leave or stay at a job?

There are a multitude of reasons:

- Professional Advancement or Development.

- Family, Location.

- Financial Stability.

- Who you work for and with.

- Administrative Stability / Support / Dysfunction.

What do you do to overcome times of struggle, burnout, or overwhelm? Who do you turn to?

I'm a faith-based person, so my petitions go to God. Conversations with friends and mentors help. The foundation on which you stand, the strength and structure of your program, and culture play a role.

What do you think about immediately after one of your athletes is injured? What is your mindset in the following week?

Health of athlete is paramount. We make a plan for return and recovery or surgery and recovery. I assess how the loss or absence of the individual will affect the play and/or dynamic of the team. Who the initial "replacement" will be.

How do you approach difficult conversations with athletes, coworkers, or your boss?

I do not have a problem speaking to people, so hard conversations, advocating for student-athletes, the program I am a part of, or otherwise, is not difficult for me. I believe what I do comes from a place of authenticity, care, and the desire to be successful, so the hard conversations are a part of it.

Do you have a "failure" that was critical to your long-term development or success?

I'm not sure because there are failures on the regular (haha). You don't succeed without them. Everything is an opportunity to learn or grow. I see lessons all around me.

What traits or skills do your most successful athletes have in common?

- Work ethic.
- Mental Toughness – They do not quit!
- Not afraid to get better. Takes teaching and critique as opportunities to improve.
- Fitness is a priority.
- They love what they do!
- Attitude is steady – Never too high, never too low.

What books or resources do you most often recommend to coaches?

The books that I recommend to coaches have to do with interpersonal work, leadership, or books dealing with the generation of student-athletes we work with. I rarely, if ever, share a book about Xs/Os.

"Those are times that you have to lean into your athletes, really embrace them because they should be the part of the job you love the most."

-Raychelle Ellsworth

Raychelle Ellsworth is a recognized Master Strength and Conditioning Coach who retired this year as the Director of Strength and Conditioning for Olympic Sports at Texas A&M, after over 25 years with the university. In her role, she was directly responsible for the Volleyball, Equestrian, and Dance programs, and also served as a Professor of Practice in the kinesiology department's master's exercise physiology program. Before returning to her alma mater, Ellsworth was an Assistant Strength and Conditioning Coach at the University of Washington, where she contributed to the Softball team's Pac-10 Championship and helped them finish as the runner-up at the 1996 NCAA Women's College Softball World Series.

Who do you go to when you need advice? Why them?

I have two male mentors who got me into this profession who have been successful, and I feel their perspective is one that can differ from mine, as well as my spouse who gives an "outside" perspective from a non-S&C lens.

What early job was pivotal in your career? Why?

Growing up on a farm, you learn to be self-reliant...no one is going to come "save you," thus you learn to persevere and to do it as close to "right" the 1st time. As a S&C coach—being a collegiate athlete because you see and experience it from the other side of things, which gives great perspective. Then, being thrown two teams to train with full autonomy as a paid intern and learning to sink or swim. No real mentorship as far as programming or organization of a workout (before the internet).

What are your first steps when you start a new job? What do you need to figure out, what do you need to get done, who do you need to get to know?

Meet with Sport coaches and get on the same page as far as their perceived needs of their team, athlete behavior, discipline. Your sports ATC not only for injury history of the student-athletes, but their insight on the student-athletes' personality, work habits, etc. Then anyone else who touches your athletes (sport psych, nutrition) to get some history of each student-athlete.

Figure out the training schedule and weight room availability with your staff and then meet with the team's academic counselor to optimize their training time (trying to go later than early morning by requesting no 8 am classes on certain days). Slowly meet everyone in the departments who touch your athletes and reach out to form relationships with janitorial crew and facility managers. Kind works and small tokens of appreciation will go a long way. Lastly, meet with your teams prior to their first scheduled workout to go over rules and expectations. Keep them simple, straightforward, and fair. Clearly state what happens if expectations aren't met. Give a little about your background and year overarching plan.

What advice do you have for a college student looking to break into coaching? Who are the best mentors in the world to work for early in your career?

Train yourself consistently. You will figure more out about training that way than in any book. The best mentors are usually genuinely good, authentic people. There is no mold...they come from all over, including some of the smaller schools and even high school settings. But if they are invested in their athletes outside of their workouts, they are worth checking out because mentors invest in people.

What goes into your decision to leave or stay at a job?

It comes down to whether you feel valued. This job is hard and often unappreciated, so being a vital part of something is critical. The second part—are there things that you value that aren't represented in a paycheck? Things like location and family, especially if you have children, is the climate favorable for what you enjoy, is it a small town or big city feel, and does that appeal to you, what is the commute look like, do you feel safe where you live, do you have flexibility in your job, what kind of boss do you work for, and of course compensation/cost of living.

What do you do to overcome times of struggle, burnout, or overwhelm? Who do you turn to?

Those are times that you have to lean into your athletes, really embrace them because they should be the part of the job you love the most. Circumstances will always change and you need to go into this field knowing it will not be all sunshine and roses, but ebbs and flows. Learn to leave work at work. Home time is sacred. Take your vacations, even if it's in non-traditional ways (take every Friday off in the summer). Find something you enjoy outside of work and look forward to.

What do you think about immediately after one of your athletes is injured? What is your mindset in the following week?

How can I get them to put this into perspective and keep them in touch with their teammates? Typically, I check in on them as soon as I know. I try to get them back in the weight room as soon as possible so they can work alongside their teammates. Even if heavily modified, there is always something they can do that can be productive. I will text them before and after surgery and then a couple of days afterwards. I want them to know someone cares and I can relate to injuries as a former collegiate athlete. Eventually, we talk about a plan of "attack" for their comeback. This will involve their PT/ATC.

How do you approach difficult conversations with athletes, coworkers, or your boss?

Directly. One of my favorite quotes is: "Accountability is not personal."

What traits or skills do your most successful athletes have in common?

Resiliency, ability to focus, to get uncomfortable, be coachable, consistency.

> **"The times in my life I feel like I've dropped the ball are almost all exclusively tied to the moments in my life where I stop prioritizing people."**
>
> ## -Dave Nedbalek

Dave Nedbalek is an Assistant Coach, Director of Player Development, and Video Coordinator for the Men's Basketball Program at Oral Roberts University, marking his second tenure with the program. During his first stint at ORU, he played a key role in helping the team win the 2021 Summit League Championship and made history as only the second No. 15 seed to reach the Sweet Sixteen. After spending a year as the Video Coordinator at Louisiana Tech, Nedbalek returned to ORU in his current role. He also has five years of experience as an Assistant Coach at the University of Texas at Tyler and another five years as the Head Boys' Basketball Coach and Athletic Director at King's Academy Christian School.

Who do you go to when you need advice? Why them?

I stole from the book *What Drives Winning* and have two groups of people in my life that I lean most heavily on. I have my Inner Circle, which is a group of men that have the freedom and authority to speak directly into any area of my life. They are my accountability and my brothers who have been with me through countless stages and seasons of life. These are men of all different ages.

I also have my Board of Directors. These are basketball/career-specific mentors that I can lean on for guidance, mentorship, brainstorming, and decision-making.

What early job was pivotal in your career? Why?

My first job at King's Academy sparked the flame of my coaching career and gave me direction and purpose professionally, but my job at UT Tyler is my most pivotal. While King's incubated my love for the game and taught me key lessons, UT Tyler unlocked levels in me professionally I didn't know existed, and that is 100% due to my first boss, Jamon Copeland. Jamon is now the Head Coach at Ave Maria University and is one of the best men I have ever met, much less know and am blessed to call a friend. He believed in me and gave me an opportunity when he had no reason to do so. He taught me to see a need and fill it before it affected the program. I learned to be proactive, a self-starter, and that no job deserves to be done less than my best.

Our assistant coach, Jake Deer (Head Coach at Columbia College), gave me two pieces of advice that I have shared with every manager or GA that I work with. Number 1: you are the way you view yourself. I was a volunteer at UT Tyler my first year and Coach Deer made sure I understood that if I viewed myself as such, then that's what I would get from it. He challenged me to carry myself in a manner worthy of the job I wanted, not the job I had. Number 2: be selfish about your development. He taught me to fight my way into every meeting, recruiting trip, department meeting, and compliance training I could. He taught me to hunt for opportunities to continue developing and to this day I have only been told no one time I've asked to sit in on a meeting.

Coach Deer and Coach Copeland breathed life into my career by giving me responsibilities and helped mentor me into the coach I am today. I would not be here without all that they did for me. I use those skills and experiences every single day in my current position. I am forever grateful Coaches!

What are your first steps when you start a new job? What do you need to figure out, what do you need to get done, who do you need to get to know?
Practically the first step for me is to create a PDF of headshots and titles of all the people on campus I need to know from A to Z. I usually study this on the plane or on breaks during the trip.

Relationally, I want to learn about the people that the program touches and identify the rhythms, traditions, and potential friction points to ensure that I am cognizant of the department norms.

Lastly, I want to learn all names and stories, beginning with those closest to my position and working my way out. My time at PGC basketball taught me the importance and impact of learning and using names in conversation. The sweetest sound in any language is your own name. Instead of calling everyone coach as a cop-out, I try to learn names, families, stories, and start integrating my own family into that equation as well.

What advice do you have for a college student looking to break into coaching? Who are the best mentors in the world to work for early in your career?
I would go back to the advice Coach Deer gave me at UT Tyler: be selfish about your development. While there may be opportunities and doors opened by being at the

highest level, there also is extreme development that happens at the mid-major and small college levels. The opportunity to get your hands dirty and touch every area of the program is invaluable. By the time I left UT Tyler, I had done opponent scouts, worked on my strength certification, fundraised, organized alumni, learned operations, been a video coordinator, organized our high school recruiting, gotten on the road recruiting, and countless others. When I transitioned to Oral Roberts for my Graduate Assistant position, I was prepared because of Division III basketball in Tyler, Texas. Prioritize great people and intentional development and it will pay off in the long run.

If you only had two 30-minute sessions a week to train your team, how would you prepare them?

As a high school coach, a veteran coach in our area told me about big picture season practice planning and that I needed to "identify what we needed to be able to do to protect ourselves by our first game." I would take those things (defensive and rebounding philosophy, ball screen coverage, transition offensive structure, transition defensive structure, press break/trap offense, and baseline out-of-bounds set) and build small-sided games utilizing specific constraints to highlight those areas. I would use film to identify areas of deficiency and continuously tweak the live play to shore up the areas most needed.

Early in my career, I thought installing set plays and offense was the name of the game. I spent the entire offseason crafting this beautiful offense and all these counters and wrinkles and schemes. Then we went and played a 2A football heavy high school in fall league and they crawled in our guys' shorts and pressed us the entire game and we couldn't run one set. That was a paradigm shift moment for me. Players need to learn how to organize and manage the messiness and the chaos of the game. I would expose them thoroughly to those elements through strategically structured small-sided play.

What goes into your decision to leave or stay at a job?

My family has always used a checklist of three items to approach job decisions:

We want to work with people of high character. I have no interest in cheating, being asked to do so, or using people or opportunities in an unethical manner. I value supremely the kind of people I surround myself and my family with.

Somewhere that I am intentionally being developed. I have never taken a job without expressing my goals, dreams, and plans to my head coach and ensuring that there is an appreciation, alignment, and understanding there. I want to be a part of a staff that has a growth mindset towards the way we operate and place growth, feedback, and learning at the center of the ecosystem.

Fair compensation. While money isn't everything, I do believe that people deserve to be compensated if they are good at something, and time is the one resource we can never get back. To trade that for something is a high cost and the reward/respect of that sacrifice is fair compensation!

What do you do to overcome times of struggle, burnout, or overwhelm? Who do you turn to?

My wife Nikki and now my son Trae are great sources of relief in my life! I try my best to do box breathing when I arrive home and clear my mind and heart. Often in my career I've shown up at home burnt out from the day and given the scraps to my most prized relationships, so I try to be intentional about my energy and how I enter my home! There was a great reel where a wife was talking about having made dinner and it being an important time for their family and her husband was late one day. She felt the holy spirit guiding her to choose whether she would be the spouse who chose life, or who brings a knife with her words. It's stuck with me to challenge myself to give my best to my family. Maxwell defines success as, "When those closest to you love you the most." There have been many days where I give my best to a job and show up with an empty tank for my family. Grateful to have had some victory in that area but still a work in progress!

Practically speaking, if I'm feeling burnt out, I try to carve out time for some of those energy giving activities for me. It could be reading a book at a coffee shop, doing some writing, hanging out with friends, going to dinner and turning off the work side of my brain for a while. It's important to have that boundary and be willing to fight for your presence in each moment—be it work or home. I also try to leave my laptop at work as often as the time of year allows it. There will ALWAYS be more work that could be done, but we will NEVER get those moments back with family.

What do you think about immediately after one of your athletes is injured? What is your mindset in the following week?

This is a great question! Admittedly, this isn't an area of technical expertise for me, but I think of them more holistically in these moments. How are they doing mentally, as a person? I remember getting injured in college and having basketball taken away from me for good and it sent me down a multi-year dark spiral of drugs, alcohol, and depression. This resurfaces when I see athletes go through major injuries because I know how easily athletes can get their identity wrapped up in sport and struggle when that is taken away, even temporarily. Helping them put together a plan of action for recovery, film, engagement challenges in practice, or retention checking after practice to ensure they don't fall behind are all ideas that come to my mind. Keeping them in the fold mentally and physically.

How do you approach difficult conversations with athletes, coworkers, or your boss?

One thing I have had to stretch myself in is not creating expectations for conversations. I remember in premarital counseling having them tell us a line that said, "Expectations are just predetermined grudges." I try to have an open mind, identify the breakdown in communication, write down what I can own, and then do my best to seek to understand rather than seek to be understood.

Do you have a "failure" that was critical to your long-term development or success?

I remember coaching my very first game in a summer league at Brook Hill high school. I was pumped, felt prepared...we got drilled by 60. I remember having a vivid thought in that moment that if I am going to do this, I need to get to work because my competitive nature would not jibe with getting dropped off so badly that they're discussing running the clock and resetting the score. As a result, I studied everything offensively I could get my hands on. I identified that as a course forward and dove headfirst into it. Fast forward five years and we're cooking. State tournament all five years, multiple All-State players, MVP's...my players hated me.

I say this in all love as we've closed this loop now, but they essentially held a meeting at our school and told our administration either he leaves or we do. This crushed me because in my mind the only objective was to get good fast, and win. I missed them as people every day. I saw them as pawns in my chess game to win and validate myself. I am so grateful to this day for those 12 guys because they manually created a fork in the road moment in my life that literally has changed my career. I was blind to how I was treating them all in the vein of "coaching the way I was coached." I am forever grateful for that school, our 45 foot carpeted practice court, and all the amazing lessons it taught me, the greatest of which is this: "People as a priority.

Always." The times in my life I feel like I've dropped the ball are almost all exclusively tied to the moments in my life where I stop prioritizing people.

What traits or skills do your most successful athletes have in common?

- Focus

  - Ability to filter through noise and distractions and stay connected to core guiding disciplines and beliefs and master the boring.

- Grit

  - At the risk of being cliché, I love the word grit. It's that grimy ability to endure through the trial aimed at something that is a deep belief or why. We have shifted to this instant gratification, microwave approach, and the best athletes stack hours on days on years of unseen work to become an overnight success. I love that quote that says, "It only took me ten years to become an overnight success."

- Gratitude

  - The athletes who lack appreciation and gratitude for the things, people, and efforts around them seem to struggle in my experience. I'm not sure what the direct correlation is here, but it seems to do something to the mind and heart of an athlete to stay zoomed in to "ME" as supreme. Inky Johnson shared a quote the other day that really grabbed me: "If you forget the language of gratitude, you will never be on speaking terms with happiness."

- Growth Mindset

  - Every great athlete I've worked with has a growth mindset. They are students of the game, students of life, inquisitive and open-minded. They DEMAND to be coached.

- Joy

  - During my time at Point Guard College, I learned the value of what they call "Spirit" or joy. They say anything worth doing in life is worthy of doing with joy. Elite athletes obviously dance on the razor's edge of high performance but they are able to enjoy the journey, to smell the roses, so to speak. I watched an interview Jayson Tatum gave during the NBA finals last year where he said Joe

Mazzula told him, "It's okay to smile during war." He elaborated he believes joy to be a competitive advantage.

- "Be the Duck" – Bill Lewit

  - This is transparently an area that I struggle with! Being coolest when the fire is hot. Coach Lewit is a legend for many reasons, not the least of which is his expansive vocabulary and witty analogies. One day a recruiting visit was going a little awry, the itinerary was getting butchered, and he could see my stress level slowly building and he said, "Coach Nedbalek, we gotta be the duck, baby. Calm on top of the water...and panicking underneath." While the analogy kind of falls apart when we think about athletes' mental state (clearly we don't want them falling apart internally during moments of pressure), but I think the concept of being cool when the fire is hot is a trait of high performers. They aren't like Will Ferrell in Old School screaming at the top of his lungs in his underwear, "WE CAN'T FREAK OUT!!!! WE GOTTA KEEP OUR COMPOSURE!!!" as he slams folding chairs into metal lockers. The best athletes have an ability to be composed in pressurized moments which exudes confidence to those around them. It reminds me of *The Last Dance* when Jordan told Doug Collins during his first game, "Take a drink, wipe that white stuff out of the corner of your mouth. I'm not gonna let you lose your first game." Imagine the boost of confidence a posture like that provided him and everyone around. The ability to be clear mentally regardless of circumstance is rare air, but absolutely a trait of the elite performers. I am a huge Sean McVay fan and I remember watching an interview where he said simply, "I want my players to be mentally free to go make big plays." I remind myself often when I feel the heat rising, "Smile" and "Be the duck, baby."

What books or resources do you most often recommend to coaches?

- **PGC Basketball**

  - PGC Coaching is some of the most intentional, holistic, and actionable coaching content I have encountered in my career. Their podcast is *Hardwood Hustle*, which is a gem as well.

- **What Drives Winning**

  - I was introduced to What Drives Winning back in 2016, and I have been hooked ever since. WDW's approach to character development in athletes as a quantifiable way to not only improve people but also to make better athletes and teammates is phenomenal. I remember getting their first book, *What Drives Winning,* and writing notes in every margin on every page. It's one of the first resources that helped me identify some hidden motivators that were causing me to coach my athletes in an unhealthy and transactional way. Paradigm shift moment reading their material and watching their videos!

- **Coaching U Live**
  - I have always wanted to attend Coaching U Live in Vegas but have never been able to, so the subscription model to stream all of their clinics has been a game changer.

- **Slappin' Glass**
  - This podcast is one of my go-to's and the SG+ subscription is a gem of content from the best basketball minds in the world.

- **Basketball Immersion**
  - Chris Oliver is a pioneer in the field of basketball training and learning methodology. He challenges the status quo and "the way it's always been done." He is a thoughtful student of the game, and a master teacher.

- **InSideOut Coaching**
  - One of the most convicting books I've ever read. Breaks down what transformational coaching versus transactional coaching looks like.

- **Doug Lemov / Teach Like a Champion**
  - Doug is a classroom educator by trade but has been on a journey of how to become a master teacher over the last decade or so. He has written several books (*Teach Like a Champion, Practice Perfect, The Coach's Guide to Teaching*) that are all centered on how students and athletes learn, how can we better teach to increase the opportunities for retention, and athletically, what does translation from training/teaching to game look like and how can we more effectively structure our practices to accomplish this.

"Rather than spending time on isolated drills, I'd immerse the team in game play, using these opportunities to coach both individual players and the team as a whole. This method ensures that the players are constantly engaged in relevant, game-like scenarios, which accelerates their learning and application of skills."

-Chris Oliver

Chris Oliver is the founder of Basketball Immersion, a leading resource for basketball coaches and players worldwide, offering *The Basketball Podcast* and immersive videos. He is a trusted authority in youth basketball development, serving as a consultant for the NBA's youth basketball programs and working with the Sierra Canyon basketball program. Oliver is renowned for his expertise in Basketball Decision Training and for educating coaches on a games-based approach to coaching. Previously, he was the Head Coach at the University of Windsor, where he won over 300 games and achieved a .750 winning percentage. Additionally, Oliver coached a team of professional players at the prestigious Jones Cup international basketball tournament, leading them to win Gold in 2018.

What advice do you have for a college student looking to break into coaching? Who are the best mentors in the world to work for early in your career?

The harder you work at it, the more you're going to learn, the more you're going to grow, and then the more information you have to share. Chronological age is not a factor in your development, so seek as many hands-on coaching experiences as possible, regardless of the level. Seek out mentors who prioritize their own growth mindset and are innovative, and even a bit different than you are. Challenging your own beliefs in critical ways helps you grow.

If you only had two 30-minute sessions a week to train your team, how would you prepare them?

I would maximize this limited time by focusing on playing the full version of the game. In basketball, this would be playing 5-on-5 every single minute of our limited time. This approach allows players to experience the game in its entirety, connecting techniques and decisions in real-time situations. Rather than spending time on isolated drills, I'd immerse the team in game play, using these opportunities to coach both individual players and the team as a whole. This method ensures that the players are constantly engaged in relevant, game-like scenarios, which accelerates their learning and application of skills.

During these sessions, I'd act as a two-way coach, guiding both offense and defense within the context of the game. This approach not only helps players understand their roles and responsibilities, but also promotes a deeper comprehension of game strategy. By cutting out the fluff drills and focusing on live play, we can make the most of our limited time, ensuring that every minute is spent on activities that directly translate to improved performance during actual games. This immersive coaching style fosters a competitive and learning-rich environment, crucial for developing well-rounded and game-ready athletes.

What traits or skills do your most successful athletes have in common?

The most successful athletes I've coached have been filled with a passionate love of their craft that has driven their effort. They are adaptable, able to problem solve, and adjust quickly. They also possess a relentless curiosity and willingness to learn, always asking questions and seeking ways to improve their understanding of how they, and their team, were the best versions possible. Lastly, they're resilient and embrace the process, not just the outcome.

> ## *"When everyone understands what you're trying to accomplish, you'll get laser focus."*
>
> ## *-Jorge Ruiz*

Jorge Ruiz is in his seventh season with the Weber State University Men's Basketball program, currently serving as an Assistant Coach. He has worked his way up through the ranks, having previously held positions as Video Coordinator and Director of Operations. During his time there, Weber State has achieved multiple 20-win seasons and secured the program's first road victory against a ranked opponent in 23 years. Ruiz has played a significant role in the development of Dillon Jones, the 2024 Big Sky MVP and first-round NBA Draft pick.

Who do you go to when you need advice? Why them?

I'm fortunate enough I can turn to Rashon Burno, Eric Daniels, and Phil Beckner. Those three have been big for my development. On and off the court they've held me to a really high standard.

What early job was pivotal in your career? Why?

Arizona State was huge for me. I learned from Coach Sendek and Coach Hurley more than I could've ever imagined. Those two showed me how hard you have to work and the amount of detail that goes into this business.

What are your first steps when you start a new job? What do you need to figure out, what do you need to get done, who do you need to get to know?

You have to find a way to provide value to the program. This can be in many different ways, such as recruiting, operations, video, etc. Keep finding a gap of where you can help and then fill it.

What advice do you have for a college student looking to break into coaching? Who are the best mentors in the world to work for early in your career?

Work as hard as you possibly can!! Work anything and get to know everyone.

Phil Beckner is one of the best to intern for. He's going to hold you to a high standard, but you're going to learn all summer long.

If you only had two 30-minute sessions a week to train your team, how would you prepare them?

We would prepare by communicating our goal and making it clear what we plan to accomplish in those 30 minutes. When everyone understands what you're trying to accomplish, you'll get laser focus.

What goes into your decision to leave or stay at a job?

Relationship and Responsibility.

- Relationship – Working for someone you know cares about you is extremely important, but also the relationship with the players. When guys are fully invested and bought in to what you're doing—it makes it so much more enjoyable every day.

- Responsibility – Making sure you'll have real responsibilities. Being trusted to get the job done and given impactful work is priceless to me.

What do you do to overcome times of struggle, burnout, or overwhelm? Who do you turn to?

I try to realign my priorities. Sometimes that is a sign for me that I need to become more efficient with my time and when I reorganize my day, it usually leads to more time for myself to unwind.

What do you think about immediately after one of your athletes is injured? What is your mindset in the following week?

Injuries are tough because they're not fair. Here is where athletes have to have the right mindset. I constantly check on them even if it's a little bothersome, just so they know I'm there, but I also work with them on developing during their injury. Remind them there are still ways to get better and grow throughout their injury.

How do you approach difficult conversations with athletes, coworkers, or your boss?

Head On. You have to rip it off like a bandaid. Don't let things manifest and become bigger than what they are. Confront it openly and honestly and let things play out as they do.

Do you have a "failure" that was critical to your long-term development or success?

I wouldn't say I had a certain failure that defined me. I try to take failures as lessons and then move on. Don't let them linger and pull you down.

On the topic of failure, I had a boss once tell me, "When you're not paranoid of getting fired, you're no longer in this business." That stuck with me pretty hard for the simple fact that everything you do should be done with pride. Do every project like your boss is over your shoulder.

What traits or skills do your most successful athletes have in common?

Discipline. The discipline to show up every single day and clock in. Those real guys that have the level of success everyone wants, they show up every day. No matter how they feel or what's going on, they go to work.

What books or resources do you most often recommend to coaches?

I keep this one pretty simple. I recommend the Bible because I believe it's the truth and you simply can't argue with it.

> *"Most people in life, athletes too, just check a box. They are not striving for greatness. The great athletes are obsessed with perfection, but also have a swagger and self-confidence when they make a mistake or lose out on a play. They don't internalize it—they just go back and try to win the next rep."*
>
> ## -David Lawrence

David Lawrence is the founder of MECA, the premier personal training and sports performance facility in Michigan. He has trained over 100 professional and Olympic athletes across 30 different sports. Lawrence specializes in taking a truly individualized approach training clients 1 on 1 for optimal results. He has served as the Head Strength Coach at Concordia University and worked as the Director of Performance for the Guyana Women's National Team. Lawrence creates incredible results with his athletes through major improvements in both body composition and sports performance, working with more than half a dozen Super Bowl winning NFL players. His work has been featured in multiple major media outlets, and he has also been a speaker at multiple seminars discussing sports performance and business management.

Who do you go to when you need advice? Why them?

For strength training I would always go to Charles Poliquin. He was one of the most successful strength coaches of all time. Charles trained athletes who had won Olympic Medals in more than a dozen sports. He was one of the smartest people I had ever met and also one of the funniest! Unfortunately he passed away in 2018. As my business has grown, I have hired many different consultants or mentors that have helped in different areas of my business and personal life.

What early job was pivotal in your career? Why?

The most pivotal experience in my life that helped me career wise was playing college football at Central Michigan University. We had a lot of success on the field, won two MAC Championships, and had over 20 guys that played professional football in the NFL and CFL. I played for two very successful coaches, Brian Kelly (LSU) and Butch Jones (formerly Tennessee). Both men were great leaders and I learned a lot from them. Being in a competitive atmosphere and trying to win at a high level was something that made a massive impact on me. I was able to learn how to work hard, how to push through adversity, and how to win. I have been able to take my experience as a college athlete and that has served me well in being an entrepreneur.

What advice do you have for a college student looking to break into coaching? Who are the best mentors in the world to work for early in your career?
Look for mentors who are doing what you want to do and reach out to them. Taking initiative and being persistent is so important. Also, offer to pay people for consultations or pay people for the opportunity to be mentored for a week. If you want to train basketball players, Preston Greene is a great strength coach (currently Clemson University Basketball). If you want to work with hockey (Ben Prentiss – Prentiss Performance in Connecticut has trained hockey players who have won every award, every medal, at every level imaginable). Jordan Shallow—Muscle Doc—has a great mentorship program for strength coaches to learn the fundamentals of anatomy, program design, and coaching. Eric Cressey in baseball—the list goes on.

Find out who is doing what you want to do and contact them. Offer to pay for the mentorship and if it goes well and you like them and want to learn more, apply for a job. Work for them for 3-5 years and immerse yourself. This is the fastest way to learn.

If you only had two 30-minute sessions a week to train your team, how would you prepare them?
Honestly I wouldn't. There is no way you can put yourself and your team in a position to be optimally successful with 60 minutes of physical preparation a week. One of the most important skills that strength coaches need to learn is the ability to negotiate time. You have to teach the sport coaches, athletic trainers, and athletes what is optimal. Two 30-minute sessions a week is not optimal.

What goes into your decision to leave or stay at a job?

1. Do I enjoy what I am doing? Does this give me juice?

2. Am I learning and growing in this role? Is this challenging me?

3. Can I have success here? Am I being supported? Can I make a positive impact on the people I am working with and working for?

4. Am I making enough income to provide for myself and my family?

5. What is my upside to staying here? Does this align with my long-term goals?

What do you do to overcome times of struggle, burnout, or overwhelm? Who do you turn to?

I think everyone has gone through burn out in their career. I usually go through it 2-3x a year personally. It's important to remember that we are not here for a long time and that some of the struggles we are going through will shape us in a great way if we let them. Struggling is how we grow, and keeping that in perspective is good.

I had an insurmountable situation that I was in about two years ago. It was one of the darkest, most difficult times of my life. It was very hard, but when I was going through it, I was able to be happy and at peace regardless of the circumstance because I knew I would come out better on the other side. It was for my good in some way. I didn't need to know the why, that wasn't actually important. But I did need to know the fact that I was here, in this place in time, and that it was meant for me to struggle and grow. That gave me a lot of comfort and peace.

How do you approach difficult conversations with athletes, coworkers, or your boss?

Running an organization with 40 plus employees—there are a lot of difficult conversations. I usually start with empathy for the other person. I try to be as calm and direct as possible and ask questions and listen. I have had to let go of many people from our organization and that is never fun. But be direct and to the point. Having compassion for the other person in the room is very important. When we give corrective feedback in our company, we use the sandwich method. Start with what that person is doing well, then provide the corrective feedback or what went wrong or what needs to be improved, then go back and finish with something positive.

What traits or skills do your most successful athletes have in common?

They are very competitive. They want to be good and are willing to do the things necessary to be good. Most people in life, athletes too, just check a box. They are not striving for greatness. In word they might, but in deed no way. The great athletes are obsessed with perfection, but also have a swagger and self-confidence when they make a mistake or lose out on a play. They don't internalize it—they just go back and try to win the next rep.

What books or resources do you most often recommend to coaches?

Find someone who is doing what you want to do or working with the population that you want to work with and try to get in with them. My first job as a strength coach was at the Poliquin Performance Center and Mike Bystol was the owner and Head Coach. My first week on the job, I was able to watch him train eight NFL athletes and multiple Super Bowl Winners. I learned more about training athletes from being mentored than I could have ever read out of a book.

The *Poliquin Principles* shaped my development as a coach. I was obsessed with helping athletes run faster and improving program design, so I sought out Charles Poliquin, went to his seminars, and paid him for consultations. He put me light years ahead and helped give me the foundation to be successful as a strength coach.

The book that has helped me out the most is *The Gap and the Gain* by Dan Sullivan and Benjamin Hardy. I think it's the best personal success book ever written. The mindset shift on focusing on and cultivating what is good and what you have accomplished in life is powerful. If you can look back and take time to count your wins in life, it gives you a lot of confidence moving forward.

"I put together a pirate map with all the essential things that would help me live a longer and more impactful life. The first thing I do is I sit down and I say, 'Is this the Dan John who Dan John said he wanted to be?'"

-Dan John

Dan John is a legendary figure in strength and conditioning, boasting over 30 years of coaching experience in the weight room as well as in football and track and field. His commitment to developing athletes has left a lasting impact, not just in their performance, but also in the broader coaching community. John has authored several influential books, including *Easy Strength*, *Never Let Go*, *40 Years With a Whistle*, and *Hardstyle Kettlebell Challenge*, among others. You will frequently find his books recommended throughout this work. Through his articles, workshops, and mentorship, Dan John continues to inspire and educate the next generation of coaches. **(John's responses were transcribed from a Zoom call)**

What early job was pivotal in your career? Why?

My senior year at Utah State, Coach Maughan called me and said, "I'd like to invite you back in the fall to take over strength training for our track and field team." There's a chance I'm the 1st collegiate track and field strength coach. There might've been somebody else, but I don't think we have a name for it then. The reason I bring this up is because Coach Maughan was part of that group of great coaches. There were great coaches like Bud Winters at San Jose State, and all these World War II vets where they're coming to the end of their career, and all those visionary coaches had seen the value of weightlifting and a number of other things. We get the Utah State discus throwing style, the wide leg, the Fosbury flop comes from this period. All the relaxation drills that everybody uses now. Coach Maughan had this piercing intellect to see what was working and what wasn't. I lucked out. I was able to pay for my master's in history by being the strength coach at Utah State and quickly I realized—and I was only about 22—I realized with absolute clarity that this body building, this body composition work, was now the tail wagging the dog of what we're trying to do out there.

I usually break things down into health, longevity, fitness, performance, and floating over all that is body composition. And I do think a 400 meter runner is probably gonna look pretty good on the beach. Yet you see that same 400 meter runner in the weight room doing nothing that will help them with their 400 meters. You see them trying to look good for the beach, but it's not going to help their performance. I lucked out very much because I was there during the big change, and I was also a voice. I just watched Dune. I'm the voice from the old, "Mahdi, Lisan al-Gaib," I am the voice from the past.

I was lucky because Coach Maughan trusted me. He knew I had an Olympic lifting background. He knew I was a self-made athlete, and I had an ability even then to teach.

What are your first steps when you start a new job? What do you need to figure out, what do you need to get done, who do you need to get to know?
My first bit of advice is don't do it, run, go find something else. Make sure you include that!

It takes a full three years to turn around the culture of a gym. It takes three years to turn around the culture of the weight room, culture of a team. Sadly, nowadays you just don't get that time. I mean, there's a Denver Bronco coach who's had some problems. And I know this will hurt the timelessness of our conversation, but it's just not working out right now because of a bad decision on hiring a quarterback. So now they're talking about firing the coach. This will be his second year and they're already, "We're done with you, time to move on." If you don't win the Super Bowl, you fire everybody. With some of the things that have changed in Division I athletics now, it's hard to change the culture. That is overwhelmingly the biggest problem.

Every place I've ever come into, when I show up there's always some level of—I don't mean to knock on the other coaches—but there's a level of disaster in there. First, generally discipline has disappeared. If you're at a university, I expect everyone to be in their gear. If you're at a high school, everyone should be in the school colors, PE uniform. You would be surprised how that takes almost a full year to turn what they wear in the weight room. Another area is the music you hear in the weight room. It's totally inappropriate. I have smashed my own stereo. I tell you one thing, when you take your fist and smash a stereo because of offensive lyrics in a song, the kids remember that for a long time. I had a student mention that from 20-plus years ago when I smashed the music maker. It stood out in their minds. If there's offensive lyrics, you can't have it, but again, that might've been my second year at the place.

I haven't gotten into equipment, have I? I haven't gotten into goblet squats versus back squats. I haven't talked about the squat depth yet. So just getting people to show up on time, wear what they're supposed to wear, speak to each other in the way they're supposed to speak, is a transition. If you don't get full buy-in from the head coaches, that just kills you.

Now, every head coach will say with their lips, "Oh, I think they all need to be in uniforms and they shouldn't say offensive things about women, or people of color, or whatever." Everybody agrees with that. But in reality, if it's their best athlete, they don't care. They have a different set of rules. That is an impossible situation, especially with an adolescent mind to work with because the adolescent struggles with that kind of thing. I'm 67 and I struggle with it, so I got to give them a break.

Once you establish little things like showing up on time, in an appropriate uniform, then you have to step back and rewire things. I like to rewire things with the warm up. I have an article called "The Warm Up is the Workout." I'm a big believer in the warm up. We do loaded carries in warm ups, we do goblet squats, we crawl, we do push up variations. I wish I'd had the tool called the hip thrust back then because we'd added it. If I have an hour and a half, which is basically an hour and 15 minutes, I might even dedicate 45 minutes as the warm up.

I might fight with you over how deep you should go on a back squat. Somebody told you that you need to back squat 500, which maybe is a good idea for what you're doing. Generally, no, that's way too much. You take the weight back and your knees sort of bend a little bit, and then you rack it and you high five, "I'm squatting 500!" I can't fight that the first year, but what I can do is get people goblet squatting deep the first year. Everyone's cheating and bouncing on bench presses, but we have what are called tick-tock pushups. It comes from Peter Pan. Every time I say tick, you move a hand. When I say tock, you do a pushup. "Tick-tock-tick-tock." Just a simple exercise. But at least I know that they're doing pushups.

After that, you start to put together programs. You need a basic global program that gets the big lifts in. You do have to spend time after you develop the program reteaching the clean, the snatch, and the Olympic lifts. I bring in kettlebells really early. I bring in tumbling really early. The number one thing I'm doing is—first we set up this discipline base. Then we try to get the warm up to be a bigger thing. The warm up becomes teaching. Yeah, you try to get a little tired and warm, so you're teaching the mobility movements you want, the flexibility movements you want, the way you want people to squat long term, all those kinds of things, and then over time, you introduce all these other pieces. It takes time. It takes about a full three years.

If you come into a high school setting, your seniors are going to fight back on you constantly. "It's not the way we used to do it." What you'll find is that the sophomore class will probably believe in you. When they're seniors, you'll own the weight room. The other thing, this sounds horrid, but you almost need to fire everybody that was around before. Just for the record, I don't believe what I'm saying, but there's always some pushback from the people who've been there before. They're comfortable with it. Every place I've ever been has the assistant coach who wears the ultra tight t-shirt, shaves his arms, sits with their arms crossed, and only talks to football players or cheerleaders. To change the weight room is an investment. It's a process and it takes time.

What advice do you have for a college student looking to break into coaching? Who are the best mentors in the world to work for early in your career?

Teaching and coaching are gifts. Literally, I think they're gifts. I'm sure you've seen it, someone who loves the sport but couldn't teach a dolphin how to swim. I think you need to have the gift. To be a strength coach is a strange kind of leadership. I do a lot of work with the military, and I was with a Marine special forces group. The guy who ran the whole thing was the first volunteer to do everything—the highest ranking officer was always the first volunteer. He was also the person to always leap up to be the test subject for anything. I learned a great lesson that weekend, because I thought to myself, "That's a great strength coach."

Great strength coaches say, "Follow me." That's probably the most powerful statement I've made in a long time. It's great if you have your head buried in a bunch of nonsense studies. How many studies that come out in weightlifting are not nonsense? I don't know if I'm nuts, none. You've got to be the person who could stand up in a room of 125 people and say, "This is how we're going to get you to the top of this mountain. Come on." You can't be up there going, "Well, I read this really interesting study from 1922, and he said..." No, no, no. "Follow me. To be great as a discus thrower we're gonna snatch, we're gonna front squat, we're gonna do suitcase carries. *What else?* If you do those, you don't need anything else!" Step one is that you have to have the gift.

One thing I would look for after that gift is—what are this person's values? To be a great strength coach, you've got to be a value first person. If you told me your number one value was being trustworthy, we can tell very quickly in the weight room whether that's true or not. Coaches gossip, athletes gossip. A trustworthy person wouldn't do that. Interestingly, my number one value is order. The way I do things is that I am as straight line as any person you ever meet in life. I just like to make sure I fill in everything you could possibly ever need, but everything I do is boom, boom, boom.

Even if you want to step back and values is too loaded of a word for you, you have to have an understanding of your systems, your structures, and how you do things. If you're an absolute slob, you're going to have a hard time being a strength coach. Interesting, a lot of strength coaches I know are absolute slobs. It's funny because you can get away with that in a one-hour workshop, a half-day certification, or a talk. But it's hard to have someone who's slovenly in their personal habits, in the way they maintain a gym, because our weight rooms are probably the most dangerous place on the campus. You can die in a weight room. The exercise is called the bench press. You can get hurt badly in the weight room. You have the one young man who fell back and broke his back because they didn't put the plates away. Make sure you have systems built into the structures in your life.

If I'm going to hire you to be my assistant, you better know kettlebells. You better know the Olympic lifts. You better know power lifts. You better know tumbling. You better have a good handle on nutrition and recovery, including advice about sleep. And that just opens the door. From there, you have to understand the sports we're supporting, because we are supporting the sports. Your knowledge might be actually number three on the list here.

When we talk about mentors, you should always capitalize the word Mentor because he's an actual person. He was Telemachus' instructor, his teacher. What a great way to go through eternity that your name becomes a noun. So if you're looking for a mentor, and I wouldn't want to mention names because then I'll forget somebody, I personally like someone who sits up straight and shows up on time. If you're working with somebody who can't answer an email, there's your sign. They have to be a professional. I haven't taught a lot of weightlifting classes in a tuxedo, but we have to be professionals in our realm, which means we have to care about hygiene. We have to care about the way we talk to our athletes. We have to care about their long-term health.

I took my shirt in recently to get dry cleaned for this wedding and one of my former athletes was there. He's 60 years old, and it was nice because as we're talking he remembered me telling them about how fast the decades go by, and don't put on a lot of body fat, get your degrees, the whole thing we always tell people, but he remembered it. You have to care about the welfare of your athletes, not just for the upcoming game, but for the next 50, 60, 70 years. Those would be the things for me when you're looking for a mentor.

I was at a workshop one time, and the person who spoke at the podium said, "I got 14,000 unanswered emails because I'm so busy." I thought to myself, "You're not busy." Then I had a word in my head that he actually was, but it wasn't busy. It's a potty word, so I'll save it for you. That to me is how you look for a mentor. I can't trust somebody to spot on a bench press who can't answer emails. That's a strange sentence to say. Think about that sentence. It's a powerful statement because if you're coaching my daughter at your university, I'm giving my most precious object in the world to you. You can't answer an email? When people wonder why I have financial success, I say because I answer my emails. "Well, but what about your business plan?" My business plan is taking care of the client. "Oh, how do you do that?" Answer emails! Answer the phone!

What goes into your decision to leave or stay at a job?

Memorize this phrase young people. Last hired, first fired. Being a strength coach, you have the pulse of every team. You are the most important cog, especially for American football and rugby. You are the person that makes the team. But when someone new comes, you're fired and they'll hire you last. I was never very good at timing my exits. I left a couple of places a little early. Only once or twice in my career did I feel like I overstayed. We always joke in the high school setting that a principal lasts about eight years. After eight years, it becomes the Charlie Brown teacher—"Womp, womp, womp." Also, we all get entrenched. There's a thing called the seven-year itch. I think it was a Marilyn Monroe movie about marriages in the seventh year. In teaching, a faculty generally works in the rule of sevens. I've been at schools who almost exactly had a third of the faculty first year through seven, a third of the faculty eighth year through about 14th, and a third of the faculty long term, 15 plus years. That's actually a healthy formula. What that means is that you've had a number of principals hire the faculty.

I know of a school that's struggling right now because the principal has been on way too long, and he's hired every person on the campus. You need rubs. You don't need conflict necessarily, but you can't have people in your organization say, "This is the way we've always done it and it must be right." In education, that's just not true. I remember using Ditto Masters when I first taught. It was this little machine, and you typed up a test. On this ditto thing, you unpeeled it and it had the ink for the machine to put the letters on the piece of paper. Well, that's just not the way it's done anymore. Every student you have probably has access to three to four computers. It's just different, things change. In our field, every time I go on Instagram, some other idiot is blathering off some stupidity that I would look at and go, "This is the dumbest thing I've seen since the last time I went on Instagram." But your discus throwers follow 100 discus throwers. If one of them does a drill that's insane—overhead squats on a BOSU ball, a chain around their neck, good plan—they'll say, "Why aren't we doing this?" And I'd respond, "I don't want you to die!"

When you leave, it's nice to have an end goal. In the high school setting, a strength coach probably has three years, six years, nine years because of the wash through on the varsity teams. After a while, it's time to hand it over because it is an exhausting job. Being a strength coach is very tiring. No matter what you do, it's wrong. The counselors are constantly pulling your athletes out because they don't think your class is very important. At the collegiate levels, you're always dealing with all kinds of, "We lost this game cause we did deadlifts last April." No, no we didn't. We lost the game because the quarterback fumbled the snap. That wasn't a deadlift issue, it was a holding the snap issue.

One thing I think is overwhelmingly important is that you have friends, and to quote Jerome K. Jerome, "Friends worthy of the name." You need to have somebody who has no skin in the game, who can talk to you and say, "I've noticed you seem tired this year. What's going on? You seem..." If you're to say to me, "You seem like you're not yourself," then the two of us have an honest conversation. I could just say, "Well, I am sick of the basketball coach driving me crazy. He doesn't want his athletes to lift. We're zero and 72 on the basketball program, and I have to listen to this moron tell me how to do my job!" You have to have a friend worthy of the name. Certainly a spouse can help, certainly someone close to you can help, but you also need someone on the campus, who's also checking the pulse of what's going on.

What do you do to overcome times of struggle, burnout, or overwhelm? Who do you turn to?

On the back of my computer here, I have this thing called my pirate map. In a pirate map, go to St. John's Island, find the white coconut tree, take seven paces to the west, dig down, there's a sunken treasure. First thing I do when I feel like my life is unwinding, I look at the things I say I'm going to do every day. Number one thing I say I'm going to do every day, before I go to bed I write my to-do list for the next day. I make coffee. I exercise every day, I eat vegetables at every single meal. I meditate for anywhere from 1 to 15 minutes every day. I read great books and every day I try to make a difference. Right now, to be honest with you, I'm trying to make a difference in your life.

The first thing I look at is, am I sticking to my pirate map? Did I write my to-do list? I've noticed when things start to fall apart in my life, I don't do that simple little thing. You're on my to do list. I went right into my journal and wrote, "Talk to John- 2:30." The first thing I do is a quick check in. Am I doing what I say I'm going to do? My long-term goal is to dance at my granddaughter Josephine's wedding. My parents were both dead before my age. People in my family don't live long.

I put together a pirate map with all the essential things that would help me live a longer and more impactful life. The first thing I do is I sit down and I say, "Is this the Dan John who Dan John said he wanted to be?" Kind of a weird sentence, but I said I was gonna exercise every day, I was gonna walk every day, I was gonna eat vegetables every meal. I was gonna make a difference. I was gonna do my to do list, make the coffee, meditate. Did I do those things? Well, no. Okay. Why am I suddenly not doing those things? Because of the stress of work. Okay, what will help me with my stress? Well, if I meditate, if I eat better, if I lift weights, if I go for a walk, all those things will help me deal with stress. "Oh..." For me, the first thing is the "Oh!"

I taught in high schools for a long time. One thing that you learn in high school is that most people don't observe people's boundaries. I wasn't very good with this and only in the last few years have I discovered the importance of having boundaries. When you get hired, you have to be very explicit on the schedule you're expected to do. What happens with strength coaches is you get hired to do about a 20 hour a week job. You got to be in the weight four hours a day for five days a week. Very quickly, they want you there at four in the morning to train the girls' football team, then they want you to teach the water polo team separately. Already you've gone through the boundaries. Obviously you expand, and that's our job. It's more than a job, it's our vocation. But boundaries is something I think we don't talk about enough in coaching. I have to be careful with how I make these comparisons, but I'm not your serf when I take a job as a coach. You're not lord of the manor. Very often, we start getting treated that way. I've talked to coaches that end up doing all the laundry. Well that's not the strength coach's job, I don't think.

The third area—I'll explain it this way using Nick Peterson's term "bumpers." The hardest thing to get a sense of is enough is enough. That's true I think with strength. Discus throwers—once you get over 400 in the squat, you're strong enough. 400 in the bench, you're strong enough. 300lb clean, high 200s in the snatch, you're strong enough to throw international distances. The first thing you have to deal with is you've got to let people know that if you're at standard, your issue in the football game isn't the weight room. Your issue is the football stuff. You can't bench press your way to making a catch. If you've got fumbleitis, doing more curls is not going to help. The other thing about bumpers is that you've got to sit back as a program and have some interesting discussions.

In high school, everyone wants to win the state championship every year, but the truth is all you've got to do is make a quick timeline—the school has been around 100 years and you've won five state championships. That means you win one every twenty years. You need to think through your bumpers. Now maybe you decide we're gonna really improve our program. Improving your program from one state championship every twenty years to one in ten is a momentous change, but how often have you ever had that conversation? I remember sitting down as a head track coach one time and saying, "My goal for this track meet is I want to fill every event." I had a real big pushback from one of the coaches. "My athletes aren't good enough to do the 4x1, we aren't fast enough." Don't take it wrong John, but I think you and I could probably both run 100m with a stick in our hand. It may not break the world record, but it's not that hard to find a human who can take a stick and go a 100. For me, my bumper was I want to fill every event at every track meet and slowly build up the program. If you have a freshman kid running the varsity leg of a relay, that's an experience that's going to inform that athlete three years later. Having the whole group go right past 'em is going to make him or her go, "Okay, I see why coach wants me to squat, do hill sprints, and work on my speed because I'm a truck, and not even a very fast truck."

What do you think about immediately after one of your athletes is injured? What is your mindset in the following week?

Every weight room injury has to be investigated. First thing I would ask would be about the exercise itself. That's one reason I don't coach the box jump anymore because of the number of shin injuries we got. They'd fall off. We had an MCL injury with someone dinking around jumping off a box. I banned box jumps. When I say that to people, especially on the internet where people who don't know anything still have a right to post—I think we can get the same qualities from a box jump that you get from a bunch of weightlifting exercises we've never had an injury with. Number one is you have to have that conversation about it. Then, how are we teaching it? Very often, guess what you find out? We're not teaching it. We put box jump x15 on the workout because we saw some lunatic online write that. We didn't teach box jumps, but we put it in the circuit. Did we teach it, did we go over it, did we discuss it?

Then we look at the equipment. Did the equipment fail on us? It happens sometimes. I love bands, but I don't use bands anymore, I use chains. They are practically idiot proof. Now when you're talking about thousands of people, saying practically idiot proof is just a challenge. The reason I got away from bands is because they degrade over time and you don't know when they're going to snap.

The third thing—you have to look at the athlete. "Well, Sydney missed 72 practices, she didn't come to any pre-season training, she constantly sneaks out, and got hurt doing a hamstring stretch." We can't blame the hamstring stretch, we've got to blame the fact that she did NOTHING!

Now on the field of play—one reason I got hired at one school was because they were having a rash of shoulder injuries. I asked, "How is that happening?" Fortunately, we actually had game film on the running backs and their shoulder injuries. With the soccer kids we were able to just ask them how they were happening. It turns out that the running backs were trying to stop the tackle by putting their hand on the ground. We stopped all the shoulder injuries not by doing things with little stretchy bands, but by learning how to tumble. Listen, if you're going to the ground, sticking your hand out isn't gonna stop you and the two tacklers. All it's going to do is pop that shoulder out of place. Roll with it, bounce up, get in the huddle and do it again. When it comes to injury on the field, I think you need to sit back and have two thoughts on injury prevention. First, is there a quality that we're not looking at? Generally, I would say it's overwhelmingly fall breaking, tumbling, rolling. You get hit, you roll, you pop up. That is almost ignored in most training programs. Adding break falling, at any level, is going to make a huge difference on some of your injuries, especially now that so many kids play on turf. Turf is tough on the joints. You've got to learn to roll on the turf.

If you're getting a plague of hamstring injuries, very often you find that they've added hamstring stretches before the game or practice. Hamstring stretches are for after practice, and on those tonic days. The way you should stretch the hamstrings, I'm a big fan of hinges. You wanna stretch your hamstrings, do Romanian Deadlifts or kettlebell swings or hang snatches.

The most important thing is that you've got to acknowledge and talk about injuries. You've got to fold your arms, be the big kids, and talk about what happened. And listen, sometimes it is the athlete's fault. You've got to know that. But if we didn't teach the athlete, then it's our fault. If we've taught everybody the proper way to do something, we've done rep after rep, but that person chose to miss those days or fool around, that's on them. That's why it's hard for some of us old timers to stick around, because I do think it's people's fault when they do stupid things.

Do you have a "failure" that was critical to your long-term development or success?

I had this athlete named Nick. Nick was a great athlete, but he had this technical flaw that I couldn't fix. It took me a couple of years to figure out what he was doing wrong. A couple of years ago he was visiting, and we had a party at Christmas. He dropped by and I said, "You know, I've got to thank you," because he should have been a 180 ft discus thrower, but he was only 130. He said, "Coach! I forgot all about that, it was not that big a deal to me." That is the great insight. I know their clock is ticking. Tick, tick, tick. *There's your eligibility. There's your high school experience. There's your professional career.* They don't. Every athlete I've ever coached is an immortal until that last game, that last play. Even then, it takes a couple of weeks for them to realize. The 50th anniversary of my last high school football game will be this Thanksgiving. I remember the week we were getting ready, one of my teammates said, "I can't wait for this to be over. *Practice?* No, football. I'm so sick of it." I remember thinking, "None of us are ever going to put on a helmet again." At one of our reunions, he was the guy talking about high school football. He was the glory days guy. I was there in real time when he said he couldn't wait for it to be over, and then years later he would do anything to have it back.

My two best athletes are redshirting this year, and I keep telling them what a joy next year it's going to be to coach them. The one athlete said to me, "Why are you so excited?" Well, because next year I'll be 68 and I don't see myself having that many more years to coach. You could see with her face the impact of what I said. My biggest failure as a coach was not being clear enough about the timeline. We have a couple of high schools here where if you play football, the coach is very clear that's the only sport you can play. To me that's idiocy. I'd much rather have a high school football team where every kid is a state wrestling champ and state sprint champ. That'd be a good football team. He wants them in the weight room, putting on weight and doing skull crushers and concentration curls because that'll make you a better athlete.

I help with this one high school over here a little bit, and a few of the kids say, "Why didn't people tell me it was this much fun? *What do you mean by that?* I never did anything else in my high school career." No drama, no debate team, no Model UN, no acappella/choir, no glee club, no chess club—just football. Then sometime in November of their senior year, it's over. I hope they learn the lesson when they go to college and get involved with as much as they can, but it's hard at that level. My biggest failure is not instilling that into every athlete. A.E. Housman's great poem about the athlete, I feel that way sometimes. I sometimes wish I just died—you know I got hit in the head with a discus my junior year, should have killed me. I remember telling somebody, "I'll tell you one thing, I'd be in the Hall of Fame if I would have died then." The poem's called "To an Athlete Dying Young." I would suggest that you might want to either read it or put it in any book you have, because that is the whole idea.

(I have included Housman's poem at the end of this chapter)

What traits or skills do your most successful athletes have in common?
Easy answer, but I want to preface it with this—my lawyer is a former athlete of mine, my doctor is a former athlete of mine, the guy over at the mortuary that I prepaid my funeral to is a former athlete of mine. There are professors in New York, in England, in Idaho, in Utah, and in Texas that are all my former athletes. Coach Maughan told me this when I first coached with him. I said, "Coach, what do you do for recruiting? What do you look for?" He goes, "Danny, I look for two things. Speed, and smarts. I can coach everything else." I'm not sure I can say it any better than Coach Ralph Maughan did at Utah State.

I have always emphasized looking for the smart athletes. Yesterday we had a group of throwers and had a high school kid come up. I asked, "How are your grades?" She goes, "They're really good." I said, "Stop, everyone come in. What question did I just ask you?" College athletes were there. She goes, "He asked me how my grades were?" I turn to my young freshman college thrower. "Have I ever asked you that question? *Almost every day Coach.* Because your academics and those goals are so much more important, and smart kids figure out ways to overcome obstacles. They don't blame anybody else. They look for options." I tell my daughters this all the time, and I do love my daughters. My daughter Kelly said to me a couple of weeks ago, "Here's the thing dad, like you always say, I just needed some options, so I went out and found them." She was having a career path decision. She found a job that paid more by searching for options.

The smart athletes are the ones that will wave you off. When you're coaching American football and you're going to send in a play, when you coach well, they'll wave you off because they know what to do. I've taken timeouts in games, ran out to the huddle and said, "What do you think?" The good teams always say, "We got this." I've taken timeouts with no other reason except I didn't want to go into the bus with a timeout in my pocket. I just talked to one athlete on the phone, and we were joking that he would wave me off. I didn't even know what I was doing there, I guess I was the guy who counted how many balls we had. We'd show up with twelve, I'd make sure we left with twelve. I look for two things. I look for speed and smarts because I can coach anything else.

I've got a buddy Stan, and he always says, "Potential? Potential is a word that means you can't do s**t, cause you've never once said potential in a positive way." Ever since he said that, every time I hear the word potential I've gone, "Wow," because you only use potential when someone is failing to live up to any standard you have. You will be at that coach's meeting, the kid walks in the room and he looks like a kid that should be in movies, a superhero. He's got the body, he's got the look, the style...but he can't show up to practice because of getting into trouble in English class. He's failing miserably on the academic side. He's a nightmare in the hallways. Every Monday you wait for the bad news to hit you for some stupid thing he did on the weekend. "OH, but the potential!" The best athlete I've ever coached is now the father of five and he sent me a Facebook post two years ago. He said, "You were in my face constantly, and I only appreciate it now." As a father of five, he understands what I was trying to tell him.

To an Athlete Dying Young

By A. E. Housman

The time you won your town the race
We chaired you through the market-place;
Man and boy stood cheering by,
And home we brought you shoulder-high.

Today, the road all runners come,
Shoulder-high we bring you home,
And set you at your threshold down,
Townsman of a stiller town.

Smart lad, to slip betimes away
From fields where glory does not stay,
And early though the laurel grows
It withers quicker than the rose.

Eyes the shady night has shut
Cannot see the record cut,
And silence sounds no worse than cheers
After earth has stopped the ears.

Now you will not swell the rout
Of lads that wore their honours out,
Runners whom renown outran
And the name died before the man.

So set, before its echoes fade,
The fleet foot on the sill of shade,
And hold to the low lintel up
The still-defended challenge-cup.

And round that early-laurelled head
Will flock to gaze the strengthless dead,
And find unwithered on its curls
The garland briefer than a girl's.

THEMES

The following sections contain themes repeated by multiple coaches. To save a few pages (it's already a pretty large book...), I did not include every reference possible for each theme.

Don't feel like you have to model your career after all these themes—plenty of coaches in this book hold opposing views. There is no one way to do it. BUT, it is helpful to see where top minds have converged.

I did not include sections for the questions about having Two 30-Minute Sessions a Week, or Common Traits of Their Most Successful Athletes. Those sections could go a million different ways.

If you find any other impactful themes, share them with me!

THEMES ON FIRST STEPS

GET TO KNOW EVERYONE—PRIORITIZE RELATIONSHIPS

Relationships are priority number one. Get to know your athletes and coaches, then admin, then everyone else. And the everyone else is NOT an afterthought, but a KEY part. The importance of building relationships with custodians, facility workers, and maintenance workers came up repeatedly.

Missy Mitchell-McBeth- "The people that run the school are the administrative assistants, maintenance workers, and custodians. These are the people you need to get to know and should always be treated with the utmost respect."

Mike Boyle- "Who do you need to get to know? Everyone. The equipment people, the custodians, the cooks. Get to know support staff and show them the respect they deserve. My dad was a high school principal. His second in command at the school was the head custodian and everyone knew it."

KNOW AND CALL PEOPLE BY NAME

Studying and learning names was a recommended method to have a great first encounter when getting to know everyone.

Darby Rich- "It may never affect a single win/loss, but you could literally make someone's day by unexpectedly addressing them by their name before you've ever met them. Make some time to go online and learn names and faces in the staff directory. Remember, you only get one chance to make a first impression."

Dave Nedbalek- "My time at PGC basketball taught me the importance and impact of learning and using names in conversation. The sweetest sound in any language is your own name. Instead of calling everyone coach as a cop-out, I try to learn names, families, stories, and start integrating my own family into that equation as well."

GET CLEAR EXPECTATIONS ON HOW YOU PROVIDE VALUE

Gain clarity on why you were hired and what your boss's expectations are. How do you provide value in your role? Not how YOU think you provide value; what did THEY hire you to do? Understanding this will steer your priorities.

Alan Bishop- "My first step is understanding why I'm there to begin with, meaning what is the head coach paying me to accomplish? Every organization has a different expectation out of their S&C, and our job is to bring as much value as possible to the organization within our role."

Erika Lambert– "As a new head coach at North Florida, I asked my Athletic Director what the top priority would be in rebuilding the Women's Basketball program. The answer was: recruiting. So in the midst of all the newness and the stress of everything that needed to get done, I knew to prioritize recruiting above everything else."

Victoria Saucedo– "Usually in my interview I'll ask, 'What do you need from my position that will get us closer to reaching X goal?' From there, I can better assess what matters, what the staff feels the team is lacking, and how to better communicate when those factors are being met or hindered."

Jeremy Anderson– "Was the position you took vacant because of success and that person moved on or because of failure? Lack of performance? Injuries and player health? That will answer a lot of what your first steps should be."

Darby Rich– "This may have been clearly outlined during the interview process, and you have clear direction and initiatives before you ever walk in the building. However, in those cases where you were being pursued, there may have been more recruiting of you than a detailed vision of what exactly was wanted from you. And while you may have received a healthy raise and lots of autonomy, nothing is more important than having a clearly defined set of expectations from your new boss. It will allow you to set a direct course for meeting those expectations, as well as giving your new boss a voice and assuring him/her they hired the right person."

"BE LIKE SPONGE"—ASK, OBSERVE, LISTEN

Many coaches emphasized that when you first join a new organization, it is more about information gathering than making drastic changes or trying to prove your value. Ask, observe, and listen more than you try to make noise. Changing everything right away is usually not received well. Learn your setting, learn what will actually provide the most value if changed in that setting, build trust, and then make change over time.

Fergus Connolly– "Before you can, as Bruce Lee said, 'Be Like Water,' you need to 'Be Like Sponge.' Watch and learn everything you can."

Molly Binetti– "Step back, don't try to do too much too soon, learn from the people around you, ask questions, and then gradually change things as you go."

Charlie Melton– "Rather than force the issue, he jumped on what they were doing and made a slow change every semester. Gradually by giving them what they wanted and getting a little bit of what he wanted, five years down the road it was the bulk of his program because he had gained their trust."

Steve McClain– "Early in your journey, be way more of a listener than you are a talker. Figure out—what can be my niche in this program? What do I bring that this program doesn't have, but they really need? Before you try to show everybody what you can do, learn what the situation needs out of you, and what your strengths can bring to that situation."

Andrew Wright– "Do not rock the boat. Learn. Have humility that your way of doing your new job may not be the only way and it likely was not the way that your predecessor did his job. The job and your new co-workers likely existed before you arrived and they may be at your place of work after you leave. They matter. Respect them by learning about the place that they hopefully care about before you storm an organization with new, possibly extreme, methods."

LEARN WHAT WORKED PREVIOUSLY

As you gather info, find out what worked before you arrived. It's easy to feel that your purpose is to provide *change* when first hired; no matter the situation, look to uncover positive things previously done.

Rod Olson– "Ask them two questions in your very first meeting with everybody. Write on one side of the notecard, what are the things that you love about this culture that we shouldn't change? These are staples and really impact you, and makes us who we are. On the backside of that note card, I want you to put down one or two things that we need to change right away in this culture."

Michael Zweifel– "The reality is every job has things that went well before you showed up. I want to keep as many things as similar as I can. I'd much rather have me adapt to a few things (language, structure, timing, etc.) than have all the athletes have to adapt to me."

I love the idea (this would probably apply more to head coaches) of learning from other coaches at the school/organization about how they have been successful within the context of that environment.

Marissa Young- "Reach out to the people that have been there and have had sustainable success at that institution. What is their cheat code, or what they've learned over the years to best navigate the environment that you're in?"

Beth O'Boyle- "It's helpful to talk with other sport coaches in the department and ask lots of questions. How do you sell the university, what places do you take recruits, what challenges have you faced, what have been the best parts?"

UNDERSTAND THE SOCIAL AND POWER DYNAMICS

Lastly, be intentional in learning the lay of the land and the social and power dynamics. Who are the players? Who has the power? Who can you trust to help you?

Bill Brogden- "I could figure out eventually who the good guys are and who is important and who is successful...That way you figure out what you need to do, what you can't do, what you should do, who you can bark at, who you can't bark at."

Lee Taft- "Figure out who's going to be an advocate and who's going to push-back. Run with the advocates and figure out how to engage those who'll resist."

Charlie Melton- "You've got to know who's got the juice, who's got the power, who's got the influence, who you can trust, who's going to not be trustworthy."

OVERVIEW

As you start your new job:

1. Get to know everyone—prioritize relationships.
2. Know and call people by name.
3. Get clear expectations on how you provide value.
4. "Be Like Sponge"—ask, observe, listen.
5. Learn what worked previously.
6. Understand the social and power dynamics.

THEMES ON BEST MENTORS

DON'T CHASE LOGOS OR NAMES

As you seek mentorship, do not seek fame. Do not seek name recognition. Do not seek the coolest, biggest logo. Seek the right mentor for YOU.

Eric Duft- "The best mentor is the one who cares about you the most. It doesn't always have to be a famous coach. Find someone who believes in you and wants to help you succeed. Don't worry about name recognition. Find the ones who want to help you."

Kyle Stark- "I would stress the importance of not chasing famous names or places, as some of the best are the furthest from the bright lights. Focus more on whether the person has a track record of success, is going to give you legitimate opportunities to grow and develop, and wants to pour into you while you're there."

Preston Greene- "The best mentors in the world are coaches who will hold you accountable and push you to become a better coach. It is not about the logo of the school or the team that they work with. You can take and learn something from everyone."

CHASE PEOPLE THAT INVEST IN YOU

Instead of pursuing someone because of their name, pursue a mentor that will genuinely invest in you. That is a critical aspect of the mentor-mentee relationship; the mentor has to pour into your development. They see the potential of who you can become and want to do everything in their power to get you there. They will coach you hard, they will deliver tough truths, but they will always support you and fight for you.

Greg Goldin- "Work for people who know where you are at, love you for where you are at, but also see great potential in you for who you are becoming."

Sundance Wicks- "The best mentors are the ones who care enough about you to help you grow and not just use you for their own gain. I don't care who your mentor(s) are, but pick someone who cares enough to invest in you achieving your dreams!"

Part of pouring into your development involves providing real opportunities for growth. You must earn those opportunities, but a good mentor will expose you to experiences above your comfort or capability level.

Hunter Eisenhower- "The best mentors are ones that will help you but not give you answers, challenge your thought process but understand where you are in your development. If you are working directly under them, giving you autonomy and a chance to fail. They need to be invested in your career, not just in the need of somebody to sweep the floors and refill the fridge."

ALIGN YOUR MENTOR WITH YOUR GOALS

There is no one-size-fits all mentor. As the mentee, what do you need? What are your goals? Understand the type of coach you are trying to become or the area you are trying to develop, search for the people that are the best in those lanes, and then seek them out.

Phil Beckner- "I would flip the question to a young coach, 'Who are the people in your life that have been impressive to you, that you want to be like, and have had success the right way, that you would want to follow or build a career similar to?' Go find those people because there are a lot of different ways to be successful, and too many times we just want to be with a Jay Wright at Villanova, Tom Izzo at Michigan State, Bill Self at Kansas, and they might be successful, but they might not be about what you're about."

David Lawrence- "Find out who is doing what you want to do and contact them. Offer to pay for the mentorship and if it goes well and you like them and want to learn more, apply for a job. Work for them for 3-5 years and immerse yourself. This is the fastest way to learn."

Brianne Brown- "Decide what is important to you: do you want to learn how to program the best? Do you want to learn how to use technology the best? Do you want to learn about nutrition and training? Once you answer that question—go out and find who you think does it the best and ask to pay for their time to learn."

LOOK AROUND YOU

As we discuss seeking mentorship, it doesn't have to be a grand journey to find someone. The mentors you need in your life might be right around you. Be open to mentorship from people in your immediate area.

Anson Dorrance- "I think most of us stumble on our mentors. They happen to be nearby and they happen to reach out. I've never been in a position where I've had to find a mentor. I've always been in positions where they were nearby, they were presented to me. When they reached out, I reached back."

Dan Hughes– "You need to look right in your life, and it doesn't have to be the biggest name on the page. A great mentor might be somebody who honestly cares, and who honestly will give you a reflection of truth. They probably need to have a common interest with you and have some experience that allows them to do that. You can have great mentors that could be your mother and father...Sometimes in life, we don't realize who really cares for us, and that might be your best mentor."

Joel Smith– "I believe the right help will come at the right time, as long as we are looking for it. The mentors who appeared in my life, such as Adarian Barr, did so at the time that was right for me. As the saying goes, 'When the student is ready, the master shall appear.'"

RESEARCH THEIR TRACK RECORD

One clue to identify a great mentor is to look at their history of developing coaches. Where have their past mentees gone on to coach? Have they had success when they moved on?

Andrew Nilo– "As for mentors, go to someone who has a good track record of producing quality mentees and has a good amount of skin in the game."

Sean Hayes– "Look for places that post and boast about where they've put their interns—places that are successful placing their interns, because that means they invest into their interns. That means they're investing in their education, helping them get certifications, and helping them prepare for the rigors. Ask questions to people that have worked for them. 'Hey, how was it working for Sean Hayes? Was he a complete jerk, or did he care?'"

OVERVIEW

Consider these criteria when seeking mentorship:

1. Don't chase logos or names.
2. Chase people that invest in you.
3. Align your mentor with your goals.
4. Look around you.
5. Research their track record.

THEMES ON SEEKING ADVICE

CONSTRUCT A BOARD OF DIRECTORS

Be intentional in building a personal Board of Directors in your life, a group of people you know you can always turn to for counsel and guidance.

Lee Taft– "The interesting aspect of this question is I have a Board of Directors of people who do not know they are on it. These are people in business, fitness, therapy, psychology, leadership, learning, financial, etc. that I simply read, listen to, or watch when I need help in a specific area."

Rod Olson– "We call it building your Mount Rushmore. Who are four people you can call anytime, anyplace, anywhere, and they'll take your call and speak truth into your life? They won't tell you what you want to hear. They're going to tell you what you need to hear for your life. They love you more than they care about your career."

Sundance Wicks– "I believe you should have a circle of 3-5 'Accurate Observers' in your life—those people who see you daily or you stay connected to more regularly than anyone else in this life. They must truly know you and know your soul and your story."

Phil Beckner– "You need someone personally, spiritually, life wise working with you; you need someone professionally, leadership wise working with you; then you need a couple people who you could trust and you could work through things together."

Joey Burton– "I have a board of advisors that I can go to regarding different aspects of life." (Spiritual/Personal mentor, a Professional mentor, and a Financial mentor)

Connor Schoepp– "In my mind, I have formed a group of people that I consider to be my council. This group is made up of people from different backgrounds, sports, experiences, and personalities. I choose them because I believe in them as people. They are genuine, honest, and have accomplished things I hope to do one day."

FIT THE PERSON TO THE TOPIC

Many coaches echoed the importance of seeking specific people for specific topics.

Joel Smith– "It depends on the advice, as I have different coaches I look for guidance on in different areas...Each of these individuals has a lifetime of honing their craft, and I highly respect the wisdom they have to offer."

Brett Bartholomew- "I don't have 1-2 'sages' that I go to for everything. Instead, I recommend that coaches build robust social capital and have a diverse range of people with varying levels of expertise, and also ensure they get around people from a wide range of professions. When you only seek the advice of a few people instead of a council, and you close yourself off to those of varying backgrounds and levels of expertise, you subsequently limit your perspective. Diversify. Diversify. Diversify."

Chuck Martin- "It depends, what is it that I'm looking for? What advice, what arena, what route, who is it, what's the topic?"

Mike Niklos- "During my internship at RMU, Todd Hamer's advice resonated with me: 'You don't need to be an expert at everything, but you do need the experts' phone numbers.' I've since tried to build a network of experts whom I can consult for advice on specific training, coaching, or technique styles."

Let's combine these two themes: Construct a Board of Directors filled with mentors that each guide you in specific areas of your life. As Brett Bartholomew said, "Diversify." One person might provide incredible guidance in a certain area, yet questionable advice in another. Understand who to go to, but also what to go to them for.

BUILD YOUR OWN PERSONAL BOARD OF DIRECTORS:

1. List out the key areas of your life that you seek advice and mentorship in.

2. List out the people you typically go to for advice.

3. Match each one of those people to one of the key areas of your life.

4. Is each area sufficiently covered? Or does one area, say Professional, have four mentors, while Financial has zero?

5. Assess where you need more formal guidance. Determine if there is someone you can "place" on your Board of Directors, or if you need to seek a new relationship to fill this spot.

6. The goal is to have key mentors in place for each impactful area of your life—your personal Board of Directors.

OTHER FREQUENTLY LISTED ANSWERS

· Faith/God.

· Family.

· Mentors.

· People that have been in similar situations.

OVERVIEW

When seeking advice:

1. Construct a Board of Directors.

2. Fit the person to the topic.

THEMES ON PIVOTAL EARLY JOBS

NON-COACHING JOBS

One overwhelming theme I did not expect to find when adding this question: many coaches listed an early job completely unrelated to coaching.

These jobs were pivotal not because of where they got them, but because of *what they taught them.* A pivotal job is not always the one that launches your rise in the coaching ranks. Sometimes it's a job you work long before you know you want to coach, but it is still preparing you to be the person you need to be to succeed.

HIGH LEVELS OF RESPONSIBILITY

An early job with high levels of responsibility—levels the coach was probably not ready for—is another major theme. These jobs were typically at smaller colleges, high schools, or middle schools. Again, these jobs were not pivotal because they were major résumé builders, but because of what they taught them. The skills they had to learn, duties they had to grow into, mistakes they were allowed to make—along with the understanding of how the many pieces of the puzzle fit together for success.

Jack Harbaugh– "My first job in 1961 in Canton, Ohio, as an Elementary Physical Education Teacher and Junior High School Football, Basketball, and Track Coach with only volunteers for help. I had to do it all—no assistants, very little administrative help, and plenty of mistakes—but working to learn and adjust every day on the job was invaluable."

Drew Long– "At that level you don't have a large staff, so you have to do everything. Recruiting, scouting, travel arrangements, expense reports, weight training, on court coaching, part-time academic advisor...you name it, I had to do it. It gave me a crash course in what coaching was all about and really challenged me to get out of my comfort zone."

Rod Olson– "I think my work ethic and my mindset were formed at that NAIA small college level where you have to do everything. It's no different than an entrepreneur or starting out as a strength coach where you're doing every sport, and I think that gives you such an advantage when you have to be a jack of all trades."

WORKING CAMPS

Similar to working at smaller schools, several coaches listed working camps as a critical piece of their development. Camps also allow for high levels of responsibility and coaching reps at a young age.

Brendan Suhr- "In the summers, I would work in basketball camps as a coach. That's how I learned how to coach. When I was 19 years old, I was working at the great Five Star Basketball Camp, which was the best basketball camp in the country. I was coaching players two years younger than me, and they were high school All-Americans. That helped me learn to connect very early with very talented guys."

Kyle Stark- "Coaching summer camps as you had to do everything, had to nail organization, and got tons of free reps coaching kids and figuring out what works and does not."

Michael Zweifel- "My dad was a college football coach and I would coach youth camps while in HS and then MS and HS camps when I was in college. I got to get my hands dirty at a young age and get a lot of exposure to coaching various levels of athletes at a young age."

SURROUNDED BY ELITE COACHES

Working around high-level people and mentors is another often cited aspect of a pivotal early job.

Fergus Connolly- "Rule 1: Early in your career is find the best Coach to work for. Later you can worry about finding the best team or club, but starting out find the best coach."

Zack Zillner- "The fact that I was there with Andrea Hudy, who is arguably the best basketball strength coach in the world, that's insane...If I didn't have that Kansas internship, I don't know where I'd be right now, probably selling insurance or something."

Jason Martinez- "Coach Ryan Horn is the best there is. The opportunity to be a sponge next to a coach and human like him every day is something I'm forever grateful for. It changed the trajectory of my career and life in the best possible way."

REVEALS WHAT YOU DON'T WANT

Lastly, some coaches listed a job because it showed them what they *didn't* want to do with their life, or who they didn't want to become as a coach.

Chad Gatzlaff– "I was working for a Fortune 500 company and had my first salary job. They were expecting me to work 60-hour weeks...and that was normal. I hated the people, I hated the work, and in that job I really started to dream about what I love. If normal was working 60 hours a week, then I wanted my normal to be FUN, EXCITING, and something I wanted to do forever!"

Debbie Hill– "That year away caused me to think a lot about who I wanted to be as a coach, who I wanted to be as a human being, and what I wanted athletes to experience through sport. I had to experience a job that, almost right away, I realized was not a fit for me and what my values were. It certainly was a defining moment."

Pat Davidson– "The most pivotal jobs I ever had were working in a grocery store, doing landscaping, and working in wholesale fish sales. Those jobs sucked so much that I knew I didn't want to work them or anything like them for the rest of my life. It motivated me to read, write, train, and work hard with my mind."

A FEW THOUGHTS ON EARLY JOBS

Here are a few thoughts to consider when choosing the first couple jobs of your career:

- Hopefully you had a job that required hard, monotonous work that instilled habits that translate to success in the everyday life of coaching. This job might have even given you the clarity or motivation to find something more purposeful to you, like coaching.

- Find the place you get to coach the most and have the most responsibility. Find the place where you are going to be required to do things you don't know how to do, and then go figure out how to do those things.

- Along with searching for responsibility, search for the best coaches to work for. As **Fergus Connolly** stated, "Rule 1: Early in your career is find the best Coach to work for. Later you can worry about finding the best team or club, but starting out find the best coach."

- Sometimes finding the best coach to work for means not having a lot of responsibility at first. I believe you need both early on, but they don't have to be at the same time. **Marissa Young** echoed some great thoughts on this:

"Find the right balance of getting in as a GA or student manager in a great program where you can learn in a successful environment, but also being in a place where maybe you're not as historically successful, but you have a lot of responsibility. You have your hands in a lot of different things that are going to give you the experience that you need to be successful. You're not going to know what you don't know until that responsibility is on your shoulders. But I also think being in a place where you have quality examples and role models, where you've been able to see people navigate the difficult things ahead of you, is really important."

- If working for a top coach, be the most curious and attentive person in the room, like **Bill Brogden** when he started out at Duke. "I took notes every day—what I liked at practice and what I didn't like, what they did say and what they didn't say. I had a suitcase full of notes from every day for a year and a half." Ask questions every day. Learn the principles of how they think and make decisions. Apply what you are learning to mock material (practice/player development plans, program design, annual plans, drawing up plays, etc.). Then, take all the knowledge you learn and go find a job with tons of responsibility. Apply what you learned, struggle, make adjustments, struggle, and then continue to refine. This process will help shape who YOU are as a coach instead of just who your first boss is.

- Working with tons of responsibility first and then going to work for a great coach has immense value as well. Because of the struggles you will face, the first experience helps create an awareness of what you need to learn and where your gaps are. If you have the awareness to identify these gaps, this can help determine who the best coach to work for is—ideally someone who is incredible in those areas. Find this coach, work with them, uncover how they operate in these areas, and then implement that new knowledge into your coaching.

- In an ideal world, you get to work for the best coach with high levels of responsibility. This could be in the same job (not likely in the beginning of your career), or you could get a job on the side where you get high levels of responsibility while still learning from the top coach. This allows you to take the knowledge you are learning from the coach and put it immediately into action. You'll get immediate feedback on what works and what doesn't, while still having the ability to go back to your coach to learn and receive guidance. This creates a rapid cycle of feedback and implementation. If you learn something from your coach and implement it the same week, observe what works and what fails, and then seek feedback, *that creates powerful and sustained learning.*

THEMES ON JOB DECISIONS

4 P'S

Job decisions are never easy, with countless variables to consider often leading to uncertainty and sleepless nights. Multiple coaches recommended using the 4P's developed by Keir Wenham-Flatt (or some variation close to it) to gain clarity in these decisions.

Scott Kuehn- "Keir Wenham-Flatt boiled down career decisions to 4 P's: Pay, Progression, Personal life, and Purpose. Pay—obvious financial compensation, but also hidden value of time demands and supporting human resources of the job, and ability to earn additional streams of income. Progression—does the opportunity move you up or down the career ladder relative to your professional goals? Personal Life—does the job add or remove from your ability to exist in the ways you want to outside of the job? Purpose—does the job give you meaningful direction and alignment with your morals and principles? If you've got all 4, you're in the dream job and should never leave; 3 out of 4, only leave for the dream job; 2 out of 4, you should be actively looking; anything less than 2 out of 4, what are you doing there?"

Greg Goldin- "First step is to read the list below and rank them for yourself, or if you are married, rank them with your partner.

- Purpose—Does what I do matter?
- People—Am I surrounded by good people?
- Personal—Do I have enough time to do the things I want to do personally?
- Professional—Am I getting better professionally?
- Pay—Can I pay my bills and save some money?
- Place—Do I like where I live?

If you have a job with 1, 2, or 3, you actively look for a job with 4. If you have 4, you are slowly yet deliberately looking for a job with 5. If you have a job with 5 you are lucky. If you have a job with 6, you never leave. After you rank them, maybe you have 4, but maybe you only have the bottom 4 of your ranking—you will most likely still be unfulfilled. These will also change throughout your life and different seasons of life."

DON'T MESS WITH HAPPY

If you're looking for a more instinctual, less systematic approach, another repeated mantra was, "Don't mess with happy."

Darby Rich- "There's an old saying, 'Don't F with happiness,' and if you are at a place in your career where money is no longer the driving force, the logo on your polo is not nearly as important as the time spent with your family."

Sundance Wicks- "Happiness—don't mess with happy."

Alan Bishop- "Remember that if you're happy in the job you've got, don't be quick to mess with happy."

THE MORNING DRIVE TO WORK

Conversely, you can use negative feelings about heading to work as a signal that it's time to go. If you dread going to sleep because that makes the morning come faster, it might be time to consider a change.

Connor Agnew- "The drive to work. If my thoughts are overly negative every morning I drive to work, it's time to find a new job."

Charlie Weingroff- "First and foremost if you dread going to work, those voices almost never get softer, so that 100% is the most important thing in leaving."

Miranda Holder- "Am I doing the job out of duty and obligation or from a place of energizing joy? This is critical in coaching, but any job goes better if you are there because it's the right one for you."

WHO

Next, WHO you work for, WHO you work with, and the alignment you have with the people writing your checks were all listed as critical factors.

Kyle Stark- "The BOSS (most people quit their boss, not their job)...WHO you are doing it with (as the what will never outweigh the WHO)."

Eric Duft- "The number one thing is alignment with the administration. If that is strong, then it's hard to leave. If it's not, then you better get out."

Tom Crean- "You've got to make decisions based on people that you know you're going to be working with. Are they going to support you in all that they're doing and that you're doing?"

GROWTH POTENTIAL

Growth potential is another key consideration. How will this new position help you and your career grow? That is not always measured in dollar bills. It can take the form of new skills, knowledge, connections, mentors, or even the ability to get the NEXT job.

Colton Rosseau- "I want my knowledge, my influence, and my salary to continue to grow throughout my career. Once I feel my potential for growth in these areas is limited, I know it is time for me to consider other options."

Steve McClain- "Am I going to learn a new system? Am I going to learn a different way of how to run a program? Every time you make a move, you should be able to justify two or three ways that it's going to help you grow as you're preparing to be a head coach. How is this helping me get to my ultimate goal of being a head coach? What am I going to learn differently in this situation? If I can't answer that question, then I shouldn't be making the move. You never want to make a move just to make a move. It has to be about growth...Even when you make the move as a head coach, is it going to allow me growth?"

Anthony Cockrill- "Growth Potential, which is a broad idea but the idea on Growth Potential was a driving factor in my move to SMU. Dallas is one of the fastest growing cities in the country, SMU is heavily invested in Athletics, for as long as I remember had been rumored to be possibly moving to a P5 conference (now happening), and what seems like the best donor support in the country. If you view these moves like investing in companies, SMU at the time was early 2000s Amazon. Obvious risk, but the potential reward outweighs the risk."

CAREER PERIODIZATION

The last thing to consider is that your key decision-making factors will evolve based on the stage of your career. Multiple coaches described making decisions based on climbing the ladder when they were young, but now they make decisions to prioritize their family. Understand what period of life you are in, who you are responsible for, and how that aligns with your goals—then decide accordingly.

Darby Rich– "Early in my career, all job-movement decisions were based around money or career advancement. Who could pay me the most, or how would this job position me to move on to my next one? After getting married and having kids, every decision now revolves around what is best for our family. Is the HC someone who will allow my boys to be around the gym or in the facility? Will my wife be happy around the other wives? Is it in a great community with excellent schools?"

Dominick Walker– "At first it was the motif of 'climbing the ladder' but now, as I get older, it's more about what's the best fit for me and my family."

OVERVIEW

When faced with leaving or staying, consider these factors:

1. The 4P's.
2. Don't mess with happy.
3. The morning drive to work.
4. Who you work with and for / Alignment.
5. Growth Potential.
6. Career Periodization.

THEMES ON OVERCOMING BURNOUT, STRUGGLE, AND OVERWHELM

DON'T ASSUME RESILIENCE

The story of Navy Seal Job Price hit me incredibly hard when delivered by **Rod Olson**: "'Job was the poster child for Navy SEALs. He was the toughest guy. He was the most skilled guy. He was a brilliant commander. We all thought he'd be an admiral some day and maybe Medal of Honor. He was the guy Rod. Every time they called him for a mission, he took it and he crushed it, and so did his team.' I go, 'Why did he kill himself?' He goes, 'Exactly...Exactly.' I asked him, 'So what's the biggest lesson you've learned in all this?' He answered, 'We've learned that even with the toughest warfighters in the world, with any kind of human, you can't assume resilience.' I think the great piece of advice here for coaches is—don't assume resilience. Don't assume that you can just keep not showing up at night, and having your wife or your spouse handle all the little kids. Don't assume she's that resilient. We've all got our breaking points. We all do."

Don't assume resilience—in others or in yourself. No matter your training. No matter your toughness. You still have a breaking point.

LEARN YOUR INDICATORS

After accepting that you can't assume resilience, start to learn and recognize the patterns, warning signs, or indicators that you're breaking down.

Rod Olson- "Figure out—what are the indicators or the yellow flags that you're starting to not be resilient? You're starting to not recover. You're starting to deplete... Everybody's gotta figure out what their own indicators are. What's your own kryptonite?"

Jorge Carvajal- "The first thing to do is to recognize what's happening—awareness is everything. Once again I reference Patrick Lencioni's *Three Signs Of A Miserable Job*. In the first burnout, I didn't recognize the three signs immediately, but I was living them every day, until I was so miserable and suffering from so many physical symptoms that I broke down—mentally, physically and spiritually...The second time I immediately recognized them."

POUR INTO OTHERS THROUGH YOUR OVERFLOW

Coaching is a service industry. Most of us coach to impact the lives of others, but this can evolve into sacrificing yourself until you have nothing left to give. It may seem counter to your mission of service, but pouring into yourself allows you to give even more to others.

Phil Beckner– "If you are ever feeling burnout, usually what's happening is you're pouring into everyone else except yourself. You have to pour into yourself, you have to fuel yourself because the best way to pour into others is through your overflow."

DRAW YOUR PIRATE MAP

Dan John's pirate map is an incredible framework for pouring into yourself:

"I put together a pirate map with all the essential things that would help me live a longer and more impactful life. The first thing I do is I sit down and I say, 'Is this the Dan John who Dan John said he wanted to be?' Kind of a weird sentence, but I said I was gonna exercise every day, I was gonna walk every day, I was gonna eat vegetables every meal. I was gonna make a difference. I was gonna do my to do list, make the coffee, meditate. Did I do those things?"

That is a powerful question. *"Is this the Dan John who Dan John said he wanted to be?"* Determine what is important to you in life, who you want to be, and then check for alignment every day. When you get away from the things you said you would do is when things start to break down.

Dan John went on to say, "Why am I suddenly not doing those things? Because of the stress of work. Okay, what will help me with my stress? Well, if I meditate, if I eat better, if I lift weights, if I go for a walk, all those things will help me deal with stress. Oh."

Start identifying the people, habits, or activities that can become part of your pirate map. Multiple other coaches listed their own pirate map without calling it that:

Tim Doyle– "My personal therapies are: journaling, working out, meditating, reading, and listening to music. Also, a 12-pack of Bud."

Tony Holler– "Reading and Running. When I am struggling, I'm always missing reading and running in my life."

Matt Aldred– "I have a checklist of daily tasks on my office wall that changes depending on the time of the year (early off-season, pre-season, in-season, etc.). Two things that are always on there—family check in and outside time."

Brett Bartholomew– "I turn to things I cannot turn into work. I get outside, sit in a hot tub, spend time with my son, and turn off my phone."

Thomas Lené– "I also get out in nature. Sit on the dock and read and write. Relax in the grass. Soak up the sun. Simply put, JUST SLOW DOWN."

MAKE YOUR OWN PIRATE MAP

1. What are five things you need to do every day to be the (your name) that (your name) said they were going to be?

2. Write these five things down.

3. Put the list somewhere you see every day (Mirror, bedside, car...).

4. During times of burnout, struggle, or overwhelm, come back to your pirate map to get back on track.

5. You can share your list with someone close to keep you accountable.

CREATE ALIGNMENT WITH WHAT'S REALLY IMPORTANT

Brett Ledbetter's book *What's Really Important* examines the struggles many highly successful coaches face when sacrificing what they value in a sprint for greatness, chasing the accomplishments that the world will applaud. Why do coaches experience depression or feel unfulfilled after winning national championships? Ledbetter highlights the need to be intentional every day in striving to align who you say you want to be with who your actions show you are. Do your stated values match what your actions demonstrate is important in your life?

Reflecting on this was a big part of my decision to leave working in collegiate athletics. I realized aspects of my life did not align with who I say I want to be and what I say is important in my life. *"Am I being the John Bloom that John Bloom said he was going to be?"* I say I value family, yet how many memories will I miss when I have children? How many events will I miss because I don't know my schedule until the week (or day) before, and we might have a recruiting visit? Do I want our family to constantly move across the country? I say I coach to impact my athletes' lives through relationships, yet things feel more and more transactional each day with the transfer

THEMES ON OVERCOMING BURNOUT, STRUGGLE, AND OVERWHELM

portal and NIL. *My own thoughts and internal feelings feel more transactional. I DON'T LIKE THAT.* When I look at the man, husband, and father I want to be in the future, is this the right setting to be that person?

I had a conversation with Kyle Stark about how to keep alignment between what we say we value and what we actually value. His answer was simple, yet profound. When looking at your values, have you truly integrated them? Are those values the lens that you view EVERYTHING through? Do you really believe this? Better yet, are you willing to be fired for this? *Do you make every decision with the thought, "Does this align with my values?"*

If you aren't making decisions and evaluating life through the lens of your values, then one of three things is true: you don't truly believe they matter that much, you aren't truthful in the order that they matter in your life, or you need to grab your pirate map and get back to those values. I believe burnout, struggle, and overwhelm occur more from too much work without purpose and alignment, rather than simply just too much work. Obviously there is a line where it can become too much work. But in many cases, if you are living your values through your work with complete alignment and purpose, struggles seem to minimize themselves.

Sundance Wicks– "Burnout happens when you do something you are not passionate about. I don't get burned out because I stay on fire for my vocation. If you are doing something because you absolutely love it and you have an insane amount of passion for it, then burnout doesn't exist."

Steve McClain– "The day it's not fun, I won't coach. The pressure will eat you up if you can't enjoy pieces of it. Somebody told me this once, and it's very true—in coaching, we don't enjoy the wins, because we're always worried about the next game. If you get to where you can't even enjoy the wins, then it means the job is eating you up. At some point, you've got to sit back and truly enjoy the wins. Enjoy the process of the wins, because it is a process. The more you can do that, then you won't have burnout. You'll walk in everyday excited to do what you do. That may sound too simple, but life's too short. You have to enjoy the process of it."

Molly Binetti– "What ultimately helped me was getting really clear on who I was while shifting my perspective on my job and what's important and what isn't."

Draw your pirate map, stick to it, and let your cup overflow with passion and purpose to impact those around you.

OTHER FREQUENTLY LISTED STRATEGIES

Here are some other highly recommended strategies throughout the book that may bleed into your pirate map:

- Faith and prayer.
- Spend time with your family.
- Mix up your routine and environment.
- Talk to other coaches about what you are going through.
- Have people in your life that can check your pulse and know when you are struggling.
- Set boundaries and learn to say no.
- Go outside and get into nature.

OVERVIEW

1. Don't assume resilience.
2. Learn your indicators.
3. Pour into others through your overflow.
4. Draw your pirate map.
5. Create alignment with what's really important.

THEMES ON INJURIES

SUPPORT THE ATHLETE MENTALLY

The athlete's mental state is always priority number one. Do not allow your focus on the process to cloud your view of *the person*. Like **Alan Bishop** said, "Remember that injuries can really mess with people. REALLY mess with people." Don't underestimate that. The psychological damage can weigh as heavy as the physical damage.

Zack Zillner- "I tore my Achilles a year and a half ago. My whole identity is being active. Run, lift, I'm always doing something. For that to be taken away, it was like a part of me was gone. I'm like, 'Dude, you're 33 and you're struggling with this, like my life's over for the next eight weeks.' Hopefully I'm more emotionally mature than an 18 or 19-year-old with an actual pro future ahead of them. I think we dismiss the mental side of things with athletes getting hurt, and they think their whole livelihood and career is done."

Charlie Melton- "One of the best things that's ever happened to me as a coach is knowing what it's like to be healthy, and knowing what it's like to have everything snatched away."

I can't think about ANYTHING else when I have an injury—big or small. And I am far from being a competitive athlete anymore. Think about how injuries can leak into all aspects of your life and consume you—your thoughts, your movement, the activities you can participate in. Now think about the mental impact when it is a person's entire career. The way they feed their family. The way they go to college. Where so much of their identity lies. Do not downplay that. Support *the person* above everything else.

Hunter Eisenhower- "Early after an injury, it's more important to take care of the athlete's psychology than their physiology. It takes time to process an injury, and shoving your RTP plan down their throat might set you back more than you know from a trust and buy in perspective."

Beth O'Boyle- "First piece is checking in and asking how they feel, what they need, and trying to stay very in the moment with them. Not on to the next part of practice or the game—in that moment, really listen and show care."

Anthony Cockrill– "My initial reaction is always a feeling of empathy for the athlete. Understand that more often than not, sport is the driving force in their current life. Serious injury is a life-altering event for any human, but it is magnified as an athlete."

DO NOT LET THE ATHLETE DRIFT AWAY

It's natural to prioritize supporting your athlete in the initial period after injury, but as time passes...responsibilities flood your schedule...it's easy to let the athlete drift from your focus.

Debbie Hill tells a powerful story about one of those times:

"I just lost track of her. I would call her and things like that, but here's the thing—she remembered none of that...She said she felt abandoned and that it was very painful for her emotionally and physically...That was a learning experience for me. I thought I had done what she needed. I did not...You can't be too careful taking care of the injured athlete's emotional AND physical needs."

Be there for them in the moments outside of their rehab and sport. Create check in systems for both the immediacy of the injury AND for the long-term rehab process.

Tim Doyle– "The following days and weeks are about establishing a support structure for that athlete. Consistent check-ins, spending time with them in the training room or at PT, going with them to appointments, ensuring they feel the same level of support and personal attachment even when their on-court abilities have been temporarily taken away. I find it's helpful to involve teammates, too. I remember we had two athletes suffer ACL injuries within three weeks of one another. We came up with a letter-writing chain where each girl with an ACL injury would receive two letters a week from two of her teammates (different each week) expressing what she meant to the team, how important she was, and words of encouragement. It's a program-wide effort to keep that person feeling valued."

Chad Gatzlaff– "I try to go to all doctor's appointments because you never know when it is going to hit them the hardest."

Erika Lambert– "I'm well aware of the increased chances of clinical depression among athletes with serious injuries, so I think it's important that coaches don't let kids on the IR list fade into the background."

CREATE A NEW ROLE FOR THE ATHLETE

Along with ensuring support and check-ins, find a way to give the athlete a new role. ENGAGE them with the team.

Stephanie Desmarais- "If it's career changing, I make it a point to continue to reach out to them throughout the season and to help solidify a new role for them on the team. It is important to make sure they still feel like they are a part of the team. They need to feel like they are still wanted and needed on the team."

Assisting with leading game day warm-ups is a role I have found meaningful to athletes. It offers a responsibility within the competition environment beyond just cheering, and their teammates usually provide lots of encouragement and hype to them throughout the warm up.

PERFORM AN AUTOPSY WITHOUT BLAME

The most common thought that immediately haunts our mind is, "What could I have done differently?" This question is often laced with guilt. But you should ask that question not to blame yourself, but to better yourself. Use it to drive your efforts in doing EVERYTHING in your power to help that athlete return to playing the sport they love. Use it to assess and adjust your program to be even better for all of your athletes. As **Matt Aldred** said, "Do an autopsy without blame."

Andrew Wright- "It is a simple fix to place blame. However, there is often not any one factor that should be held responsible unless utter negligence has occurred...If questions as to 'why' the injury occurred, speculation doesn't do anyone any favors in formal conversations. It occurred. It's unfortunate. But, it's part of athletics and, aside from negligence, there is no use in placing responsibility towards anyone."

I love this 24-hour rule offered by **Missy Mitchell-McBeth:**

"I give myself the same 24-hour pouting window that my good friend and G.O.A.T. athletic trainer Val Hairson gave to our athletes. After the 24 hours have expired, we no longer focus on the injury, only the recovery."

Sean Hayes: "If you start blaming yourself, getting negative, and overthinking it—you're doing your team a disservice. If you start over-correcting, your athletes are smart. They'll be like, 'What is this guy doing?'"

Improve your processes, improve your program, but don't sit in guilt. That doesn't help anyone. Take the next step to audit your program and decision-making with the mindset **Scott Kuehn** offers, "A delicate balance of introspection and acceptance of uncontrollable factors."

Jeremy Anderson- "I stay process oriented. Audit what happened, try to understand why, and then try to improve in any areas I found that were lacking or deficient."

Colton Rosseau- "I sometimes also have a peer assess my program and ask for their input on any potential blind spots I may have. After that re-examination, I will try to rationally determine if a change in volume, intensity, or exercise selection is necessary."

WHAT CAN WE DO NOW?

After auditing your program and decision making, get to *WHAT CAN WE DO NOW?*

Henry Barrera- "I operate on a 3D process that I've been working on for a while. Discover, Develop, and Deliver. Learn as much as possible about the injury and recovery process, develop a plan of action, and deliver that on a day-to-day basis."

Steve McClain- "We have to worry about how we are going to get better every day. You try to turn what is a negative situation in the beginning into, 'Okay, now we gotta get ready to grow.' How are we going to grow and get better from this and not let it become a crutch that holds us back even farther?"

Jason Martinez- "We shift our focus on what the athlete CAN do and not on what they CAN'T do."

CREATE CLARITY

As we support the athlete, engage them with the team, and put a plan in place, also create clarity. What does progress actually look like? I've seen athletes go through rehab, do the same things every day, not know why they are doing them or what they are trying to achieve, and become mentally disengaged. Part of why athletes love sports is because of the competitiveness, the goals, the accomplishments. We can still provide those aspects for the athlete. Create a space for them to not think about their limitations, but to work hard and FEEL progress, to feel one step closer to returning.

Philip Farmer- "In those moments, that's where I love being a coach. I enjoy being there for them and picking them up. Helping a player get from A to B, helping them improve, helping them gain confidence and overcome tough times in their careers. From tough losses, to setbacks, to even injuries, that's where I thrive in lifting them up and being there for them. Keeping them upbeat and positive while looking at the big picture of where we're going. Let's find a solution to the problem. Let's come up with some new goals and let's stay positive."

Phil Beckner- "We're providing clarity, and then we could develop this mindset, this confidence, this relentless work ethic within that framework. Having a plan for that kid and showing them—that increases hope, that increases confidence, that allows them to not feel left out."

Lee Taft- "It's about how can we get this athlete's mindset off the injury and into training mode so they feel competitive still and like they are working towards something."

HELP YOUR TEAM OVERCOME THAT MOMENT AND RECALIBRATE

The last theme relates most closely to head coaches. As the head coach, it is their responsibility to focus on preparing the team to win after the initial jolt of the injury. Despite their internal feelings, they must inspire confidence and belief in the team while making tactical adjustments. Does that mean they don't care about the athlete or are cold-hearted? Of course not. But they have a responsibility to every other member of that team to help them overcome that moment.

Tom Crean- "You immediately have to be cognizant of how you look, how you sound. That doesn't mean you're not concerned. I've had to get a team going again, and I had tears in my eyes. That's part of it. You have got to give them a belief that the rest of them can still win, that the rest of them can still do what they have to do, that the player is in a position to be helped because of the medical staff. This is what we have to do. You've got to get them there because they're all concerned too, if they care about the teammate. You have to get them back focused on the task at hand."

Eric Duft- "The mindset better be one of strength and confidence, no matter how you actually feel. The team will pick up on any doubts that the leader has."

Tim Doyle– "'Continue mission.' There's no good time for it to happen. And when it does, our team always has something 'more important' in that moment for them to focus on. The team comes first. So I encourage everyone to press pause, get their mind right, then be ready to step back up to the plate and take action. There will come a time after the 'mission' to sympathize, spend time with, and exhibit our compassion. But not in that moment."

OVERVIEW

In the painful times of injury:

1. Support the athlete mentally.

2. Do not let the athlete drift away—create touchpoints from you and the team.

3. Create a new role for the athlete.

4. Perform an autopsy without blame and make adjustments if needed.

5. What can we do now? Create an action plan to help the athlete return better than before.

6. Create clarity in the rehab process—create new goals, new milestones; let them be competitive and WORK HARD.

7. If it is your role, help your team overcome that moment and recalibrate.

THEMES ON DIFFICULT CONVERSATIONS

DIRECT, HONEST, AND ASAP

You read it over and over—have these conversations as soon as possible and be direct and honest.

Brianne Brown– "Being direct and honest is the best way to go about difficult conversations. Some of the best advice I've been given is to speak to facts, not feelings."

Dominick Walker– "James Baldwin said, 'Not everything that is faced can be changed, but nothing can be changed until it is faced.' Difficult conversations are a part of life, so if they need to be had then we have to engage. Of course, how I go about them will be different depending on the person, but I tend to have difficult conversations as soon as possible. You don't want that feeling to linger."

Jon McDowell– "The best way to have difficult conversations is to address them head-on, as soon as it happens. The worst can be when things build up over time, then someone explodes and the entire situation unfolds badly."

UNDERSTAND THE LONG-TERM CONSEQUENCES OF DELAYING

No matter how many times it was repeated to immediately face these conversations with directness and honesty...it doesn't make DOING that any easier. Remind yourself—how much worse will the situation become if I choose the temporary relief of delaying the conversation versus having the courage to face the discomfort?

Erika Lambert– "If there's a talk that needs to happen but I really am not looking forward to it, I try to remember what things will look like in a week or two, or a month or two, if I don't do the hard thing. Author Brene Brown calls these meetings 'Rumbles.' As the boss of my small company, I have to be intentional about rumbling."

Fergus Connolly– "The longer you leave something unsaid, the more combinations and permutations your mind runs through. Most are inaccurate and just speculative. With that time and speculation comes pressure you're only putting on yourself. You end up making mountains out of molehills."

Sean Hayes– "If you don't have that conversation and you avoid it, there is a bomb waiting around the corner."

Joel Smith– "The older I get, the more I realize that we often get tied up in inter-webs of comfort and fear of potential pain. Oftentimes we are sharing those chains in some way, and communicating our problems sets us free. So often, the difficult conversation is a gateway to leveling up a relationship, as well as one's own abilities and belonging in the workplace."

APPROACH WITH EMPATHY

As you find the courage to face these conversations directly, approach with empathy. Do not approach with brutality in the name of honesty. You will get much further using honesty AND empathy together.

Rod Olson– "The first question we have to ask to make sure we put ourselves in an empathetic state is, 'What's it like to meet with me right now?' What's it like to be pulled in by the head coach and be reprimanded? What's it like to miss four workouts and now he might kick me off the team? What's it like to get a DUI and now I have to meet with the head coach? I'll do it with my wife in the middle of a disagreement. We've been married for almost 35 years and in the middle of the conversation, I'll think to myself, 'What's it like to argue with me right now?' Because I'm an ass. I don't want to lose when I get into those situations."

Tom Crean– "It's really hard to be a leader. But if you don't have empathy, if you don't have conviction of what you're doing, if you're not flexible enough to change, if you can't look across the table and see their point of view—it doesn't mean you accept it, but you have to see it. If you can't confront and demand, you will not be a leader for very long."

David Lawrence– "I usually start with empathy for the other person. I try to be as calm and direct as possible and ask questions and listen. I have had to let go of many people from our organization and that is never fun. But be direct and to the point. Having compassion for the other person in the room is very important."

RELATIONSHIPS MAKE THESE TALKS EASIER

This is something you probably all instinctively know but is still worth repeating: the better the relationship you have with the other person, the easier and more productive the conversation will run.

Sundance Wicks– "Become a truth teller by first establishing a trustworthy connection with those under your supervision or care. It sounds cliché, but there can be no correction without first a connection."

Steve McClain- "If you have a relationship, difficult conversations aren't difficult. Difficult conversations usually become easy once the other person knows you care about them and you're only trying to help them."

Approaching the conversation with the mindset of "We" instead of "Me/You" will also lead to greater results. When we think with the lens of "We," success looks like *both* sides succeeding, while "Me/You" typically results in one winner and one loser (or two losers).

Andrew Wright- "'We' and 'Us' always instead of 'You.' We walk this walk with whomever we speak, if it's a conversation worth having. If we didn't care about them, we likely would not have the conversation to begin with."

Jeremy Anderson- "I always try to approach conflict or difficult conversations as US against the problem, not me vs you. 90% of the time this re-shifts the focus to a solutions oriented approach instead of who is right or wrong."

Let's get into six practical strategies to use before and during these difficult conversations:

STEP BACK AND REMOVE EMOTION

Molly Binetti- "Our ego gets involved and clouds judgment sometimes, and it's easy to get mad if something's not the way that you want it to be. But just take a deep breath, let it die down, and approach the situation when you're in a better state of mind, coming from a place of curiosity and a place of trying to find the solution to the problem."

Steven Greek- "It is important not to communicate when one or both parties are angry or upset or emotional. We have a 24-hour rule in our program that encourages athletes, parents, coaches, and leaders to get a good night's sleep, gather their thoughts, and set up a time to visit in person or by phone to share what is on their heart."

Evan VanBecelaere- "The passion behind coaching is a good thing, but our passions can quickly influence our emotions. When emotions drive your decisions, your clarity for what you want to get out of the conversation becomes muddled."

DO YOUR HOMEWORK / COME WITH DATA

Anson Dorrance– "Most of my player conference is done with data, so it's very easy. Numbers that are data driven aren't my personal opinions. It's what the kid has achieved in practice. Since everything we do is data driven, it's me and the player against the data. This way, the player feels fully supported. So the hard conversation—a player conference based on opinion—is completely stripped away."

Ethan Gold– "For lack of a better way of putting it, do your homework. Ask around, 'How is this athlete/coach/coworker viewed? Who do they hangout with?' Understand that listening and paying attention to the ones you're trying to communicate with is pivotal to the success of any hard conversation."

LEAN ON ESTABLISHED EXPECTATIONS

Tim Doyle– "With ANYONE, I find these conversations easiest when falling back on a previously established expectation or standard, explicitly defined. This is why group sessions on culture and leadership are so important. When I can bring an athlete in and say, 'Go to page 3. See what the position expectations are? And the criteria for me making a decision? How can I go against that?' It makes the conversation much easier."

Mike Niklos– "It's essential to establish trust, respect, and clear standards long before difficult situations arise to handle them effectively. When standards are well-defined, addressing issues becomes more straightforward."

Kyle Keese– "I've seen a lot of those issues resolved by clearly defining the expectation before it gets to that point. If you clearly define the expectations, then people know where you stand."

ASK QUESTIONS AND BE OPEN-MINDED

Marissa Young– "I've done a much better job over the years of going in with an open mind and asking questions so that we can work collectively towards a common goal."

Phil Beckner– "It's great to ask them questions first. You think about it, even Jesus would ask people questions first, let them kind of tell on themselves without being manipulative, but ask them or give them feedback."

DECIDE WHEN AND WHERE

Phil Beckner– "When do you tell them? When do you have this conversation? Where do you have the conversation? Is it on the court? Is it in the classroom? Some guys will be way less insecure and willing to hear it if everyone's getting warmed up, and you could have it at half court. Some other people are going to flip their lid and not be able to do it."

THIRD PARTY PRESENT

Heidi Henke– "I always like to have a third party present for any and all tough conversations. That way, nothing can be misconstrued or misquoted."

Erika Lambert– "From a practical standpoint, I rarely have difficult conversations with my athletes alone. Another coach is usually present in the meeting."

CHOOSE YOUR BATTLES

Lastly, choose your battles wisely. How many bullets do you have within your organization's social and power dynamics? This will vary by person and role, but fighting everything diminishes your influence when you REALLY need it. What battles will provide the greatest return on investment if won? What smaller issues should you let go to lose the battle but win the war?

Missy Mitchell-McBeth– "Choose your battles. An overarching question I try to consider: what action would I like the other party to take as a result of this exchange? If I'm not able to answer that, it's likely not a conversation that needs to happen."

OVERVIEW

Consider these strategies when facing difficult conversations:

1. Direct, Honest, and ASAP.
2. Understand the long-term consequences of delaying.
3. Approach with empathy.
4. Relationships make these talks easier.
5. Step back and remove emotion.
6. Do your homework / Come with data.
7. Lean on established expectations.
8. Ask questions and be open-minded.
9. Decide when and where.
10. Third party present.
11. Choose your battles.

THEMES ON FAILURE

ESSENTIAL TO GROWTH

Many of these coaches, people we view as wildly successful, say they live a life filled with failures. No matter who you are, no matter how many championships you win, you WILL encounter failure. Like **Pat Davidson** said, "I've failed more times than I can count. Most of my life has been failures. They don't matter. You just push on."

These failures are not just an unfortunate part of the journey, they are *essential* to the journey. Failure, both macro and micro, is an opportunity to learn and progress. Failure teaches lessons that success cannot.

Scott Kuehn– "Failures are opportunities to learn and grow by learning what something isn't, or via negativa; there is very little about this field we know with 100% certainty, but there is infinitely more knowledge to be gained by learning what not to do or what doesn't work."

Thomas Lené– "I allowed myself to know that this will happen at some point, but I did not and do not allow myself to let it be defining or permanent. I use failure as a tool and not an outcome."

Andrew Wright– "Everyone has that moment or moments that serve as teachers seared into our memory."

Sundance Wicks– "Getting over the fear of getting fired was pivotal for me early in my career. You never fully become the best version of yourself until you have felt what it was like to be the worst version of yourself."

Velaida Harris– "You don't succeed without them. Everything is an opportunity to learn or grow. I see lessons all around me."

Jorge Carvajal– "Failure is a common part of coaching. It's what you do with that failure that redefines what it means. You're going to make mistakes—count on it. Failure has to be thought of as an opportunity to learn from the experience."

Brett Bartholomew– "Ultimately, it's these dark moments where we get to know ourselves the best."

Fergus Connolly– "But 'The man who never made a mistake never made anything.' I have no problem with mistakes providing two things: (1) the intent was sincere and well-intentioned and (2) the mistake is learned from and isn't repeated…You find ways that work, ways that don't work—but it's a process of constant iterative improvement. That's not an excuse to recklessly make change, you're taking probability based risks to explore possible improvement."

STRUGGLES, NOT FAILURES

Taking it one step further, multiple coaches choose not to even label events as failures.

Kevin Eastman– "I actually never think of things as failures. I have always just assessed an outcome and tried to do better the next time I face that situation. I 100% believe in lesson learned more than game lost."

Bill Brogden– "I felt that if I was doing my job, then I'd get through it and everything would be alright. It's never as bad as you think it is. Somebody always has it worse than you do. You're not an extreme, you're not an example. Most of the time it's just a tough situation, whatever that might be. I feel like I was blessed, because I never really thought of it as a failure."

Chuck Martin– "I made a decision to become the head coach at Marist. It didn't work. I can't view it like it's a failure. You made a decision. You took the job. It didn't work. Stop. Learn from it. Move on."

Brendan Suhr– "I don't call them failures, I call them disappointments and adversity."

REDIRECTION

Not only is failure essential to growth, it also has the ability to positively reroute the direction of your career.

Joel Smith– "I generally failed as a recruiter at Wilmington College in my first three years. This led to a lot of stress and difficulty with my job security there, and motivated me to start the Just Fly Sports brand. If not for the failure, I very well may have stayed in the NCAA track coaching circuit, which on a level would have been enjoyable, but ultimately was not my highest calling."

Failure can also reroute us not by changing our career necessarily, but by causing *us* to change internally.

Tony Holler- "I've had millions of failures. Probably most important was my experience as a head basketball coach when I was in my twenties. My record in my first five years was 28-90. This forced me to become a lifelong learner. I feel sorry for coaches who have immediate success."

Drew Long- "I had a medical emergency that took me out of coaching for several years. When I was young, I sacrificed family to climb the ladder at all costs. Becoming a head coach was the only goal I had. After my cancer diagnosis and treatment I had a completely different outlook on life and coaching. It allowed me to enjoy the process but also understand that you don't have to immerse yourself in it 24 hrs/day."

Joey Burton- "I was the farthest I've ever been from my professional goals. This was a critical time because it forced me to develop my belief system. It created my foundation and philosophy, and it realigned me with my purpose. Without this season in my life, I wouldn't be where I'm at today with the impact I'm having."

OVERVIEW

Rather than viewing failure as a negative, these coaches view failure as:

1. Essential to growth.

2. Struggles, not failures.

3. Redirection.

BOOK RECOMMENDATIONS

My original plan was to include two lists: one with the top five most recommended non-strength and conditioning books, and one with the top five most recommended strength and conditioning books (I know non-strength coaches probably don't want to crack open *Supertraining.* Strength coaches will get that...). I made a document with the books every coach recommended and started tallying them up. I ended up finding so many books that were recommended 3-4 times...so I scrapped the list.

Instead, I'm going to give you a list of books that I think are really impactful—in no specific order. I've also included a brief description of each book. I didn't list books specific to one type of coach—each book applies across sport and domain. Enjoy!

The Coach's Guide to Teaching - Doug Lemov

Doug Lemov took lessons learned from teaching in a classroom and transformed them into a masterclass on teaching in sport. The lessons—both micro and macro— on developing athletes AND developing an environment and culture of learning are endlessly useful. I ran through multiple highlighters reading this book.

What Drives Winning (All of their books) - Brett Ledbetter

Brett Ledbetter's books should be required reading, especially if you are in college athletics with the portal and NIL. He discusses how to develop the person AND the player, how to develop successful teams and environments, and how to create value alignment in your life as a coach. (Mentioned in the Themes on Overcoming Burnout)

Range: Why Generalists Triumph in a Specialized World - David Epstein

This one rocked my world when it first came out. I could not stop thinking about the ideas in this book, and they dramatically impacted my views on learning, thinking, and development. Epstein highlights the importance of looking outside our silo for solutions and how having "Range" is critical in problem solving.

The Talent Lab: How to Turn Potential into World-Beating Success - Owen Slot

I discovered this book from the reference list in *Range*. Absolute gem. I've never heard another coach talk about or even know about this book. It contains incredible insight into how Great Britain rose to Olympic success in 2012 and 2016.

Principles - Ray Dalio

Principles contains an extraordinary amount of wisdom on leadership, managing, problem solving, personality types, and living by both life and work principles.

Game Changer: The Art of Sports Science - Dr. Fergus Connolly

This book will change your view on how to prepare your athletes and team for sport. Fergus Connolly delivers a holistic view of how so many variables come together to achieve success. *Game Changer* shifted how I viewed preparing athletes for success in games and helped me see the importance of integration between all aspects of an organization in sports preparation.

Hidden Potential: The Science of Achieving Greater Things - Adam Grant

An extremely thought-provoking and inspiring book that reveals new ways to think about developing both yourself and others. Adam Grant has many outstanding books, but this one is personally my favorite.

Shoe Dog - Phil Knight

Shoe Dog tells the inspiring story of how Phil Knight started Nike and overcame numerous setbacks, risks, and failures to grow the company into the giant it is today.

The Art of Impossible: A Peak Performance Primer - Steven Kotler

This book is filled with tons of practical steps to perform at your highest level and how to set up your daily life to get in Flow State, develop at a rapid rate, and dominate your goals. I've gone back to this one MANY times.

The Quadrant System: Navigating Stress in Team Sport - Daniel Bove

The *Quadrant System* has been one of the most practically helpful books that I've continued to utilize since reading. Learn how to align the stress of practice, skill-development, and sports performance each day and holistically periodize your weeks and months.

Never Split The Difference: Negotiating As If Your Life Depended On It - Chris Voss

A super actionable book where you get to learn directly from a former FBI top hostage negotiator the best practices for negotiating in daily life.

The Comfort Crisis: Embrace Discomfort to Reclaim Your Wild, Happy, Healthy Self - Michael Easter

The Comfort Crisis is an eye-opener on how the comforts of modern society negatively impact our health and quality of life, diving into strategies to combat the harmful effects.

The Art of Learning: An Inner Journey to Optimal Performance - Josh Waitzkin

This is a fascinating book filled with insights from someone who became a national champion in chess, walked away, and then became a world champion in martial arts. There is so much gold in the methods and philosophy he uses to develop himself.

Conscious Coaching: The Art and Science of Building Buy-In - Brett Bartholomew

A powerful and practical guide on how to engage and influence different personality types to build trust and buy-in. I read this book during my first year of coaching and it influenced not only how I coached but also the understanding of *why I coached.*

Mastery - Robert Greene

A masterful book discussing strategies to work towards mastery in whatever pursuit you choose.

Tribe of Mentors: Short Life Advice from the Best in the World - Tim Ferriss

Strength In Numbers wouldn't be here without *Tribe of Mentors.* On top of that, this book has so much wide-ranging wisdom in it from all types of top performers in the world.

Everybody, Always: Becoming Love in a World Full of Setbacks and Difficult People - Bob Goff

This is a powerful book on living a life guided by the principle of loving everyone—no matter how difficult they are or how they wrong you. Christian or not, the stories and lessons in this book are powerful. I am always convicted each time I read it.

I Am Pilgrim / The Year of the Locust - Terry Hayes

For a while, I only read "useful" books—books that delivered specific knowledge to help me become a better coach. But over the last two years, I've started reading fiction again before bed. It helps shut my mind off from work to sleep better while also helping me read more when I've found a great book (always a good thing). These two thrillers by Terry Hayes are some of the most incredibly crafted stories I've ever read. If you are looking for a book to get your mind away from coaching for a little bit, I can't recommend these two enough.

ACKNOWLEDGEMENTS

Strength In Numbers doesn't exist without each coach choosing to share their experiences. I cannot thank each contributor enough for their time, openness, and authenticity. These coaches shared their journey to success, but many also shared their darkest moments. Their vulnerability made this book REAL, and I am so grateful for that. Thank you.

This book came to life through connections. The pages are filled with coaches contacted through personal relationships or MANY (and I mean MANY) cold reach outs. But this book wouldn't be here without the people willing to connect me to other coaches. To the coaches who went out of their way to recommend a colleague, share a contact, or personally introduce me to another coach, thank you.

Thank you to my mentors who have served as guides in my young coaching journey, selflessly pouring into my development. To the mentors I have worked with directly—Alex Peña, Brandon Decker, and Darby Rich—and to the many mentors who have influenced me from afar. I am not sure where in life I would be without each one of you.

Thank you Miranda Holder, who served as my coach and an incredible guide as I transitioned from collegiate coaching to starting my own business and writing this book.

Thank you to the many people who gave feedback or sparked ideas for this book along the way.

Finally, thank you to my family for their endless support. From growing up, to beginning to coach, to starting a business—they have been there for me through it all. I have never had to doubt their love or support in anything I have set out to do in life. Thank you.

And to my wife Josie, the woman who inspires and loves me every day. You are my biggest encourager. Watching the way you live your life pushes me to be a better man, husband, and Christian in this world. I am blessed beyond measure to call you my wife, and I thank God for each day I get to spend by your side.

NOTES

Ferriss, T. (2017). *Tribe of mentors: Short life advice from the best in the world.* Houghton Mifflin Harcourt.

Grant, A. (2023). *Hidden potential: The science of achieving greater things.* Viking.

Housman, A. E. (1896). *To an athlete dying young.* Poetry Foundation. https://www.poetryfoundation.org/poems/52772/to-an-athlete-dying-young

Ledbetter, B. (2022). *What's really important: Lessons on leading and living.* Win, Build, Learn Publishing.

ABOUT THE AUTHOR

John Bloom has worked as a sports performance coach at Abilene Christian, Weber State, Texas Tech, and Oral Roberts before founding Elevated Athlete Development LLC. John's mission is to provide holistic development for athletes in the Dallas-Fort Worth area while creating platforms for coaches to learn, connect, and build *Strength In Numbers.*

Learn more at:

JohnBloomCoaching.com

If you have questions about the book, coaching, or life in general, I would love to hear from you! You can contact me at info@johnbloomcoaching.com, and I'll get back to you!

I'm not famous or special . . . I'm just an average guy that was willing to ask people for help. But what started as an interesting idea evolved into something I believe can make a massive difference in the lives of so many people.

I told myself that even if no one buys the book or everyone hates it, the countless hours putting it together would all be worth it if one life is changed by reading it.

And I really hope that life is yours.

If *Strength In Numbers* has impacted your life in any way, please consider leaving a review on Amazon to help others discover it. Your review helps this book reach more people—and might just guide someone who needs it most to find it. Your feedback is so valuable, and even a few words can make a massive difference.

Scan the QR Code Below to Review *Strength In Numbers*

Made in the USA
Las Vegas, NV
11 December 2024

13771028R00319